CONTEMPORARY MARXIST LITERARY CRITICISM

Edited and Introduced by

FRANCIS MULHERN

Longman Group UK Limited,
Longman House, Burnt Mill,
Harlow, Essex CM20 2JE, England
and Associated Companies throughout the world.

Published in the United States of America
by Longman Publishing, New York

© Longman Group UK Limited 1992

First published 1992

ISBN 0 582 05977 1 CSD
ISBN 0 582 05976 3 PPR

British Library Cataloguing-in-Publication Data
A catalogue record for this book is
available from the British Library

Library of Congress Cataloging-in-Publication Data
Contemporary Marxist literary criticism / edited and introduced by
    Francis Mulhern.
        p.   cm. – (Longman critical reader)
    Includes bibliographical references and index.
    ISBN 0–582–05977–1 (csd). – ISBN 0–582–05976–3 (ppr)
    1. Marxist criticism.   I. Mulhern, Francis.   II. Series.
PN98.C6C66   1992
801'.95'0904 – dc20   92–8878
                                                                            CIP

Set 9k in 9/11½ pt Palatino
Produced by Longman Singapore Publishers (Pte) Ltd.
Printed in Singapore

Contents

General Editors' Preface

The outlines of contemporary critical theory are now often taught as a standard feature of a degree in literary studies. The development of particular theories has seen a thorough transformation of literary criticism. For example, Marxist and Foucauldian theories have revolutionized Shakespeare studies, and 'deconstruction' has led to a complete reassessment of romantic poetry. Feminist criticism has left scarcely any period of literature unaffected by its searching critiques. Teachers of literary studies can no longer fall back on a standardized, received, methodology.

Lecturers and teachers are now urgently looking for guidance in a rapidly changing critical environment. They need help in understanding the latest revisions in literary theory, and especially in grasping the practical effects of the new theories in the form of theoretically sensitized new readings. A number of volumes in the series anthologize important essays on particular theories. However, in order to grasp the full implications and possible uses of particular theories it is essential to see them put to work. This series provides substantial volumes of new readings, presented in an accessible form and with a significant amount of editorial guidance.

Each volume includes a substantial introduction which explores the theoretical issues and conflicts embodied in the essays selected and locates areas of disagreement between positions. The pluralism of theories has to be put on the agenda of literary studies. We can no longer pretend that we all tacitly accept the same practices in literary studies. Neither is a *laissez-faire* attitude any longer tenable. Literature departments need to go beyond the mere toleration of theoretical differences: it is not enough merely to agree to differ; they need actually to 'stage' the differences openly. The volumes in this series all attempt to dramatize the differences, not necessarily with a view to resolving them but in order to foreground the choices presented by different theories or to argue for a particular route through the impasses the differences present.

The theory 'revolution' has had real effects. It has loosened the grip of traditional empiricist and romantic assumptions about language and literature. It is not always clear what is being proposed as the new agenda for literary studies, and indeed the very notion of 'literature' is questioned by the post-structuralist strain in theory. However, the uncertainties and obscurities of contemporary theories appear much less worrying when we see what the best critics have been able to do with them in practice. This series aims to disseminate the best of recent criticism, and to show that it is possible to re-read the canonical texts of literature in new and challenging ways.

RAMAN SELDEN AND STAN SMITH

The Publishers and fellow Series Editor regret to record that Raman Selden died after a short illness in May 1991 at the age of fifty-three. Ray Selden was a fine scholar and a lovely man. All those he has worked with will remember him with much affection and respect.

Preface

The purpose of this volume is to illustrate the more significant lines of development in the Marxist literary criticism of the past twenty-odd years. The substantive implications of this undertaking are explored in the Introduction. However, it may be helpful to say a few words about the design of the collection, in a more strictly editorial spirit.

I have tried to represent the _diversity_ of the Marxist tradition: the international character of its activity; its distinct theoretical lineages; its complex relations with other intellectual currents (political or not); the versatility of Marxist analytic procedures; and the range of its inquiries across the spaces, times and registers of cultural history. I have sought at the same time to emphasize Marxism's fundamental _continuities_, without which it would not really be a tradition at all.

For an editor, ideas are brutally practical things. An infinity of conceptual discriminations must submit, in the end, to the pattern of a few decisions. One of the main problems of this project was foreseeable, because generic: how to achieve an acceptable minimum of diversity within a strictly limited space? There is always more than one answer to this question, and seldom, if ever, a truly compelling one. All I would add to my outline of intent is that I have tried to minimize the illusions of retrospect, wishing to cite the period as it has been, not as any particular interest may have preferred it to be. The second major problem seems obvious now, but had to be discovered along the way. It is possible, in the abstract and always in the certain expectation of challenge, to define a 'Marxist' intellectual identity. But it is another matter to match this definition with a given range of writers and texts. In the majority case, where declared Marxists produce recognizably Marxist work, there is no difficulty beyond the ordinary pressure to select. But it is a notable feature of our period that there are Marxists who, for one or another reason, do not contribute to specifically Marxist traditions of inquiry and debate; while others, in opposite fashion, decline the title and precise commitments of Marxism yet write in close and manifest affinity with it. As an aspect of everyday left culture, this is enriching, on the whole – but anthologists must draw lines where others need not, and wherever the issue arose, I resolved it on the basis of texts rather than signatures.

The eleven texts gathered here are, with one exception, unabridged reprintings of essays and chapters. Some have been lightly retouched to eliminate confusing references to earlier formats of publication or for local clarification. A few non-authorial interpolations have been made, normally in the form of expanded or additional notes; these are given in square brackets and signed thus: [– *Ed*. or – *Trans*.] Except in chapters 2, 5 and 9, where editorial subtitles have been added for the sake of information, titles (and subtitles) are as in the originals; the bracketed dates, also editorial, mark the year of first publication or, in some cases, of composition. Full details of provenance are given in the individual headnotes, which also offer brief introductions to their respective texts. The arrangement of the texts is largely by chronological order of subject matter, and shows some tendency to move from more general to more specialized topics. It is in all other respects random, and is not proposed emphatically as an order of reading.

The time for second thoughts has run out, and others will decide whether my choices have been made wisely. It remains for me only to insist that editorial responsibility for the volume is mine alone; none of my decisions or statements implicates any of the contributing authors, whose texts, in turn, should be read as expressing their views at the time of composition. I offer the same warrant of exemption, along with my thanks, to Clara Connolly, Aoibhinn O'Kane, Peter Osborne, Stan Smith, Jean Tonini and Peter Widdowson, who in various ways supported my work on the book.

Autumn 1991

Acknowledgements

We are grateful to the following for permission to reproduce copyright
material:
Blackwell Publishers for ch.1 'Free Particulars' by Terry Eagleton from
The Ideology of the Aesthetic and 'Jane Austen and Empire' by Edward Said
from *Raymond Williams: Critical Perspectives* ed. Terry Eagleton; the Editor,
Literature and History for the article 'Marxism and Popular Fiction' by
Tony Bennett in *Literature and History* Vol 7, No 2 1981, pp. 138–65; John
Logie Baird Centre for the editorial group of *Screen* and the Author,
Stephen Heath for his article 'Lessons from Brecht' from *Screen* Vol 15,
Summer 1974. © Stephen Heath; Manchester University Press/University
of Minnesota Press/Suhrkamp Verlag for ch. 2 'Theory of the Avant-
Garde pp. 15–34 & notes pp. 109–12; the Editor, *Oxford Literary Review*
for the article 'On Literature as an Ideological Form: Some Marxist
Propositions' by Etienne Balibar and Pierre Macherey in *Oxford Literary
Review* 3:1 (1978), pp. translated by Ian McLeod, 4–12, © 1978 *Oxford
Literary Review*; Routledge for 'Licensed to Look' by Michael Denning
from *Cover Stories: Narrative and Ideology in the British Spy Thriller* pp.
91–113, 160–61, London Routledge 1986, © Michael Denning; Routledge/
University of Minnesota Press for 'Beyond the Cave: Demystifying the
Ideology of Modernism' by Fredric Jameson from *The Ideologies of Theory:
Essays 1971–1986, Volume 2 Syntax of History*, pp. 115–32, 215–16,
London, Routledge 1988. Copyright © 1988 by the University of
Minnesota; Verso Editions for 'The Moment of Truth' by Franco Moretti
from *Signs Taken for Wonders* rev. edn. pp. 249–261, London Verso 1988.
© Franco Moretti; 'Pandora's Box: Subjectivity, Class and Sexuality in
Socialist Feminist Criticism' by Cora Kaplan from *Sea Changes*, pp.
147–76, London Verso 1986. © Cora Kaplan; and 'The Bloomsbury
Fraction' by Raymond Williams from *Problems in Materialism and Culture*,
pp. 148–69, London Verso 1986. © Estate of Raymond Williams.

Introduction

'Contemporary Marxist literary criticism' is a plain enough title, and as nearly accurate as most.[1] Yet none of its terms is self-explanatory. The periodizing term has no agreed usage; 'literature' and 'criticism' no longer mark off a stable community of interest and procedure; and the meanings of 'Marxism' continue to be the most disturbing in twentieth-century culture. Some preliminary clarifications are necessary, therefore, both for practical guidance and as tokens of interest and intent.

'Literary criticism' is used colloquially here, referring to any kind of discourse on written texts – mainly those made for reading but also texts written for oral delivery or performance, and above all the kind of text conventionally assigned to 'literature'. Theoretical, historical and sociological styles of work coexist here with various types of textual analysis in freedom from strict classification and without discrimination of rank. (The nearly complete restriction to one medium is a matter of publishing circumstance. The relations between writing and other media, and the many transfers of theory, method and substantive analysis from one area of work to another have been fundamentally important; but in a volume like this, designed for a large series, they cannot be a major focus.)

'Marxism' might be encapsulated in the manner of the later Engels as (i) a general theory of modes of production, the forms of their development, crisis and transformation, and their structuring role in human history; and specifically (ii) a theory of the capitalist mode of production, its fundamental classes and their antagonisms, and of the organic relationship between working-class struggles against capital and the historical possibility of socialism.[2] These have been the constitutive themes of historical materialism, the 'real foundation' upon which the specifically cultural constructions of Marxist thought have been raised. They are the minima of a Marxist identity, the core elements that make it meaningful to affirm a continuing tradition at all. Yet they have never had the character of a singular, univocal doctrinal code: even in the darkest years of this century, diversity and contention did not disappear from Marxist intellectual life. And besides, a Marxist culture is always something more than its inherited canon, various and evolving as this may be. Marxism is historical not merely because it is subject to change but because it is itself fully a part of the history it seeks to understand and act in. History is as much a part of Marxism as Marxism is of it; they inhabit one another, in unending tension.

To understand this is to perceive that there is more than one question to be asked about the bearings of 'contemporary' as used here. The first question may be answered simply. Its chronological reference is, roughly, to the years since 1968. There is wide agreement that the later 1960s saw the end of a cultural period, and it seemed to me obvious, on practical grounds, that the distinctive work of the next twenty years would not be represented adequately if made to compete for space with the great names of earlier generations. The second question is more taxing. The critical culture of these past decades has been, by any comparative reckoning, a turbulent one. The merest inventory of the ideas, forces, projects and institutions whose time has come – or gone – since 1968 is a sufficient index of this. Wholly involved in this turbulence, 'contemporary Marxist literary criticism' is not a stable entity, or even a phase in the history of a settled lineage. It is a field of forces drawn and redrawn by the shifting contentions of all four terms. The decades ahead will be especially testing for Marxism in all its forms and areas of engagement, and not least in this one. Marxism has not 'arrived', nor has it 'departed'. It persists, theoretically and practically, in a continuing history whose outcome is uncertain. The texts gathered here stand as representatives of a formidable collective achievement – but less as milestones than as resources, and resources are a strength but not a guarantee.

The task of this introduction is to assist evaluation of these resources, and its method is historical. The past is the prehistory of the present, and as tradition it is itself an actor in the present; without historical understanding we can neither explain the present nor evaluate the options it offers us. In returning, as I do in sections 1–3 below, to analyse the courses of Marxist literary thinking over the past 150 years, I am attempting not only to provide historical 'background' but to clarify the conditions, terms and purposes of future work – the topic of section 4. Rather than comment directly on individual contributions as if from an editorial dais, the considerations of this closing section move among them, seeking to elucidate some major bearings in a collective development of thought.

This history is not easy to construct. Even a brief reminder of its outlines – all that is offered here – must proceed by caveat. Three phases of initiative and elaboration can be distinguished, but it is misleading to imagine these as 'stages' in an upward movement, or even as separable 'periods' in a less triumphalist sequence. All the familiar schemes of history occur here: development and decline, continuation but also break and recombination, supersession but also stasis and return. With such cautions kept in view, it is possible to mark a *classical* or *scientific-socialist* phase, initiated by Marx and Engels, continuing strongly throughout the later nineteenth century and into the first half of the twentieth; a self-styled *critical* phase originating in the 1920s, maturing and diversifying over the next three decades and establishing a 'norm of heterodoxy' by the 1960s; and then a phase at first pledged to a *critical classicism* announced in the early 1960s and vigorously propagated in the succeeding decade, but then rapidly and variously redefined under such spacious headings as 'materialism' and 'anti-humanism', in a process that continues today.

1. Classical perspectives: towards scientific socialism

Marx and Engels were deeply cultivated men, and keenly interested in the implications of their theory for the status and practice of literature. The standard compendium of their writings 'on literature and art' runs to some 500 pages (and the authoritative account of Marx's personal literary culture is nearly as long).[3] No developed theory emerges from them. A number of latter-day theorists have maintained that the basic categories of historical materialism themselves imply an aesthetics, but in substantive terms so deeply contrasted that, paradoxically, they serve mainly to emphasize the philological fact of absence.[4] However, a general theory of social structures and their transformations bears with the utmost logical force on our understanding of the cultural practices within them; and the associated politics, assessing every kind of cultural commitment in the terms of classes and their struggles, can scarcely forgo comment on the actual and possible courses of literary production. These minimum considerations framed Marx and Engels's diverse writings on culture, and while they do not amount to a theory, they defined a perspective that has held ever since.

The terms of the perspective were both analytic and political, and in both senses *critical*. Historical materialism would refound the knowledge of cultural life, asserting its own basic theses and their implications against received understandings; and would clarify and promote cultural tendencies favouring the objectives of socialism as theory and movement. Engels's writings furnish the plainer and more systematic instances of this commitment. In a text like *Ludwig Feuerbach and the End of Classical German Philosophy* (1886), he set out to illustrate the material reality of 'spirit' as one activity among others in an integrated social–historical process governed ultimately by the dynamics of modes of production. His late sequence of letters to Bloch, Schmidt, Mehring and others sought to defend and enhance the explanatory claims of historical materialism, distancing Marx and himself from any belief in mechanical determinism and arguing that the evidence of autonomy in intellectual life, far from controverting their basic claims, was itself a specific effect of historical development in their sense.[5] A structured culture was not necessarily a passive one, Engels maintained, and such episodes in constructive aesthetics as his letters to Lassalle and Harkness bear witness to the quite practical spirit of his claim. The broad realism he advocated here (as did Marx in his own response to Lassalle's play) was not a matter of 'reflection', nor simply an animated version of theoretical abstractions, but a project of historical construction achieved in a critical deployment of the repertoire of dramatic and narrative forms.[6]

However, the single most telling adumbration of the classic perspective occurs in the closing passage of Marx's draft 'Introduction to the Critique of Political Economy' (1857), where he turns from his main concern to reflect on a crux in literary history:

In the case of the arts, it is well known that certain periods of their flowering are out of all proportion to the general development of society, hence also to the material foundation, the skeletal structure as it were, of its organization. For example, the Greeks compared to the moderns or also Shakespeare. It is even recognized that certain forms of art, e.g., the epic, can no longer be produced in their world epoch-making, classical stature as soon as the production of art, as such, begins; that is, that certain significant forms within the realm of the arts are possibly only at an undeveloped stage of artistic development. If this is the case with the relation between different kinds of art within the realm of the arts, it is already less puzzling that it is the case in the relation of the entire realm to the general development of society. The difficulty consists only in the general formulation of these contradictions. As soon as they have been specified, they are already clarified.

Let us take e.g. the relation of Greek art [. . .] to the present time. It is well known that Greek mythology is not only the arsenal of Greek art but also its foundation. Is the view of nature and of social relations on which the Greek imagination and hence Greek [mythology] is based possible with self-acting mule spindles and railways and locomotives and electrical telegraphs? What chance has Vulcan against Roberts & Co., Jupiter against the lightning-rod and Hermes against the Crédit Mobilier? All mythology overcomes and dominates and shapes the forces of nature in the imagination and by the imagination; it therefore vanishes with the advent of real mastery over them. [. . .] Greek art presupposes Greek mythology. [. . .] This is its material. [. . .]

But the difficulty lies not in understanding that the Greek arts and epic are bound up with certain forms of social development. The difficulty is that they still afford us artistic pleasure and that in a certain respect they count as a norm and as an unattainable model.

A man cannot become a child again, or he becomes childish. But does he not find joy in the child's naiveté, and must he himself not strive to reproduce its truth at a higher stage? [. . .] Why should not the historic childhood of humanity, its most beautiful unfolding, as a stage never to return, exercise an eternal charm? [. . .] The charm of [Greek] art for us is not in contradiction to the undeveloped stage of society on which it grew. [It] is its result, rather, and is inextricably bound up, rather, with the fact that the unripe social conditions under which it arose, and could alone arise, can never return.[7]

The very occasion of these sentences is eloquent: a study in political economy turns suddenly towards cultural analysis, illustrating the inborn drive of a strong general theory to assert itself throughout its domain of application. That this drive is critical rather than dogmatic is attested by the distinctive movement of Marx's reflection. There is little here of Engels's didactic manner. Rather, Marx opens with an evocation of a basic materialist analysis, which he takes to be persuasive, and then presses on to 'the real problem' presented by his exemplary case: not the historical conditions of *formation* of a culture but those of its *persistence*. Writing in the months before 'the materialist conception of history' received its first, classic formulation, Marx was already imagining the analytic agendas of his posterity a century on. But the bathos of his conclusion tells a less heroic story. The appeal to 'the historic childhood of humanity', a mystified trope bearing no substantive relation to his own concepts, prompts a second look at the concrete terms of his particular 'case', which in truth was less a piece of evidence than a preconstituted cultural topic. Marx's theoretical insight was valid and important: the problem of persistence (or active anachronism, or tradition) is central to any history of politics or culture. But his phrasing of this 'real problem' in fact rewrote one of the great commonplaces of literary culture in his day: the belief that ancient Greek culture was 'a norm and an unattainable model'.

That 'truth' has long since passed away, as has the genre of explanation that it called forth; the theoretical issue remains. The fusion of the two in Marx's prose illustrates a general point about the terms and conditions of Marxist intellectual work. Here as in the areas of their more emphatic concern, Marx and Engels drafted a prospectus of theoretical and historical inquiry: what is implied in the iconoclastic thesis that literature, like all cultural phenomena, is fundamentally 'determined' by its economic conditions of existence? How can this claim be substantiated, and in what kind of analytic procedure? And what would be the corresponding bent of a socialist 'literary politics' concerned not only to explain and interpret but also to develop a partisan tendency in the practical life of culture? As rational ventures, such questions are properly tackled in the light of critical reason alone. However, any intellectual practice internalizes its cultural conditions of existence to some extent – even when, like Marx's, it aims at 'the unsparing criticism of all that exists', the political and cultural conditions in and against which it moves are always already a part of its own being.

So it was that as a succeeding generation pursued the effort to extend and systematize the theoretical work of Marx and Engels, they did so under the banner of 'science'. The intellectual project that they sought to further – perhaps to complete – was irresistible in its grand, simple ambition. The middle years of the nineteenth century had witnessed decisive advances in the historical sciences of nature – Lyell's geology and Darwin's evolutionary biology. They also saw major initiatives in the scientific study of social organization, in its oldest forms (Morgan's ethnology) and its most modern (Mill's political economy or Marx's *Capital*). Against a background of prolific capitalist development and as yet unbroken liberal confidence, an entrancing – and attainable – horizon came into view: it now seemed possible to make a concerted scientific assault on all history, to devise a scheme of knowledge unified in method and integrated in its results, capable of mastering the evolutionary and structural ascent from protein to poetry in a single cognitive operation. This positivist goal was pursued in more than one kind of philosophical or political conviction: Spencer's *Evolutionary Sociology* and Duhring's *System* . . . are two of its better-remembered initiatives. And in Marxism, too, the spirit of scientific encyclopaedism worked strongly. The great expression of Marxist positivism was by all standards a latecomer: Kautsky's *Materialist Conception of History* (1927). However, in its very *passéisme* and its status as the culminating effort of fifty years' intellectual labour, this treatise of nearly 2,000 pages bore witness to the deep, early formation of its author.

Art found its necessary but modest place in this macroscopic scheme; the nature of the work dictated some consideration of it, but the bent of Kautsky's personal interest ensured that this would be minimal. The cultural temper of late-nineteenth-century Marxism is more fully illustrated in the writings of his Russian peer and co-thinker G. V. Plekhanov. The rhetorical mode of his *Unaddressed Letters* (a sequence begun in 1899 and never completed) itself embodies the didacticism of much Marxist work in this period: suasion is as important a goal as discovery. Plekhanov takes for granted the power of 'art' as a value and so sees it as a particularly rewarding 'test' of his 'general view of history': a science that can raise its standard on the highest ground of culture must be recognized as a great intellectual power. His analysis recapitulates the putative order of life, beginning with the natural world as seen by Darwin, moving on to an ethnological account of early social forms, and thus to a materialist social psychology in which art appears as a primarily 'utilitarian' activity conditioned by the 'mentality' appropriate to a given 'situation' whose determining component is the forces and relations of production. Plekhanov's contribution to 'scientific theorizing on aesthetics' was ambiguous in outcome. The manner and substance of his analysis was at odds with the prevailing ethos of art, but its political suggestions were quite unthreatening. Positivism in theory led, here as also in the later *Art and Social Life* (1912), to fatalism in practice. The idea of intervention in the course of artistic practice did not arise.[8]

Within years, however, intervention had become the leitmotif of Marxist discourse on art. The scientific encyclopaedism of Kautsky and Plekhanov was conventionally honoured by the younger generation of theoreticians, but not much imitated. Political organization, the strategy and tactics of revolutionary struggle and the awesome novelty of socialist construction were the fated preoccupations of Lenin, Trotsky, Luxemburg and their peers: the topics of their most important writings and the determining context of their thinking about art and culture. Lenin's articles on Tolstoy (1908–11) were polemical in character, political interventions in the ideological controversies of the anti-Tsarist revolution. Trotsky's later *Literature and Revolution* (1923) was a more ambitious work, by someone in whom artistic interests ran more deeply; but again its guiding concerns were the practical ones of cultural orientation and policy in the new revolutionary society. The cultural vision of the Proletkult Movement was indeed bold and systematic, but in a spirit that Kautsky and Plekhanov expressly repudiated: with its voluntaristic commitment to a synthetic 'proletarian' culture wholly new and disconnected from the past, it was antithetical to the positivism of the elders.

The most significant literary–theoretical initiatives of these years were not Marxist in origin, though their bearers were often actively revolutionary in sympathy and in some cases worked for an intellectual *rapprochement* with Marxism. These were the work of the trend that came to be known as Formalism. The shaping context of Formalism was the brilliant culture of late Imperial Russia, with its pattern of innovation and departure right across the sciences and arts. Its specific identity emerged in the confluence of two such currents of innovation: linguistic and literary research and the avant-garde poetry of the Futurists. Led by such figures as Viktor Shklovsky, Yuri Tynjanov, Boris Eikhenbaum and

Roman Jakobson, the Formalists fashioned a 'scientific' agenda for poetics: a new object ('literariness') with its specific modes of existence and change, a distinctive cultural motivation ('making strange'), and, implicitly, a new canon of criticism and literary practice. Formalist themes made their contribution to the extraordinary intellectual and artistic turbulence of early Soviet Russia, and were in turn remade by it; towards the end of the 1920s there emerged a current of 'post-formalism' associated with the names of Bakhtin, Vološinov and Medvedev, deeply critical of its parent tradition and closer to historical materialism. But the time for free debate had passed. Marxism was being reduced to a code of intellectual rectitude, as Stalin moved to eliminate what remained of political opposition and cultural pluralism in party and society. The new orientation was both exclusive and traditionalist, fusing the cultural traditions of the Tsarist state with those of its intellectual opponents in an official doctrine of ('socialist') realism.

By the middle 1930s, the situation of Marxist culture had been transformed. The corpus of revolutionary political thought had been expurgated and codified as 'Leninism', Marx's theory of history had achieved the metaphysical finish of 'dialectical materialism' – and both were in the keeping of a state now embarked on a course of domestic terror. In response to the gathering European crisis, the Communist International called for the creation of people's fronts whose overriding purpose would be to oppose fascism and war. This was the narrow and deceptive setting in which the important intellectual radicalizations of the 1930s occurred. Popular-frontism promoted the etiquettes of open cultural dialogue but did little to renew the spirit of rational debate. At worst, the studied forbearance of Communist 'humanism' was a sectarian's gambit, the tax that Truth must pay to Circumstance. The truly critical intelligences of the Communist tradition worked far from its authorized venues, victims of Stalin's purges (Trotsky) or fascist repression (Gramsci). Airless and embattled, this was not an environment in which intellectual energies ran strong and free. But let the life of Christopher Caudwell serve as a cameo of how much was ventured and how much lost in those years. Caudwell was perhaps the last notable encyclopaedist in the Marxist tradition. Reprocessing the enormous yield of his reading in natural sciences, philosophy, anthropology, psychoanalysis and literature by means of his new-found theoretical apparatus, he attempted to synthesize a Marxist vision of reality. Physics and poetry – the fundamental science and the most elevated art of language – were, significantly, the matter of his most elaborate studies. A book on the novel and two volumes devoted to the logic of capitalism's 'dying culture' stood beside them. All this and more in something like four years. But Caudwell was a devoted rank-and-file Communist, not merely a radicalized literatus; and so he joined the

International Brigades in Spain, where, within weeks, he died in action, not yet thirty years old.

2. Critical departures

However, Marxism was already something more than the theoretical outlook of organized communism (official or other). Numerous intellectual varieties had emerged in the revolutionary climate of 1917–23 and survived, sometimes in the margins of party life but more often in quite different settings, where they followed distinctive lines of development. Similar episodes of diversification were to occur after the Second World War. The generic resemblance in these minority Marxisms was their avowedly *critical* character, and this in two senses. They offered a *philosophical critique* of what was now commonly known as 'orthodox' Marxism; and their intellectual energies were devoted primarily to culture, above all to art and literature. Whereas Plekhanov's generation had tended to address 'the literary question' (a label it might aptly have borne) as a dramatic test case for a general theory, the exponents of 'critical' Marxism made it their special concern. Out of their various initiatives came a wealth of theoretical, historical and textual analysis; entire modes, genres, periods and movements were studied; 'culture' was anatomized, both as an idea and as a changing historical formation; there was recurring controversy over the ethics and politics of contemporary art. The long reign of party dogmatism, through the decades of Stalinism proper and beyond, was also a golden age of Marxist aesthetics.[9]

To generalize further than this is to run a continuous risk of error. 'Critical Marxism' is at best an ideal–typical construction with no perfect incarnation, at worst a legend. The short list of its variably ascribed membership is itself a caution: Georg Lukács; the so-called Frankfurt School of Theodor Adorno, Herbert Marcuse and others; Walter Benjamin; Jean-Paul Sartre; Lucien Goldmann – and, sometimes, the earlier Raymond Williams. Not a great deal unites these heterogeneous thinkers except their distance from 'orthodoxy'; and even then it must be added that the distinction between 'critical' and 'orthodox' Marxism has commonly been broadcast in deeply *un*critical ways. However, there are real relationships and affinities here, defining important shifts in Marxism's cultural sensibility.

The 'critical' tradition yielded nothing to the 'orthodox' in the measure of intellectual ambition, but its projects were normally conceived in a different register. The temper of Plekhanov's time had been positivist: the paragon of knowledge was natural science imagined as the progressive disclosure, by induction, of a law-bound reality. The answering appeal of the 'critical' tradition was to the philosophical legacy of Hegel – less to 'materialism' than to 'dialectics'. 'The truth is the whole', Hegel had declared, so epitomizing his vision of history as a dynamic unity. The method proper to Marxism, Lukács continued, in the inspirational text of this tradition, *History and Class Consciousness* (1923), is 'the point of view of totality'.[10]

Lukács was in important respects a deviant among 'critical' Marxists. He was a lifelong Communist, notoriously willing to pay a heavy intellectual price for his party membership when circumstances demanded it; and the signature of his literary studies from the later 1920s onwards was an exclusive sponsorship of realism, which intensified the appearance of conformism. Yet the pattern of his intellectual development suggests a different emphasis. Lukács came to Marxism as a relatively mature professional intellectual with already formed commitments in the philosophical and artistic arenas of his day; his early writings belong, by his own account, to the late-Romantic culture of 'despair'. Similarly, Walter Benjamin's idiom was lastingly shaped by his early interest in Judaic theology and French symbolism. Herbert Marcuse's political conversion came early, through involvement in the German revolutionary crisis of 1918–19, but his counterpart intellectual orientations were to avant-garde art and Heidegger's phenomenology. Theodor Adorno learned musicology from Schönberg and Webern and wrote a critical study of Kierkegaard before gravitating to Marxism in the later 1920s. Lukács's aggressive anti-modernism was less egregious than it may appear to have been in this setting. Modernism, as it featured in his historical design, was the subjectivist 'other' of a more enduring negative preoccupation: the para-scientific culture of *naturalism*. His advocacy of realism was, among more familiar things, a modified continuation of his early rebellion against bourgeois positivism.

Just as once Marxist theory had been forwarded as the culmination of a wider movement of scientific enlightenment, so now it was reconstrued in the terms of a far less confident, more conflict-ridden cultural phase. 'Critical' Marxism took shape in the tumult of Europe's second Thirty Years War.[11] It is normally, and correctly, maintained that the privileged phenomena of 'critical' reflection were those to which any alert and responsible Marxism would have turned its attention. The containment and reversal of revolution; the antithetical novelties of avant-gardism and 'the culture industry'; the dialectics of liberal traditions in the era of fascism; the courses of subjectivity in landscapes of organized happiness, and the meaning of reason itself in conditions of 'scientific' barbarism: these historical realities explain and vindicate the agendas of the new Marxisms, and the ethos of paradox and tragedy that set their characteristic tone. Yet Marxism is no more capable than any other thought of being assumed body and soul from history into Truth. What must be added, with equal emphasis, is that bourgeois culture thematized its crises for itself, in philosophical and aesthetic modes that actively formed the intellectuals who went on to create the new 'critical' repertoire. The achievements of Lukács, Adorno, Benjamin and Marcuse – to cite only these – are unforgettable. To them twentieth-century Marxism owes its boldest synopses of intellectual and artistic history, its most acute assessments of culture in developed capitalism, its whole sense of what liberation from such a condition might demand and promise. But this work should not be abstracted as the reward of a heroically 'unorthodox' insistence on the moment of the new; rather, it made articulate the internalized dialogue of historical–materialist tradition with self-critical bourgeois culture in a distinctively modernist Marxism.[12]

Frankfurtian Critical Theory, the leading form of this tradition, remained productive long after the Second World War, and became deeply influential both on its native ground, where Adorno – returned from wartime exile in New York and California – taught and wrote for a further twenty years, and in the USA, where Marcuse went on to do his most important work (becoming, for a season, notorious as the 'prophet' of the student revolt). The post-war period also saw new critical departures, this time originating in France, in the work of Jean-Paul Sartre and Lucien Goldmann. Goldmann was a direct descendant of the inter-war tradition. For him, still more than for Adorno or Benjamin, Lukács's early writings were a key reference. Drawing on these and on his engagement with Piaget's psychology, he elaborated an expressly 'anti-scientistic' historical sociology of literature and culture, to which he gave the name 'genetic structuralism'. Sartre's affiliations were distinct, but the pattern of his relations with Marxism was, if anything, hyperbolically typical. He entered the field of Marxist culture as a formed and distinguished philosopher and novelist of 'existence'; the constant sense of his intervention was a militantly anti-positivist insistence on human freedom; his philosophical *summa* derived a Marxist anthropology from the rigorously individualist premises of his early thought, and his culminating achievement was a study of Flaubert, whose ethos was not merely an old preoccupation in Sartre's writing but – arguably – an element in its distinctive personality.

English-language culture can claim to have contributed to the 'critical' tradition in the person of Raymond Williams. Expressly at odds with the perceived positivism of historical–materialist tradition and unconcerned to claim the title of Marxist, deeply attentive to Romantic and other ethical lineages of social criticism and particularly engaged with the positions of F. R. Leavis, Williams's earlier writings are indeed a part of this mid-century constellation. But the ulterior logic of his work led beyond its common terms, as was to become apparent in a new phase, whose opening may be marked by the symbolic date of 1968.

3. Critical classicism and since

The main intellectual energies of 'scientific socialism' were directed to the positivistic goal of demonstrating the laws of social nature. The 'totality' of the later phase, in contrast, was philosophically conceived, not so much the last horizon of discovery as the precondition of validity in critical analysis and judgement. Both kinds of work continued well after their defining periods, in both pure and hybrid forms, and neither tradition is spent. However, by the later 1960s, the culture of Marxist theory was entering a new, and fateful, phase of reconstruction. The signature of the third phase, as of the first, was 'science', though now without the cosmological inflection of the nineteenth century; like the second, the new phase was to be 'critical', though not in the spirit of Hegel, who now assumed the role of ceremonial outcast. The intellectual agenda announced by the French Communist philosopher Louis Althusser dictated a 'return to Marx', or, precisely, to the science of history that must at last be disengaged from the heterogeneous mass of Marx's writings and their posterity of unrigorous commentary – in a phrase, *a critical classicism*.

The motives and conditions of this new departure were in significant measure political. Althusser's unfamiliar, often scandalizing Marxism – an 'anti-humanist', 'anti-historicist' 'theoretical practice' formed and sustained in a 'break' with the ordinary world of ideology – was deliberately pitched against what he saw as the mistaken bearings of official communism at home and internationally. But its main register was philosophical, and its decisive effects were felt in the intellectual sphere. Althusser's most important substantive intervention in historical materialism was a new analysis of the canonical 'base–superstructure' relation, an abiding crux in literary and other cultural theory.[13] Marx's 'totality' was structurally *complex*, he insisted. It contained no master contradiction to which all social reality could be reduced, whether along a chain of mechanical effects (the positivist error) or as simple expression (the characteristic assumption of left Hegelianism). It was, rather, a dynamic ensemble of 'relatively autonomous' practices, each possessing a 'specific effectivity' and entering with all the others into 'overdetermined' configurations (or 'conjunctures'), which the economy determined only 'in the last instance'. The immediate implication and the promise of Althusser's rereading were obvious. It was unnecessary, and probably mistaken, to analyse literature as the complicated appearance of the essentially simple reality of classes and their struggles. Rather, it must be grasped as a distinct practice, carried on by specific means and with specific ideological effects, within an always complex social history. The further implication, half-silenced by the characteristic apocalypticism of Althusserian discourse but soon to make itself heard with lasting effect, was that while historical materialism was the general science of history, it was not therefore theoretically competent to construct the 'regional' sciences of specific historical practices: the definitive entry into scientificity entailed renunciation of the belief in Marxism as a self-sufficient world view.

Althusser's opening was quickly taken. His collaborator Pierre Macherey (see ch. 1) ventured a specific theory of literary production, and Terry Eagleton (see ch. 2) followed, at a critical distance, with a more comprehensive analysis centred on the notion of the literary as work in and on ideology. An Althusserian pattern of intellectual dependency was also visible in these ventures. Where Althusser had paid some attention to structural linguistics and was substantially committed to psychoanalysis, so both Macherey and Eagleton appealed to structuralist and kindred traditions in linguistics and poetics, and to a Freud who seemed exemplary as a reader of texts born out of antagonism. Of course, such borrowings were neither so new nor so distinctive as legend would have it. The history of Marxist attraction to psychoanalysis is a long and varied one: reference to Freud was canonical in the Frankfurt tradition (which seeded a remarkable synthesis of Marxist and psychoanalytic theory in the form of Marcuse's visionary *Eros and Civilization*). Italy witnessed a wholly independent, and rather earlier, development of anti-Hegelian Marxism under the aegis of Galvano Della Volpe, whose aesthetic treatise *Critique of Taste* (1960) made systematic use of structural linguistics. And Franco Moretti (see ch. 5), a critic of Della Volpean background whose early work coincides with these Althusserian excursions, was from the outset closely, though quite differently, engaged with formalist and structuralist poetics and with psychoanalysis. Nevertheless, it was only in the early 1970s, and most often in Althusserian accents, that reference to linguistics and psychoanalysis became habitual in Marxist literary theorizing. The 'return to Marx', in this intellectual zone, meant a turning *out* into a new phase of inquiry and debate.

The work that now began to appear was, by any comparative standard, remarkable in its versatility and ambition – the present volume is no more than an evocation of the record. The analytic potential of a Marxist–psychoanalytic–semiotic trinity (promoted in France by the influential *Tel Quel* group) was explored with greatest concentration and impact in the collaborative work of the London quarterly *Screen*, which also reassessed the legacies of German and Russian revolutionary culture, in the context of its central concern with the dominant and oppositional cinemas of the present (see Heath, Ch. 11). The contrasting 'Hegelian' coloration of much North American Marxism was visible in the project of the *Telos* group, and remains so in the writings of Fredric Jameson (see ch. 8), who at the same time has sustained a strong relationship with French avant-garde theory. On Hegel's home territory, meanwhile, the Frankfurt tradition was reanimated by a new generation of theorists (see Bürger, ch. 7). The dramatic return of feminism, initially in the form of the Women's Liberation Movement, confounded every kind of common sense, not exempting that of left culture, where groups like the Marxist–Feminist Literature Collective set out to reconstruct inherited analytic and political perspectives (see Kaplan, ch. 3). Within instituted literary studies, Raymond Williams's work (see ch. 6) reached a crucial point of development in the formulation of a Marxist 'cultural materialism'. And the gathering significance of these eddies and currents of thought – as, in effect, a collective re-formation – was given concrete and sustained form in such venues as *Literature and History*, *Red Letters* and *Radical Philosophy*, and in intellectual 'movements' like History Workshop and Literature Teaching Politics.

There were familiar ways of describing the new critical styles: they were 'sociological', 'historical' and 'political' in 'approach'. But these were reductive (and often defensive) characterizations. The diverse undertakings of this phase were far more radical in their implications – in truth, fateful for the old world of literary criticism. At their most concerted, they undermined the deep taxonomy and criteriology that founded the discipline and in this way – fitting climax in a literary battle – unmade its corporate imagination. 'Literature' and 'criticism' themselves were called into question (see Bennett, ch. 9). The *domain* of inquiry was now reconstructed by the inclusion of other written materials, 'non-literary' or 'popular' (see Denning, ch. 10); work in other media; and wider, more challenging notions of historical 'context' (see Said, ch. 4). New analytic *objects* were proposed, displacing 'the literary' as self-evident value or genus: the social formations of writing, for example (see Williams, ch. 6), or the historical–spatial morphology of its great modes (see Moretti, ch. 5). The basic *norms* of analysis – say, explanation, interpretation, evaluation – were redefined or reordered or displaced altogether, in new strategies of reading. An enlarged domain, new objects, revised norms, and, framing these, new terms of identity. The emerging formation of (post-)literary studies was, in all its varieties, theoretically 'materialist'; its ethos was 'political'; and its summarizing commitment, polarized against the sovereign value of bourgeois culture, was 'anti-humanist'.

*

14

But these last paragraphs smack a little of Whig history. . . . They exaggerate the institutional strength and, more important, the intellectual authority of the emerging formation – as many of its exponents have been symptomatically prone to do. And they are written as if from the confident centre of the new collective identity – which, however, has been ever less inclined to think of itself as Marxist. For those of us who remain Marxists – others will judge according to their different lights – the emerging pattern of this third phase has been thought provoking in more ways than one.

The defining initiatives of the new formation were launched by Marxists, with expressly Marxist intellectual and political motives. The general project of *New Left Review*, whose publishing initiatives were decisive in this, was to foster a left culture informed about its past and unbewitched by it, versatile and capable in its own socialist and other contexts; and so to help free and focus intellectual energies for the development of a contemporary revolutionary politics. The call to 'theory', the broad rubric of 'materialism' and the always more controversial slogan of 'anti-humanism' were, in an important respect, the keywords of an ecumenical terminology intended to facilitate productive, though duly critical, exchanges with other radical movements and with the human sciences. Marxist cultural theory benefited significantly from this conjuncture of ideas and activity, learning to explore aspects of subjectivity and signification that were, with good but still limiting cause, only partially conceptualized within historical materialism strictly understood. Hybridization was one natural consequence of all this, and – irrespective of the widely differing merits of particular instances – a sign of general growth; Marxism, and more so its individual adherents, could not expect to emerge unchanged from engagements with unfamiliar ideas and demands. At the same time, it was to Marxism that the new formation owed its widest perspectives. In so far as anything united the proliferating critical culture of the early-to-middle 1970s (not only the specifically theoretical trends but also the new movements of social emancipation, and notably feminism), it was a spontaneous orientation to one or another variety of Marxist historical reason and politics. Out of this came the recognizable collective idiom of radical literary and cultural studies; but the continuity of such phatic signals as 'materialism', 'theory', 'anti-humanism' and the rest served mainly to ease a steady reordering of investments. Historical materialism was not only hybridized; it was relativized, marginalized or simply anathematized, as the heterogeneous intellectual avant-gardes of the preceding decades (eponymically: Barthes–Derrida–Foucault–Lacan) were recruited to a new canon of subversion, the counter-enlightenment thematics of 'post-structuralism'. The 'return to Marx' was not only a salutary turning out from Marxist autarky; for many it was a roundabout turning away.

As a passage of intellectual debate, this shift must be evaluated in properly conceptual terms. But as a collective tendency it calls rather for historical interpretation. And in this perspective, the new formation of radical literary studies appears as a creature of paradox – the paradox of its legendary moment of origin, May 1968. For a whole generation of intellectual radicals, the French May was the blazing symbol of revolutionary possibility. The Cold War had ended. Imperialism was weakening, fought to a standstill in the revolutionary theatres of the Third World and challenged in its heartlands by a dramatic renewal of working-class combativity and an international explosion of student revolt. Repressive political structures were at the point of collapse all along the periphery of bourgeois Europe, from Ireland to Greece – and perhaps also in the East, where the crisis of Stalinism was overt. In such conditions, socialist revolution seemed a quite concrete, short-term possibility. Such was the widespread expectation (and for too many of this generation, it has to be said, the crux of a tacit personal deal with history), and it proved false.

Flatly reckoned, May 1968 was after all a defeat. And the modal political experiences of its intellectual progeny were hope and set-back, misadventure, poisoned victories, moderated ambition encountering still more painful rebuff – a pattern that continues today. Thus, the cultural innovation of 'sixty-eight' – the making of a numerous and versatile leftist intelligentsia – was unmatched by any comparable political advance of the left or workers' movement generally, with results that became unambiguous in the worsened conditions of the 1980s. Dismayed by the lengthening experience of political frustration and supported less and less by independent cultural structures and practices (which, inevitably, were directly affected by the general downturn), left intellectuals became increasingly exposed to the norms and priorities of the dominant order, and particularly those of the academy, where so many of them worked. Rightly determined to master and criticize bourgeois culture on its own best terms, to challenge and where possible reconstruct the given order and substance of learning, at the same time they were now vulnerable to an academic remaking of their politics. In effect, political and academic desiderata became hard to distinguish. The political demand for fresh thinking could be recoded as the academy's positivistic requirement of 'progress in research'; and this, recoded in reverse, facilitated an inappropriately abstract valorization of political revision (always in the sense of greater moderation). The ambient culture of the capitalist market, in years largely voided of general challenge to its values, then sealed this compact in the vacuous idiom of fashion.

And so it came about that 'new' and 'old' began to circulate, tendered and accepted without irony or shame, as terms of intellectual and political judgement. The denominator of 'materialism' remains current but (except in the case of the 'cultural materialism' deriving from Williams) with little differential meaning other than 'not liberal-humanist but not/not really/no longer Marxist'. The 'political' posture of radical literary studies is, at worst, a residual group mannerism; more typically, it combines a fanciful belief in 'subversion' *ordinaire* with a knowing disdain for revolutionary ideas, in a mutant creed that might be called anarcho-reformism. And at the centre of this subculture stands its legendary achievement, a thing that no one, of whatever particular persuasion, would have thought to design: the institutional chimera named 'Theory'.

Theoretical work is indispensable to all fruitful inquiry, and must be defended as such. But the latter-day culture of 'Theory' is an academic mystification, a factitious singular that tends to relativize and equalize the heterogeneous ideas it entertains, to inhibit understanding of the antagonisms and sheer incommensurabilities of the real world of theories (plural). Rational theories submit only to stronger theories, which may but also may not be newer ones, and almost certainly will not be more accommodating. But 'Theory', mistaking professional collegiality for a meaningful consensual standard of judgement, beckons its votaries into a 'politics' of adaptive novelty. If this ungenerous summary has any net justification, it is in that it serves to emphasize the need to assert the distinct identity and purposes of Marxism within radical literary studies, whose spontaneously evolving life in a narrow, unyielding environment is not only a positive resource and not ever a binding pattern of conduct.[14]

4.   Results and prospects: notes for now

The historical impression offered here is of a tradition that, though strong, is not autarkic. It lives under its own law: history has no 'outside', from which it can be known and managed absolutely. The subculture of Marxism, like any other, is intertextual in character.[15] And in so far as it acts consistently in the spirit of science, Marxism acknowledges its necessary cognitive incompleteness. As Freud once observed, 'world views' are theological, not scientific goals.[16] Marxism's claim has to do with modes of production and their functioning in the structure and courses of social history. This is its power and its self-defined limitation: the first in so far as it therefore asserts a critical check on all theses concerning the social; the second in that it is, therefore, not competent to generate an exhaustive knowledge of the social from within

17

its own conceptual resources. Marxism has always drawn on other knowledges, whether avowedly or not. It fares better when it acknowledges its cognitive dependencies, and understands its appropriate 'world view' not as the acme of self-elaboration but as the changing horizon of sciences in critical solidarity.[17]

The same anti-triumphalist qualifications apply in internal affairs. There is no unalloyed truth of Marxism, against which to measure the deficiencies of other aspirants. Marxism's history has been irreducibly various and agonistic; nothing in that history is simply 'past', and the temptation to judge and act as though it were otherwise bespeaks a damaging parochialism of spirit. So then, in going on to sketch some orientations in Marxist literary studies in the years ahead, I do not claim either certainty or consensual authority. It would of course be legitimate to propose a distinctive programme, but that suggests a measure of originality that I cannot claim either. All I offer here are some annotations – at times commonplace, at others idiosyncratic – of our current theoretical culture. Their manner will seem to belie the profession of modesty. But this is partly the effect of brevity, and partly a mark of the belief that discussion is served better by clear statements, vulnerable though they may be, than by a fog of defensive qualifications.

Rhetorics in history is an inclusive but still pointed definition of our field. Rhetoric is often remembered, in this post-Romantic literary culture, as taxonomania, a tireless cataloguing of schemes and tropes, as the art of 'mere' eloquence. But in its full ambition it was, simply, the study of language in action. Of *language* and thus of forms and meanings; of language in *action* and thus also of its occasions, purposes and effects. Invoked in this sense the tradition of rhetoric is not merely the depository of a certain knowledge; it furnishes a critical example for the present. Specifically, it displaces without simply liquidating two persistent literary-critical cruces, which Marxism has not been spared.

The first concerns the relation between 'form' and 'content'. Everyone has learned the correct response to this metaphorical couple; yet the received solution – 'the unity of form and content' – is either gestural or, more interestingly, tendentious. 'Form' and 'content' are alternative analytic abstractions from a singular signifying practice. The idea that they could be other than a 'unity' is the merest fiction of uncertainty, an ideological feint. What is in question, as Balibar and Macherey, among others, insist (see ch. 1), is whether the text is – or can be – in either aspect unitary in the required sense. In the tradition of rhetoric, forms are always–already meaningful and meanings are always–already shaped; discourses are intertextual in nature, working in and across existing formations of sense (the topics and commonplaces, the fallacies and so on), understood thus as *specific organizations of social meaning*.

The second concerns the relation between the text and its exterior. The notion of textual autonomy has been a tenet of literary culture in this century, Jameson reminds us (see ch. 8), and for Marxism, the chief mystification. But it is not sufficiently countered by efforts, however sophisticated, to demonstrate a relationship 'between' the text 'and' history. Textual practice is internal to history, which inhabits it. The tradition of rhetoric assumes just this: linguistic practice is discourse, situated and motivated utterance, organized in and organizing specific relations of culture. To explore the historicity of the text is, then, not simply to relate a frail singularity to the broad design of a period; it is also to investigate its direct social relations (see Williams, ch. 6), the formations of writing and reading – and these not as 'context' or 'background' but as substantive elements of the practice itself.[18]

This theoretical orientation implies a distinctive pattern of inquiry and exposition. Marxist criticism has characteristically paid special attention to the larger units of literary history, privileging period and genre in contrast with the dominant preference for individual texts and corpuses – Lukács's *The Historical Novel* and Benjamin's *The Origin of German Tragic Drama* are classic instances. Other, less familiar objects, collective or intertextual in character, must also be written into a developing Marxist scheme: the *conventions*, as Williams terms them, the 'techniques' or topics which, forming an order distinct from the received classification of literary kinds, are the deeper organization of the culture; and the *repertoire*, the changing array of conventions, of possible and 'preferred' writing options, which is arguably the true actor in literary history.[19] Such undertakings tend to displace the individual text from its traditionally central position, and in doing so, disturb one of the strongest and 'politically' most serviceable intuitions of the critical profession. That is, the conviction that the normal mode of critical attention – inquiry and *also* commentary – is the reading of a given text: this *form* of discourse is the visible sign and the indispensable warrant of 'relevance'. This is, in Barthes's sense of the term, a myth, whose operation deserves a little (homeopathic) close reading.[20] The presiding trope in this critical convention is metaphor: the elementary distinction between the order of research and the order of exposition, familiar from all intellectual work, is occluded, the latter dissolved into the former in an expository mode that simulates a primal act of discovery. Thus, the exposition validates itself and in the same gesture naturalizes its underlying norms of inquiry. Reading is reading, and its protocols are given and validated by the kind of text being read – a text embodying the distinctive quality conveyed in one word: literature.

Literature, in its ordinary sense of an inherently valuable canon of imaginative writing, has been and remains a potent cultural value. As a norm, it has been institutionalized in public bodies and internalized by countless individuals, organizing the whole culture of writing and reading, inflecting the course of practice in other media, and validating major traditions of discourse. An enormous amount of important work has been done under its sign. The historical reality and productivity of 'literature' are not in dispute. The interesting question is, rather, whether it can make a legitimate claim of privilege either as an object of analysis or as a norm of subjectivity. Balibar, Macherey, Bennett and Williams have been notable in maintaining – correctly – that it cannot. The claim that the study of written culture should continue as the study of 'literature' is dogmatic and obscurantist. Literary studies so conceived are an authoritarian defence of certain received cultural values, within preset limits of debate and discovery. 'Literature gives us wisdom', goes one definition-cum-defence I have personally encountered. It is memorable as an act of self-exposure: the verb erases reading as an active process; 'wisdom' displaces debatable knowledge in favour of humbling revelation; and the appeal to an indeterminate 'us' simply cancels the existing order of human relations and interests. Procedural openness to the whole field of writing and a pluralist corporate ethos are the minimum conditions of genuinely 'critical' literary study. It may be that there are important and very general qualitative distinctions to be made within the material range of writing, yet it is doubtful whether 'literature' will feature among them. The scientific search for the objective properties and functions of the poetic has run a paradoxical course. 'Literariness' is both too general and too variable to fulfil its all-important specifying role: it may indeed exist and flourish in language but it does not vindicate the received hypothesis of 'literature'. On the other hand, the function of 'the literary' as a norm of subjectivity seems clear. 'Literature' (and more generally 'art') is, in Freud's sense, fetishistic. Exactly in the manner of its profane counterpart, 'entertainment', it mediates a disavowal, acknowledging a process of meaning in the practice it designates, yet suggesting that such meaning is somehow not really implicated in the secular divisions of meaning that are the ordinary substance of culture. The conventional riposte to the onset of 'ideological' questioning ('but as *literature* . . .') is seldom if ever the formalism that it might decently be (on the contrary: formalism in literary studies is scarcely less barbarous than 'sociology'). It is, rather, an appeal to an ideological 'elsewhere' – in literal translation, an *alibi*.

The material sign of this elsewhere is 'form', and the essence of form is 'unity' or 'closure'. The moral integrity of 'literature' is incarnated as material ('aesthetic') completeness. Again, there is no need to doubt the potent reality of this modern tradition of the aesthetic. Eagleton (see ch. 2) accords it a key role in the constitution of bourgeois culture as such – and it has been taken over and indeed reaffirmed by many Marxists, most notably Herbert Marcuse. Rhetorical closure, connoting unity, harmony, reconciliation, has been the sovereign norm of most artistic practice for two centuries or more, as also of the world of critical commentary and valuation in which it lives. Deviant rhetorics are recent and minoritarian, or, in one sense or another, primitive, and in all cases disturbing to deep collective intuitions. But closure is, in strict principle, unattainable. The practical infinity of language and the intertextual character of signifying processes forbid it, in 'aesthetic' as in all other sense-making activity. Even the most concentrated trope of language, the pun, is, precisely, equivocal: it is, according to perspective, a binding of meaning, or an uncontrollable accretion of it – like a tryst made awkward by unwanted company. The action of 'the aesthetic' has been valued by Marcuse and, latterly, Jameson for its Utopian moment – the closure effect as anticipating a healed existence. It can be interpreted, less grandly, as a privileged occasion of unconscious desire – artistic language as a recovery of infantile pleasures. But such proposals give no comfort to traditionalism. 'The aesthetic' and 'the literary', so defined, are non-identical with the canons defended in their name. Anything but norms, they bear witness rather to the inextinguishable strain of perversity in social life.[21]

Reading as well as writing is implicated in the vicissitudes of 'closure'. The notion of a 'correct' reading, in its simplest form, is philosophically humanist, presupposing a shared essence that guarantees the possibility of perfect communication between writer and reader. But subjectivity is mobile and self-divided, composed and recomposed in ways that it seldom chooses and often does not or cannot recognize. Even where writerly deliberation is at its most consequent, the text is necessarily deficient in author-ity over the reader – who, reciprocally, is condemned to read without the warrant of innocence and propriety. Extrapolated over the ordinary distances of history, the necessary discrepancies of the writing–reading relationship become marked. Texts are 'iterable': they function in spaces and times quite remote from their primary conditions of existence, and, in doing so, are in effect rewritten–reread, acquiring further or different meanings, undergoing alterations in status, suffering fluctuations of imputed value. Textual productivity is unending, as is the variability of reading. There is no 'text-in-itself' and no 'reader-as-such' to appropriate it.[22]

The difficulty with this now-familiar view is not that it is false – in its own terms it is persuasive – but that it is abstract and, at worst, trivial. To insist on the constitutional non-identity of writing and of subjectivity is to be returned, as though by counter-suggestion, to the abundant historical evidence for stability and continuity in culture. It may be true in principle that 'you(?) can't read the same text twice'; but what is then all the more striking is how relatively little, and how weightlessly, this enforced liberty is exercised in concrete cultural relations. Meaning and inter-subjectivity have no absolute ground, yet they are *orderly*, strongly consensualist in tendency and rather predictable in their patterns of antagonism and discrepancy. They are shaped and held in historical formations of writing and reading that constrain textuality, that are, precisely, *authoritative*.

If the idea of a perennially self-identical text is a humanist dogma, the antithetical idea of an ever-self-differing text is an academic–libertarian trifle. Neither is adequate for the purposes of historical inquiry, for which some notion of *context* is indispensable. Yet to say only so much is to say very little: everything depends on how 'context' is understood. The generic claim that meaning is context-determined is uninteresting: it amounts to saying that there is no culture without society, a truism for all but the most other-worldly perennialist. What, then, counts as an interesting context? A characteristic response (familiar not only in recent literary studies but also, and over a longer period, in the history of political thought[23]) is to privilege the most limited contexts, beyond which a text is quickly 'self-estranged', and thus to assert an extreme relativism of meaning – and again, but this time for sheer want of plausibility, to weaken the challenge to common-sense perennialism. The preference for narrow contexts reproduces the tacit misapprehension of the generic claim: both rest on a tacit reduction of *history* to *change* – a kind of hyper-history. This is the most understandable of polemical habits, but it perpetuates a confusing half-truth. History is also – and decisively, for its greater part – *continuity*. The historical process is differential: it is patterned by a plurality of rhythms and tempos, some highly variable, some very little so, some measured by clocks and calendars, others belonging to the practical eternity of 'deep time'. Historical structures and events – the substance of what we invoke as 'contexts' – are thus necessarily complex in character, never belonging to a single mode (continuity/discontinuity) or temporality. Contexts are brief and narrow (a generation, a political crisis) but they are also long and wide (a language, a mode of production, sex-gender privilege), and all of these at once.[24] Perennialist reading – across continents and centuries – is no more pure fancy than hyper-historical relativism is pure enlightenment. The appeal to 'context' does not suffice either to discredit the one or to establish the other. The concept of 'context', putative determinant of meaning, is itself under-determined, acquiring critical value only within a specific understanding of history.

History, and so, for good or for ill, historical materialism. All contemporary reflection on history is a declared or tacit response to the legacy of Marx. That this should be so testifies to the crucial character of Marx's theoretical claims, but also to their ambiguities. Thus any statement on behalf of historical materialism is, at the same time, an intervention within it.

The oldest ambiguities – and in the present connection, the most stressful – inhere in the very notion of a *materialist* conception of history. 'Materialism', in the Marxist tradition, is a complex idea, incorporating three variably related claims. The first asserts an ontological monism: reality is homogeneous, without residue, consisting of so many modes of materiality. The second claim is already historical in implication, positing a reality so structured that its 'lower' modes constrain its 'higher' ones, which, though irreducible as systems, are none the less consubstantial with them: biological existence does not outstrip physico-chemical regularities, nor human sociality the biological. Finally, as these claims imply, 'materialist' epistemology is broadly realist, affirming the existence of an object-world independent of thought and accessible to it. These three claims have shared the common space of 'materialism' since the 1840s, peaceably for much of the time but often, and certainly in recent years, in a state of antagonism.

'Materialism' in the first sense has motivated – or, at least, glossed – significant developments in Marxist thinking about culture.[25] Ideology as material practice; meaning as the effect of work in language, as textual production; the notion of culture as, quite literally, *making* sense – these have become common themes in Marxist discourse, in some cases through initiatives within the tradition, in others through the assimilation of various kinds of semiotic theory. Marxism's habits of theory and analysis have been residually dualist, it is said (by Williams, for example). Historical materialism has redefined the *social status* of culture but has not been commensurately active in rethinking its specificity as a *practice*; the old cultural spirituality lingers, humbled but not banished, in a theory which, to that extent, remains unequal to its own materialist rule of life. That this has often been so is undeniable, even if the historical record as a whole is more varied, and less flawed, than some latter-day generalizations admit. Marxist cultural analysis has, in the past twenty years, finally come to terms with its 'erstwhile philosophical consciousness', thinking through and beyond essentialist understandings of the literary and the aesthetic and displacing such equivocal categories as 'expression' and 'reflection' in new forms of attention to discourse and representation in their material specificity.

However, 'materialism' in this sense has often been taken to imply a further critical objection – one which, pursued to a finish, strikes Marxism at its theoretical core. If cultural practice is truly understood as material (the monist thesis), then perhaps there is no longer any strong reason to endorse the structural–historical thesis ('materialism' in its second sense) that social reality is subject to a hierarchy of constraint. Marx's privileging of the economic, the notorious theory of 'base and superstructure', itself embodies the old dualism. Althusser's attempt to resolve its cruces through the notion of 'relative autonomy' was a late, and insufficient, improvisation; 'determination in the last instance' is no determination at all, as he himself conceded in his famous quip, 'the last instance never comes'.

This appeal to consistency is itself fallacious and philosophically inconsistent. 'To say . . . that an object is material is still to say nothing,' Lucio Colletti once wrote: 'materiality as such does not specify, it is rather a *generic* attribute, a property common to *all* things.'[26] In other words, to say that a given reality is material is merely to assert its ontological unity with other realities, not to imply anything, one way or another, about its relations with them. Even if the notion of a social hierarchy of constraint is misconceived, it cannot be rebutted by an appeal to ontological 'materialism' – which, as deployed on occasions like this, betrays its own kind of dualism. The literary 'materialism' of recent times remains true to custom in its tacit special pleading on behalf of humanity. Arguments over the relations between cultural and economic practice are conducted in abstraction, as though humans, whether as poets or as farmers, were not wholly a part of nature – where the reality of hierarchical constraint, of 'relative autonomy', in effect, is manifest, and understood as such in the materialist knowledge of the sciences generally. 'Relative autonomy' – or, more precisely and tellingly, *conditional* autonomy – encapsulates that unity of specificity and generic dependence that characterizes the relationship of more to less complex modes of nature. Thus, animal behaviours are specific, but effectively so only in and in conformity with physico-chemical nature. Human history exhibits unique specificities, but is not exceptional. Biological self-reproduction is the permanent condition of all social practice, whose real and effective power of variation is correspondingly limited. The historical means of self-reproduction – the organization of economic relations – are, for any given place and time, a 'second nature' that systematically favours certain social variations over others, and, as an essential part of this, fosters a 'common sense' which, though never homogeneous and often contested, is the given substance of our perceptions, imaginings and valuations – which is, in a word, the historically specific reality of our *culture*, in its ordinary and specialized modes alike. Culture is omnipresent, it is pointed out, as a necessary element of all social practice: the idea that it is determined by 'something else' is confused. It is indeed omnipresent, and for just that reason can *not* be represented, contrariwise, as a strong independent variable. It is, moreover, subject to two constraints which, though not normally existing in an a-cultural state, are finally impervious to meaning: *force*, the ultimate resort of the political, and *need*, the unanswerable daily 'argument' of the economy, which in this fundamental sense must always 'determine' human life 'in the last instance'.

But 'the last instance', as we all remember, 'never comes'. . . . This, the rhetorical highlight of Althusser's career, is better seen as a moment of damaging theoretical confusion. Evoking the pattern and dynamic of the October Revolution, Althusser affirmed the necessary complexity of the social whole, and excluded, in principle, the possibility of a climactic simplification of struggle to the pure terms of capital and labour – in short, he excluded a *politico-temporal* 'last instance'.[27] But the irreducible complexity of Russian revolutionary politics was based precisely on the complexity of the Tsarist socio-economic formation: a decaying feudalism interlocked with a dynamic but subaltern capitalist sector in conditions of aggressive inter-imperialist rivalry to determine the configuration of the crisis, its protagonists and its finite array of possibilities. 'The last instance' in this *structural* sense did not 'fail' to come: it was present from the start, as the *condition* of October. Althusser's *mot* intended a useful but limited political caution (even if as a judgement on the general notion of a temporal 'last instance' it seems ill considered, simply overlooking the ordinary cycles of systematized commodity production). But it mistakes and compromises the lesson of its own illustration, which – not retreating from Marx's thesis but reinforcing it – bears on the *structure* of the social *as such*, and on the differential effectivity of economic relations within it.

Modes of production are ultimately decisive in the formations and transformations of human history, and the ordering of social agency in which a mode of production humanly consists – its system of *classes* – is correspondingly central for theory and politics. The strength of this claim is perhaps better appreciated, in current conditions, through a reminder of its limitations. It does not entail the essentialist belief that the economy is the simple truth of complex appearances, or that class furnishes the exhaustive meaning of social being. No consistent historical materialist can evade the specific reality of sexual dimorphism and the relatively autonomous regimes and cultures of gender that have been constructed upon it, not to speak of other, historically more limited, forms of human bonding and antagonism such as race; and only an alchemist will maintain that these are so many base metals to be transmuted into the gold of class struggle. Concrete social beings are necessarily involved in all such forms of relationship, among which none is their 'essence' – not class *or* sex *or* race *or* nationality *or* generation. Cora Kaplan emphasizes the complex inter-coding of all these determinations in subjectivity and its representations (see ch. 3). If the problematic of class remains crucial for Marxists, this is not out of hidebound devotion to an old cause but because of the fundamental thesis that in the overdetermined totality of social life, the dominant mode of production plays a decisive structuring role, confirming or adapting or remaking the given human relations in accordance with its own logic, patterning both the necessary conditions of its existence and the forces capable of transforming it.

It has frequently been said that this thesis is fatally dogmatic; the very assumption that social relations constitute a totality is unwarrantably speculative; 'historical materialism' is the culmination of idealist philosophy of history. The charge of dogmatism, it may be retorted, is a projection. Indeed there is no ultimate guarantee. Marxism's theoretical propositions are necessarily fallible, and open to displacement by a stronger theory. But this is the normal situation of rational knowledge. The dogmatism lies rather in the ethos of the objection, which tacitly holds that uncertain knowledge is worthless. Here as often, metaphysics is safe in the keeping of the disenchanted.

The Marxist vision of socialism as an historical possibility evolved but locked within capitalism, and of labour – the exploited collective producer – as its indispensable revolutionary agency, does not affect the status of revelation. It is a rational challenge, as bold and as exposed as all genuine challenges must be. There are many on the left who would sooner say that it is a bluff that has now been called. As it was called in the 1890s? And again in the 1950s? Nothing is more suspect than the apocalyptic *Now*. 'The crisis of Marxism' has been a recurring theme of the past century, and not only for the predictable, transient reasons. Marxism is wholly involved in the crises it seeks to understand and resolve. And precisely because of this, it is the more necessary to recall another recurring phenomenon. Not a few attempts have been made to 'go beyond' Marxism; and all have entailed regression to earlier, more limited positions.[28] Thus, for instance, the 'new' ethics and tactics of 'identity', which are nowadays urged against the 'old', oppressive generalities of 'class' (and 'woman' and 'black'), turn out to be a post-modern variant of a long-familiar radical liberalism. Marxism remains what it has always been: incomplete, fallible, a tradition in process – but for all that, as Sartre once wrote, the unsurpassable horizon of thought in our time.

'*Cultural politics*' is Marxism's activist mode in this domain, and, like all lucid practice, not so much a release from the ink-horn preoccupations of theory as a tense rediscovery of them.

The very idea of 'cultural politics' is monstrous, according to the liberal–humanist tradition. Culture is what hesitates before politics, resists it, in the name of values that transcend the ordinary interests and antagonisms of social life. To believe and act as though it were otherwise is morally stupid, if not criminal. The record of communism betrays the dismal truth of 'cultural politics'. Routine docketing of all art according to its 'progressive' or 'reactionary' tendency, administered creation, a repertoire of edifying kitsch – these are the images that haunt the liberal imagination (and also the collective memory of socialists) and they cannot be wished away. Yet the recent course of left cultural politics has led in the opposite direction. 'Culture' understood as the moment of meaning in social relations is obviously not the entity enshrined in liberal tradition, but it is commonly granted a similar kind of authority. Far from subject to external political tests, culture is in itself already political, it is said, and this in a fuller sense than the narrow conventions of parties and programmes can comprehend. The innate meta-political ambition of liberal humanism has been reborn on the left, in the reductionist analytics and practice of *culturalism*.

This is not a logically necessary outcome of 'cultural studies' or 'cultural materialism'; its favouring condition has been the historical situation evoked earlier in these pages. But it is facilitated also by specifically theoretical difficulties, which in practice collude with objective circumstances, and which we do well to try to resolve.

The culturalist temptation is a spontaneous effect of current theoretical preferences. If the instance of culture is coextensive with sociality, it must encompass the political. Even on the closer definition of culture as the ensemble of those practices whose *principal* function is signification, the specificity of politics appears questionable. Culture is the necessary element of politics, whose means, moreover, are often strictly cultural. And thus, by simple elision, culture absorbs politics and assumes its titles. The attempt to affirm the political nature of culture leads, from its opposite beginnings, to a familiar conclusion: the dissolution of politics.

The conceptual germ of this confusion is, however, not so much an overweening sense of 'culture' as a deficient understanding of politics, which as a practice is always irreducible to the cultural, even when it moves wholly within its dimension. It is not that political discourse speaks of 'different' matters – let alone that culture is the province of 'higher' or 'deeper' (or 'ordinary') realities. In this respect there really is no final distinction between them. The object of politics is the totality of social relations in a given space, and this, however defined and inventoried, has also been a *topos* in important cultural traditions. But the discursive object of politics is also a practical field: more precisely defined, it is the *determination* (maintenance or alteration) of the totality. Thus, even as word and image, political practice is *modally* distinct from other kinds of discourse – and, finally, more than them. Political discourse is functionally specialized: it is essentially *deliberative* in character, moving always towards the question, What is to be done – and how? Its rhetoric is correspondingly distinctive: oriented towards the elaboration of contentious demands, the language of politics is in an especially strong sense 'performative', couched always, in effect, in the *imperative.*[29] And the decisive resources of this deliberative–imperative practice, lacking which it is something less than itself, are no longer simply cultural at all, but *coercive*: political discourse is systemically bonded with the actual or potential sanction of force, be that exercised through the state apparatuses or through the counter-power of mass action.

Thus, it is certainly necessary to insist that all culture is shot through with political values; necessary to insist at the same time that these, as meanings, are cultural; but it is therefore all the more necessary to understand that the two are mutually irreducible, and that their relationship is most fraught when it is closest, in notions of 'cultural politics'. The co-ordination of values implied in such phrases can perfect itself only in an illusion of identity that compromises both culture and politics. Any culture is more various than its corresponding politics. It will explore and promote solidarities and differences of value according to its own spontaneous dynamics, heedless of the regular discipline of deliberative reason; and such solidarities and differences are, in this mode, quasi-absolute – as Lukács once observed, there is no peaceful coexistence in the realm of ideas.[30] Political discourse also explores and promotes solidarities and antagonisms, but while these are necessarily asserted as, if not absolute then certainly decisive, they can never simply replicate the pattern of a coexistent culture. The simplest illustration of this comes from political culture itself: party forums debate (many) analyses but vote only on (a few) programmatic conclusions. Culture and politics are thus both sectarian and 'ecumenical' with respect to one another; each routinely makes excessive demands on the other, and that is how it must be.[31] In the field of cultural politics the only 'solutions' are bad ones.

The record of Marxist cultural politics itself points the moral here. Scientific positivism and artistic realism emerged as the cardinal values of the first phase. There were good reasons for this, transcending the force of cultural context. But in the historical outcome the function of these values, neither scientific nor realistic, was to orchestrate the deathly culture of bureaucratic omniscience and optimism. Realism found new defenders in the second phase, but now in the persons of such deeply anti-scientistic philosophers as Lukács and Sartre. Most 'critical' Marxism was similarly aloof from science but, contrastingly, well disposed towards modernism – again, in keeping with the ambient high culture of the time. This release from 'orthodoxy', a tonic in itself, stimulated invaluable work, but also recharged a delphic late-Romantic ethos of pessimism and abstract refusal. Neither 'solution' was empty, neither was adequate; and both, inevitably, were deeply conditioned by politico-cultural circumstances. Today, somewhere in the history of the third phase, having seen 'science' come again and go, having relived the 'realism–modernism debate' as a climactic novelty, understanding 'at last' that truth has gone the way of all modernity, we cannot delude ourselves that there is, for now, life outside the dominant culture, but we might at least learn to maintain a critical distance from its passing absolutes.[32]

In the smaller world of academic literary studies, the recurring flashpoint of cultural politics is the question of 'literary value'. I have already suggested the shortcomings of the counter-'ideological' appeal to 'literature' and 'literary value'. As a defence of *generic literariness*, it leads logically to a wider valorization of, say, story-telling or linguistic play, which works against the putative specificity of 'literature'. As a defence of *differential value*, it recedes towards a purely technical judgement unequal to its own moral pretensions. In either case, it fails in its objective purpose, which is to defend specific traditions of writing and to contain discussion of them through a disavowal of their substantive burden of meaning. We need not deny the experience of literary pleasure and unpleasure, complex and opaque as this often is, in order to maintain that 'value' is always transitive, *for* given subjects *in* given conditions, and that it is finally moral, in the ethical or the political stress of the word. And we need not promote a meaningless equality of all texts in order to maintain that received mystifications concerning 'quality' are not a fit basis for a discipline of rational inquiry. Far from this, the academic–liberal commitment to 'great literature' is only a nuance removed from the authoritarian–deferential middlebrow cult of 'a good book' (which every literary intellectual knows how to despise). It is enough that the writings enshrined in 'the canon', along with the greater body of writings whose cultural substance is indissociable from theirs, are richly *interesting* (in the strong sense, that is: engaging actual interests) as objects of rhetorical and other analysis, as interlocutors, as occasions of debate, as the available repertoire of writing today and tomorrow.

Expertise was Walter Benjamin's term for the cultural orientation suggested here, which implies more than skilled practice, for its contrary, in his analysis, was not 'incompetence' but *taste*.[33] 'Taste' is a relationship to culture (consumption) conditioned by estrangement from its processes of production. The inherited formations of literary study are another form of this estrangement, which tends to limit its students to the deprived accomplishment of (informed) taste. 'Expertise' might be the watchword of a cooler and not at all deferential relation to work in this field, as much for those who do not themselves aim to invent stories or song lyrics as for those who do. The distinction between 'criticism' and 'creation' has lain deep in literary studies, as it does in the wider culture, but it has no final authority. The Marxist tradition – including some of the contributors to this volume – has looked, and often acted, beyond its alienated terms. And so it is appropriate that the closing essay should be devoted to Benjamin's friend Brecht, who gave practical meaning to the conviction that for a developed Marxist cultural politics the point is not only to interpret rhetorics in history but to change them.

Notes

1. The relative slightness of reference in these notes is the effect of a writing format that discourages particular textual engagements, and does not adequately identify my debts, which are owing to many of the authors listed in Further Reading, not least the contributors to this volume, and others besides.

2. 'Socialism: Utopian and Scientific', in KARL MARX and FREDERICK ENGELS, *Selected Works* (London: Lawrence and Wishart, 1970), pp. 375–428. A *mode of production*, the central concept of Marxist theory, is a determinate combination of *forces* and *relations* of production. The former include the existing *means* of production, including not only technologies and raw materials but also the developed powers of living men and women; the latter include the relations of appropriation of the means and products of economic activity and also the systemic objective of production. Thus, in contrast with the narrowly technical idea of 'the economy' that predominates in bourgeois culture, a mode of production is *in itself* a fully *social* organization. And to argue for its determining role in social life is to point to the effects of *structured relationships*, not – again contrary to bourgeois ideology – to some essential human acquisitiveness.

3. MARX and ENGELS, *On Literature and Art* (Moscow: Progress Publishers, 1976); S.S. PRAWER, *Karl Marx and World Literature* (Oxford: Clarendon Press, 1976).

4. See MIKHAIL LIFSCHITZ, *The Philosophy of Art of Karl Marx* [1933] (London: Pluto Press, 1973); GEORG LUKÁCS, *Record of a Life: an Autobiographical Sketch* (London: Verso, 1983), pp. 163–4; RAYMOND WILLIAMS, 'Marxism and Culture' and 'Lukács: a Man Without Frustration' (a review of the foregoing) in his *What I Came to Say* (London: Hutchinson Radius, 1989), pp. 195–225 and 267–74 respectively.

5. 'Ludwig Feuerbach . . .', *Selected Works*, pp. 584–622; Letters to C. Schmidt (1890), J. Bloch (1890) and F. Mehring (1893), *Selected Works*, pp. 678–80 and 684–9; 682–3; 689–93.

6. MARX (19 April 1859) and ENGELS (18 May 1859) to Lassalle, *Collected Works*, vol. 40 (London: Lawrence and Wishart, 1983), pp. 419–20 and 441–6 respectively; ENGELS to Harkness (April 1888), *Marx and Engels on Literature and Art*, ed. Lee Baxandall and Stefan Morawski (New York: International General, 1974), pp. 115–17.

7. *Grundrisse* (Harmondsworth: Penguin, 1973), pp. 110–11.

8. PLEKHANOV, *Unaddressed Letters and Art and Social Life* (Moscow: Progress Publishers, 1957); cf. KARL KAUTSKY, *The Materialist Conception of History*, ed. John H. Kautsky (New Haven and London: Yale University Press, 1988), pp. 101–2.

9. PERRY ANDERSON's *Considerations on Western Marxism* (London: NLB, 1976) is the outstanding reconstruction of this history. My indebtedness to it will be evident to anyone who reads it. My main disagreement here is that whereas

Anderson regards a strong orientation to contemporaneous bourgeois culture as distinctively 'Western Marxist', I see it as historically normal – though not therefore a matter of indifference.

10. *History and Class Consciousness* (London: Merlin Press, 1971), p. xx.

11. This is ARNO MAYER's telling designation for the period 1914–45: see his *The Persistence of the Old Regime* (London: Croom Helm, 1981).

12. The standard account of the Frankfurt School is MARTIN JAY, *The Dialectical Imagination* (London: Heinemann, 1973); see also EUGENE LUNN, *Marxism and Modernism* (London: Verso, 1985).

13. See 'Contradiction and Overdetermination' (1962) in his *For Marx* (London: NLB, 1977), pp. 89–128.

14. A passage like this one, which quotes the breeze rather than signed and dated texts, must seem indiscriminate, and even unjust in respect of particular persons. My generalizations refer not to a totality of individuals but the stronger tendencies of the milieu they currently inhabit. They focus, moreover, on a particular 'generation' (of work and experience, not necessarily of age) and may be inapplicable to students, teachers and writers of more recent formation.

15. Here and later I use the term 'intertextual/intertextuality' in the sense of Julia Kristeva's original coinage, meaning: the presence within a text of 'other' texts of its culture. It does not mean simple 'influence' and does not bear only on the special case of 'allusion', but rather is part of a redefinition of textuality *as such*. This sense must be distinguished from a more recent one, marked only by the insertion of a vulnerable hyphen (inter-textuality) and referring to the effect, in reading, of a given text's changeable associations with other existing texts (see TONY BENNETT and JANET WOOLLACOTT, *Bond and Beyond*, London: Macmillan, 1987, pp. 6–8).

16. 'The Question of a *Weltanschauung*', *New Introductory Lectures*, Standard Edition of the Complete Psychological Works, Vol. XXII (London: The Hogarth Press, 1964), p. 158.

17. See SEBASTIANO TIMPANARO, *On Materialism* (London: NLB, 1975).

18. The analysis of 'reading formations' is developed in BENNETT and WOOLLACOTT, *Bond and Beyond*.

19. The Soviet/Estonian semiotician YURI M. LOTMAN proposes the concept of *repertoire*, but with specific reference to 'text-oriented cultures', which he distinguishes from 'grammar-oriented' cultures governed, contrastingly, by *system* (see his *Universe of the Mind: a Semiotic Theory of Culture*, London: I.B. Tauris, 1990, and Umberto Eco's 'Introduction'). This analytic option seems to me to spare Romantic notions of culture just when it is poised to displace them. A distinction between, say, 'prescribed' and 'discretionary' repertoires might be a less tendentious way of acknowledging the historical differences he has in view.

20. See ROLAND BARTHES, *Mythologies* (London: Paladin, 1973), especially the concluding essay, 'Myth Today', pp. 109–59.

21. See FREDRIC JAMESON, *The Political Unconscious* (Ithaca, NY: Cornell University Press, 1981), ch. 6; FREUD, *Jokes and Their Relation to the Unconscious* (Harmondsworth: Penguin, 1976); JULIA KRISTEVA, *Desire in Language*, ed. Leon S. Roudiez (Oxford: Basil Blackwell, 1980. PERRY ANDERSON is among those Marxists who resist the displacement of the literary/aesthetic and of canon-defined fields of study, discerning in it a well-meaning ('democratic' and

'egalitarian') but misjudged liquidation of the practice of judgement and, above all, a denial of differential technical accomplishment ('A Culture in Contraflow – II', *New Left Review*, 182, 1990, pp. 85–137, at pp. 85–97). His case does not convince, either as criticism or as recommendation, founded as it is on certain stock associations of ideas. Decisions concerning the *range* of inquiry do not necessarily dictate the *nature* of the inquiry itself; and the issue of the literary/aesthetic as a category is logically distinct from that of generic or differential textual 'value'. The recall of technical achievement is insufficient as a defence of historic canons (some traditionalists would shun it, fearing damnation by faint praise) and, more importantly, as a corrective for the future: to deny differential 'skill' is simple populism, but to privilege it as an object of study is simple connoisseurism. The truly democratic and egalitarian demand for the widest possible learning of skills imagines a culture no longer deformed by the mutually confirming antipathies of populist and connoisseur.

22. For an interesting discussion see 'The "Text in Itself"', *Southern Review* (Adelaide), 17 (1984), a symposium led off by Terry Eagleton and Tony Bennett, and continuing with interventions by Noel King, Ian Hunter, Peter Hulme, Catherine Belsey and John Frow (cf. Further Reading, below).

23. The classic statement, much debated over the past twenty years, is QUENTIN SKINNER, 'Meaning and Understanding in the History of Ideas', *History and Theory*, 8, 1969. Skinner's polemical precedent was, aptly enough, literary-critical: the debate between F. R. Leavis and the 'contextualist' F. W. Bateson in *Essays in Criticism*, III (1953) and *Scrutiny*, 19 (1953).

24. These sentences draw freely on ALTHUSSER, *Reading Capital* (London: NLB, 1971); some historiographical themes of the *Annales* school (see PIERRE VILAR, 'Marxist History, a History in the Making: Dialogue With Althusser, *New Left Review*, 80 (1973), pp. 65–106); and on STEPHEN JAY GOULD's explorations of the structures and processes of natural history (see, for example, *Time's Arrow, Time's Cycle: Myth and Metaphor in the Discovery of Geological Time*, Cambridge, Mass: Harvard University Press, 1987).

25. ROSALIND COWARD and JOHN ELLIS, *Language and Materialism* (London: RKP, 1977) and RAYMOND WILLIAMS, *Marxism and Literature* (Oxford: Oxford University Press, 1977) are in their different ways influential statements of this general tendency. See also TERRY EAGLETON's critical assessment 'Base and Superstructure in Raymond Williams', in Terry Eagleton, ed., *Raymond Williams: Critical Perspectives* (Oxford: Polity, 1989), pp. 165–75.

26. 'Marxism as a Sociology' (1958), in his *From Rousseau to Lenin* (London: NLB, 1972), p. 5.

27. 'Contradiction and Overdetermination', *For Marx*, pp. 95–8, 113.

28. Cf. TIMPANARO, *On Materialism*, 2nd edn (London: Verso, 1980), p. 261.

29. *Gerundive* ('expressing the idea of necessity or fitness': *OED*) would be better here: that is, to take the old textbook illustration, the exhortation 'Carthage must be destroyed' rather than the simple command 'Destroy Carthage'. But I leave this point as an aside.

30. Cited in FRANCO FORTINI, *Verifica dei poteri* (Milan: Il Saggiatore/Garzanti, 1974), p. 158.

31. This is how I interpret Gramsci's remarks on Paul Nizan (*Selections From Cultural Writings*, ed. David Forgács and Geoffrey Nowell-Smith, London: Lawrence and Wishart, 1985, pp. 99–102). See also NIZAN, *Pour une nouvelle culture* (Paris: Grasset, 1971).

32. The nostrum of 'anti-humanism' calls for particular attention. 'Anti-humanism' is confident in rejecting the notion of a human essence (its principal definition) and the putatively bourgeois conception of the subject as self-transparent originator of meaning (its longest-running theme); yet as a contributor to radical social thought, it belongs to a broad historical tradition that affirms the possibility and value of human self-development, and is in that sense 'humanist'. This ambiguity is more than superficial and more than contemplative; it bespeaks theoretical deficiency and promotes practical confusion. The critique of essentialism, pursued unilaterally, is itself idealist, denying our common and relatively stable reality as a natural species; and too-euphoric a dissolution of the humanist subject may reduce all programmes of emancipation to a Babel in which ideas of 'need' and 'right' are merely positional gambits. 'Anti-humanism' is defiantly 'historical' – but historical understanding is practised whole or not at all. Human time is complex, syncopated but also regular, rapid but also unobservably slow; and even if our history does not move towards a preinscribed *telos*, it does not follow that all ideas of development are 'modern' fictions. Among the numerous imperatives of the struggle for human emancipation is the need to clarify (in properly historical and materialist ways) the terms of a general interest. And in this sense, 'humanism' may prove to be, as Marxism was for Sartre, an 'unsurpassable horizon'.

33. *Charles Baudelaire: a Lyric Poet in the Era of High Capitalism* (London: NLB, 1973), pp. 104–6.

1 On Literature as an Ideological Form* (1974)

ETIENNE BALIBAR AND PIERRE MACHEREY

Etienne Balibar (b. 1942) and Pierre Macherey teach philosophy at the University of Paris. Balibar is the co-author, with Louis Althusser, of *Reading Capital* (1971), a selection from the larger *Lire le Capital* (1965), to which Macherey and others also contributed. Macherey is the author of *A Theory of Literary Production* (1966; trans. 1978).

Balibar and Macherey here return to the classic question 'What is literature?' in order to displace it as an illegitimate intrusion into Marxist theory. Drawing upon Althusser's later theory of ideology, they propose instead a view of literature as a specific mode of ideological practice, whose material effects derive from its role in the reproduction of the 'national' (common and class-divided) language and in the bourgeois educational apparatuses whose basic practice this is. The 'literary effect' dramatizes ideological antagonisms in such a way that their resolution is already given. As a norm, 'literature' sustains inequality and domination within linguistic practice itself, staging but also confirming the contradiction between 'writ-ing'–'reading' and merely 'knowing how to read and write'. The mythic liberties of the literary – authorship, appreciation and so on – are the deceptive signs of its institutionalized conservative ideological function.

Is there a Marxist theory of literature? In what could it consist? This is a classic question, and often purely academic. We intend to reformulate it in two stages and suggest new propositions.

---

* Reprinted from *Oxford Literary Review*, 3 (1978), pp. 4–12. Translated by Ian McLeod, John Whitehead and Ann Wordsworth.

Marxist theses on literature and the category of 'reflection'

Can there be a 'Marxist aesthetic'?

It is not our intention to give an account of the attempts which have been made to substantiate this idea or of the controversies which have surrounded it. We will merely point out that to constitute an aesthetic (and particularly a literary aesthetic) has always presented Marxism with two kinds of problem, which can be combined or held separate: (i) How to explain the specific ideological mode for 'art' and the 'aesthetic' effect. (ii) How to analyse and explain the class position (or the class positions, which may be contradictory in themselves) of the author and more materially the 'literary text', within the ideological class struggle.

The first problem is obviously brought in, imposed on Marxism by the dominant ideology so as to force the Marxist critic to produce his own aesthetic and to 'settle accounts' with art, the work of art, the aesthetic effect, just like Lessing, or Hegel, or Taine, or Valéry et al. Since the problem is imposed on Marxism from outside, it offers two alternatives: to reject the problem and so be 'proved' unable to explain, not so much a 'reality' as an absolute 'value' of our time, which is now supreme since it has replaced religious value; or to recognise the problem and therefore be forced to acknowledge aesthetic 'values', i.e. to submit to them. This is an even better result for the dominant ideology since it thereby makes Marxism yield to the 'values' of the dominant class within its own problematic – a result which has great political significance in a period when Marxism becomes the ideology of the working class.

The second problem meanwhile is induced from within the theory and practice of Marxism, on its own terrain, but in such a way that it can remain a formal and mechanical presentation. In this case the necessary criterion is that of practice. In the first place, of scientific practice: the question for Marxism should be, does the act of confronting literary texts with their class positions result in the opening of new fields of knowledge and in the first place simply in the siting of new problems? The proof of the right formulation would be whether it makes objectively clear within historical materialism itself whole sets of unsolved and sometimes as yet unrecognised problems.[1]

In the second place, the criterion of political practice itself, in so far as it is operative within literature. The least one should therefore ask of a Marxist theory is that it should bring about real transformation, new practice, whether in the production of texts and 'works of art' or in their social 'consumption'. But is this a real transformation, even if at times it does have an immediate political effect – the simple fact of endowing the practitioners of art (writers and artists, but also teachers and students) with a Marxist ideology of the form and social function of art (even if this operation may sometimes have a certain immediate political interest)? Is it enough simply to give Marxism and its adherents their turn to taste and consume works of art in their own way? In effect experience proves that it is perfectly possible to substitute new 'Marxist' themes, i.e. formulated in the language of Marxism, for the ideological notions dominant in 'cultural life', notions that are bourgeois or petit-bourgeois in origin, and yet not alter at all the place of art and literature within social practice, nor therefore the practical relationship of individuals and classes to the works of art they produce and consume. The category of art in general dominates production and consumption, which are conceived and practised within this mode – whether 'committed', 'socialist', 'proletarian', or whatever.

Yet in the Marxist classics there were elements which can open a path (*frayer la voie*). Of course they do not constitute an 'aesthetic' or a 'theory of literature', any more than a 'theory of knowledge'. Yet through their mode of practising literature and the implications of a theoretical position based ultimately on revolutionary class practice, they pose certain theses about literary effects, which, worked within the problematic of historical materialism, can contribute to a scientific and therefore historical analysis of literary effects.[2]

These very general premises are enough to show at once that the two types of problem between which Marxist attempts are divided are really one and the same. To be able to analyse the nature and expression of class positions in literature and its output (the 'texts', 'works' perceived as literature) is simultaneously to be able to define and know the ideological mode of literature. But this means that the problem must be posed in terms of a theory of the history of literary effects, clearly showing the primary elements of their relation to their material base, their progressions (for they are not eternal) and their tendential transformations (for they are not immutable).

The materialist category of reflection

Let us be clear. The classic Marxist theses on literature and art set out from the essential philosophical category of reflection. To understand this category fully is therefore the key to the Marxist conception of literature.

In the Marxist texts on this materialist concept, Marx and Engels on Balzac, Lenin on Tolstoy, it is *qua* material reflection, reflection of objective reality, that literature is conceived as an historic reality – in its very form, which scientific analysis seeks to grasp.

In the 'Talks at the Yenan Forum on Literature and Art', Mao Tse-Tung writes, 'Works of literature and art, as ideological forms, are the product of the reflection in the human brain of the life of a given society.'[3] So the first implication of the category of reflection for Marxist theoreticians is to provide an index of reality of literature. It does not 'fall from the heavens', the product of mysterious 'creation', but is the product of social practice (rather, a particular social practice); it is not an 'imaginary' activity, although producing imaginary effects, but inescapably part of a material process, 'the product of the reflection . . . of the life of a given society'.

The Marxist conception thus inscribes literature in its place in the unevenly determined system of real social practices: one of several ideological forms within the ideological superstructures, corresponding to a base of social relations of production which are historically determined and transformed, and historically linked to other ideological forms. Be sure that in using the term ideological forms no reference to formalism is intended – the historical materialist concept does not refer to 'form' in opposition to 'content', but to the objective coherence of an ideological formation – we shall come back to this point. Let us note too that this first, very general but absolutely essential premise, has no truck with queries about what ideological form is taken by literature within the ideological instance. There is no 'reduction' of literature to morality, religion, politics, etc.

The Marxist concept of reflection has suffered from so many misinterpretations and distortions that we must stop here for a moment. The conclusions reached by Dominique Lecourt through an attentive reading of Lenin's *Materialism and Empiriocriticism* will be useful to us.[4]

Dominique Lecourt shows that the Marxist and Leninist category of reflection contains two propositions which are combined within a constitutive order – or better, two successive articulated problems. (Thus according to Lecourt there is not one simple thesis, but a double thesis of the reflection of things in thought.)

The first problem, which materialism always re-establishes in its priority, is that of the objectivity of reflection. It poses the question: 'Is there an existent material reality reflected in the mind which determines thought?' And consequently it has the rider, 'Is thought itself a materially determined reality?' Dialectical materialism asserts the objectivity of the reflection and the objectivity of thought as reflection, i.e. the determinance of the material reality which precedes thought and is irreducible to it, and the material reality of thought itself.

The second problem, which can only be posed correctly on the basis of the first, concerns the scientific knowledge of the exactitude of the reflection. It poses the question, '*If* thought reflects an existent reality how accurate is its reflection?' or better, 'Under what conditions (i.e. historical conditions whereby the dialectic between "absolute truth" and "relative truth" intervenes) can it provide an accurate reflection?' The answer lies in the analysis of the relatively autonomous process of the history of science. In the context, it is clear that this second problem poses the question, 'What form does the reflection take?' But it only has a materialist implication once the first question has been posed and the objectivity of the reflection affirmed.

The result of this analysis, which we have only given in outline, is to show that the Marxist category of 'reflection' is quite separate from the empiricist and sensualist concept of the image, reflection as 'mirroring'. The reflection, in dialectical materialism, is a 'reflection without a mirror'; in the history of philosophy this is the only effective destruction of the empiricist ideology which calls the relation of thought to the real a specular (and therefore reversible) reflection. This is thanks to the complexity of the Marxist theory of 'reflection': it poses the separate nature of two propositions and their articulation in an irreversible order within which the materialist account is realised.

These observations are central to the problem of the 'theory of literature'. A rigorous use of this complex structure eliminates the seeming opposition of two contrary descriptions: that between formalism and the 'critical' or 'normative' use of the notion of 'realism'. That is, on one side an intention to study the reflection 'for itself', independent of its relationship to the material world; on the other, a confusion of both aspects and an assertion of the primacy of thought, a reversal of the materialist order.[5]

Hence the advantage of a rigorous definition like Lenin's, for it is then possible to articulate, in theory as in fact, two aspects which must be both kept separate and in a constitutive order: literature as an ideological form (amongst others), and the specific process of literary production.

Literature as an ideological form

It is important to 'locate' the production of literary effects historically as part of the ensemble of social practices. For this to be seen dialectically rather than mechanically, it is important to understand that the relationship of 'history' to 'literature' is not like the relationship or 'correspondence' of two 'branches', but concerns the developing forms of an internal contradiction. Literature and history are not external to each other (not even as the history *of* literature versus social and political history), but are in an intricate and connected relationship, the historical condition of existence of anything like a literature. Very generally, this internal relationship is what constitutes the definition of literature as an ideological form.

But this definition is significant only in so far as its implications are then developed. Ideological forms, to be sure, are not straightforward systems of 'ideas' and 'discourses', but are manifested through the workings and history of determinate practices in determinate social relations, what Althusser calls the Ideological State Apparatuses (ISAs). The objectivity of literary production is therefore inseparable from given social practices in a given ISA. More precisely, we shall see that it is inseparable from a given linguistic practice (there is a 'French' literature because there is a linguistic practice 'French', i.e. a contradictory ensemble making a national tongue), in itself inseparable from an academic or schooling practice which defines both the conditions for the consumption of literature and the very conditions of its production also. By connecting the objective existence of literature to this ensemble of practices, one can define the material anchoring points which make literature an historic and social reality.

First, then, literature is historically constituted in the bourgeois epoch as an ensemble of language – or rather of specific linguistic practices – inserted in a general schooling process so as to provide appropriate fictional effects, thereby reproducing bourgeois ideology as the dominant ideology. Literature submits to a threefold determination: 'linguistic', 'pedagogic', and 'fictive' (*imaginaire*) – we must return to this point, for it involves the question of a recourse to psychoanalysis for an explanation of literary effects. There is a linguistic determination because the work of literary production depends on the existence of a common language codifying linguistic exchange, both for its material and for its aims – in so far as literature contributes directly to the maintenance of a 'common language'. That it has this starting point is proved by the fact that divergences from the common language are not arbitrary but determined. In our introduction to the work of Renée Balibar and Dominique Laporte, we sketched out an explanation of the historical process by which this 'common language' is set up.[6] Following their line of thought, we stressed that the common language, i.e. the national language, is bound to the political form of 'bourgeois democracy' and is the historical outcome of particular class struggles. Like bourgeois right, its parallel, the common national language is needed to unify a new class domination, thereby universalising it and providing it with progressive forms throughout its epoch. It refers therefore to a social contradiction, perpetually reproduced via the process which surmounts it. What is the basis of this contradiction?

It is the effect of the historic conditions under which the bourgeois class established its political, economic and ideological dominance. To achieve hegemony, it had not only to transform the base, the relations of production, but also radically to transform the superstructure, the ideological formations. This transformation could be called the bourgeois 'cultural revolution' since it involves not only the formation of a new ideology, but its realisation as the dominant ideology, through new ISAs and the remoulding of the relationships between the different ISAs. This revolutionary transformation, which took more than a century but which was preparing itself for far longer, consisted in making the schooling apparatus the means of forcing submission to the dominant ideology – individual submission, but also, and more importantly, the submission of the very ideology of the dominated classes. Therefore in the last analysis, all ideological contradictions rest on the contradictions of this apparatus, and become contradictions subordinated and internal to the form of schooling.

We are beginning to work out the form taken by social contradictions in the schooling apparatus. It can only establish itself through the formal unity of a 'single' and 'unifying' educational system, the product of this same unity, which is itself formed from the co-existence of two systems or contradictory networks: those which, by following the institutional division of 'levels of teaching' which in France has long served to materialise this contradiction, we could call the apparatus of 'basic education' (*primaire-professionnel*) and that of 'advanced education' (*secondaire-supérieur*).[7]

This division in schooling, which reproduces the social division of a society based on the sale and purchase of individual labour-power, while ensuring the dominance of bourgeois ideology through asserting a specifically national unity, is primarily and pervasively based on a linguistic division. Let us be clear: there as well, the unifying form is the essential means of the division and of the contradiction. The linguistic division inherent in schooling is not like the division between different 'languages' observable in certain pre-capitalist social formations – those languages being a 'language of the common people' (dialect, patois or argot), and a 'language of the bourgeoisie' – on the contrary, the division presupposes a common language, and is the contradiction between different practices of the same language. Specifically, it is in and through the educational system that the contradiction is instituted – through the contradiction between the basic language (*français élémentaire*), as taught at primary school, and the literary language (*français littéraire*) reserved for the advanced level of teaching. This is the basis of the contradiction in schooling techniques, particularly between the basic exercise of 'rédaction–narration', a mere training in 'correct' usage and the reporting of 'reality', and the advanced exercise of comprehension, the 'dissertation-explication de textes', so-called 'creative' work which presupposes the incorporation and imitation of literary material. Hence the contradictions in schooling practice, and in ideological practice and in social practice. What thus appears as the basis of literary production is an unequal and contradictory relation to the same ideology, the dominant one. But this contradiction would not exist if the dominant ideology did not have to struggle all the time for its priority.

From this analysis, given in mere outline, there is an essential point to be grasped: the objectivity of literature, i.e. its relation to objective reality by which it is historically determined, is not a relation to an 'object' which it represents, is not representational. Nor is it purely and simply the instrument for using and transforming its immediate material, the linguistic practices determined within the practice of teaching. Precisely because of their contradictions, they cannot be used as a simple primary material: thus all use is an intervention, made from a standpoint, a declaration (in a general sense) from within the contradiction and hence a further development of it. So, the objectivity of literature is its necessary place within the determinate processes and reproduction of the contradictory linguistic practices of the common tongue, in which the effectivity of the ideology of bourgeois education is realised.

This siting of the problem abolishes the old idealist question, 'What is literature?', which is not a question about its objective determination, but a question about its universal essence, human and artistic.[8] It abolishes it because it shows us directly the material function of literature, inserted within a process which literature cannot determine even though it is indispensable to it. If literary production has for its material and specific base the contradictions of linguistic practices in schooling taken up and internalised (through an indefinitely repeated labour of fiction), it is because literature itself is one of the terms of the contradiction whose other term is determinately bound to literature. Dialectically, literature is simultaneously product and material condition of the linguistic division in education, term and effect of its own contradictions. It is not surprising, therefore, that the ideology of literature, itself a part of literature, should work ceaselessly to deny this objective base: to represent literature supremely as 'style', as individual genius, conscious or natural, as creativity, etc., as something outside (and above) the process of education, which is merely able to disseminate literature, and to comment on it exhaustively, though with no possibility of finally capturing it. The root of this constitutive repression is the objective status of literature as an historic ideological form, its relation to the class struggle. And the first and last commandment in its ideology is: 'Thou shalt describe all forms of class struggle, save that which determines thine own self.'

By the same token, the question of the relation of literature to the dominant ideology is posed afresh – escaping a confrontation of universal essences, in which many Marxist discussions have been trapped. To see literature as ideologically determined is not – cannot be – to 'reduce' it to moral ideologies or to political, religious, even aesthetic ideologies which are definable outside literature. Nor is it to make ideology the content to which literature brings form – even when there are themes and ideological statements which are more or less perfectly separable. Such a pairing is thoroughly mechanical, and, moreover, serves to corroborate the way in which the ideology of literature by displacement misconstrues its historic determination. It merely prolongs the endless false dialectic of 'form' and 'content' whereby the artificially imposed terms alternate so that literature is sometimes perceived as content (ideology), sometimes as form ('real' literature). To define literature as a particular ideological form is to pose quite another problem: the specificity of ideological effects produced by literature and the means (techniques) of production. This returns us to the second question involved in the dialectical materialist concept of reflection.

The process of production of aesthetic effects in literature

By now, thanks to the proper use of the Marxist concept of reflection, we are able to avoid the false dilemma of the literary critic (should we analyse literature on its own ground – search out its essence – or from an external standpoint – find out its function?). Once we know better than to reduce literature either to something other than itself or to itself, but instead analyse its ideological specificity,[9] helped by the conclusions of Renée Balibar, we can attempt to trace the material concepts which appear in this analysis. Of course such a sketch has only a provisional value – but it helps us to see the consistency of our materialist concept of literature and its conceptual place within historical materialism.

As we see it, these concepts have three moments. They refer simultaneously to (i) the contradictions which literary ideological formations (texts) realise and develop; (ii) the mode of ideological identification produced by the action of fiction; and (iii) the place of literary aesthetic effects in the reproduction of the dominant ideology. Let us deal with each one schematically.

The specific complexity of literary formations – ideological contradictions and linguistic conflicts

The first principle of a materialist analysis would be: literary productions must not be studied in their unity, which is illusory and false, but in their material disparity. One must not look for unifying effects but for signs of the contradictions (historically determined) which produced them and which appear as unevenly resolved conflicts in the text.

So, in searching out the determinant contradictions, the materialist analysis of literature rejects on principle the notion of 'the work' – i.e. the illusory presentation of the unity of a text, its totality, self-sufficiency and perfection (in both senses of the word: success and completion). More precisely, it recognises the notion of 'the work' (and its correlative, 'the author') only in order to identify both as necessary illusions written into the ideology of literature, the accompaniment of all literary production. The text is produced under conditions which represent it as a finished work, providing a requisite order, expressing either a subjective theme or the spirit of the age, according to whether the reading is a naive or a sophisticated one. Yet in itself the text is none of these things: on the contrary, it is materially incomplete, disparate and diffuse, the conflictual contradictory effect of overriding real processes which cannot be abolished in it except in an imaginary way.[10]

To be more explicit: literature is produced finally through the effect of one or more ideological contradictions precisely because these contradictions cannot be solved within ideology, i.e. in the last analysis through the effect of contradictory class positions within ideology, as such irreconcilable. Obviously these contradictory ideological positions are not in themselves 'literary' – that would lead us back into the closed circle of 'literature'. They are ideological positions within theory and practice, covering the whole field of the ideological class struggle, i.e. religious, juridical and political, and they correspond to the conjunctures of the class struggle itself. But it would be pointless to look in the texts for the 'original' bare discourse of these ideological positions, as they were 'before' their 'literary' realisations, for these ideological positions can only be formed in the materiality of the literary text. That is, they can only appear in a form which provides their imaginary solution, or better still, which displaces them by substituting imaginary contradictions soluble within the ideological practice of religion, politics, morality, aesthetics and psychology.

Let us approach this phenomenon more closely. We shall say that literature 'begins' with the imaginary solution of implacable ideological contradictions, with the representation of that solution: not in the sense of representing i.e. 'figuring' (by images, allegories, symbols or arguments) a solution which is really there (to repeat, literature is produced because such a solution is impossible) but in the sense of providing a 'mise en scène', a presentation as solution of the very terms of an insurmountable contradiction, by means of various displacements and substitutions. For there to be a literature, it must be the very terms of the contradiction (and hence of the contradictory ideological elements) that are enunciated in a special language, a language of 'compromise', realising in advance the fiction of a forthcoming conciliation. Or better still, it finds a language of 'compromise' which presents the conciliation as 'natural' and so both necessary and inevitable.

In *A Theory of Literary Production*, with reference to Lenin's work on Tolstoy, and Verne and Balzac, the attempt was made to use materialist principles to show the complex contradictions which produce the literary text: in each case, specifically, what can be identified as the ideological project of the author, the expression of one determinate class position, is only one of the terms of the contradiction of whose oppositions the text makes an imaginary synthesis despite the real oppositions which it cannot abolish. Hence the idea that the literary text is not so much the expression of ideology (its 'putting into words') as its staging, its display, an operation which has an inbuilt disadvantage since it cannot be done without showing its limits, thereby revealing its inability to subsume a hostile ideology.

But what remained unclear in *A Theory* is the process of literary production, the textual devices which present the contradictions of an ideological discourse as the same as the fiction of its unity and its reconciliation, conditionally upon this same fiction. What still evades us, in other words, is the specific mechanism of the literary 'compromise', in so far as the materialist account is still too general. The work of Renée Balibar makes it possible to surmount this difficulty and so not only complete the account but also correct and transform it.

What does Renée Balibar show us? That the discourse, literature's own special 'language', in which the contradictions are set out, is not outside ideological struggles as if veiling them in a neutral, neutralising way. Its relation to these struggles is not secondary but constitutive; it is always already implicated in producing them. Literary language is itself formed by the effects of a class contradiction. This is fundamental, bringing us back to the material base of all literature. Literary language is produced in its specificity (and in all permitted individual variants) at the level of linguistic conflicts, historically determined in the bourgeois epoch by the development of a 'common language' and of an educational system which imposes it on all, whether cultured or not.

This, schematically put, is the principle of the complex nature of literary formations, the production of which shares the material conditions necessary to the bourgeois social formation and transforms itself accordingly. It is the imaginary solution of ideological contradictions in so far as they are formulated in a special language which is both different from the common language and within it (the common language itself being the product of an internal conflict), and which realises and masks in a series of compromises the conflict which constitutes it. It is this displacement of contradictions which Renée Balibar calls 'literary style' and whose dialectic she has begun to analyse. It is a remarkable dialectic, for it succeeds in producing the effect and the illusion of an imaginary reconciliation of irreconcilable terms by displacing the ensemble of ideological contradictions on to a single one, or a single aspect, the linguistic conflict itself. So the imaginary solution has no other 'secret' than the development, the redoubling of the contradiction: this is surely, if one knows how to analyse it and work it out, the proof of its irreconcilable nature.

We are now ready to outline the principal aspects of the aesthetic effect of literature as an ideological device.

Fiction and realism: the mechanism of identification in literature

Here we must pause, even if over-schematically, to consider a characteristic literary effect which has already been briefly mentioned: the identification effect. Brecht was the first Marxist theoretician to focus on this, showing how the ideological effects of literature (and of the theatre, with the specific transformations that implies) materialise via an identification process between the reader or the audience and the hero or anti-hero – the simultaneous mutual constitution of the fictive 'consciousness' of the character with the ideological 'consciousness' of the reader.[11]

But it is obvious that any process of identification is dependent on the constitution and recognition of the individual as 'subject' – to use a very common ideological notion lifted by philosophy from the juridical and turning up in various forms at all other levels of bourgeois ideology. Now all ideology, as Althusser shows in his essay 'Ideology and Ideological State Apparatuses', must in a practical way 'hail or interpellate individuals as subjects': so that they perceive themselves as such, with rights and duties, the obligatory accompaniments. Each ideology has its specific mode: each gives to the 'subject' – and therefore to other real or imaginary subjects who confront the individual and present him with his ideological identification in a personal form – one or more appropriate names. In the ideology of literature, the nomenclature is: Authors (i.e. signatures), Works (i.e. titles), Readers, and Characters (with their social background, real or imaginary). But in literature, the process of constituting subjects and setting up their relationships of mutual recognition necessarily takes a detour via the fictional world and its values, because that process (i.e. of constitution and setting up) embraces within its circle the 'concrete' or 'abstract' 'persons' which the text stages. We now reach a classic general problem: what is specifically 'fictional' about literature? We shall preface our solution with a parenthesis.

Speaking of 'fiction' in literature usually entails singling out certain genres privileged as such: the novel, tale, short story. More generally, it indicates something which, whatever its traditional genre, can be appealed to as novelistic: it 'tells a story', whether about the teller himself or about other characters, about an individual or an idea. In this sense the idea of fiction becomes allegorically the definition of literature in general, since all literary texts involve a story or a plot, realistic or symbolic, and arrange in a 'time', actual or not, chronological or quasi-chronological, a sequence of events which do or do not make sense (in formalist texts, order can be reduced to a verbal structure only). All description of literature in general, as of fiction, seems to involve this primary element: the dependence on a story which is analogous to 'life'.

But this characteristic involves another, more crucial still: the idea of confronting a model. All 'fiction', it seems, has a reference point, whether to 'reality' or to 'truth', and takes its meaning from that. To define literature as fiction means taking an old philosophical position, which since Plato has been linked with the establishing of a theory of knowledge, and confronting the fictional discourse with a reality, whether in nature or history, so that the text is a transposition, a reproduction, adequate or not, and valued accordingly and in relation to standards of verisimilitude and artistic licence.

There is no need to go further into details: it is enough to recognise the consistency which links the definition of literature as fiction with a particular appropriation of the category 'realism'. As everyone knows, realism is the key-word of a school: that in favour of a realist 'literature' in place of 'pure fiction', i.e. bad fiction. This too implies a definition of literature in general: all literature must be realist, in one way or another, a representation of reality, even and especially when it gives reality an image outside immediate perception and daily life and common experience. The 'shores' of reality can stretch to infinity. And yet the idea of realism is not the opposite of fiction: it scarcely differs from it. It too has the idea of a model and of its reproduction, however complex that may be – a model outside the representation, at least for the fleeting instant of evaluation – and of a norm, even if it is nameless.

After this digression, we can get back to the problem we had set ourselves. Marxist propositions, provisional and immature as they may be, are nevertheless bound to effect a profound critical transformation of the classic idealist problematic. Let us have no doubt, for instance, that the classics of Marxism, not to speak of Brecht and Gramsci, who can be our guides here, never dealt with literature in terms of 'realism'. The category of reflection, central to the Marxist problematic as we have shown, is not concerned with realism but with materialism, which is profoundly different. Marxism cannot define literature in general as fiction in the classic sense.

Literature is not fiction, a fictive image of the real, because it cannot define itself simply as a figuration, an appearance of reality. Literature is the production, by a complex process, of a certain reality – not indeed (one cannot over-emphasise this) an autonomous reality, but a material reality – and of a certain social effect (we shall conclude with this). Literature is not therefore fiction, but the production of fictions: or better still, the production of fiction-effects (and in the first place the provider of the material means for the production of fiction-effects).

Similarly, as the 'reflection of the life of a given society', historically given (Mao), literature is still not providing a 'realist' reproduction of it, even and least of all when it proclaims itself to be such, because even then it cannot be reduced to a straight mirroring. But it is true that the text does produce a reality-effect. More precisely it produces simultaneously a reality-effect and a fiction-effect, emphasising first one and then the other, interpreting each by each in turn but always on the basis of their dualism.

So, it comes to this once more: fiction and realism are not the concepts for the production of literature but, on the contrary, notions produced by literature. But this leads to remarkable consequences, for it means that the model, the real referent 'outside' the discourse which both fiction and realism presuppose, has no function here as a non-literary non-discursive anchoring point predating the text. (We know by now that this anchorage, the primacy of the real, is different from and more complex than a 'representation'.) But it does function as an effect of the discourse. So, the literary discourse itself institutes and projects the presence of the 'real' in the manner of an hallucination.

How is this materially possible? How can the text so control what it says, what it describes, what it sets up (or 'those' it sets up) with its sign of hallucinatory reality, or contrastingly, its fictive sign, diverging, infinitesimally perhaps, from the 'real'? On this point too, the works we have used supply the material for an answer. Once more they refer us to the effects and forms of the fundamental linguistic conflict.

In a study of 'modern' French literary texts, carefully dated in each case according to their place in the history of the common language and of the educational system, Renée Balibar refers to the production of 'imaginary French' (*français fictif*). What does this mean? Clearly not pseudo-French, elements of a pseudo-language, seeing that these literary instances do also appear in certain contexts chosen by particular individuals, e.g. by compilers of dictionaries who illustrate their rubrics only with literary quotations. Nor is it simply a case of the language being produced in fiction (with its own usages, syntax and vocabulary), characters in a narrative making an imaginary discourse in an imaginary language. Instead, it is a case of expressions which always diverge in one or more salient details from those used in practice outside the literary discourse, even when both are grammatically 'correct'. These are linguistic 'compromise formations', compromising between usages which are socially contradictory in practice and hence exclude each other. In these compromise formations there is an essential place, more or less disguised but recognisable, for the reproduction of 'simple' language, 'ordinary' language, French 'just like that', i.e. the language which is taught in elementary school as the 'pure and simple' expression of 'reality'. In Renée Balibar's book there are numerous examples which 'speak' to everyone, re-awakening or reviving memories which are usually repressed (it is their presence, their reproduction – the reason for a character or his words and for what the 'author' makes himself responsible for without naming himself – which produces the effect of 'naturalness' and 'reality', even if it is only by a single phrase uttered as if in passing). In comparison, all other expressions seem 'arguable', 'reflected' in a subjectivity. It is necessary that first of all there should be expressions which seem objective: these are the ones which in the text itself produces the imaginary referent of an elusive 'reality'.

Finally, to go back to our starting point: the ideological effect of identification produced by literature or rather by literary texts, which Brecht, thanks to his position as a revolutionary and materialist dramatist, was the first to theorise. But there is only ever identification of one subject with another (potentially with 'oneself': 'Madame Bovary, c'est moi', familiar example, signed Gustave Flaubert). And there are only ever subjects through the interpellation of the individual as a subject by a naming Subject, as Althusser shows: 'tu es Un tel, et c'est à toi que Je m'adresse'; 'Hypocrite lecteur, mon semblable, mon frère', another familiar example, signed Charles Baudelaire. Through the endless functioning of its texts, literature unceasingly 'produces' subjects, on display for everyone. So, paradoxically, using the same schema, we can say: literature endlessly transforms (concrete) individuals into subjects and endows them with a quasi-real hallucinatory individuality. According to the fundamental mechanism of the whole of bourgeois ideology, to produce subjects ('persons' and 'characters') one must oppose them to objects, i.e. to things, by placing them in and against a world of 'real' things, outside it but always in relation to it. The realistic effect is the basis of this interpellation which makes characters or merely discourse 'live' and which makes readers take up an attitude towards imaginary struggles as they would towards real ones, though undangerously. They flourish here, the subjects we have already named: the Author and his Readers, but also the Author and his Characters, and the Reader and his Characters via the mediator, the Author – the Author identified with his Characters, or 'on the contrary' with one of their Judges, and likewise for the Reader. And from there, the Author, the Reader, the Characters opposite their universal abstract subjects: God, History, the People, Art. The list is neither final nor finishable: the work of literature, by definition, is to prolong and expand it indefinitely.

The aesthetic effect of literature as ideological domination-effect

The analysis of literature (its theory, criticism, science, etc.) has always had as its given object either – from a spiritualist perspective – the essence of Works and Authors, or better of the Work (of Art) and of Writing, above history, even and especially when seeming its privileged expression; or – from an empiricist (but still idealist) perspective – the ensemble of literary 'facts', the supposedly objective and documentary givens which lend biographical and stylistic support to 'general facts', the 'laws' of genres, styles and periods. From a materialist point of view, one would analyse literary effects (more precisely, aesthetic literary effects) as effects which cannot be reduced to ideology 'in general' because they are particular ideological effects, in the midst of others (religious, juridical, political) to which they are linked but from which they are separate.

This effect must finally be described at a threefold level, relating to the three aspects of one social process and its successive historical forms: (1) its production in determinate social conditions; (2) its moment in the reproduction of the dominant ideology; (3) and, consequently, as in itself an ideological domination-effect. To demonstrate this: the literary effect is socially produced in a determined material process. This is the process of constitution, i.e. the making and composing of texts, the 'work' of literature. Now, the writer is neither supreme creator, founder of the very conditions to which he submits (in particular, as we have seen, certain objective contradictions within ideology), nor its opposite – expendable medium, through whom is revealed the nameless power of inspiration, or history, or period, or even class (which comes to the same thing). Rather, he is a material agent, an intermediary inserted in a particular place, in conditions he has not created, in submission to contradictions which by definition he cannot control, through a particular social division of labour, characteristic of the ideological superstructure of bourgeois society, which individuates him.[12]

The literary effect is produced as a complex effect, not only, as shown, because its determinant is the imaginary resolution of one contradiction within another, but because the effect produced is simultaneously and inseparably the materiality of the text (the arrangement of sentences), and its status as a 'literary' text, its 'aesthetic' status. That is, it is both a material outcome and a particular ideological effect, or rather the production of a material outcome stamped with a particular ideological effect which marks it ineradicably. It is the status of the text in its characteristics – no matter what the terms, which are only variants: its 'charm', 'beauty', 'truth', 'significance', 'worth', 'profundity', 'style', 'writing', 'art', etc. Finally, it is the status of the text per se, quite simply, for in our society only the text is valid in itself, revealer of its true form; equally, all texts deemed to be 'written' are valued as 'literary'. This status extends as well to all the historically indissociable modes of *reading* texts: the 'free' reading, reading for the pure 'pleasure' of letters, the critical reading giving a more or less theorised, more or less 'scientific' commentary on form and content, meaning, 'style', 'textuality' (revealing neologism!) – and behind all readings, the explication of texts by academics which conditions all the rest.

Therefore, the literary effect is not just produced by a determinate process, but actively inserts itself within the reproduction of other ideological effects: it is not only itself the effect of material causes, but is also an effect on socially determined individuals, constraining them materially to treat literary texts in a certain way. So, ideologically, the literary effect is not just in the domain of 'feeling', 'taste', 'judgment', and hence of aesthetic and literary ideas; it sets up a process itself: the rituals of literary consumption and 'cultural' practice.

That is why it is possible (and necessary) when analysing the literary effect as produced *qua* text and by means of the text, to treat as equivalents the 'reader' and the 'author'. Equivalent too are the 'intentions' of the author – what he expresses whether in the text itself (integrated within the 'surface' narrative) or alongside the text (in his declarations or even in his 'unconscious' motives as sought out by literary psychoanalysis) – and the interpretations, criticism and commentaries evoked from readers, whether sophisticated or not.

It is not important to know whether the interpretation 'really' identifies the author's intention (since the latter is not the cause of literary effects but is itself one of them). Interpretations and commentaries reveal the (literary) aesthetic effect, precisely, in full view. Literariness is what is recognised as such, and it is recognised as such precisely in the time and to the extent that it activates the interpretations, the criticisms and the 'readings'. This way a text can very easily stop being literary or become so under new conditions.

Freud was the first to follow this procedure in his account of the dream-work, and more generally in his method of analysing the compromise formations of the unconscious; he defined what must be understood by the 'text' of the dream. He gave no importance to restoring the manifest content of the dream – to a careful, isolated reconstruction of the 'real' dream. Or at least he acceded to it only through the intermediary of the 'dream narrative', which is already a transposition through which, via condensation, displacement and dream symbolism, repressed material makes its play. And he posited that the text of the dream was both the object of analysis and, simultaneously, through its own contradictions, the means of its own explanation: it is not just the manifest text, the narrative of the dream, but also all the 'free' association (i.e. as one well knows, the forced associations, imposed by the psychic conflicts of the unconscious), the 'latent thoughts' for which the dream (or symptom) can serve as a pretext and which it arouses.

In the same way, criticism, the discourse of literary ideology, an endless commentary on the 'beauty' and 'truth' of literary texts, is a train of 'free' associations (in actuality forced and predetermined) which develops and realises the ideological effects of a literary text. In a materialist account of the text one must take them not as located above the text, as the beginnings of its explication, but as belonging to the same level as the text, or more precisely to the same level as the 'surface' narrative whether that is figurative, allegorically treating certain general ideas (as in the novel or autobiography) or straightforwardly 'abstract', non-figurative (as in the moral or political essay). They are the tendential prolongation of this façade. Free from all question of the individuality of the 'writer', the 'reader' or the 'critic', these are the same ideological conflicts, resulting in the last instance from the same historic contradictions, or from their transformations, that produce the form of the text and of its commentaries.

Here is the index of the structure of the process of reproduction in which the literary effect is inserted. What is in fact 'the primary material' of the literary text? (But a raw material which always seems to have been already transformed by it.) It is the ideological contradictions which are not specifically literary but political, religious, etc.; in the last analysis, contradictory ideological realisations of determinate class positions in the class struggle. And what is the 'effect' of the literary text (at least on those readers who recognise it as such, those of the dominant cultured class)? Its effect is to provoke other ideological discourses which can sometimes be recognised as literary ones but which are usually merely aesthetic, moral, political, religious discourses in which the dominant ideology is realised.

We can now say that the literary text is the agent for the reproduction of ideology in its ensemble. In other words, it induces by the literary effect the production of 'new' discourses which always reproduce (under constantly varied forms) the same ideology (with its contradictions). It enables individuals to appropriate ideology and make themselves its 'free' bearers and even its 'free' creators. The literary text is a privileged operator in the concrete relations between the individual and ideology in bourgeois society and ensures its reproduction. To the extent that it induces ideological discourse to leave its subject matter, which has always already been invested as the aesthetic effect, in the form of the work of art, it does not seem a mechanical imposition, forced, revealed like a religious dogma, on individuals who must repeat it faithfully. Instead it appears as if offered for interpretations, a free choice, for the subjective private use of individuals. It is the privileged agent of ideological subjection, in the democratic and 'critical' form of 'freedom of thought'.[13]

Under these conditions, the aesthetic effect is also inevitably an effect of domination: the subjection of individuals to the dominant ideology, the dominance of the ideology of the ruling class.

It is inevitably therefore an uneven effect, which does not operate uniformly on individuals and particularly does not operate in the same way on different and antagonistic social classes. 'Subjection' must be felt by the dominant class as by the dominated but in two different ways. Formally, literature as an ideological formation realised in the common language is provided and destined for all, and makes no distinctions between readers, unless in relation to their own differing tastes and sensibilities, natural or acquired. But concretely, subjection means one thing for the members of the educated dominant class – 'freedom' to think within ideology, a submission which is experienced and practised as if it were a mastery – but another for those who belong to the exploited classes: manual workers or even skilled workers, employees, those who according to official statistics never 'read' or rarely. These find in reading nothing but the confirmation of their inferiority: subjection means domination and repression by literary discourse of a discourse deemed 'inarticulate' and 'faulty' and inadequate for the expression of complex ideas and feelings.

This point is vital to an analysis. It shows that the difference is not set up after the event as a straightforward inequality of reading power and assimilation, conditioned by other social inequalities. It is implicit in the very production of the literary effect and materially inscribed in the constitution of the text.

But one might say, how is it clear that what is implicit in the structure of the text is not just the discourse of those who practise literature but also, most significantly, the discourse of those who do not know the text and whom it does not know; i.e. the discourse of those who 'write' (books) and 'read' them, and the discourse of those who do not know how, although they 'know how to read and write' – a play of words and a profoundly revealing double usage? One can understand this only by reconstituting and analysing the linguistic conflict in its determining place as that which produces the literary text and which opposes two antagonistic usages, equal but inseparable, of the common language: on one side, 'literary' French which is studied in higher education (*l'enseignement secondaire et supérieur*) and on the other, 'basic', 'ordinary' French which far from being natural, is also taught at the other level (*à l'école primaire*). It is 'basic' only by reason of its unequal relation to the other, which is 'literary' by the same reason. This is proved by a comparative and historical analysis of their lexical and syntactical forms – which Renée Balibar is one of the first to undertake systematically.

So, if in the way things are, literature can and must be used in secondary education both to fabricate and simultaneously dominate, isolate and repress the 'basic' language of the dominated classes, it is only on condition that that same basic language should be present in literature, as one of the terms of its constitutive contradiction – disguised and masked, but also necessarily given away and exhibited in the fictive reconstructions. And ultimately this is because literary French embodied in literary texts is both tendentially distinguished from (and opposed to) the common language and placed within its constitution and historic development, so long as this process characterises general education because of its material importance to the development of bourgeois society. That is why it is possible to assert that the use of literature in schools and its place in education is only the converse of the place of education in literature, and that therefore the basis of the production of literary effects is the very structure and historical role of the currently dominant ideological state apparatus. And that too is why it is possible to denounce as a denial of their own real practice the claims of the writer and his cultured readers to rise above simple classroom exercises, and evade them.

The effect of domination realised by literary production presupposes the presence of the dominated ideology within the dominant ideology itself. It implies the constant 'activation' of the contradiction and its attendant ideological risk – it thrives on this very risk which is the source of its power. That is why, dialectically, in bourgeois democratic society, the agent of the reproduction of ideology moves tendentially via the effects of literary 'style' and linguistic forms of compromise. Class struggle is not abolished in the literary text and the literary effects which it produces. They bring about the reproduction, as dominant, of the ideology of the dominant class.

Notes

1. [In the Althusserian formulation, 'science' is distinguished from 'ideology' not so much by what it 'knows' as by the fact that it produces new 'problematics', new objects of possible knowledge and new problems about them. The effect of ideology, according to Althusser, is the reverse of this; it contains any problems or contradictions by masking them with fictional or imaginary resolutions. – *Trans.*]

2. Lenin shows this clearly in his articles on Tolstoy. [Lenin's articles on Tolstoy, written 1908–11, are reprinted as an appendix to MACHEREY's *A Theory of Literary Production*, (London: Routledge and Kegan Paul, 1978), pp. 299–323.]

3. *Selected Readings from the Works of Mao Tse-Tung (A)*, (Peking: Foreign Language Press, 1971), p. 250.

4. DOMINIQUE LECOURT, *Une crise et son enjeu (Essai sur la position de Lénine en philosophie)* (Paris: Maspero, 1973).

5. [Macherey and Balibar here refer to structuralism (and also, by implication, to the journal *Tel Quel*), and to the concept of realism, as espoused by Lukács – *Trans.*]

6. RENÉE BALIBAR and DOMINIQUE LAPORTE, *Le français national (constitution de la langue nationale commune à l'époque de la révolution démocratique bourgeoise)* (Paris: Hachette, 1974) [Introduced by Etienne Balibar and Pierre Macherey.]

7. Readers are referred to the first two chapters of J. BAUDELOT and R. ESTABLET, *L'Ecole capitaliste en France* (Paris: Maspero, 1972).

8. [Macherey and Balibar are referring here to SARTRE's *What is Literature?* (1948). In an interview with *Red Letters*, 5 (1977), Macherey adds: 'He was looking for a definition, a theory of what literature *is*, and in my view, this sort of enterprise is really very traditional and not very revolutionary. The question "what is literature?" is as old as the hills; it revives . . . an idealist and conservative aesthetic. If I had a single clear idea when I began my work, it was that we must abandon this kind of question because "what is literature?" is a false problem. Why? Because it is a question which already contains an answer. It implies that literature is *something*, that literature exists as a *thing*, as an eternal and unchangeable thing with an essence.' – *Trans.*]

9. See *A Theory of Literary Production*.

10. Rejecting the mythical unity and completeness of a work of art does not mean adopting a reverse position – that of seeing the work of art as anti-nature, a violation of order (as in *Tel Quel*). Such reversals are characteristic of conservative ideology: 'For oft a fine disorder stems from art' (Boileau)!

11. [See *Brecht on Theatre*, trans. John Willett (London: Methuen, 1964). – *Trans.*]

12. [On the category of the author, see also MICHEL FOUCAULT, 'The Order of Discourse', in Robert M. Young, ed., *Untying the Text*, (London, Routledge, 1981); 'What Is an Author?', in *Language, Counter-Memory, Practice*, ed. and trans. Donald F. Bouchard, (Ithaca: Cornell, 1977), pp. 113–38; and Roland Barthes, 'The Death of the Author', in *Image–Music–Text*, essays selected and translated by Stephen Heath, (London; Fontana, 1977), pp. 142–8. – *Trans.*]

13. One could say that there is no religious literature proper; at least there was not before the bourgeois epoch, by which time religion had been instituted as a form (subordinate and contradictory) of bourgeois ideology itself. Rather, literature itself and aesthetic ideology played a decisive part in the struggle against religion, the ideology of the dominant feudal class.

2 Free Particulars: The Rise of the Aesthetic* (1990)

TERRY EAGLETON

Terry Eagleton (b. 1943) is Warton Professor of English Literature in the University of Oxford. His many publications include *Criticism and Ideology* (1976), *The Rape of Clarissa* (1982), *Against the Grain* (1986) and *The Ideology of the Aesthetic* (1990). Long identified as Althusserian in derivation, Eagleton's Marxism has in fact availed of a much wider theoretical repertoire, including the Frankfurtian thematic noticeably present in this essay.

Since the Enlightenment, aesthetics has been the mode in which philosophy strives to penetrate 'the life-world'. The aesthetic has been understood and valorized as a realm in which the potentially conflicting demands of universal and particular, duty and inclination, reason and bodily impulse are composed under 'the law of the heart'. The modern history of the aesthetic has been fundamentally political, Eagleton argues, in part an allegory of the relationship between bourgeois civil society and its constitutional setting, in part the practical means by which a specifically bourgeois subjectivity is fashioned. The aesthetic is irreducibly ambivalent, at once, or variously, conformist and critical, but in either aspect it has been the privileged mode of bourgeois ideology.

Aesthetics is born as a discourse of the body. In its original formulation by the German philosopher Alexander Baumgarten, the term refers not in the first place to art, but, as the Greek *aisthesis* would suggest, to the whole region of human perception and sensation, in contrast to the more rarified domain of conceptual thought. The distinction which the term 'aesthetic' initially enforces in the mid-eighteenth century is not one

---

* Reprinted from Terry Eagleton, *The Ideology of the Aesthetic* (Oxford: Blackwell, 1990), pp. 13–30.

between 'art' and 'life', but between the material and the immaterial: between things and thoughts, sensations and ideas, that which is bound up with our creaturely life as opposed to that which conducts some shadowy existence in the recesses of the mind. It is as though philosophy suddenly wakes up to the fact that there is a dense, swarming territory beyond its own mental enclave which threatens to fall utterly outside its sway. That territory is nothing less than the whole of our sensate life together – the business of affections and aversions, of how the world strikes the body on its sensory surfaces, of that which takes root in the gaze and the guts and all that arises from our most banal, biological insertion into the world. The aesthetic concerns this most gross and palpable dimension of the human, which post-Cartesian philosophy, in some curious lapse of attention, has somehow managed to overlook. It is thus the first stirrings of a primitive materialism – of the body's long inarticulate rebellion against the tyranny of the theoretical.

The oversight of classical philosophy was not without its political cost. For how can any political order flourish which does not address itself to this most tangible area of the 'lived', of everything that belongs to a society's somatic, sensational life? How can 'experience' be allowed to fall outside a society's ruling concepts? Could it be that this realm is impenetrably opaque to reason, eluding its categories as surely as the smell of thyme or the taste of potatoes? Must the life of the body be given up on, as the sheer unthinkable other of thought, or are its mysterious ways somehow mappable by intellection in what would then prove a wholly novel science, the science of sensibility itself? If the phrase is nothing more than an oxymoron, then the political consequences are surely dire. Nothing could be more disabled than a ruling rationality which can know nothing beyond its own concepts, forbidden from enquiring into the very stuff of passion and perception. How can the absolute monarch of Reason retain its legitimacy if what Kant called the 'rabble' of the senses remains forever beyond its ken? Does not power require some ability to anatomize the feelings of what it subordinates, some science or concrete logic at its disposal which would map from the inside the very structures of breathing, sentient life?

The call for an aesthetics in eighteenth-century Germany is among other things a response to the problem of political absolutism. Germany in that period was a parcellized territory of feudal–absolutist states, marked by a particularism and idiosyncrasy consequent on its lack of a general culture. Its princes imposed their imperious diktats through elaborate bureaucracies, while a wretchedly exploited peasantry languished in conditions often little better than bestial. Beneath this autocratic sway, an ineffectual bourgeoisie remained cramped by the nobility's mercantilist policies of state-controlled industry and tariff-protected trade, overwhelmed by the conspicuous power of the courts, alienated from the degraded masses and bereft of any corporate influence in national life. The Junkerdom, rudely confiscating from the middle class their historic role, themselves sponsored much of what industrial development there was for their own fiscal or military purposes, leaving a largely quiescent middle class to do business with the state, rather than force the state to shape its policies to their own interests. A pervasive lack of capital and enterprise, poor communications and locally based trade, guild-dominated towns marooned in a backward countryside: such were the unpropitious conditions of the German bourgeoisie in this parochial, benighted social order. Its professional and intellectual strata, however, were steadily growing, to produce for the first time in the later eighteenth century a professional literary caste; and this group showed all the signs of exerting a cultural and spiritual leadership beyond the reach of the self-serving aristocracy. Unrooted in political or economic power, however, this bourgeois enlightenment remained in many respects enmortgaged to feudalist absolutism, marked by that profound respect for authority of which Immanuel Kant, courageous *Aufklärer* and docile subject of the king of Prussia, may be taken as exemplary.

What germinates in the eighteenth century as the strange new discourse of aesthetics is not a challenge to that political authority; but it can be read as symptomatic of an ideological dilemma inherent in absolutist power. Such power needs for its own purposes to take account of 'sensible' life, for without an understanding of this no dominion can be secure. The world of feelings and sensations can surely not just be surrendered to the 'subjective', to what Kant scornfully termed the 'egoism of taste'; instead, it must be brought within the majestic scope of reason itself. If the *Lebenswelt* is not rationally formalizable, have not all the most vital ideological issues been consigned to some limbo beyond one's control? Yet how can reason, that most immaterial of faculties, grasp the grossly sensuous? Perhaps what makes things available to empirical knowledge in the first place, their palpable materiality, is also in a devastating irony what banishes them beyond cognition. Reason must find some way of penetrating the world of perception, but in doing so must not put at risk its own absolute power.

It is just this delicate balance which Baumgarten's aesthetics seek to achieve. If his *Aesthetica* (1750) opens up in an innovative gesture the whole terrain of sensation, what it opens it up to is in effect the colonization of reason. For Baumgarten, aesthetic cognition mediates between the generalities of reason and the particulars of sense: the aesthetic is that realm of existence which partakes of the perfection of reason, but in a 'confused' mode. 'Confusion' here means not 'muddle' but 'fusion': in their organic interpenetration, the elements of aesthetic representation resist that discrimination into discrete units which is characteristic of conceptual thought. But this does not mean that such representations are obscure: on the contrary, the more 'confused' they are – the more unity-in-variety they attain – the more clear, perfect and determinate they become. A poem is in this sense a perfected form of sensate discourse. Aesthetic unities are thus open to rational analysis, though they demand a specialized form or idiom of reason, and this is aesthetics. Aesthetics, Baumgarten writes, is the 'sister' of logic, a kind of *ratio inferior* or feminine analogue of reason at the lower level of sensational life. Its task is to order this domain into clear or perfectly determinate representations, in a manner akin to (if relatively autonomous of) the operations of reason proper. Aesthetics is born of the recognition that the world of perception and experience cannot simply be derived from abstract universal laws, but demands its own appropriate discourse and displays its own inner, if inferior, logic. As a kind of concrete thought or sensuous analogue of the concept, the aesthetic partakes at once of the rational and the real, suspended between the two somewhat in the manner of the Lévi-Straussian myth. It is born as a woman, subordinate to man but with her own humble, necessary tasks to perform.

Such a mode of cognition is of vital importance if the ruling order is to understand its own history. For if sensation is characterized by a complex individuation which defeats the general concept, so is history itself. Both phenomena are marked by an irreducible particularity or concrete determinateness which threatens to put them beyond the bounds of abstract thought. 'Individuals', wrote Baumgarten, 'are determined in every respect . . . particular representations are in the highest degree poetic.'[1] Since history is a question of 'individuals', it is 'poetic' in precisely this sense, a matter of determinate specificities; and it would therefore seem alarmingly to fall outside the compass of reason. What if the history of the ruling class were itself opaque to its knowledge, an unknowable exteriority beyond the pale of the concept? Aesthetics emerges as a theoretical discourse in response to such dilemmas; it is a kind of prosthesis to reason, extending a reified Enlightenment rationality into vital regions which are otherwise beyond its reach. It can cope, for example, with questions of desire and rhetorical effectivity: Baumgarten describes desire as 'a sensate representation because a confused representation of the good',[2] and examines the ways in which poetic sense-impressions can arouse particular emotive effects. The aesthetic, then, is simply the name given to that hybrid form of cognition which can clarify the raw stuff of perception and historical practice, disclosing the inner structure of the concrete. Reason as such pursues its lofty ends far removed from such lowly particulars; but a working replica of itself known as the aesthetic springs into being as a kind of cognitive underlabourer, to know in its uniqueness all that to which the higher reason is necessarily blind. Because the aesthetic exists, the dense particulars of perception can be made luminous to thought, and determinate concretions assembled into historical narrative. 'Science', writes Baumgarten, 'is not to be dragged down to the region of sensibility, but the sensible is to be lifted to the dignity of knowledge.'[3] Dominion over all inferior powers, he warns, belongs to reason alone; but this dominion must never degenerate into tyranny. It must rather assume the form of what we might now, after Gramsci, term 'hegemony', ruling and informing the senses from within while allowing them to thrive in all of their relative autonomy.

Once in possession of such a 'science of the concrete' – 'a contradiction in terms', Schopenhauer was later to call it – there is no need to fear that history and the body will slip through the net of conceptual discourse to leave one grasping at empty space. Within the dense welter of our material life, with all its amorphous flux, certain objects stand out in a sort of perfection dimly akin to reason, and these are known as the beautiful. A kind of ideality seems to inform their sensuous existence from within, rather than floating above it in some Platonic space; so that a rigorous logic is here revealed to us in matter itself, felt instantly on the pulses. Because there are objects which we can agree to be beautiful, not by arguing or analysing but just by looking and seeing, a spontaneous consensus is brought to birth within our creaturely life, bringing with it the promise that such a life, for all its apparent arbitrariness and obscurity, might indeed work in some sense very like a rational law. Such, as we shall see, is something of the meaning of the aesthetic for Kant, who will look to it for an elusive third way between the vagaries of subjective feeling and the bloodless rigour of the understanding.

For a modern parallel to this meaning of the aesthetic, we might look less to Benedetto Croce than to the later Edmund Husserl. For Husserl's purpose in *The Crisis of European Sciences* is precisely to rescue the life-world from its troubling opacity to reason, thereby renewing an Occidental rationality which has cut alarmingly adrift from its somatic, perceptual roots. Philosophy cannot fulfil its role as the universal, ultimately grounding science if it abandons the life-world to its anonymity; it must remember that the body, even before it has come to think, is always a sensibly experiencing organism positioned in its world in a way quite distinct from the placing of an object in a box. Scientific knowledge of an objective reality is always already grounded in this intuitive pre-givenness of things to the vulnerably perceptive body, in the primordial physicality of our being-in-the-world. We scientists, Husserl remarks with faint surprise, are after all human beings; and it is because a misguided rationalism has overlooked this fact that European culture is in the crisis it is. (Husserl, victim of fascism, is writing in the 1930s.) Thought must thus round upon itself, retrieving the *Lebenswelt* from whose murky depths it springs, in a new 'universal science of subjectivity'. Such a science, however, is not in fact new in the least:

when Husserl admonishes us that we must 'consider the surrounding life-world concretely, in its neglected relativity . . . the world in which we live intuitively, together with its real entities',[4] he is speaking, in the original sense of the term, as an aesthetician. It is not, of course, a question of surrendering ourselves to 'this whole merely subjective and apparently incomprehensible "Heraclitean flux"'[5] which is our daily experience, but rather of rigorously formalizing it. For the life-world exhibits a general structure, and this structure, to which everything that exists relatively is bound, is not itself relative. 'We can attend to it in its generality and, with sufficient care, fix it once and for all in a way equally accessible to all.'[6] Indeed it turns out conveniently enough that the life-world discloses just the same structures that scientific thought presupposes in its construction of an objective reality. Higher and lower styles of reasoning, in Baumgartenian terms, manifest a common form. Even so, the project of formalizing the life-world is not a simple one, and Husserl is frank enough to confess that 'one is soon beset by extraordinary difficulties . . . every "ground" that is reached points to further grounds, every horizon opened up awakens new horizons'.[7] Pausing to console us with the thought that this 'endless whole, in its infinity of flowing movement, is oriented towards the unity of one meaning', Husserl brutally undoes this solace in the next breath by denying that this is true 'in such a way that we could ever simply grasp and understand the whole'.[8] Like Kafka's hope, it would appear that there is plenty of totality, but not for us. The project of formalizing the life-world would seem to scupper itself before getting off the ground, and with it the proper grounding of reason. It will be left to Maurice Merleau-Ponty to develop this 'return to living history and the spoken word' – but in doing so to question the assumption that this is simply 'a preparatory step which should be followed by the properly philosophical task of universal constitution'.[9] From Baumgarten to phenomenology, it is a question of reason deviating, doubling back on itself, taking a *detour* through sensation, experience, 'naivety' as Husserl calls it in the Vienna lecture, so that it will not have to suffer the embarrassment of arriving at its *telos* empty-handed, big with wisdom but deaf, dumb and blind into the bargain.

Such a detour through sensation is politically necessary. If absolutism does not wish to trigger rebellion, it must make generous accommodation for sensual inclination. Yet this turn to the affective subject is not without its perils for an absolutist law. If it may succeed in inscribing that law all the more effectively on the hearts and bodies of those it subjugates, it may also, by a self-deconstructive logic, come to subjectivize such authority out of existence, clearing the ground for a new concept of legality and political power altogether. In a striking historical irony recorded by Karl Marx, the very idealist cast into which conditions of social backwardness had forced the thinking of the late eighteenth-century German middle class led to the prefiguration in the mind of a bold new model of social life as yet quite unachievable in reality. From the depths of a benighted late feudal autocracy, a vision could be projected of a universal order of free, equal, autonomous human subjects, obeying no laws but those which they gave to themselves. This bourgeois public sphere breaks decisively with the privilege and particularism of the *ancien régime*, installing the middle class, in image if not in reality, as a truly universal subject, and compensating with the grandeur of this dream for its politically supine status. What is at stake here is nothing less than the production of an entirely new kind of human subject – one which, like the work of art itself, discovers the law in the depths of its own free identity, rather than in some oppressive external power. The liberated subject is the one who has appropriated the law as the very principle of its own autonomy, broken the forbidding tablets of stone on which that law was originally inscribed in order to rewrite it on the heart of flesh. To consent to the law is thus to consent to one's own inward being. 'The heart', writes Rousseau in *Émile*, 'only receives laws from itself; by wanting to enchain it one releases it; one only enchains it by leaving it free.'[10] Antonio Gramsci will write later in the *Prison Notebooks* of a form of civil society 'in which the individual can govern himself without his self-government thereby entering into conflict with political society – but rather becoming its normal continuation, its organic complement'.[11] In a classic moment in *The Social Contract*, Rousseau speaks of the most important form of law as one 'which is not graven on tablets of marble or brass, but on the hearts of the citizens. This forms the real constitution of the State, takes on every day new powers, when other laws decay or die out, restores them or takes their place, keeps a people in the ways it was meant to go, and insensibly replaces authority by the force of habit. I am speaking of morality, of custom, above all of public opinion; a power unknown to political thinkers, on which nonetheless success in everything else depends.'[12]

The ultimate binding force of the bourgeois social order, in contrast to the coercive apparatus of absolutism, will be habits, pieties, sentiments and affections. And this is equivalent to saying that power in such an order has become *aestheticized*. It is at one with the body's spontaneous impulses, entwined with sensibility and the affections, lived out in unreflective custom. Power is now inscribed in the minutiae of subjective experience, and the fissure between abstract duty and pleasurable inclination is accordingly healed. To dissolve the law to custom, to sheer unthinking habit, is to identify it with the human subject's own pleasurable well-being, so that to trangress that law would signify a deep self-violation. The new subject, which bestows on itself self-referentially a law at one with its immediate experience, finding its freedom in its necessity, is modelled on the aesthetic artefact.

This centrality of custom, as opposed to some naked reason, lies at the root of Hegel's critique of Kantian morality. Kant's practical reason, with its uncompromising appeal to abstract duty as an end in itself, smacks rather too much of the absolutism of feudalist power. The aesthetic theory of the *Critique of Judgement* suggests, by contrast, a resolute turn to the subject: Kant retains the idea of a universal law, but now discovers this law at work in the very structure of our subjective capacities. This 'lawfulness without a law' signifies a deft compromise between mere subjectivism on the one hand, and an excessively abstract reason on the other. There is indeed for Kant a kind of 'law' at work in aesthetic judgement, but one which seems inseparable from the very particularity of the artefact. As such, Kant's 'lawfulness without a law' offers a parallel to that 'authority which is not an authority' (*The Social Contract*) which Rousseau finds in the structure of the ideal political state. In both cases, a universal law of a kind lives wholly in its free, individual incarnations, whether these are political subjects or the elements of the aesthetic artefact. The law simply *is* an assembly of autonomous, self-governing particulars working in spontaneous reciprocal harmony. Yet Kant's turn to the subject is hardly a turn to the *body*, whose needs and desires fall outside the disinterestedness of aesthetic taste. The body cannot be figured or represented within the frame of Kantian aesthetics; and Kant ends up accordingly with a formalistic ethics, an abstract theory of political rights, and a 'subjective' but non-sensuous aesthetics.

It is all of these which Hegel's more capacious notion of reason seeks to sweep up and transform. Hegel rejects Kant's stern opposition between morality and sensuality, defining instead an idea of reason which will encompass the cognitive, practical and affective together.[13] Hegelian Reason does not only apprehend the good, but so engages and transforms our bodily inclinations as to bring them into spontaneous accord with universal rational precepts. And what mediates between reason and experience here is the self-realizing *praxis* of human subjects in political life. Reason, in short, is not simply a contemplative faculty, but a whole project for the hegemonic reconstruction of subjects – what Seyla Benhabib has called 'the successive transformation and reeducation of inner nature'.[14] Reason works out its own mysterious ends through human beings' sensuous, self-actualizing activity in the realm of *Sittlichkeit* (concrete ethical life) or Objective Spirit. Rational moral behaviour is thus inseparable from questions of human happiness and self-fulfilment; and if this is so then Hegel has in some sense 'aestheticized' reason by anchoring it in the body's affections and desires. It is not of course aestheticized *away*, dissolved to some mere hedonism or intuitionism; but it has lapsed from the lofty Kantian domain of Duty to become an active, transfigurative force in material life.

The 'aesthetic' dimension of this programme can best be disclosed by suggesting that what Hegel confronts in emergent bourgeois society is a conflict between a 'bad' particularism on the one hand, and a 'bad' universalism on the other. The former is a matter of civil society: it stems from the private economic interest of the solitary citizen, who as Hegel comments in the *Philosophy of Right* is each his own end and has no regard for others. The latter is a question of the political state, where these unequal, antagonistic monads are deceptively constituted as abstractly free and equivalent. In this sense, bourgeois society is a grotesque travesty of the aesthetic artefact, which harmoniously interrelates general and particular, universal and individual, form and content, spirit and sense. In the dialectical medium of *Sittlichkeit*, however, the subject's participation in universal reason takes the shape at each moment of a unified, concretely particular form of life. It is through '*Bildung*', the rational education of desire through *praxis*, or as we might say a programme of spiritual hegemony, that the bond between individual and universal is ceaselessly constituted. Knowledge, moral practice and pleasurable self-fulfilment are thus coupled together in the complex interior unity of Hegelian Reason. The ethical, Hegel remarks in the *Philosophy of Right*, appears not as law but as custom, an habitual form of action which becomes a 'second nature'. Custom is the law of the spirit of freedom; the project of education is to show individuals the way to a new birth, converting their 'first' nature of appetites and desires to a second, spiritual one which will then become customary to them. No longer torn asunder between blind individualism and abstract universalism, the reborn subject lives its existence, we might claim, aesthetically, in accordance with a law which is now entirely at one with its spontaneous being. What finally secures social order is that realm of customary practice and instinctual piety, more supple and resilient than abstract rights, where the living energies and affections of subjects are invested.

That this should be so follows necessarily from the social conditions of the bourgeoisie. Possessive individualism abandons each subject to its own private space, dissolves all positive bonds between them and thrusts them into mutual antagonism. 'By "antagonism"', writes Kant in his 'Idea for a Universal History', 'I mean the unsociable sociability of men, i.e. their propensity to enter into society bound together with a mutual opposition which constantly threatens to break up the society.'[15] In a striking irony, the very practices which reproduce bourgeois society also threaten to undermine it. If no positive social bonds are possible at the level of material production or 'civil society', one might perhaps look to the political arena of the state to bear the burden of such interrelationship. What one finds here, however, is a merely notional community of abstractly symmetrical subjects, too rarefied and theoretic to provide a rich *experience* of consensuality. Once the bourgeoisie has dismantled the centralizing political apparatus of absolutism, either in fantasy or reality, it finds itself bereft of some of the institutions which had previously organized social life as a whole. The question therefore arises as to where it is to locate a sense of unity powerful enough to reproduce itself by. In economic life, individuals are structurally isolated and antagonistic; at the political level there would seem nothing but abstract rights to link one subject to the other. This is one reason why the 'aesthetic' realm of sentiments, affections and spontaneous bodily habits comes to assume the significance it does. Custom, piety, intuition and opinion must now cohere an otherwise abstract, atomized social order. Moreover, once absolutist power has been overturned, each subject must function as its own seat of self-government. An erstwhile centralized authority must be parcellized and localized: absolved from continuous political supervision, the bourgeois subject must assume the burden of its own internalized governance. This is not to suggest that absolutist power itself requires no such internalization: like any successful political authority, it demands complicity and collusion from those it subordinates. It is not a question of some stark contrast between a purely heteronomous law on the one hand, and an insidiously consensual one on the other. But with the growth of early bourgeois society, the ratio between coercion and consent is undergoing gradual transformation: only a rule weighted towards the latter can effectively regulate individuals whose economic activity necessitates a high degree of autonomy. It is in this sense, too, that the aesthetic moves into the foreground in such conditions. Like the work of art as defined by the discourse of aesthetics, the bourgeois subject is autonomous and self-determining, acknowledges no merely extrinsic law but instead, in some mysterious fashion, gives the law to itself. In doing so, the law becomes the form which shapes into harmonious unity the turbulent content of the subject's appetites and inclinations. The compulsion of autocratic power is replaced by the more gratifying compulsion of the subject's self-identity.

To rely on sentiment as a source of one's social cohesion is not as precarious a matter as it looks. The bourgeois state, after all, still has its coercive instruments at the ready should this project falter; and what bonds could in any case be stronger, more unimpeachable, than those of the senses, of 'natural' compassion and instinctive allegiance? Such organic liaisons are surely a more trustworthy form of political rule than the inorganic, oppressive structures of absolutism. Only when governing imperatives have been dissolved into spontaneous reflex, when human subjects are linked to each other in their very flesh, can a truly corporate existence be fashioned. It is for this reason that the early bourgeoisie is so preoccupied with *virtue* – with the lived habit of moral propriety, rather than a laborious adherence to some external norm. Such a belief naturally demands an ambitious programme of moral education and reconstruction, for there is no assurance that the human subjects who emerge from the *ancien régime* will prove refined and enlightened enough for power to found itself on their sensibilities. It is thus that Rousseau writes the *Émile* and the *Nouvelle Heloïse*, intervening in the realms of pedagogy and sexual morality to construct new forms of subjectivity. Similarly, the law in *The Social Contract* has behind it a Legislator, whose role is the hegemonic one of educating the people to receive the law's decrees. 'The [Rousseauian] state', comments Ernst Cassirer, 'does not simply address itself to already existing and given subjects of the will; rather its first aim is to *create* the sort of subjects to whom it can address its call.'[16] Not just any subject can be 'interpellated', in Althusserian phrase;[17] the task of political hegemony is to produce the very forms of subjecthood which will form the basis of political unity.

The virtue of Rousseau's ideal citizen lies in his passionate affection for his fellow citizens and for the shared conditions of their common life. The root of this civic virtue is the pity we experience for each other in the state of nature; and this pity rests on a kind of empathetic imagination, 'transporting ourselves outside ourselves, and identifying ourselves with the suffering animal, leaving our being, so to speak, in order to take his . . . Thus no one becomes sensitive except when his imagination is animated and begins to transport himself outside of himself.'[18] At the very root of social relations lies the aesthetic, source of all human bonding. If bourgeois society releases its individuals into lonely autonomy, then only by such an imaginative exchange or appropriation of each other's identities can they be deeply enough united. Feeling, Rousseau claims in *Émile*, precedes knowledge; and the law of conscience is such that what I *feel* to be right is right. Even so, social harmony cannot be grounded in such sentiments alone, which suffice only for the state of nature. In the state of civilization, such sympathies must find their formal articulation in law, which invokes a similar 'exchange' of subjects: 'Each of us puts his person and all his power in common under the supreme direction of the general will, and, in our corporate capacity, we receive each member as an indivisible part of the whole.'[19] In Rousseau's view, for the subject to obey any law other than one it has personally fashioned is slavery; no individual is entitled to command another, and the only legitimate law is thus of a self-conferred kind. If all citizens alienate their rights entirely to the community, 'each man, in giving himself to all, gives himself to nobody', and so receives himself back again as a free, autonomous being. The citizen surrenders his 'bad' particularism – his narrowly selfish interests – and through the 'general will' identifies instead with the good of the whole; he retains his unique individuality, but now in the form of a disinterested commitment to a common well-being. This fusion of general and particular, in which one shares in the whole at no risk to one's unique specificity, resembles the very form of the aesthetic artefact – though since Rousseau is not an organicist thinker, the analogy is only approximate. For the mystery of the aesthetic object is that each of its sensuous parts, while appearing wholly autonomous, incarnates the 'law' of the totality. Each aesthetic particular, in the very act of determining itself, regulates and is regulated by all other self-determining particulars. The enheartening expression of this doctrine, politically speaking, would be: 'what appears as my subordination to others is in fact self-determination'; the more cynical view would run: 'my subordination to others is so effective that it appears to me in the mystified guise of governing myself.'

The emergent middle class, in an historic development, is newly defining itself as a universal subject. But the abstraction this process entails is a source of anxiety for a class welded in its robust individualism to the concrete and the particular. If the aesthetic intervenes here, it is as a dream of reconciliation – of individuals woven into intimate unity with no detriment to their specificity, of an abstract totality suffused with all the flesh-and-blood reality of the individual being. As Hegel writes of classical art in his *Philosophy of Fine Art*: 'Though no violence is done . . . to any feature of expression, any part of the whole, and every member appears in its independence, and rejoices in its own existence, yet each and all is content at the same time to be only an aspect in the total evolved presentation.'[20] Rousseau's general will, as a kind of mighty totalizing artefact, might be seen as imaginative empathy assuming a rational, objective form.

Rousseau does not think that feeling can simply replace rational law; but he does hold that reason in itself is insufficient for social unity, and that to become a regulative force in society it must be animated by love and affection. It is thus that he quarrelled with the Encyclopaedists, whose dream of reconstructing society from pure reason seemed to him simply to erase the problem of the subject. And to overlook the subject is to ignore the vital question of political hegemony, which the ultra-rationalism of the Enlightenment is powerless in itself to address. 'Sensibility', then, would seem unequivocally on the side of the progressive middle class, as the aesthetic foundation of a new form of polity. Yet if the conservative Edmund Burke found Rousseau's sentimentalism offensive, he was also revolted by what he saw as his impious rationalism. Such rationalism seemed to Burke just that effort to reconstruct the social order from metaphysical first principles which was most calculated to undermine an organic cultural tradition of spontaneous pieties and affections.[21] Rationalism and sentimentalism do indeed in this sense go together: if a new social order is to be constructed on the basis of virtue, custom and opinion, then a radical rationalism must first of all dismantle the political structures of the present, submitting their mindless prejudices and traditionalist privileges to disinterested critique. Conversely, both rationalism and an appeal to feeling can be found on the political right. If the given social order defends itself in Burkeian fashion through 'culture' – through a plea for the values and affections richly implicit in national tradition – it will tend to provoke an abrasive rationalism from the political left. The left will round scathingly on the 'aesthetic' as the very locus of mystification and irrational prejudice; it will denounce the insidiously naturalizing power which Burke has in mind when he comments that customs operate better than laws, 'because they become a sort of Nature both to the governors and the governed'.[22] If, however, the existing order ratifies itself by an appeal to absolute law, then the 'subjective' instincts and passions which such law seems unable to encompass can become the basis of a radical critique.

The form which these conflicts take is partly determined by the nature of the political power in question. In late eighteenth-century Britain, an evolved tradition of bourgeois democracy had produced a social order which sought on the whole to work 'hegemonically', however savagely coercive it could also show itself. Authority, as Burke recommends, has regard to the senses and sentiments of at least some of its subjects; and in this situation two alternative counter-strategies become available. One is to explore the realm of affective life which authority seeks to colonize and turn it against the insolence of power itself, as in some eighteenth-century cults of sensibility. A new kind of human subject – sensitive, passionate, individualist – poses an ideological challenge to the ruling order, elaborating new dimensions of feeling beyond its narrow scope. Alternatively, the fact that power utilizes feelings for its own ends may give rise to a radical rationalist revolt against feeling itself, in which sensibility is assailed as the insidious force which binds subjects to the law. If, however, political dominance assumes in German fashion more openly coercive forms, then an 'aesthetic' counter-strategy – a cultivation of the instincts and pieties over which such power rides roughshod – can always gather force.

Any such project, however, is likely to be deeply ambivalent. For it is never easy to distinguish an appeal to taste and sentiment which offers an alternative to autocracy from one which allows such power to ground itself all the more securely in the living sensibilities of its subjects. There is a world of political difference between a law which the subject really does give to itself, in radical democratic style, and a decree which still descends from on high but which the subject now 'authenticates'. Free consent may thus be the antithesis of oppressive power, or a seductive form of collusion with it. To view the emergent middle-class order from either standpoint alone is surely too undialectical an approach. In one sense, the bourgeois subject is indeed mystified into mistaking necessity for freedom and oppression for autonomy. For power to be individually authenticated, there must be constructed within the subject a new form of inwardness which will do the unpalatable work of the law for it, and all the more effectively since that law has now apparently evaporated. In another sense, this policing belongs with the historic victory of bourgeois liberty and democracy over a barbarously repressive state. As such, it contains within itself a genuinely utopian glimpse of a free, equal community of independent subjects. Power is shifting its location from centralized institutions to the silent, invisible depths of the subject itself; but this shift is also part of a profound political emancipation in which freedom and compassion, the imagination and the bodily affections, strive to make themselves heard within the discourse of a repressive rationalism.

The aesthetic, then, is from the beginning a contradictory, double-edged concept. On the one hand, it figures as a genuinely emancipatory force – as a community of subjects now linked by sensuous impulse and fellow-feeling rather than by heteronomous law, each safeguarded in its unique particularity while bound at the same time into social harmony. The aesthetic offers the middle class a superbly versatile model of their political aspirations, exemplifying new forms of autonomy and self-determination, transforming the relations between law and desire, morality and knowledge, recasting the links between individual and totality, and revising social relations on the basis of custom, affection and sympathy. On the other hand, the aesthetic signifies what Max Horkheimer has called a kind of 'internalised repression', inserting social power more deeply into the very bodies of those it subjugates, and so operating as a supremely effective mode of political hegemony. To lend fresh significance to bodily pleasures and drives, however, if only for the purpose of colonizing them more efficiently, is always to risk foregrounding and intensifying them beyond one's control. The aesthetic as custom, sentiment, spontaneous impulse may consort well enough with political domination; but these phenomena border embarrassingly on passion, imagination, sensuality, which are not always so easily incorporable. As Burke put it in his *Appeal from the New to the Old Whigs*: 'There is a boundary to men's passions when they act from feeling; none when they are under the influence of imagination.'[23] 'Deep' subjectivity is just what the ruling social order desires, and exactly what it has most cause to fear. If the aesthetic is a dangerous, ambiguous affair, it is because there is something in the body which can revolt against the power which inscribes it; and that impulse could only be eradicated by extirpating along with it the capacity to authenticate power itself.

Notes

1. ALEXANDER BAUMGARTEN, *Reflections on Poetry*, trans. K. Aschenbrenner and W. B. Holther (Berkeley, 1954), p. 43. For a useful recent essay on Baumgarten, see RODOLPHE GASCHÉ, 'Of aesthetic and historical determination', in *Post-Structuralism and the Question of History*, ed. D. Attridge, G. Bennington and R. Young (Cambridge: CUP, 1987). See also DAVID E. WELLBERY, *Lessing's Laocoön: Semiotics and Aesthetics in the Age of Reason* (Cambridge: CUP, 1984), chapter 2, and K.E. GILBERT and H. KUHN, *A History of Esthetics* (New York, 1939), ch. 10. For a splendid survey of English and German aesthetics from which I have benefited a good deal in chs. 1 and 2, see HOWARD CAYGILL, 'Aesthetics and Civil Society: Theories of Art and Society 1640–1790', unpublished Ph.D. thesis, University of Sussex, 1982; and see CAYGILL, *Art of Judgement* (Oxford 1989).

2. BAUMGARTEN, *Reflections on Poetry*, p. 38.

3. Quoted by ERNST CASSIRER, *The Philosophy of the Enlightenment* (Princeton: Princeton UP, 1951), p. 340.

4. EDMUND HUSSERL, *The Crisis of European Sciences and Transcendental Phenomenology* (Evanston: Northwestern UP, 1970), p. 156.

5. HUSSERL, *Crisis of European Sciences*, p. 156.

6. HUSSERL, *Crisis of European Sciences*, p. 139.

7. HUSSERL, *Crisis of European Sciences*, p. 170.

8. HUSSERL, *Crisis of European Sciences*, p. 170.

9. MAURICE MERLEAU-PONTY, *Signs* (Evanston: Northwestern UP, 1964), p. 110.

10. JEAN-JACQUES ROUSSEAU, *Émile ou de l'éducation* (Paris: Gallimard, 1961), vol. IV, p. 388.

11. ANTONIO GRAMSCI, *Selections from the Prison Notebooks*, ed. Q. Hoare and G. Nowell Smith (London: Lawrence and Wishart, 1971), p. 268.

12. JEAN-JACQUES ROUSSEAU, *The Social Contract and Discourses*, ed. G.D.H. Cole (London: Dent, 1938), p. 48.

13. See SEYLA BENHABIB, *Critique, Norm, and Utopia* (New York, 1986), pp. 80–4. For the relation between custom and law in the Enlightenment, see I.O. WADE, *The Structure and Form of the French Enlightenment* (Princeton: Princeton UP, 1977), vol. 1, Part II.

14. BENHABIB, *Critique, Norm, and Utopia*, p. 82.

15. IMMANUEL KANT, 'Idea for a Universal History', in I. Kant, *On History*, ed. Lewis White Beck (Indianapolis: Bobbs-Merrill, 1963), p. 15.

16. ERNST CASSIRER, *The Question of Jean-Jacques Rousseau* (Bloomington: Indiana UP, 1954), pp. 62–3.

17. See LOUIS ALTHUSSER, 'Ideology and Ideological State Apparatuses', in *Lenin and Philosophy* (London: NLB, 1971).

18. ROUSSEAU, *Émile*, vol. IV, p. 261.

19. ROUSSEAU, *The Social Contract*, p. 15.

20. G.W.F. HEGEL, *The Philosophy of Fine Art* (London, 1920), vol. 11, p. 10 (translation slightly amended).

21. See ANNIE MARIE OSBORN, *Rousseau and Burke* (London: OUP, 1940), a work

which at one point strangely speaks of Burke as an Englishman. See also, for Rousseau's political thought, J. H. BROOME, *Rousseau: A Study of his Thought* (London: Arnold, 1963); STEPHEN ELLENBURG, *Rousseau's Political Philosophy* (Ithaca: Cornell UP, 1976); ROGER D. MASTER, *The Political Philosophy of Rousseau* (Princeton: Princeton UP, 1968); LUCIO COLLETTI, *From Rousseau to Lenin* (London: NLB, 1972), Part 3.

22. EDMUND BURKE, *An Abridgement of English History*, quoted in W.J.T. Mitchell, *Iconology* (Chicago: U Chicago Press, 1986), p. 140.

23. *The Works of Edmund Burke*, ed. George Nichols (Boston, 1865–67), vol. 4, p. 192.

3 Pandora's Box: Subjectivity, Class and Sexuality in Socialist Feminist Criticism* (1985)

CORA KAPLAN

Cora Kaplan (b. 1940) is Professor of English Literature at Rutgers University. Based in England for many years, she taught at Sussex University, and was a member of the Marxist–Feminist Literature Collective and a member of the editorial teams of *Feminist Review* and *New Formations*. Her publications include the anthology *Salt and Bitter and Good: Three Centuries of English and American Women Poets* (1975), a new edition of Elizabeth Barrett Browning's *Aurora Leigh* (1978), and *Sea Changes* (1986).

Psychoanalysis and semiotics are key references in Kaplan's discussion of subjectivity and its representations and positionings in writing. Insisting on the divisions and instabilities of the psyche and on its necessary implication in specifically social relations, understanding textual meaning as a process of construction, her analysis presses beyond the binaries of reason/passion and gender/class that have variously informed humanist and essentialist feminism and androcentric Marxism. Identities are formed in narrative logics that associate the meanings of gender, sexuality, class and race in complex patterns of inter-definition; to read any one of these in categorial abstraction is to misread them all. Kaplan's critical interlocutors here are feminists, but her theses bear equally upon the customary inclinations of Marxist literary analysis.

Feminist criticism, as its name implies, is criticism with a Cause, engaged criticism. But the critical model presented to us so far is merely engaged to be married. It is about to contract what can only be a *mésalliance* with bourgeois modes of thought and the critical

* Reprinted from Cora Kaplan, *Sea Changes: Culture and Feminism* (London: Verso, 1986), pp. 147–76.

categories they inform. To be effective, feminist criticism cannot become simply bourgeois criticism in drag. It must be ideological and moral criticism; it must be revolutionary.[1]

The 'Marriage' of marxism and feminism has been like the marriage of husband and wife depicted in English common law: marxism and feminism are one, and that is marxism . . . we need a healthier marriage or we need a divorce.[2]

I

In spite of the attraction of matrimonial metaphor, reports of feminist nuptials with either mild-mannered bourgeois criticism or macho mustachioed Marxism have been greatly exaggerated. Neither liberal feminist criticism decorously draped in traditional humanism, nor her red-ragged rebellious sister, socialist feminist criticism, has yet found a place within androcentric literary criticism, which wishes to embrace feminism through a legitimate public alliance. Nor can feminist criticism today be plausibly evoked as a young deb looking for protection or, even more problematically, as a male 'mole' in transvestite masquerade. Feminist criticism now marks out a broad area of literary studies, eclectic, original and provocative. Independent still, through a combination of choice and default, it has come of age without giving up its name. Yet Lilian Robinson's astute pessimistic prediction is worth remembering. With maturity, the most visible, well-defined and extensive tendency within feminist criticism had undoubtedly bought into the white, middle-class heterosexist values of traditional literary criticism, and threatens to settle down on her own in its cultural suburbs. For, as I see it, the present danger is not that feminist criticism will enter an unequal dependent alliance with any of the varieties of male-centred criticism. It does not need to, for it has produced an all too persuasive autonomous analysis which is in many ways radical in its discussion of gender, but implicitly conservative in its assumptions about social hierarchy and female subjectivity, the Pandora's box for all feminist theory.

This reactionary effect must be interrogated and resisted from within feminism and in relation to the wider socialist feminist project. For, without the class and race perspectives that socialist feminist critics bring to the analysis both of literary texts and of their conditions of production, liberal feminist criticism, with its emphasis on the unified female subject, will unintentionally reproduce the ideological values of mass-market romance. In that fictional landscape the other structuring relations of society fade and disappear, leaving us with the naked drama of sexual difference as the only scenario that matters. Mass-market romance tends to represent sexual difference as natural and fixed – a constant, transhistorical femininity in libidinized struggle with an equally 'given' universal masculinity. Even where class difference divides lovers, it is there as narrative backdrop or minor stumbling-block to the inevitable heterosexual resolution. Without overstraining the comparison, a feminist literary criticism that privileges gender in isolation from other forms of social determination offers us a similarly partial reading of the role played by sexual difference in literary discourse, a reading bled dry of its most troubling and contradictory meanings.

The appropriation of modern critical theory – semiotic with an emphasis on the psychoanalytic – can be of great use in arguing against concepts of natural, essential and unified identity: against a static femininity and masculinity. But these theories about the production of meaning in culture must engage fully with the effects of other systems of difference than the sexual, or they too will produce no more than an anti-humanist avant-garde version of romance. Masculinity and femininity do not appear in cultural discourse, any more than they do in mental life, as pure binary forms at play. They are always, already, ordered and broken up through other social and cultural terms, other categories of difference. Our fantasies of sexual transgression as much as our obedience to sexual regulation are expressed through these structuring hierarchies. Class and race ideologies are, conversely, steeped in and spoken through the language of sexual differentiation. Class and race meanings are not metaphors for the sexual, or vice versa. It is better, though not exact, to see them as reciprocally constituting each other through a kind of narrative invocation, a set of associative terms in a chain of meaning. To understand how gender and class – to take two categories only – are articulated together transforms our analysis of each of them.

The literary text too often figures in feminist criticism as a gripping spectacle in which sexual difference appears somewhat abstracted from the muddy social world in which it is elsewhere embedded. Yet novels, poetry and drama are, on the contrary, peculiarly rich discourses in which the fused languages of class, race and gender are both produced and re-presented through the incorporation of other discourses. The focus of feminist analysis ought to be on that heterogeneity within the literary, on the intimate relation there expressed between all the categories that order social and psychic meaning. This does not imply an attention to content only, but also entails a consideration of the linguistic processes of the text as they construct and position subjectivity within these terms.

For without doubt literary texts do centre the individual as object and subject of their discourse. Literature has been a traditional space for the exploration of gender relations and sexual difference, and one in which women themselves have been formidably present. The problem for socialist feminists is not the focus on the individual that is special to the literary, but rather the romantic theory of the subject so firmly entrenched within the discourse. Humanist feminist criticism does not object to the idea of an immanent, transcendent subject but only to the exclusion of women from those definitions which it takes as an accurate account of subjectivity rather than as an historically constructed ideology. The repair and reconstitution of female subjectivity through a rereading of literature becomes, therefore, a major part, often unacknowledged, of its critical project. Psychoanalytic and semiotically oriented feminist criticism has argued well against this aspect of feminist humanism, emphasizing the important structural relation between writing and sexuality in the construction of the subject. But both tendencies have been correctly criticized from a socialist feminist position for the neglect of class and race as factors in their analysis. If feminist criticism is to make a central contribution to the understanding of sexual difference, instead of serving as a conservative refuge from its more disturbing social and psychic implications, the inclusion of class and race must transform its terms and objectives.

II

The critique of feminist humanism needs more historical explication than it has so far received. Its sources are complex, and are rooted in that moment almost 200 years ago when modern feminism and Romantic cultural theory emerged as separate but linked responses to the transforming events of the French Revolution. In the heat and light of the revolutionary decade 1790–1800, social, political and aesthetic ideas already maturing underwent a kind of forced ripening. As the progressive British intelligentsia contemplated the immediate possibility of social change, their thoughts turned urgently to the present capacity of subjects to exercise republican freedoms – to rule themselves as well as each other if the corrupt structures of aristocratic privilege were to be suddenly razed. Both feminism as set out in its most influential text, Mary Wollstonecraft's *A Vindication of the Rights of Woman* (1792), and Romanticism as argued most forcefully in Wordsworth's introduction to *Lyrical Ballads* (1800) stood in intimate, dynamic and contradictory relationship to democratic politics. In all three discourses the social and psychic character of the individual was centred and elaborated. The public and private implications of sexual difference as well as of the imagination and its products were both strongly linked to the optimistic, speculative construction of a virtuous citizen subject for a brave new egalitarian world. Theories of reading and writing – Wollstonecraft's and Jane Austen's as well as those of male Romantic authors – were explicitly related to contemporary politics as expressed in debate by such figures as Tom Paine, Edmund Burke and William Godwin.

The new categories of independent subjectivity, however, were marked from the beginning by exclusions of gender, race, and class. Jean-Jacques Rousseau, writing in the 1750s, specifically exempted women from his definition; Thomas Jefferson, some twenty years later, excluded Blacks. Far from being invisible ideological aspects of the new subject, these exclusions occasioned debate and polemic on both sides of the Atlantic. The autonomy of inner life, the dynamic psyche whose moral triumph was to be the foundation of republican government, was considered absolutely essential as an element of progressive political thought.

However, as the concept of the inner self and the moral psyche from the eighteenth century onwards was used to denigrate whole classes, races and genders, late nineteenth-century socialism began to de-emphasize the political importance of the psychic self, and redefine political morality and the adequate citizen subject in primary social terms. Because of this shift in emphasis, a collective moralism has developed in socialist thought which, instead of criticizing the reactionary interpretation of psychic life, stigmatizes sensibility itself, interpreting excess of feeling as regressive, bourgeois and non-political.

Needless to say, this strand of socialist thought poses a problem for feminism, which has favoured three main strategies to deal with it. In the first, women's psychic life is seen as being essentially identical to men's, but distorted through vicious and systematic patriarchal inscription. In this view, which is effectively Wollstonecraft's, social reform would prevent women from becoming regressively obsessed with sexuality and feeling. The second strategy wholly vindicates women's psyche, but sees it as quite separate from men's, often in direct opposition. This is frequently the terrain on which radical feminism defends female sexuality as independent and virtuous between women, but degrading in a heterosexual context. It is certainly a radical reworking of essentialist sexual ideology, shifting the ground from glib assertions of gender complementarity to the logic of separatism. The third strategy has been to refuse the issue's relevance altogether – to see any focus on psychic difference as itself an ideological one.

Instead of choosing any one of these options, socialist feminist criticism must come to grips with the relationship between female subjectivity and class identity. This project, even in its present early stages, poses major problems. While socialist feminists have been deeply concerned with the social construction of femininity and sexual difference, they have been uneasy about integrating social and political determinations with an analysis of the psychic ordering of gender. Within socialist feminism, a fierce and unresolved debate continues about the value of using psychoanalytic theory, because of the supposedly ahistorical character of its paradigms. For those who are hostile to psychoanalysis, the meaning of mental life, fantasy and desire – those obsessive themes of the novel and poetry for the last two centuries – seems particularly intractable to interpretation. They are reluctant to grant much autonomy to the psychic level, and often most attentive to feeling expressed in the work of non-bourgeois writers, which can more easily be read as political statement. Socialist feminism still finds unlocated, unsocialized psychic expression in women's writing hard to discuss in non-moralizing terms.

On the other hand, for liberal humanism, feminist versions included, the possibility of a unified self and an integrated consciousness that can transcend material circumstance is represented as the fulfilment of desire, the happy closure at the end of the story. The psychic fragmentation expressed through female characters in women's writing is seen as the most important sign of their sexual subordination, more interesting and ultimately more meaningful than their social oppression. As a result, the struggle for an integrated female subjectivity in nineteenth-century texts is never interrogated as ideology or fantasy, but seen as a demand that can actually be met, if not in 1848, then later.

In contrast, socialist feminist criticism tends to foreground the social and economic elements of the narrative and socialize what it can of its psychic portions. Women's anger and anguish, it is assumed, should be amenable to repair through social change. A positive emphasis on the psychic level is viewed as a valorization of the anarchic and regressive, a way of returning women to their subordinate ideological place within the dominant culture, as unreasoning social beings. Psychoanalytic theory, which is by and large morally neutral about the desires expressed by the psyche, is criticized as a confirmation and justification of them.

Thus semiotic or psychoanalytic perspectives have yet to be integrated with social, economic and political analysis. Critics acknowledge the importance of both and the need to relate them. A comparison of two admirable recent essays on Charlotte Brontë's *Villette*, one by Mary Jacobus and the other by Judith Lowder Newton, both informed by socialist feminist concerns, can illustrate this difficulty.

Jacobus uses the psychoanalytic and linguistic theory of Jacques Lacan to explore the split representations of subjectivity that haunt *Villette*, and calls attention to its anti-realist gothic elements. She relates Brontë's feminized defence of the imagination, and the novel's unreliable narrator-heroine, to the tension between femininity and feminism that reaches back to the eighteenth-century debates of Rousseau and Wollstonecraft. Reading the ruptures and gaps of the text as a psychic narrative, she also places it historically in relationship to nineteenth-century social and political ideas. Yet the social meanings of *Villette* fade and all but disappear before 'the powerful presence of fantasy', which 'energizes *Villette* and satisfies that part of the reader which also desires constantly to reject reality for the sake of an obedient, controllable, narcissistically pleasurable image of self and its relation to the world'.[3] In Jacobus's interpretation, the psyche, desire and fantasy stand for repressed, largely positive elements of a forgotten feminism, while the social stands for a daytime world of Victorian social regulation. These social meanings are referred to rather than explored in the essay, a strategy that renders them both static and unproblematically unified. It is as if, in order to examine how *Villette* represents psychic reality, the dynamism of social discourses of gender and identity must be repressed, forming the text's new 'unconscious'.

Judith Lowder Newton's chapter on *Villette* in her impressive study of nineteenth-century British fiction, *Women, Power, and Subversion* (1981), is also concerned with conflicts between the novel's feminism and its evocation of female desire.[4] Her interpretation privileges the social meanings of the novel, its search for a possible *détente* between the dominant ideologies of bourgeois femininity and progressive definitions of female autonomy. For Newton, 'the internalized ideology of women's sphere' includes sexual and romantic longings – which for Jacobus are potentially radical and disruptive of mid-Victorian gender ideologies. The psychic level as Newton describes it is mainly the repository for the worst and most regressive elements of female subjectivity: longing for love, dependency, the material and emotional comfort of fixed class identity. These desires which have 'got inside' are predictably in conflict with the rebellious, autonomy-seeking feminist impulses, whose source is a rational understanding of class and gender subordination. Her reading centres on the realist text, locating meaning in its critique of class society and the constraints of bourgeois femininity.

The quotations and narrative elements cited and explored by Jacobus and Newton are so different that even a reader familiar with *Villette* may find it hard to believe that each critic is reading the same text. The psychic level exists in Newton's interpretation, to be sure, but as a negative discourse, the dead weight of ideology on the mind. For her, the words 'hidden', 'private' and 'longing' are stigmatized, just as they are celebrated by Jacobus. For both critics, female subjectivity is the site where the opposing forces of femininity and feminism clash by night, but they locate these elements in different parts of the text's divided selves. Neither Newton nor Jacobus argues for the utopian possibility of a unified subjectivity. But the *longing* to close the splits that characterize femininity – splits between reason and desire, autonomy and dependent security, psychic and social identity – is evident in the way each critic denies the opposing element.

III

My comments on the difficulties of reading *Villette* from a materialist feminist stance are meant to suggest that there is more at issue in the polarization of social and psychic explanation than the problem of articulating two different forms of explanation. Moral and political questions specific to feminism are at stake as well. In order to understand why female subjectivity is so fraught with *Angst* and difficulty for feminism, we must go back to the first full discussion of the psychological expression of femininity, in Mary Wollstonecraft's *A Vindication of the Rights of Woman*. The briefest look will show that an interest in the psychic life of women as a crucial element in their subordination and liberation is not a modern, post-Freudian preoccupation. On the contrary, its long and fascinating history in 'left' feminist writing starts with Wollstonecraft, who set the terms for a debate that is still in progress. Her writing is central for socialist feminism today, because she based her interest in the emancipation of women as individuals in revolutionary politics.

Like so many eighteenth-century revolutionaries, she saw her own class, the rising bourgeoisie, as the vanguard of the revolution, and it was to the women of her own class that she directed her arguments. Her explicit focus on the middle class, and her concentration on the nature of female subjectivity, speaks directly to the source of anxiety within socialist feminism today. For it is at the point when women are released from profound social and economic oppression into greater autonomy and potential political choice that their social and psychic expression becomes an issue, and their literary texts become sites of ambivalence. In their pages, for the last 200 years and more, women characters seemingly more confined by social regulation than women readers today speak as desiring subjects. These texts express the politically 'retrograde' desires for comfort, dependence and love as well as more acceptable demands for autonomy and independence.

It is Mary Wollstonecraft who first offered women this fateful choice between the opposed and moralized bastions of reason and feeling, which continues to determine much feminist thinking.[5] The structures through which she developed her ideas, however, were set for her by her mentor Jean-Jacques Rousseau, whose writing influenced the political and social perspectives of many eighteenth-century English radicals. His ideas were fundamental to her thinking about gender as well as about revolutionary politics. In 1792, that highly charged moment of romantic political optimism between the fall of the Bastille and the Terror when *A Vindication* was written, it must have seemed crucial that Rousseau's crippling judgement of female nature be refuted. How else could women freely and equally participate in the new world being made across the Channel? Rousseau's ideas about subjectivity were already immanent in Wollstonecraft's earlier book *Mary: A Fiction* (1788). Now she set out to challenge directly his offensive description of sexual difference which would leave women in post-revolutionary society exactly where they were in unreformed Britain, 'immured in their families, groping in the dark'.[6]

Rousseau had set the terms of the debate in his *Emile* (1762),[7] which describes the growth and education of the new man, progressive and bourgeois, who would be capable of exercising the republican freedoms of a reformed society. In Book V, Rousseau invents 'Sophie' as a mate for his eponymous hero, and here he outlines his theory of sexual asymmetry as it occurs in nature. In all human beings passion was natural and necessary, but in women it was not controlled by reason, an attribute of the male sex only. Women, therefore, 'must be subject all their lives to the most constant and severe restraint, which is that of decorum; it is therefore necessary to accustom them early to such confinement that it may not afterwards cost them too dear . . . we should teach them above all things to lay a due restraint on themselves.'[8]

To justify this restraint, Rousseau allowed enormous symbolic power to the supposed anarchic, destructive force of untrammelled female desire. As objects of desire Rousseau made women alone responsible for male 'suffering'. If they were free agents of desire, there would be no end to the 'evils' they could cause. Therefore the family, and women's maternal role within it, were, he said, basic to the structure of the new society. Betrayal of the family was thus as subversive as betrayal of the state; adultery in *Emile* is literally equated with treason. Furthermore, in Rousseau's regime of regulation and restraint for bourgeois women, their 'decorum' – the social expression of modesty – would act as an additional safeguard against unbridled, excessive male lust, should its natural guardian, reason, fail. In proscribing the free exercise of female desire, Rousseau disarms a supposed serious threat to the new political as well as social order. To read the fate of a class through the sexual behaviour of its women was not a new political strategy. What is modern in Rousseau's formulation is the harnessing of these sexual ideologies to the fate of a new progressive bourgeoisie, whose individual male members were endowed with radical, autonomous identity.

In many ways, Mary Wollstonecraft, writing thirty years after *Emile*, shared with many others the political view of her master. Her immediate contemporary Thomas Paine thought Rousseau's work expressed 'a loveliness of sentiment in favour of liberty', and it is in the spirit of Rousseau's celebration of liberty that Wollstonecraft wrote *A Vindication*. Her strategy was to accept Rousseau's description of adult women as suffused with sensuality, but to ascribe this unhappy state of things to culture rather than nature. It was, she thought, the vicious and damaging result of Rousseau's punitive theories of sexual difference and female education when put into practice. Excessive sensuality was for Wollstonecraft, in 1792 at least, as dangerous if not more so than Rousseau had suggested, but she saw the damage and danger first of all to women themselves, whose potential and independence were initially stifled and broken by an apprenticeship to pleasure, which induced psychic and social dependency. Because Wollstonecraft saw pre-pubescent children in their natural state as mentally and emotionally unsexed as well as untainted by corrupting desire, she bitterly refuted Rousseau's description of innate infantile female sexuality. Rather, the debased femininity she describes is constructed through a set of social practices which by constant reinforcement become internalized parts of the self. Her description of this process is acute: 'Every thing they see or hear serves to fix impressions, call forth emotions, and associate ideas, that give a sexual character to the mind . . . This cruel association of ideas, which every thing conspires to twist into all their habits of thinking, or, to speak with more precision of feeling, receives new force when they begin to act a little for themselves.'[9]

For Wollstonecraft, female desire was a contagion caught from the projection of male lust, an ensnaring and enslaving infection that made women into dependent and degenerate creatures, who nevertheless had the illusion that they acted independently. An education that changed women from potentially rational autonomous beings into 'insignificant objects of desire' was, moreover, rarely reversible. Once a corrupt subjectivity was constructed, only a most extraordinary individual could transform it, for 'so ductile is the understanding and yet so stubborn, that the association which depends on adventitious circumstances, during the period that the body takes to arrive at maturity, can seldom be disentangled by reason'.[10]

What is disturbingly peculiar to *A Vindication* is the undifferentiated and central place that sexuality as passion plays in the corruption and degradation of the female self. The overlapping Enlightenment and Romantic discourses on psychic economy all posed a major division between the rational and the irrational, between sense and sensibility. But they hold sensibility *in men* to be only in part an antisocial sexual drive. Lust for power and the propensity to physical violence were also, for men, negative components of all that lay on the other side of reason. Thus sensibility in men included a strong positive element too, for the power of the imagination depended on it, and in the 1790s the Romantic aesthetic and the political imagination were closely allied. Sexual passion controlled and mediated by reason, Wordsworth's 'emotion recollected in tranquility', could also be put to productive use in art – by men. The appropriate egalitarian subjects of Wordsworth's art were 'moral sentiments and animal sensations' as they appeared in everyday life.[11] No woman of the time could offer such an artistic manifesto. In women the irrational, the sensible, even the imaginative are all drenched in an overpowering and subordinating sexuality. And in Wollstonecraft's writing, especially in her last, unfinished novel *Maria, or the Wrongs of Woman* (1798), which is considerably less punitive about women's sexuality in general than *A Vindication*, only maternal feeling survives as a positively realized element of the passionate side of the psyche. By defending women against Rousseau's denial of their reason, Wollstonecraft unwittingly assents to his negative, eroticized sketch of their emotional lives. At various points in *A Vindication* she interjects a wish that 'after some future revolution in time' women might be able to live out a less narcissistic and harmful sexuality. Until then they must demand an education whose central task is to cultivate their neglected 'understanding'.

It is interesting and somewhat tragic that Wollstonecraft's paradigm of women's psychic economy still profoundly shapes modern feminist consciousness. How often are the maternal, romantic-sexual and intellectual capacity of women presented by feminism as in competition for a fixed psychic space. Men seem to have a roomier and more accommodating psychic home, one which can, as Wordsworth and other Romantics insisted, situate all the varieties of passion and reason in creative tension. This gendered eighteenth-century psychic economy has been out of date for a long time, but its ideological inscription still shadows feminist attitudes towards the mental life of women.

The implications of eighteenth-century theories of subjectivity were important for early feminist ideas about women as readers and writers. In the final pages of *A Vindication*, decrying female sentimentality as one more effect of women's psychic degradation, Wollstonecraft criticizes the sentimental fictions increasingly written by and for women, which were often their only education. 'Novels' encouraged in their mainly young, mainly female audience 'a romantic twist of the mind'. Readers would 'only be taught to look for happiness in love, refine on sensual feelings and adopt metaphysical notions respecting that passion'. At their very worst the 'stale tales' and 'meretricious scenes' would by degrees induce more than passive fantasy. The captive, addicted reader might, while the balance of her mind was disturbed by these erotic evocations, turn fiction into fact and 'plump into actual vice'.[12] A reciprocal relationship between the patriarchal socialization of women and the literature that supports and incites them to become 'rakes at heart' is developed in this passage.

While Wollstonecraft adds that she would rather women read novels than nothing at all, she sets up a peculiarly gendered and sexualized interaction between women and the narrative imaginative text, one in which women become the ultimately receptive readers easily moved into amoral activity by the fictional representation of sexual intrigue.

The political resonance of these questions about reader response was, at the time, highly charged. An enormous expansion of literacy in general, and of the middle-class reading public in particular, swelled by literate women, made the act of reading in the last quarter of the eighteenth century an important practice through which the common sense and innate virtue of a society of antonomous subject-citizens could be reached and moulded. An uncensored press, cheap and available reading matter and a reading public free to engage with the flood of popular literature, from political broadsheets to sensational fiction, was part of the agenda and strategy of British republicanism. 'It is dangerous', Tom Paine warned the government in the mid-1790s after his own writing had been politically censored, 'to tell a whole people that they shall not read.' Reading was a civil right that supported and illustrated the radical vision of personal independence. Political and sexual conservatives, Jane Austen and Hannah More, as well as the republican and feminist left, saw reading as an active, not a passive function of the self, a critical link between the psychic play of reason and passion and its social expression. New social categories of readers, women of all classes, skilled and unskilled working-class males, are described in this period by contemporaries. Depending on their political sympathies, observers saw these actively literate groups as an optimistic symptom of social and intellectual progress or a dire warning of imminent social decay and threatened rebellion.

Wollstonecraft saw sentiment and the sensual as reinforcing an already dominant, approved and enslaving sexual norm, which led women to choose a subordinate social and subjective place in culture. The damage done by 'vice' and 'adultery', to which sentimental fiction was an incitement, was a blow to women first and to society second. Slavish legitimate sexuality was almost as bad for women in Wollstonecraft's view as unlicensed behaviour. A more liberal regime for women was both the goal and the cure of sentimental and erotic malaise. In *A Vindication* women's subjection is repeatedly compared to all illegitimate hierarchies of power, but especially to existing aristocratic hegemony. At every possible point in her text, Wollstonecraft links the liberation of women from the sensual into the rational literally and symbolically to the egalitarian transformation of the whole society.

'Passionlessness', as Nancy Cott has suggested, was a strategy adopted both by feminists and social conservatives.[13] Through the assertion that women were not innately or excessively sexual, that on the contrary their 'feelings' were largely filial and maternal, the imputation of a degraded subjectivity could be resisted. This alternative psychic organization was represented as both strength and weakness in nineteenth-century debates about sexual difference. In these debates, which were conducted across a wide range of public discourses, the absence of an independent, self-generating female sexuality is used by some men and women to argue for women's right to participate equally in an undifferentiated public sphere. It is used by others to argue for the power and value of the separate sphere allotted to women. And it is used more nakedly to support cruder justifications of patriarchal right. The idea of passionlessness as either a natural or a cultural effect acquires no simple ascendancy in Victorian sexual ideology, even as applied to the ruling bourgeoisie.

As either conservative or radical sexual ideology, asexual femininity was a fragile, unstable concept. It was constructed through a permanently threatened transgression, which fictional narrative obsessively documented and punished. It is a gross historical error to infer from the regulatory sexual discourses in the novel the actual 'fate' of Victorian adulteresses, for novels operated through a set of highly punitive conventions in relation to female sexuality that almost certainly did not correspond to lived social relations. However, novels do call attention to the difficulty of fixing such a sexual ideology, precisely because they construct a world in which there is no alternative to it.

IV

One of the central weaknesses of humanist criticism is that it accepts the idea advanced by classical realism that the function of literature is mimetic or realistic representation. The humanist critic identifies with the author's claim that the text represents reality, and acts as a sympathetic reader who will test the authenticity of the claim through the evidence of the text. The Marxist critic, on the other hand, assumes that author and text speak from a position within ideology – that claims about fictional truth and authenticity are, in themselves, to be understood in relation to a particular historical view of culture and art that evolved in the Romantic period. Semiotic and psychoanalytic theories of representation go even further in rejecting the possibility of authentic mimetic art. They see the literary text as a system of signs that constructs meaning rather than reflecting it, inscribing simultaneously the subjectivity of speaker and reader. Fiction by bourgeois women writers is spoken from the position of a class-specific femininity. It constructs us as readers in relation to that subjectivity through the linguistic strategies and processes of the text. It also takes us on a tour, so to speak, of a waxworks of other subjects-in-process – the characters of a dream, as constituent structures of the narrative of the dreamer, not as correct reflections of the socially real.

It is hard for feminism to accept the implications of this virtual refusal of textual realism, if only because literature was one of the few public discourses in which women were allowed to speak themselves, where they were not the imaginary representations of men. None the less, the subjectivity of women of other classes and races and with different sexual orientations can never be 'objectively' or 'authentically' represented in literary texts by the white, heterosexual, middle-class woman writer, however sympathetically she invents or describes such women in her narrative. The nature of fiction and the eccentric relation of female subjectivity itself both to culture and to psychic identity, as understood from a psychoanalytic perspective, defeats that aim. We can, however, learn a great deal from women's writing about the cultural meanings produced from the splitting of women's subjectivity, especially their sexuality, into class and race categories. But before we say more about this way of reading women's writing we need a more precise working definition of 'class'.

Unlike subjectivity, 'class' has been a central category for socialist feminist criticism, but remains somewhat inert within it, if not within socialist feminist theory as a whole. Socialist critics hesitate to identify their own object of study, the literary text, as a central productive site of class meaning, because it seems too far away from 'real' economic and political determinations. The same worry, conversely, can induce a compensatory claim that *all* the material relations of class can be discovered within the discourse; indeed, that they are most fully represented there, because language is itself material. These positions, which I confess I have parodied a little, remain unresolved in current debate, although efforts at *détente* have been made. They indicate the uneasy relationship between the political and the literary in the Marxist critical project, an unease shared by socialist feminists too.

Among socialist historians in the last few years the understanding of the history of class has undergone vigorous reappraisal in response to debates about the changing composition and politics of the working class in modern capitalist societies. In a recent collection of essays, *The Language of Class*, the British historian of the nineteenth century, Gareth Stedman Jones, proposes some radical approaches to that history which have an immediate relevance for the analysis of representation. First of all, Stedman Jones asks for a more informed and theoretical attention by historians to the linguistic construction of class. '"Class" is a word embedded in language and should be analysed in terms of its linguistic content,' he states. In the second place, 'class' as a concept needs to be unpacked, and its differential construction in discourse recognized and given a certain autonomy: 'because there are different languages of class, one should not proceed upon the assumption that "class" as an elementary counter of official social description, "class" as an effect of theoretical discourse about distribution or productive relations, "class" as the summary of a cluster of culturally signifying practices or "class" as a species of political or ideological self-definition, share a single reference point in anterior social reality.'[14]

This formulation helps to break down the oppressively unitary character of class as a concept. Through it class can be seen as defined in different terms at different levels of analysis. However we still need to understand in more detail how class is experienced by class subjects. 'Anterior social reality' hangs slightly loose in Stedman Jones' model. How does it exist, if it exists at all, as a site where these conflicting and competing discourses meet? Class is lived, after all, as if it were a set of coherent social relations. Yet, at the same time there is a gap between what people think they are doing, and what they are actually doing, and it is important to think about what happens in that gap both in the everyday and at moments of crisis in class relations. Take, for example that most visible instance of working class protest, the strike. Most strikes do not set out to challenge capitalism, but rather to gain specific demands from employer and state. Yet strikes do disrupt the smooth running of capitalism at a macrocosmic level, and in consequence shift the terms in which capitalism is perceived for the striking community itself. Indeed the field of meaning of social and economic relations and not incidentally of the subjectivity of strikers and owners is changed by a strike. Whether the strike is lost or won a partly new paradigm, though not necessarily a more radical one for the striking community, is constructed. This process is not marked by a simple progression from one position or one subjectivity to another. Rather it is characterized by an oscillation between moments of relative incoherence – the breaking-up of old political languages and positions – and moments when new formulations – often tentative and transitory – are being realised. Nor are these processes of transformation always or even mostly, wilful, argued through, fully conscious realignments. Class is 'made' and 'lived' in both conscious and unconscious registers through a variety of languages and practices at any given point in history.

How can this pulling apart of the languages of class help socialist feminist critics to put class and gender, the social and the psychic together in a non-reductive way? First of all, these distinctions put a useful space between the economic overview of class – the Marxist or socialist analysis – and the actual rhetoric of class as it appears in a novel. The class language of a nineteenth-century novel is not only or even primarily characterized by reference to the material circumstances of the protagonists, though that may be part of its representation there. The language of class in the novel foregrounds the language of the self, the inner discourse of the subject *as* class language, framing that discourse through the dissonant chorus of class voices that it appropriates and invents. In the novel, class discourse *is* gendered discourse; the positions of 'Emile' and 'Sophie' are given dramatic form. Class is embodied in fiction in a way that it never is either in bourgeois economic discourse or in Marxist economic analysis. In those discourses of class, *gender* is mystified, presented in ideological form. In fiction, though difference may be presented through sexual ideologies, its immanent crucial presence in the social relations of class, as well as its psychic effects, is strongly asserted. Fiction refuses the notion of a genderless class subjectivity, and resists any simple reduction of class meaning and class identity to productive forces. This refusal and resistance cannot be written off, or reduced to the humanist ideologies of transcendence that those fictions may also enunciate, for the presence of gendered subjectivity in nineteenth-century fiction is always 'in struggle' with the Romantic ideologies of unified identity.

Within socialist feminist cultural analysis it has been easier to describe the visual or linguistic fusion of class and gender meanings in representation than it has been to assess the role such fusion plays in the construction of either category. Let us assume that in these signifying practices class is powerfully defined through sexual difference, and vice versa, and that these representations are constitutive of certain class meanings, not merely a distorted or mendacious reflection of other languages. 'Class' needs to be read through an ensemble of these languages, often contradictory, as well as in terms of an economic overview. The overpowering presence of gender in some languages of class and its virtual absence in others needs to be related not to a single anterior definition of class reality, but to the heterogeneous and contradictory nature of that reality.

Literature is itself a heterogeneous discourse, which appropriates, contextualizes and comments on other 'languages' of class and gender. This process of intertextuality – the dialogic, as the Russian critic Bakhtin called it, undermines the aspirations of the text towards a unifying definition.[15] The language of class in the nineteenth-century novel obsessively inscribes a class system whose divisions and boundaries are at once absolute and impregnable and in constant danger of dissolution. Often in these narratives it is a woman whose class identity is at risk or problematic; the woman and her sexuality are a condensed and displaced representation of the dangerous instabilities of class and gender identity for both sexes. The loss and recuperation of female identity within the story – a favourite lost-and-found theme from *Mansfield Park* to *Tess* – provides an imaginary though temporary solution to the crisis of both femininity and class. Neither category – class or gender – was ever as stable as the ideologies that support them must continually insist. The many-layered, compacted representations of class and gender found in imaginative literature are not generic metaphors, peculiar to fiction, drama and poetry, though in them they are given great scope. They occur in many other nineteenth-century discourses – metonymic, associative tropes linked by incomparable similarities, through a threat to identity and status that inheres to both sets of hierarchies, both structures of difference.

The class subjectivity of women and their sexual identity thus became welded together in nineteenth-century discourses and took on new and sinister dimensions of meaning. Ruling groups had traditionally used the sexual and domestic virtue of their women as a way of valorizing their moral authority. By focusing on the issue and image of female sexual conduct, questions about the economic and political integrity of dominant groups could be displaced. When the citizen–subject became the crucial integer of political discourse and practice, this type of symbolization, which was always 'about' sexual difference as well as 'about' the political, took on new substantive, material meaning. The moral autonomy of individuals and the moral behaviour of social groups now converged in a political practice and theory – liberal, constitutional and legitimated through an expanding franchise – in which the individual voter was the common denominator of the political. Women, as we have seen, were explicitly excluded from these political practices, but, as we have also seen, attempts to naturalize that exclusion were never wholly successful. Feminism inserted itself into the debate just at the point where theories of innate difference attempted to deny women access to a full political identity. The debate about women's mental life signalled, as I have suggested, a more general anxiety about non-rational, unsocial behaviour. Female subjectivity, or its synecdochic reference, female sexuality, became the displaced and condensed site for the general anxiety about individual behaviour that republican and liberal political philosophy stirred up. It is not too surprising that the morality of the class as a whole was better represented by those who exercised the least power within it, or that the punishment for female sexual transgression was fictionally represented as the *immediate* loss of social status.

The ways in which class is lived by men and women, like the ways in which sexual difference is lived, are only partly open to voluntary self-conscious political negotiation. The unconscious processes that construct subjective identity are also the structures through which class is lived and understood, through which political subjection and rebellion are organized. Arguing for the usefulness of psychoanalysis in historical analysis, Sally Alexander emphasizes that its theories do not imply a universal human nature. Rather, 'Subjectivity in this account is neither universal nor ahistorical. First structured through relations of absence and loss, pleasure and unpleasure, difference and division, these are simultaneous with the social naming and placing among kin, community, school, class which are always historically specific.'[16]

Literary texts give these simultaneous inscriptions narrative form, pointing towards and opening up the fragmentary nature of social and psychic identity, drawing out the ways in which social meaning is psychically represented. It is this symbolic shaping of class that we should examine in fiction. Literary texts tell us more about the intersection of class and gender than we can learn from duly noting the material circumstances and social constraints of characters and authors.

However mimetic or realistic the aspirations of fiction, it always tells us less about the purely social rituals of a class society organized around the sexual division of labour than about the powerful symbolic force of class and gender in ordering our social and political imagination. The doubled inscription of sexual and social difference is the most common, characteristic trope of nineteenth-century fictions. In these texts, the difference between women is at least as important an element as the difference between the sexes, as a way of representing both class and gender. This salient fact often goes unnoticed in the emphasis of bourgeois criticism on male/female division and opposition. In turn, this emphasis on heterosexual antagonisms and resolutions effaces the punitive construction of alternative femininities in women's writing. If texts by women reveal a 'hidden' sympathy between women, as radical feminist critics often assert, they equally express positive femininity through hostile and denigrating representations of women. Imperilled bourgeois femininity takes meaning in relation to other female identities, and to the feminized identities of other social groups that the novel constructs and dialogizes. The unfavourable symbiosis of reason and passion ascribed to women is also used to characterize both men and women in the labouring classes and in other races and cultures. The line between the primitive and the degraded feminine is a thin one, habitually elided in dominant discourse and practically used to limit the civil and political rights of all three subordinated categories: Blacks, women and the working class.

Through that chain of colonial associations, whole cultures became 'feminized', 'blackened' and 'impoverished' – each denigrating construction implying and invoking the others. 'True womanhood' had to be protected from this threatened linguistic contamination, not only from the debased subjectivity and dangerous sexuality of the lower-class prostitute, but from all other similarly inscribed subordinate subjectivities. The difference between men and women in the ruling class had to be written so that a slippage into categories reserved for lesser humanities could be averted. These fragmented definitions of female subjectivity were not only a mode through which the moral virtue of the ruling class was represented in the sexual character of its women; they also shaped, and were shaped by, the ways in which women of the middle and upper classes understood and represented their own being. It led them towards projecting and displacing on to women of lower social standing and women of colour, as well as on to the 'traditionally' corrupt aristocracy, all that was deemed vicious and regressive in women as a sex.

It is deeply troubling to find these projected and displaced representations in the writing of sexual and social radicals, and in the work of feminists from Wollstonecraft to Woolf, as well as in conservative sexual and social discourses. They are especially marked in those texts and writers who accept in whole or in part the description of mental life and libidinal economy of the Enlightenment and the moral value attached to it. In *A Vindication*, working-class women are quite unselfconsciously constructed as prostitutes and dirty-minded servants corrupting bourgeois innocence. Turn the page over and you will also find them positioned in a more radical sense as the most brutalized victims of aristocratic and patriarchal despotism. Note the bestial descriptions of the female poor in Elizabeth Barrett Browning's *Aurora Leigh*. Remember the unhappy, ambivalent and contradictory relationship to black subjectivity, male and female, of many mid-nineteenth-century American feminists and abolitionists. Most distressing of all, because nearer to us in time, think about the contrast between Woolf's public polemical support of working-class women and the contempt with which the feelings and interests of her female servants are treated in her diaries, where they exist as lesser beings. These representations are neither natural nor inevitable. They are the historic effects of determinate social divisions and ideologies worked through psychic structures, worked into sexual and social identity. If they are understood they can be changed.

In Ann Radcliffe's *Mysteries of Udolpho*, one of the most popular of the Enlightenment gothic novels of the 1790s, the heroine, Emily, flees from the sinister importunities of her titled foreign host. The scene is rural Italy, as far away as possible from genteel British society. Emily's flight from the castle is precipitous, and in her terror and haste she forgets her hat. Within the world of the text, Emily's bare head threatens her identity as pure woman, as surely as do the violent, lascivious attentions of her pursuer. Both the narrative and her flight are interrupted while Emily restores her identity by purchasing 'a little straw hat' from a peasant girl. A woman without a hat was, in specular terms, a whore; the contemporary readership understood the necessary pause in the story. They understood too that the hat, passed from peasant to lady, securing the class and sexual status of the latter, was not only a fragment of domestic realism set against gothic fantasy. Hat and flight are part of a perfectly coherent psychic narrative in which aristocratic seducer, innocent bourgeois victim, peasant girl and straw hat play out the linked meanings of class and sexuality.[17]

Stories of seduction and betrayal of orphaned, impoverished heroines of uncertain class origin, provided a narrative structure through which the instabilities of class and gender categories were both stabilized and undermined. Across the body and mind of 'woman' as sign, through her multiple representations, bourgeois anxiety about identity is traced and retraced. A favourite plot, of which *Jane Eyre* is now the best-known example, sets the genteel heroine at sexual risk as semi-servant in a grand patriarchal household. This narrative theme allowed the crisis of middle-class femininity to be mapped on to the structural sexual vulnerability of all working-class servants in bourgeois employment. Such dramas were full of condensed meanings in excess of the representation of sexuality and sexual difference. A doubled scenario, in which the ideological and material difference between working-class and bourgeois women is blurred through condensation, it was popular as a plot for melodrama with both 'genteel' and 'vulgar' audiences.

We do not know very much so far about how that fictional narrative of threatened femininity was understood by working-class women, although it appeared in the cheap fiction written for servant girls as well as in popular theatre. Nineteenth-century bourgeois novels like *Jane Eyre* tell us almost nothing about the self-defined subjectivity of the poor, male or female. For, although they are rich sources for the construction of dominant definitions *of* the inner lives of working classes, they cannot tell us anything about how even these ideological inscriptions were lived *by* them. For an analysis of the subjectivity of working-class women we need to turn to non-literary sources, to the discourses in which they themselves spoke. That analysis lies outside the project of this chapter but is, of course, related to it.

I want to end this chapter with an example of the kind of interpretative integration that I have been demanding of feminist critics. No text has proved more productive of meaning from the critic's point of view than Charlotte Brontë's *Jane Eyre*. I have referred to the condensation of class meanings through the characterization and narrative of its heroine, but now I want to turn to that disturbing didactic moment in volume 1, chapter 12, which immediately precedes the entry of Rochester into the text. It is a passage marked by Virginia Woolf in *A Room of One's Own*, where it is used to illustrate the negative effect of anger and inequality on the female imagination. Prefaced defensively – 'Anybody may blame me who likes' – it is a passage about need, demand and desire that exceed social possibility and challenge social prejudice. In Jane's soliloquy, inspired by a view reached through raising the 'trap-door of the attic', the Romantic aesthetic is reasserted for women, together with a passionate refusal of the terms of feminine difference. Moved by a 'restlessness' in her 'nature' that 'agitated me to pain sometimes', Jane paces the top floor of Thornfield and allows her 'mind's eye to dwell on whatever bright visions rose before it': 'to let my heart be heaved by the exultant movement which, while it swelled it in trouble, expanded it with life; and, best of all, to open my inward ear to a tale that was never ended – a tale my imagination created, and narrated continuously; quickened with all of incident, life, fire, feeling, that I desired and had not in my actual existence.'[18]

This reverie is only partly quoted by Woolf, who omits the 'visionary' section, moving straight from 'pain . . .' to the paragraph most familiar to us through her citation of it:

> It is in vain to say that human beings ought to be satisfied with tranquillity; they must have action; and they will make it if they cannot find it. Millions are condemned to a stiller doom than mine, and millions are in silent revolt against their lot. Nobody knows how many rebellions besides political rebellions ferment in the masses of life which people earth. Women are supposed to be very calm generally: but women feel just as men feel; they need exercise for their faculties, and a field for their efforts as much as their brothers do; they suffer from too rigid a restraint, too absolute a stagnation, precisely as men would suffer; and it is narrow-minded in their more privileged fellow-creatures to say that they ought to confine themselves to making puddings and knitting stockings, to playing on piano and embroidering bags. It is thoughtless to condemn them, or laugh at them, if they seek to do more or learn more than custom has pronounced necessary for their sex.
> When thus alone I not unfrequently heard Grace Poole's laugh . . . [19]

This shift from feminist polemic to the laugh of Grace Poole is the 'jerk', the 'awkward break' of 'continuity' that Woolf criticizes. 'The writer of such a flawed passage will never get her genius expressed whole and entire. Her books will be deformed and twisted. She will write in a rage where she should write calmly. She will write foolishly where she should write wisely. She will write of herself when she should write of her characters. She is at war with her lot. How could she help but die young, cramped and thwarted?'[20]

It is a devastating, controlled, yet somehow uncontrolled indictment. What elements in this digression, hardly a formal innovation in nineteenth-century fiction, can have prompted Woolf to such excess? Elaine Showalter analyses this passage and others as part of Woolf's

91

ndrogyny', that aesthetic chamber where masculine and
inds meet and marry. Showalter's analysis focuses on Woolf's
s an effect of her inability to come to terms with her sexuality,
sexual difference itself. Showalter's analysis is persuasive in
individual terms, but it does not deal with all of the questions thrown up
by Brontë's challenge and Woolf's violent response to it. In the sentences
that Woolf omits in her own citation, Brontë insists that even the
confined and restless state could produce 'many and glowing' visions.
Art, the passage maintains, can be produced through the endless
narration of the self, through the mixed incoherence of subjectivity
spoken from subordinate and rebellious positions within culture. It was
this aesthetic that Woolf as critic explicitly rejected.

However, the passage deals with more than sexual difference. In the
references to 'human beings' and to unspecified 'millions', Brontë
deliberately and defiantly associates political and sexual rebellion even as
she distinguishes between them. In the passage the generic status of
'men' is made truly trans-class and trans-cultural when linked to
'masses', 'millions' and 'human beings', those larger inclusive terms. In
1847, on the eve of the second great wave of modern revolution, it was a
dangerous rhetoric to use.

Its meaningful associations were quickly recognized by contemporary
reviewers, who deplored the contiguous relationship between revolution
and feminism. Lady Eastlake's comments in the *Quarterly Review* of 1849
are those most often quoted: 'We do not hesitate to say, that the tone of
mind and thought which has overthrown authority and violated every
code human and divine abroad, and fostered chartism and rebellion at
home is the same which has also written *Jane Eyre*.'

Yet Charlotte Brontë was no political radical. How is it then that she is
pulled towards the positive linking of class rebellion and women's revolt
in this passage, as she will be again in *Shirley*? Perhaps my earlier
example of the process through which class meaning is transformed for
class subjects during a strike is helpful here. For this passage does not
mark out a moment of conscious reformulation of Brontë's class politics.
Rather it is a significant moment of incoherence, where the congruence
between the subordination of women and the radical view of class
oppression becomes, for a few sentences, irresistible. It is a tentative,
partial movement in spite of its defiant rhetoric, a movement which
threatens to break up the more general, self-conscious class politics of the
text. And it brings with it, inexorably, its own narrative reaction which
attempts, with some success, to warn us quite literally that the
association of feminism and class struggle leads to madness. For Jane's
vision is checked, instantly, by the mad mocking female laughter, and
turned from its course a few pages later by the introduction of Rochester
into the narrative.

For Woolf, Jane's soliloquy spoils the continuity of the narrative with its 'anger and rebellion'. Woolf turns away, refuses to comprehend the logical sequence of the narration at the symbolic level of the novel.

Jane's revolutionary manifesto of the subject, which has its own slightly manic register, invokes that sliding negative signification of women that we have described. At this point in the story the 'low, slow ha' ha!' and the 'eccentric murmurs' that 'thrilled' Jane are ascribed to Grace Poole, the hard-featured servant. But Grace is only the laugh's minder, and the laugh later becomes correctly ascribed to Rochester's insane wife, Bertha Mason. The uncertain source of the laughter, the narrator's inability to predict its recurrence – 'There were days when she was quite silent; but there were others when I could not account for the sounds she made' – both mark out the 'sounds' as the dark side of Romantic female subjectivity.[21]

Retroactively, in the narrative the laughter becomes a threat to all that Jane had desired and demanded in her roof-top reverie. Mad servant, mad mistress, foreigner, nymphomaniac, syphilitic, half-breed, aristocrat, Bertha turns violently on keeper, brother, husband and, finally, rival. She and her noises become the condensed and displaced site of unreason and anarchy as it is metonymically figured through dangerous femininity in all its class, race and cultural projections. Bertha must be killed off, narratively speaking, so that a moral, Protestant femininity, licensed sexuality and a qualified, socialized feminism may survive. Yet the text cannot close off or recuperate that moment of radical association between political rebellion and gender rebellion, cannot shut down the possibility of a positive alliance between reason, passion and feminism. Nor can it disperse the terror that speaking those connections immediately stirs up – for Woolf in any case.

Woolf was at her most vehement and most contradictory about these issues, which brought together for her, as for many other feminists before and after, a number of deeply connected anxieties about subjectivity, class, sexuality and culture. Over and over again in her critical writing, Woolf tries to find ways of placing the questions inside an aesthetic that disallows anger, unreason and passion as productive emotions. Like Wollstonecraft before her, she cannot quite shake off the moral and libidinal economies of the Enlightenment. In 'Women and Fiction' (1929) she frames the question another way:

> In *Middlemarch* and in *Jane Eyre* we are conscious not merely of the writer's character, as we are conscious of the character of Charles Dickens, but we are conscious of a woman's presence – of someone resenting the treatment of her sex and pleading for its rights. This brings into women's writing an element which is entirely absent from a man's, unless, indeed, he happens to be a working man, a Negro, or

one who for some other reason is conscious of disability. It introduces a distortion and is frequently the cause of weakness. The desire to plead some personal cause or to make a character the mouthpiece of personal discontent or grievance always has a distressing effect, as if the spot at which the reader's attention is directed were suddenly two-fold instead of single.[22]

Note how the plea for a sex, a class, a race becomes reduced to individual, personal grievance, how subordinate position in a group becomes immediately pathologized as private disability, weakness. Note too how 'man' in this passage loses its universal connotation, so that it only refers normatively to men of the ruling class. In this passage, as in *Jane Eyre*, degraded subjectivities are metonymically evolved – 'disability', 'distortion' – and degradation is expressed as an effect of subordination, not its rationale nor its cause. But the result is still a negative one. For the power to resist through fictional language, the language of sociality and self; the power to move and enlighten, rather than blur and distress through the double focus, is denied. Instead, Woolf announces the death of the feminist text, by proclaiming, somewhat prematurely, the triumph of feminism. 'The woman writer is no longer bitter. She is no longer angry. She is no longer pleading and protesting as she writes . . . She will be able to concentrate upon her vision without distraction from outside.'[23] This too is a cry from the roof-tops of a desire still unmet by social and psychic experience.

Although the meanings attached to race, class and sexuality have undergone fundamental shifts from Wollstonecraft's (and Woolf's) time to our own, we do not live in a post-class society any more than a post-feminist one. Our identities are still constructed through social hierarchy and cultural differentiation, as well as through those processes of division and fragmentation described in psychoanalytic theory. The identities arrived at through these structures will always be precarious and unstable, though *how* they will be so in the future we do not know. For the moment, women still have a problematic place in both social and psychic representation. The problem for women of woman-as-sign has made the self-definition of women a resonant issue within feminism. It has also determined the restless inability of feminism to settle for humanist definitions of the subject, or for materialism's relegation of the problem to determinations of class only. I have emphasized in this chapter some of the more negative ways in which the Enlightenment and Romantic paradigms of subjectivity gave hostages to the making of subordinate identities, of which femininity is the structuring instance. Although psychoanalytic theories of the construction of gendered subjectivity stress difficulty, antagonism and contradiction as necessary parts of the production of identity, the concept of the unconscious and the psychoanalytic view of sexuality dissolve in great part the binary divide between reason and passion that dominates earlier concepts of subjectivity. They break down as well the moralism attached to those libidinal and psychic economies. Seen from this perspective, 'individualism' has a different and more contentious history within feminism than it does in androcentric debates.

That is the history we must uncover and consider, in both its positive and its negative effects, so that we can argue convincingly for a feminist rehabilitation of the female psyche in non-moralized terms. Perhaps we can come to see it as neither sexual outlaw, social bigot nor dark hiding-place for treasonable regressive femininity waiting to stab progressive feminism in the back. We must redefine the psyche as a structure, not as a content. To do so is not to move away from a feminist politics that takes race and class into account, but to move towards a fuller understanding of how social divisions and the inscription of gender are mutually secured and given meaning. Through that analysis we can work towards change.

Notes

1. Lillian S. Robinson, 'Dwelling in Decencies: Radical Criticism and the Feminist Perceptive', in *Sex, Class and Culture* (Bloomington: Indiana UP, 1978), pp. 3–21.

2. Heidi Hartmann, 'The Unhappy Marriage of Marxism and Feminism: Towards a more Progressive Union', in *The Unhappy Marriage of Marxism and Feminism: A Debate on Class and Patriarchy*, ed. Lydia Sargent (London: Pluto, 1981), pp. 1–42.

3. Mary Jacobus, 'The Buried Letter: Feminism and Romanticism in *Villette*' in *Women Writing and Writing about Women*, ed. Mary Jacobus (London: Croom Helm, 1979), p. 51.

4. Judith Lowder Newton, *Women, Power, and Subversion: Social Strategies in British Fiction 1778–1860* (Athens, Ga.: U Georgia Press, 1981).

5. Mary Wollstonecraft, *A Vindication of the Rights of Woman* (New York: 1975).

6. Wollstonecraft, *A Vindication*, p. 5.

7. Jean-Jacques Rousseau, *Emile* (London: Dent, 1974).

8. Rousseau, *Emile*, p. 32.

9. Wollstonecraft, *A Vindication*, p. 177.

10. Wollstonecraft, *A Vindication*, p. 116.

11. William Wordsworth and Samuel Taylor Coleridge, *Lyrical Ballads*, ed. R.L. Brett and A.R. Jones (London: Methuen, 1971), p. 261.

12. Wollstonecraft, *A Vindication*, p. 183.

13. NANCY F. COTT, 'Passionlessness: An Interpretation of Victorian Sexual Ideology, 1790–1850', *Signs*, 2 (2), pp. 219–33.

14. GARETH STEDMAN JONES, *Languages of Class: Studies in English Working Class History 1832–1982* (Cambridge: CUP, 1983), pp. 7–8.

15. M.M. BAKHTIN, *The Dialogic Imagination: Four Essays*, ed. Michael Holquist (Austin, Tex.: U Texas Press, 1981).

16. SALLY ALEXANDER, 'Women, Class and Sexual Difference', *History Workshop Journal*, 17, (1984), pp. 125–49.

17. ANN RADCLIFFE, *The Mysteries of Udolpho* (London: OUP, 1966).

18. CHARLOTTE BRONTË, *Jane Eyre*, ed. Margaret Smith (London: OUP, 1976), p. 110.

19. BRONTË, *Jane Eyre*, pp. 110–11.

20. VIRGINIA WOOLF, *A Room of One's Own* (Harmondsworth: Penguin, 1973), p. 70.

21. BRONTË, *Jane Eyre*, p. 111.

22. VIRGINIA WOOLF, 'Women and Fiction', in *Women and Writing*, ed. Michèle Barrett (London 1979), p. 47.

23. WOOLF, 'Women and Fiction', p. 47.

4 Jane Austen and Empire*
(1989)

EDWARD W. SAID

Edward W. Said is Parr Professor of English and Comparative
Literature at Columbia University. His numerous books include
Orientalism (1978) and *The World, the Text, and the Critic* (1983).

The issues posed by Said's reading of *Mansfield Park* are historical
and rhetorical, and in both cases, ultimately, political. The dating of
British culture's imperialist phase must be revised backwards from
the beginning of formal Empire into the eighteenth century, he
argues. And its traces must be sought in an under-explored dimension of narrative: its 'moral geography', its *space*. Said analyses the
drama of place in Austen's novel and shows how the composition of
domestic order in it depends on a reorganized and internalized
elsewhere – the absent world of the Caribbean colonies. Writing in
solidarity with Marxism rather than as a declared exponent – his main
theoretical reference has been to Foucault – Said emphasizes the
constructive role of discourse in historical systems; assigning Austen
to a lineage of writing that will later include Conrad and Kipling, he
reinserts the humane traditions of English culture in their ambiguous
role in the unfolding of Britain's colonial history.

We are on solid ground with V. G. Kiernan when he says that 'empires
must have a mould of ideas or conditioned reflexes to flow into, and
youthful nations dream of a great place in the world as young men
dream of fame and fortunes.'[1] It is, I believe, too simple and reductive a
proposition to argue that everything in European and American culture
is therefore a preparation for, or a consolidation of, the grand idea of
empire that took over those societies during 'the age of empire' after 1870

---

* Reprinted from *Raymond Williams: Critical Perspectives*, ed. Terry Eagleton
(Oxford: Polity, 1989), pp. 150–64.

but, conversely, it will not do to ignore those tendencies found in narrative, or in political theory, or in pictorial technique that enable, encourage, and otherwise assure the readiness of the West during the earlier parts of the nineteenth century to assume and enjoy the experience of empire. Similarly, we must note that if there was cultural resistance to the notion of an imperial mission there was not much support for such resistance in the main departments of cultural thought. Liberal though he was, John Stuart Mill – as a particularly telling case in point – could still say that 'the sacred duties which civilized nations owe to the independence and nationality of each other, are not binding towards those to whom nationality and independence are certain evil, or at best a questionable good.'[2]

Why that should be so, why sacred obligation on one front should not be binding on another, are questions best understood in the terms of a culture well grounded in a set of moral, economic and even metaphysical norms designed to approve a satisfying local, that is European, order in connection with the denial of the right to a similar order abroad. Perhaps such a statement appears preposterous, or extreme. In fact, I think, it formulates the connection between a certain kind of European well-being and cultural identity on the one hand, and, on the other, the subjugation of imperial realms overseas in too fastidious and circumspect a fashion. Part of the difficulty today in accepting any sort of connection at all is that we tend to collapse the whole complicated matter into an unacceptably simple causal relationship, which in turn produces a rhetoric of blame and consequent defensiveness. But I am *not* saying that the major thing about early nineteenth century European culture was that it *caused* late nineteenth century imperialism, and I am not therefore implying that all the problems of the contemporary non-European, formerly colonial, world should be blamed on Europe. I am saying, however, that European culture often, if not always, characterized itself in such a way as simultaneously to validate its own preferences while also advocating those preferences in conjunction with distant imperial rule. Mill certainly did: he always recommended that India not be given independence. When for a variety of reasons imperial rule occupied Europe with much greater intensity after 1880, this schizophrenic practice became a useful habit.

The first thing to be done now is more or less to jettison the simple causal mode of thinking through the relationship between Europe and the non-European world. This also requires some lessening of the hold on our thought of the equally simple sequence of temporal consecutiveness. We must not admit any notion, for instance, of the sort that proposes to show that Wordsworth, Jane Austen and Hazlitt because they wrote before 1857 actually caused the establishment of formal British government rule over India. What we should try to discern instead is a counterpoint between overt patterns in British writing about Britain and representation of what exists in the world beyond the British Isles. The inherent mode for this counterpoint therefore is not temporal, but spatial. How do writers in the period before the great age of explicit and programmatic colonial expansion in the late nineteenth century – the scramble for Africa say – situate and see themselves and their work in the larger world? We will find some striking but careful strategies employed, most of them deriving from expected sources – the positive ideas of home, of a nation and its language, of proper order, good behaviour, moral values.

But positive ideas of this sort do more than validate 'our' world. They also tend to devalue other worlds and, perhaps more significantly from a retrospective point of view, they do not prevent or inhibit or provide a resistance to horrendously unattractive imperialist practices. No, we are right to say that cultural forms like the novel or the opera do not cause people to go out and imperialize; perhaps Carlyle did not drive Rhodes directly, and he certainly cannot be 'blamed' for the problems of today's South Africa. But the genuinely troubling issue is how little the great humanistic ideas, institutions, and monuments, which we still celebrate as having the power ahistorically to command our approving attention, how little they stand in the way of an accelerating imperial process during the nineteenth century. Are we not entitled to ask therefore how this body of humanistic ideas coexisted so comfortably with imperialism, and why until the resistance to imperialism *in the imperial domain*, among Africans, Asians, Latin Americans, developed, there was little significant opposition or deterrence to empire at home? May we suspect that what had been the customary way of distinguishing 'our' home and order from 'theirs' grew into a harsh political rule for accumulating more of 'them' to rule, study and subordinate? Do we not have in the great humane ideas and values promulgated by mainstream European culture precisely that 'mould of ideas and conditioned reflexes' of which V. G. Kiernan speaks, into which the whole business of empire would later flow?

The extent to which these ideas are actually invested in distinctions between real places has been the subject of Raymond Williams's richest book, *The Country and the City*. His argument concerning the interplay between the rural and the urban in England admits of the most extraordinary transformations, from the pastoral populism of Langland, through Ben Jonson's country-house poems, the picture of Dickens's London, right up to visions of the metropolis in twentieth-century literature. And while he does tackle the export of England into the colonies Williams does so, in my opinion, less centrally, less expansively than the practice actually warrants. Near the end of *The Country and the City*, Williams suggests that 'from at least the mid-nineteenth century, and with important instances earlier, there was this large context [the relationship between England and the colonies, and its effects on the English imagination which, Williams correctly says, 'have gone deeper than can easily be traced'] within which every idea and every image was consciously and unconsciously affected.' He goes on quickly to list 'the idea of emigration to the colonies' as one such image prevailing in various novels by Dickens, the Brontës, Gaskell, and he quite rightly shows that 'new rural societies', all of them colonial, enter the imaginative metropolitan economy of English literature via Kipling, early Orwell, Somerset Maugham. After 1880 there comes a 'dramatic extension of landscape and social relations': this corresponds more or less exactly with the great age of empire.[3]

It is dangerous to disagree with Williams. Yet I would venture to say that if one began to look for something like an imperial map of the world in English literature it would turn up with amazing centrality and frequency well before the middle of the nineteenth century. And not only turn up with an inert regularity that might suggest something taken for granted, but – much more interestingly – threaded through, forming a vital part of the texture of linguistic and cultural practice. For there were established English interests in America, the Caribbean and Asia from the seventeenth century on, and even a quick inventory will reveal poets, philosophers, historians, dramatists, novelists, travel writers, chroniclers, and fabulists for whom these interests were to be traced, cared for, prized, and regarded with a continuing concern. A similar argument could be made for France, Spain and Portugal, not only as overseas powers in their own right, but as competitors with the British. How then can we examine these interests at work in England *before* the age of empire that officially occurred during the last third of the nineteenth century?

We would do well to follow Williams's lead, and look at that period of crisis following upon wide-scale land enclosure at the end of the eighteenth century. Not only are old organic communities dissolved, and new ones forged under the impulse of parliamentary activity, industrialization, and demographic dislocation, but, I would suggest, there occurs a new process of relocating England (and in France, France) within a much larger circle of the world map. During the first half of the eighteenth century, Anglo-French competition in India was intense; in the second half there were numerous violent encounters between them in the Levant, the Caribbean and of course in Europe itself. Much of what we read today as major pre-Romantic literature in France and England contains a constant stream of references to the overseas dominions: one thinks not only of various encyclopaedists, the Abbé Reynal, de Brosses, and Volney, but also of Edmund Burke, Beckford, Gibbon, and William Jones.

In 1902 J. A. Hobson described imperialism as the expansion of nationality, implying that the process was understandable mainly by considering *expansion* to be the more important of the two terms, since 'nationality' was a fixed quantity.[4] For Hobson's purposes nationality was in fact fully formed, whereas a century before it was in the process of *being formed*, not only at home, but abroad as well. Between France and Britain in the late eighteenth century there were two contests: the battle for strategic gains in such places as India, the Nile delta and the Caribbean islands, and the battle for a triumphant nationality. Both battles place 'Englishness' in contrast with 'the French', and no matter how intimate and closeted such factors as the supposed English or French 'essence' appear to be, they were almost always thought of as being (as opposed to already) made, and being fought out with the other great competitor. Thackeray's Becky Sharp, for example, is as much an upstart as she is because of her half-French heritage. Earlier, the upright abolitionist posture of Wilberforce and his allies developed partly out of a desire to make life harder for French hegemony in the Antilles.[5]

These considerations, I think, suddenly provide a fascinatingly expanded dimension to *Mansfield Park*, by common acknowledgement the most explicit in its ideological and moral affirmation of all Austen's novels. Williams once again is in general dead right: Austen's novels all express an 'attainable quality of life', in money and property acquired, moral discriminations made, the right choices put in place, the correct 'improvement' implemented, the finely nuanced language affirmed and classified. Yet, Williams continues,

> What [Cobbett] names, riding past on the road, are classes. Jane Austen, from inside the houses, can never see that, for all the intricacy of her social description. All her discrimination is, understandably, internal and exclusive. She is concerned with the conduct of people who, in the complications of improvement, are repeatedly trying to make themselves into a class. But where only one class is seen, no classes are seen.[6]

As a general description of how by the effect of her novels Austen manages to elevate certain 'moral discriminations' into 'an independent value', this is excellent. Where *Mansfield Park* is concerned, however, a good deal more needs to be said and in what follows I should like to be understood as providing greater explicitness and width to Williams's fundamentally correct survey. Perhaps then Austen, and indeed, pre-imperialist novels generally, will appear to be more implicated in the rationale for imperialist expansion than at first sight they have been.

After Lukács and Proust, we have become so accustomed to regarding the novel's plot and structure as constituted mainly by temporality that we have overlooked the fundamental role of space, geography and location. For it is not only Joyce's very young Stephen Dedalus who sees himself in a widening spiral at home, in Ireland, in the world, but every other young protagonist before him as well. Indeed we can say without exaggeration that *Mansfield Park* is very precisely about a whole series of both small and large dislocations in space that must occur before, at the end of the novel, Fanny Price, the niece, becomes the mistress of Mansfield Park. And that place itself is precisely located by Austen at the centre of an arc of interests and concerns, spanning the hemisphere, two major seas, and four continents.

As in all of Austen's novels, the central group that finally emerges with marriage and property 'ordained' is not based principally upon blood. What her novel enacts is the disaffiliation (in the literal sense) of some members of a family, and the affiliation between others and one or two chosen and tested outsiders: in other words, blood relationships are not enough for the responsibilities of continuity, hierarchy, authority. Thus Fanny Price – the poor niece, the orphaned child from the outlying port city of Portsmouth, the neglected, demure and upright wallflower – gradually acquires a status commensurate with, and even superior to, her more fortunate relatives. In this pattern of affiliation and of assumption of authority, Fanny Price is relatively passive. She resists the misdemeanours and the importunings of others, and very occasionally she ventures actions on her own: all in all, though, one has the impression that Austen has designs for her that Fanny herself can scarcely comprehend, just as throughout the novel Fanny is thought of by everyone as 'comfort' and 'acquisition' despite herself. Thus, like Kim O'Hara, Fanny is both device and instrument in a larger pattern, as well as novelistic character.

Fanny, like Kim, requires direction, requires the patronage and outside authority that her own impoverished experience cannot provide. Her conscious connections are to some people and to some places, but as the novel reveals there are *other* connections of which she has faint glimmerings that nevertheless demand her presence and service. What she comes into is a novel that has opened with an intricate set of moves all of which taken together demand sorting-out, adjustment and re-arrangement. Sir Thomas Bertram has been captivated by one Ward sister, the others have not done well, and so 'an absolute breach' opens up; their 'circles were so distinct', the distances between them were so great that they have been out of touch for eleven years (*MP*, p. 42);[7] fallen on hard times, the Prices seek out the Bertrams. Gradually, and even though she is not the eldest, Fanny becomes the new focus of attention as she is sent to Mansfield Park, there to begin her new life. Similarly, the Bertrams have given up London (the result of Lady

Bertram's 'little ill health and a great deal of indolence') and come to reside entirely in the country.

What sustains this life materially is the Bertram estate in Antigua, which is not doing well. Austen takes considerable pains to show us two apparently disparate but actually convergent processes; the growth of Fanny's importance to the Bertrams' economy, including Antigua, and Fanny's own steadfastness in the face of numerous challenges, threats and surprises. In both processes, however, Austen's imagination works with a steel-like rigour through a mode that we might call geographical and spatial clarification. Fanny's ignorance, when as a frightened ten-year-old she arrives at Mansfield, is signified by her inability to 'put the map of Europe together' (*MP*, p. 54), and for much of the first half of the novel the action is concerned with a whole range of things whose common denominator, misused or misunderstood, is space. Not only is Sir Thomas in Antigua to make things better there and at home, but at Mansfield Park Fanny, Edmund, and her Aunt Norris negotiate where she is to live, read and work, where fires are to be lit, the friends and cousins concern themselves with the improvement of the estates, and the importance of chapels (of religious authority) to domesticity is debated and envisioned. When, as a device for stirring things up, the Crawfords (the tinge of France that hangs over their background is significant) suggest a play, Fanny's discomfiture is polarizingly acute. She cannot participate, although with all its confusion of roles and purposes, the play, Kotzebue's *Lovers' Vows*, is prepared for anyway.

We are to surmise, I think, that while Sir Thomas is away tending his colonial garden, a number of inevitable mis-measurements (associated explicitly with feminine 'lawlessness') will occur. Not only are these apparent in innocent strolls through a park, in which people lose and catch sight of each other unexpectedly, but most clearly in the various flirtations and engagements between the young men and women left without true parental authority, Lady Bertram being too indifferent, Mrs Norris unsuitable. There is sparring, there is innuendo, there is a perilous taking on of roles: all of this of course is crystallized in preparations for the play, in which something dangerously close to libertinage is about to be (but never is) enacted. Fanny, whose earlier sense of alienation, distance and fear all derive from her first uprooting, has now assumed a sort of surrogate consciousness of what is right and how far is too much. Yet she has no power to implement her uneasy awareness, and until Sir Thomas suddenly returns from 'abroad' the rudderless drift continues.

When he does appear, preparations for the play are immediately stopped, and in a passage remarkable for its executive dispatch, Austen narrates the reestablishment of Sir Thomas's local rule:

It was a busy morning with him. Conservation with any of them occupied but a small part of it. He had to reinstate himself in all the wonted concerns of his Mansfield life, to see his steward and his bailiff – to examine and compute – and, in the intervals of business, to walk into his stables and his gardens, and nearest plantations; but active and methodical, he had not only done all this before he resumed his seat as master of the house at dinner, he had also set the carpenter to work in pulling down what had been so lately put up in the billiard room, and given the scene painter his dismissal, long enough to justify the pleasing belief of his being then at least as far off as Northampton. The scene painter was gone, having spoilt only the floor of one room, ruined all the coachman's sponges, and made five of the under-servants idle and dissatisfied; and Sir Thomas was in hopes that another day or two would suffice to wipe away every outward memento of what had been, even to the destruction of every unbound copy of 'Lovers' Vows' in the house, for he was burning all that met his eye. (*MP*, p. 206)

The force of this paragraph is unmistakable. This is not only a Crusoe setting things in order: it is also an early Protestant eliminating all traces of frivolous behaviour. There is nothing, however, in *Mansfield Park* that would contradict us were we to assume that Sir Thomas does exactly the same things – on a larger scale – in Antigua. Whatever was wrong there, and the internal evidence garnered by Warren Roberts suggests that economic depression, slavery, and competition with France were at issue[8] – Sir Thomas was able to fix, thereby maintaining his control over his colonial domain. Thus more clearly than anywhere else in her fiction Austen synchronizes domestic with international authority, making it plain that the values associated with such higher things as ordination, law and propriety must be grounded firmly in actual rule over and possession of territory. What she sees more clearly than most of her readers is that to hold and rule Mansfield Park is to hold and rule an imperial estate in association with it. What assures the one, in its domestic tranquillity and attractive harmony, is the prosperity and discipline of the other.

Before both can be fully secured, however, Fanny must become more actively involved. For this, I believe, Austen designed the second part of the book, which contains not only the failure of the Edmund–Mary Crawford romance as well as the disgraceful profligacy of Lydia and Henry Crawford, but Fanny Price's rediscovery and rejection of her Portsmouth home, the injury and incapacitation of Tom (the eldest) Bertram, the launching of William Price's naval career. This entire ensemble of relationships and events is finally capped with Edmund's marriage to Fanny, whose place in Lady Bertram's household is taken by

Susan Price, her sister. I do not think it is an exaggeration to interpret the concluding sections of *Mansfield Park* as the coronation of an arguably *unnatural* (or at the very least, illogical) principle at the heart of a desired English order. The audacity of Austen's vision is disguised a little by her voice, which despite its occasional archness is understated and notably modest. But we should not misconstrue the limited references to the outside world, her lightly stressed allusions to work, process and class, her apparent ability to abstract (in Raymond Williams's phrase) 'an everyday uncompromising morality which is in the end separable from its social basis'. For in fact Austen is far less diffident, far more severe than that.

The clues are to be found in Fanny, or rather in how rigorously we wish to consider Fanny. True, her visit home upsets the aesthetic and emotional balance she had become accustomed to at Mansfield Park, and true, she had begun to take for granted the wonderful luxuries there as something she cannot live without. These things, in other words, are fairly routine and natural consequences of getting used to a new place. But Austen is talking about two other matters we must not mistake. One is Fanny's newly enlarged sense of what it means to be at home; this is not merely a matter of expanded space.

> Fanny was almost stunned. The smallness of the house, and thinness of the walls, brought every thing so close to her, that, added to the fatigue of her journey, and all her recent agitation, she hardly knew how to bear it. *Within* the room all was tranquil enough, for Susan having disappeared with the others, there were soon only her father and herself remaining; and he taking out a newspaper – the customary loan of a neighbour, applied himself to studying it, without seeming to recollect her existence. The solitary candle was held between himself and the paper, without any reference to her possible convenience; but she had nothing to do, and was glad to have the light screened from her aching head, as she sat in bewildered, broken, sorrowful contemplation.
>
> She was at home. But alas! it was not such a home, she had not such a welcome, as – she checked herself; she was unreasonable . . . A day or two might shew the difference. *She* only was to blame. Yet she thought it would not have been so at Mansfield. No, in her uncle's house there would have been a consideration of times and seasons, a regulation of subject, a propriety, an attention towards every body which there was not here. (*MP*, pp. 375–6)

In too small a space you cannot see clearly, you cannot think clearly, you cannot have regulation or attention of the proper sort. The fineness of Austen's detail ('the solitary candle was held between himself and the paper, without any reference to her possible convenience') renders very precisely the dangers of unsociability, of lonely insularity, of diminished awareness that are rectified in larger and better administered spaces.

That such spaces are not available by direct descent, by legal title, by propinquity, contiguity or adjacence (Mansfield Park and Portsmouth are after all separated by many hours' journey) is precisely Austen's point. To earn the right to Mansfield Park you must first leave home as a kind of indentured servant, or to put the case in extreme terms, as a kind of transported commodity; this clearly is the fate of Fanny and William, but it also contains the promise for them of future wealth. I think Austen saw what Fanny does as a domestic or small-scale movement in space that corresponds to the longer, more openly colonial movements of Sir Thomas, her mentor, the man whose estate she inherits. The two movements depend on each other.

The second matter about which Austen speaks, albeit indirectly, is a little more complex, and raises an interesting theoretical issue. To speak about Austen's awareness of empire is obviously to speak about something very different, very much more alluded to almost casually, than Conrad's or Kipling's awareness of empire. Nevertheless, we must concede that Antigua and Sir Thomas's trip there play a definitive role in *Mansfield Park*, a role which, I have been saying, is both incidental, because referred to only in passing, and absolutely important, because although taken for granted it is crucial to the action in many ways. How then are we to assess the few references to Antigua, and as exactly as possible what are we to make of them interpretively?

My contention is that Austen genuinely presages Kipling and Conrad, and that far from being a novelist only dedicated to the portrayal and elucidation of domestic manners, Austen by that very odd combination of casualness and stress reveals herself to be *assuming* (just as Fanny assumes, in both senses of the word) the importance of empire to the situation at home. Let me go further. Since Austen refers to and uses Antigua as she does in *Mansfield Park*, there needs to be a commensurate effort on the part of her readers to understand concretely the historical valences in the reference. To put it differently, we should try to understand *what* she referred to, why she gave it the role she did, and why, in a certain sense, she did not avoid the choice, keeping in mind that she might *not* have made use of Antigua. Let us now proceed to calibrate the signifying power of the references to Antigua in *Mansfield Park*; how do *they* occupy the place they do, what are they doing there?

According to Austen, no matter how isolated and insulated the English *place* is (e.g. Mansfield Park), it requires overseas sustenance. Sir Thomas's property in the Caribbean would have had to be a sugar plantation maintained by slave labour (not abolished until the 1830s): these are not dead historical facts but, as Austen certainly knew, the results of evident historical processes. Before the Anglo-French competition to which I referred earlier, there is for Britain the major distinguishing characteristic between its empire and all earlier ones (the Spanish and Portuguese principally, but also the Roman). That was that earlier empires were bent, as Conrad puts it, on loot, the transport of treasure from the colonies to Europe, with very little attention to development, organization, system; Britain and, to a lesser degree, France were deeply concerned with how to make the empire a long-term profitable and, above all, an on-going concern. In this enterprise the two countries competed, nowhere with more observable results than in the slave colonies of the Caribbean, where the transport of slaves, the functioning of large sugar plantations dedicated exclusively to sugar production, the whole question of sugar markets which raised problems of protectionism, monopolies, and price: all these were more or less constantly, competitively at issue.

Far from being something 'out there', British colonial possessions in the Antilles and Leeward Islands were during the last years of the eighteenth century and the first third of the nineteenth a crucial setting for Anglo-French colonial competition. Not only was the export of revolutionary ideas from France there to be registered, but there was a steady decline in British Caribbean profits: the French sugar plantations were producing more sugar at less cost. By the end of the century, however, the slave rebellions generated in and out of Haiti were incapacitating France and spurring British interests to more intervention, and greater power locally. Yet compared with their prominence for the home market during the eighteenth century, the British Caribbean sugar plantations of the nineteenth century were more vulnerable to such countervailing forces as the discovery of alternative sugar supplies in Brazil and Mauritius, the emergence of a European beet-sugar industry, and the gradual dominance of free trade (as opposed to monopolistic) ideology and practice.

In *Mansfield Park* – and I speak here both of its formal characteristics as well as its contents – a number of all these currents converge. The most important of course is the complete subordination of colony to metropolis. Sir Thomas is absent from Mansfield Park, and is never seen as *present* in Antigua, which requires at most a half dozen references in the novel, all of them granting the island the merest token importance to what takes place in England. There is a passage from John Stuart Mill's *Principles of Political Economy* which catches the spirit of Austen's use of Antigua:

> These are hardly to be looked upon as countries, carrying on an exchange of commodities with other countries, but more properly as outlying agricultural or manufacturing estates belonging to a larger

community. Our West Indian colonies, for example, cannot be regarded as countries with a productive capital of their own . . . [but are, rather,] the place where England finds it convenient to carry on the production of sugar, coffee and a few other tropical commodities. All the capital employed is English capital; almost all the industry is carried on for English uses; there is little production of anything except for staple commodities, and these are sent to England, not to be exchanged for things exported to the colony and consumed by its inhabitants, but to be sold in England for the benefit of the proprietors there. The trade with the West Indies is hardly to be considered an external trade, but more resembles the traffic between town and country.[9]

To some extent Antigua is like London or Portsmouth, a less desirable urban setting than the country estate at Mansfield Park. Unlike them, however, it is a place producing goods, sugar, to be consumed by all people (by the early nineteenth century every Britisher used sugar), although owned and maintained by a small group of aristocrats and gentry. The Bertrams and the other characters in *Mansfield Park* constitute one sub-group within the minority, and for them the island is wealth, which Austen regards as being converted to propriety, order, and at the end of the novel, comfort, an added good. But why 'added'? Because Austen tells us pointedly in the final chapters, she wants to 'restore every body, not greatly in fault themselves, to tolerable comfort, and to have done with all the rest' (*MP*, p. 446).

This can be interpreted to mean, first, that the novel has done enough in the way of destabilizing the lives of 'everybody', and must now set them at rest: actually Austen does say this explicitly as a bit of meta-fictional impatience. Second, it can mean what Austen implicitly suggests, that everybody may now be finally permitted to realize what it means to be properly at home, and at rest, without the need to wander about or to come and go. Certainly this does not include young William, who, we are right to assume, will continue to roam the seas in the British navy on whatever missions, commercial and political, may still be required. Such matters draw from Austen only a last brief gesture (a passing remark about William's 'continuing good conduct and rising fame'). As for those finally resident in Mansfield Park itself, more in the way of domesticated advantages is given to these now fully acclimatized souls, and to none more than to Sir Thomas. He understands for the first time what has been missing in his education of his children, and he understands it in the terms paradoxically provided for him by unnamed outside forces so to speak, the wealth of Antigua and the imported example of Fanny Price. Note here how the curious alternation of outside and inside follows the pattern identified by Mill of the outside *becoming* the inside by use and to use Austen's word, 'disposition':

> Here [in his deficiency of training, of allowing Mrs Norris too great a role, of letting his children dissemble and repress feeling] had been grievous mismanagement; but, bad as it was, he gradually grew to feel that it had not been the most direful mistake in his plan of education. Some thing must have been wanting *within*, or time would have worn away much of its ill effect. He feared that principle, active principle, had been wanting, that they had never been properly taught to govern their inclinations and tempers, by that sense of duty which can alone suffice. They had been instructed theoretically in their religion, but never required to bring it into daily practice; to be distinguished for elegance and accomplishments – the authorized object of their youth – could have had no useful influence that way, no moral effect on the mind. He had meant them to be good, but his cares had been directed to the understanding and manners, not the disposition; and of the necessity of self-denial and humility, he feared they had never heard from any lips that could profit them. (*MP*, p. 448).

What was wanting *within* was in fact supplied by the wealth derived from a West Indian plantation and a poor provincial relative, both brought in to Mansfield Park and set to work. Yet on their own, neither the one nor the other could have sufficed; they require each other and then, more important, they need executive disposition, which in turn helps to reform the rest of the Bertram circle. All of this Austen leaves to her reader to supply in the way of literal explicitation.

And that is what reading her necessarily entails. But all these things having to do with the outside brought in, seem to me unmistakably *there* in the suggestiveness of her allusive and abstract language. A 'principle wanting within' is, I believe, intended to evoke for us memories of Sir Thomas's absences in Antigua, or the sentimental and near-whimsical vagary on the part of the three variously deficient Ward sisters by which a niece is displaced from one household to another. But that the Bertrams did become better if not altogether good, that some sense of duty was imparted to them, that they learned to govern their inclinations and tempers, and brought religion into daily practice, directed disposition: all of this did occur because outside (or rather outlying) factors were lodged properly inward, became native to Mansfield Park, Fanny, the niece, its final spiritual mistress, Edmund, the second son, its master.

An additional benefit is that Mrs Norris is dislodged from the place: this is described as 'the great supplementary comfort of Sir Thomas's life' (*MP*, p. 450). For once the principles have been interiorized, the comforts follow: Fanny is settled for the time being at Thornton Lacey 'with every attention to her comfort'; her home later becomes 'the home of affection and comfort'; Susan is brought in 'first as a comfort to Fanny, then as an auxiliary, and at last as her substitute' (*MP*, p. 456), when the new import takes Fanny's place by Lady Bertram's side. Clearly the pattern established at the outset of the novel continues, only now it has what the novel has intended to give it all along, an internalized and retrospectively guaranteed rationale. This is the rationale that Raymond Williams describes as 'an everyday, uncompromising morality which is in the end separable from its social basis and which, in other hands, can be turned against it.'

I have tried to show that the morality in fact is not separable from its social basis, because right up to the last sentence of the novel Austen is always affirming and repeating a geographical process involving trade, production, and consumption that pre-dates, underlies, and guarantees the morality. Most critics have tended to forget or overlook that process, which has seemed less important to the morality than in devising her novel Austen herself seemed to think it was. But interpreting Jane Austen depends on *who* does the interpreting, *when* it is done, and no less important, from *where* it is done. If with feminists, with great Marxist critics sensitive to history and class like Williams, with historical and stylistic critics, we have been sensitized to the issues their interests raise, we should now proceed to regard geography – which is after all of significance to *Mansfield Park* – as not a neutral fact (any more than class and gender are neutral facts) but as a politically charged one too, a fact beseeching the considerable attention and elucidation its massive proportions require. The question is thus not only how to understand and with what to connect Austen's morality and its social basis, but *what* to read of it.

Take the casual references to Antigua, the ease with which Sir Thomas's needs in England are met by a Caribbean sojourn, the uninflected, unreflective citations of Antigua (or the Mediterranean, or India, which is where Lady Bertram in a fit of distracted impatience requires that William should go 'that I may have a shawl. I think I will have two shawls' – *MP*, p. 308). They stand for something significant 'out there' that frames the genuinely important action *here*, but not for something too significant. Yet these signs of 'abroad' include, even as they repress, a complex and rich history, which has since achieved a status that the Bertrams, the Prices and Austen herself would not, could not recognize. To call this status 'the Third World' begins to deal with its realities, but it by no means exhausts its history with regard to politics or cultural activities.

There are first some prefigurations of a later English history as registered in fiction to be taken stock of. The Bertram's usable colony in *Mansfield Park* can be read proleptically as resulting in Charles Gould's San

Tome mine in *Nostromo*, or as the Wilcoxes' Anglo-Imperial Rubber Company in Forster's *Howards End*, or indeed as any of these distant but convenient treasure spots in *Great Expectations*, or in Jean Rhys's *Wide Sargasso Sea*, or *Heart of Darkness*, resources to be visited, talked about, described or appreciated – for domestic reasons, for local metropolitan benefits. Thus Sir Thomas's Antigua already acquires a slightly greater density than the discrete, almost reticent appearances it makes in the pages of *Mansfield Park*. And already our reading of the novel begins to distend and open up at those points where ironically Austen was most economical and her critics most (dare one say it?) negligent. Her 'Antigua' is therefore not just a slight but definite way of marking the outer limits of what Williams calls domestic improvements, or as a quick allusion to the mercantile venturesomeness of acquiring overseas dominions as a source for local fortunes, or one reference among many attesting to a historical sensibility suffused not just with manners and curtsies but with contests of ideas, struggles with Napoleonic France, awareness of seismic economic and social change. Not just those things, but also strikingly early anticipation of the official age of Empire, which Kipling, Conrad and all the others will realize a full three-quarters of a century later.

Second, we must see 'Antigua' as a reference for Austen held in its precise place in her moral geography, and in her prose, by a series of historical changes that her novel rides like a vessel sitting on a mighty sea. The Bertrams could not have been possible without the slave trade, sugar, and the colonial planter class; as a social type Sir Thomas would have been familiar to eighteenth- and early nineteenth-century readers who knew the powerful influence of the class in domestic British politics, in plays (like Cumberland's *The West Indian*), and in numerous other public ways. As the old system of protected monopoly gradually disappeared, and as a new class of settler-planter displaced the old absentee system, the West Indian interest lost its dominance: cotton manufacture, open trade, abolition reduced the power and prestige of people like the Bertrams whose frequency of sojourn in the Caribbean decreased appreciably.

Thus in *Mansfield Park* Sir Thomas's infrequent trips to Antigua as an absentee plantation-owner *precisely* reflect the diminishment of his class's power, a reduction immediately, directly conveyed in the title of Lowell Ragatz's classic *The Fall of the Planter Class in the British Caribbean, 1763–1833* (published in 1928). But we must go further and ask whether what is hidden or allusive in Austen – the reasons for Sir Thomas's rare voyages – are made sufficiently explicit in Ragatz? Does the aesthetic silence or discretion of a great novel in 1814 receive adequate explication in a major work of historical research written a full century later? If so, can we assume that the process of interpretation is thereby fulfilled, or must we go on to reason that it will continue as newer material comes to light?

111

Consider that for all his learning Ragatz still finds it in himself to speak of 'the Negro race' as having the following characteristics: 'he stole, he lied, he was simple, suspicious, inefficient, irresponsible, lazy, superstitious, and loose in his sexual relations.'[10] Such 'history' as this therefore gave way (as Austen gave way to Ragatz) to the revisionary work of Caribbean historians like Eric Williams and C. L. R. James, works in which slavery and empire are seen directly to have fostered the rise and consolidation of *capitalism* well beyond the old plantation monopolies, as well as a powerful ideological system whose original connection to actual economic interests may have passed, but whose effects continued for decades.

> The political and moral ideas of the age are to be examined in the very closest relation to the economic development . . .
> An outworn interest, whose bankruptcy smells to heaven in historical perspective, can exercise an obstructionist and disruptive effect which can only be explained by the powerful services it had preciously rendered and the entrenchment previously gained . . .
> The ideas built on these interests continue long after the interests have been destroyed and work their old mischief, which is all the more mischievous because the interests to which they correspond no longer exist.[11]

Thus Eric Williams in *Capitalism and Slavery* (1961). The question of interpretation, and indeed of writing itself, is tied to the question of interests, which we have seen are at work in aesthetic as well as historical work, then and now. We cannot easily say that since *Mansfield Park* is a novel, its affiliations with a particularly sordid history are irrelevant or transcended, not only because it is irresponsible to say that, but because we know too much to say so without bad faith. Having read *Mansfield Park* as part of the structure of an expanding imperialist venture, it would be difficult simply to restore it to the canon of 'great literary masterpieces' – to which it most certainly belongs – and leave it at that. Rather, I think, the novel points the way to Conrad, and to theorists of empire like Froude and Seeley, and in the process opens up a broad expanse of domestic imperialist culture without which the subsequent acquisition of territory would not have been possible.

Notes

1. V.G. KIERNAN, *Marxism and Imperialism* (London: Edward Arnold, 1974), p. 100.
2. J.S. MILL, *Disquisitions and Discussions*, vol. III (London: Longmans Green, Reader & Dyer, 1875), pp. 167–8.

3. RAYMOND WILLIAMS, *The Country and the City* (London: Chatto and Windus, 1973), p. 281.

4. J.A. HOBSON, *Imperialism* (1902; repr. Ann Arbor, U Michigan Press, 1972), p. 6.

5. This is most memorably discussed in C.L.R. JAMES, *The Black Jacobins: Toussaint L'Ouverture and the San Domingo Revolution* (1938; repr. New York, 1963; London: Allison and Busby, 1980), especially ch. II, 'The Owners'.

6. WILLIAMS, *The Country and the City*, p. 117.

7. JANE AUSTEN, *Mansfield Park*, ed. Tony Tanner (1814; repr. Harmondsworth: Penguin, 1966). All references to this edition of the novel are indicated parenthetically after the citation as *MP*. The best account of the novel is in Tony Tanner's *Jane Austen* (Cambridge, Mass. and London: Macmillan, 1986).

8. WARREN ROBERTS, *Jane Austen and the French Revolution* (London: Macmillan, 1979), pp. 97–8. See also AVROM FLEISHMAN, *A Reading of Mansfield Park: An Essay in Critical Synthesis* (Minneapolis: U Minnesota Press, 1967), pp. 36–9, and *passim*.

9. J.S. MILL, *Principles of Political Economy*, vol. III, ed. J.M. Robson (Toronto: U Toronto Press, 1965), p. 693. The passage is quoted in SIDNEY W. MINTZ, *Sweetness and Power: The Place of Sugar in Modern History* (New York: Sifton, 1985), p. 42.

10. LOWELL JOSEPH RAGATZ, *The Fall of the Planter Class in the British Caribbean, 1763–1833: A Study in Social and Economic History* (1928; repr. New York: Octagon, 1963), p. 27.

11. ERIC WILLIAMS, *Capitalism and Slavery* (New York, 1961), p. 211.

5 The Moment of Truth: the Geography of Modern Tragedy* (1986)

FRANCO MORETTI

Franco Moretti (b. 1950) has been Professor of Comparative Literature at the University of Verona, and is now Professor of English Literature at Columbia University. He has written *Signs Taken For Wonders* (1983) and *The Way of the World: the Bildungsroman in European Culture* (1987).

Primarily Della Volpean and formalist–structuralist in its earlier stages, Moretti's work has developed towards a kind of cultural analysis whose inspirational precedents are the *Annales* school's 'total history' and the genre criticism of Georg Lukács. The summarizing theme of his writing is bourgeois civilization and its (literary) symbolic forms.

Here he explores the geographical differentiation of West European culture into two great zones, one (Anglo-French) dominated by the novel, the other (German–Scandinavian) by tragedy. The novelistic and the tragic are the contrasting rhetorics of largely incompatible world views, he argues: the former deals in the national and the everyday, gravitating towards 'compromise', while the latter, implacably estranged from 'life' in this sense, presses always towards an abstract 'moment of truth'. The spacing of these antagonistic sensibilities is itself historical, conditioned by the divergent political courses of Europe's nation-states. The essay concludes, characteristically, with a meditation on the tragicism of New Left culture and politics in the 1970s.

Literary genres have temporal boundaries, and the current definition of *modern* tragedy is an evident if vague acknowledgement of this fact. But they have spatial boundaries too, which may be at times even more

---

* Reprinted from Franco Moretti, *Signs Taken for Wonders*, 2nd expanded edn (London: Verso, 1988), pp. 249–61.

revealing – *historically* revealing – than temporal ones.[1] Such is the case with modern tragedy, whose own geography has the striking peculiarity of being the reverse of the novel's. Henrik Ibsen, who is usually considered (rightly so, in my opinion) the key figure of modern tragedy, belonged to a Scandinavian culture which has been left virtually untouched by the novel. The same culture also produced Kierkegaard, whose philosophy was to offer a variety of themes and accents to tragic world-views, and Strindberg, whom contemporaries perceived as Ibsen's alter ego. Conversely, the areas of Europe where Ibsen met with the fiercest resistance – 'poison', 'loathsome sore unbandaged', 'open drain', 'lazar house', as contemporary newspapers put it – were France and England; strongholds of the novel, but the most barren contributors to the new drama. Still, the most revealing example of cultural geography in the modern period is Germany. Modern tragedy, and modern tragic theory, are simply unthinkable without it, to the extent that even Kierkegaard, Ibsen and Strindberg achieved world-historical significance only through German mediation. In 1915 – drafting his rabid nationalistic pamphlet, *The Blight of Ibsenism* – James Leatham was obviously wrong in holding Ibsen and Strindberg (and Nietzsche) responsible for 'German methods in the battlefields of Belgium'. But that 'these three philosophers have nowhere a larger following than in Germany' was a well-known fact – and a fact, as we shall see, with its own disturbing implications.

Germany: battlefield of modernity

Germany's centrality for modern tragedy is also, symmetrically, modern tragedy's centrality in the developments of German culture. Initially, as it happens, this relationship was an antagonistic one, and German philosophy was the first and most thorough in theorizing, two centuries ago, the *anti*-tragic orientation of the modern aesthetic sphere. Kant's third *Kritik*, designed as the 'middle term' between the first two, was an explicit attempt to heal through the aesthetic sphere the potentially tragic laceration between the domain of knowledge and the domain of ethics; and the same can be said for Schiller's *Letters on the Aesthetic Education of Man*, where art is asked to restore a disrupted harmony, 'tempering' the painful one-sidedness of human faculties and social institutions. Goethe also criticized tragedies, maintaining that they leave our minds 'perturbed' and 'unsettled'. In *Faust* he circumscribed tragedy to individual existence, thereby deleting it from the progress of universal history. This rhetorical choice, or 'plot', was of course Hegel's as well, in whose thought, as Hayden White has pointed out, a sequence of

115

tragedies ultimately reveals a cosmic comedy. This anti-tragic thrust inspired not only Hegel's conception of historical movement, but the very inner form of his philosophy. In his dialectical logic, where the meaninglessness of whatever is 'one-sided' yields to the symmetrically opposite claim that 'only the Whole is the True', the tragic form is deprived of any cognitive value whatsoever.

In the first fifty years of Modernity, then, a great battle against tragic culture was fought – and won – on German soil. But in the long run, the weight of tragedy proved too strong: Lessing, Schiller, Hölderlin, Kleist, Büchner, Hebbel, Wagner, Hauptmann, Wedekind, Hofmannsthal, Schopenhauer, Kierkegaard, Nietzsche, Schmitt, Benjamin, Heidegger; even, in some ways, Marx, Weber and Freud . . .

Germany, then. But why Germany? The most common answer points to the destructive heritage of the religious wars of early modern Europe – both international and civil wars. Why Germany? Because Germany, in Thomas Mann's words, has always been 'the battlefield of Europe': the physical battlefield, and even more so the spiritual one, where conflicts have 'little, if any, national content: they are almost entirely European in character'. In this light Germany is a sort of Magic Stage, where the symbolic antagonisms of European culture achieve a metaphysical intractability, and clash irreconcilably. It is the centre and catalyst of the integrated historical system we call Europe; but it is so in a paradoxical way, as its 'systemic' role – Mann again, in his *Reflections of an Unpolitical Man* – is one and the same with its lack of 'national bonds' and 'spiritual unity'. Unlike France or England, Germany's international function is not the consequence of its national power, but is inversely proportional to it: it is the product of national *weakness*: in Freiligrath's mid-nineteenth-century metaphor for the absence of spiritual unity, '*Deutschland ist Hamlet*'.

I have just mentioned the notion of Europe as an 'integrated system', and we tend to take the European setting for granted whenever we discuss transnational genres or movements like Modernism, the novel, or tragedy. We should be aware, however, that in each case 'Europe' is a different system, with its distinctive socio-geographic configuration. The Europe of the novel is the well-differentiated system of self-enclosed nation-states, with a typically national interplay of city and countryside, and a solid bourgeois core in England and France. The Europe of modern tragedy, for its part, is the Europe of war: a far more abstract and homogeneous oppositional field, of which Germany is not so much the 'core' as the no-man's-land where universal dramas can be acted out. As for the Europe of Modernism, it is transnational in a different way still, as a constellation of metropolises: Paris, Petrograd, Berlin, London, Zürich, Milan, Vienna, Prague and even Dublin – each became, under Modernism, an archetype. In contrast to the two previous 'Europes', this is a punctuated, and hence far more open, pattern ready to incorporate New York, Los Angeles, Buenos Aires, Bombay. For this very reason Modernism has become, in the course of our century, the first real *world*-system of literature. (So much so that for the first time in modern history Europe has been pushed towards the periphery.)

This spatial partition of the three different Europes is easily discernible within the social institution most closely interwoven with space and boundaries: language. Here, we move from the rich and varied national languages of the novel, loaded with local peculiarities and idioms, to the abstract, barren, always-translatable speech of modern tragedy; and finally to the inter-cultural mélange of Modernism, foreshadowed perhaps by the aberrant yet all-inclusive English of *Finnegans Wake*. All these configurations suggest that the 'theory of temporal spaces' envisaged by Fernand Braudel for economic history may be just as necessary and promising for literary history: we should try to think of literary epochs not only as segments in time, but as figures in space, too. A geography of symbolic forms: isn't that a quite stimulating prospect?

But back to tragedy. That question – why Germany? – has a second possible answer, which centres on Germany's relationship with the politics of Modernity. In all major capitalist countries, Modernity was no doubt a destabilizing, unpredictable, painful process, but it never called for radical political alternatives. As a rule, fundamental political choices pre-dated capitalist modernity, and the ensuing regimes enjoyed a basic stability. The political trajectories of Britain and the United States were set in the 17th and 18th centuries respectively. As for France, its many political crises (1789, 1830, 1848) saw the clash of Modernity and the *ancien régime*: but the conflict was not the product of Modernity, nor did it point beyond it. (The Commune is the manifest exception: but its historical relevance may have been exaggerated by the [German] political theorist who saw in it a universal paradigm.) In Britain, France and the United States, then, the bourgeois-democratic state remained fundamentally unchallenged: but not so in Germany. Here, not only did the creation of the national state occur comparatively very late, but in just fifteen years – from 1918 to 1933 – the political order was shaken *twice*, and in wholly *opposite* directions. No other industrial power has ever been on the brink of a socialist revolution, or under fascist rule: Germany has experienced *both*, as if to reveal a hidden and fatal bifurcation of Modernity – a truly tragic choice lying beneath that ordinary administration to which other Western countries had grown used.

Earlier, I mentioned Mann's thesis, according to which the centrality of tragedy in German culture is the consequence of national weakness. Now we can be more specific, and claim that the symbolic power of tragic form is inversely proportional to the real power of the state. When the state is stable and strong, a national culture does not have to bother about it, and it evolves in a fundamentally unpolitical fashion: whence the anti-heroic conventions of the novelistic world-view, one of the greatest stabilizing factors of Modernity. But where the state is unsettled and weak, culture tends fatally to 'fill the void': dismissing the novelistic everyday as a realm of vain appearances. This world-view finds its centre not just in politics, but in a tragic version of political struggle. In the notion of conflict as something which must inevitably lead to a crisis, and of *crisis as the moment of truth*.

Crisis as the moment of *truth*: only when engaged in a conflict to the death do social actors manifest their real nature. Hence the epistemological superiority of exceptional over ordinary circumstances: 'Exception', writes Carl Schmitt in 1922, 'is more interesting than the normal case. The latter proves nothing, the former everything . . . In the state of exception, the strength of real life breaks the hardened crust of mechanical repetition.' Crisis as *the moment* of truth: the abolition of the ordinary rhythm of everyday life implies that metaphysical contraction of time – 'time deprived of temporality' – envisaged by Lukács in *Soul and Form*. 'This moment,' Lukács goes on, 'is a beginning and an end, and from it no consequence concerning existence can descend.'

Tragedy versus the novel

Before discussing the connection between the notion of 'the moment of truth' and twentieth-century politics, however, we must examine more closely some formal features of modern tragedy. In its progress towards what it calls truth, this genre has a new antagonist, unknown to Ancient and Renaissance tragedy alike. It is neither blindness, nor passion, nor Fate, nor a conflicting value. It is, quite simply, *life*. 'Speaking in a strictly human sense', writes Kierkegaard in the fifth issue of *The Moment* in July 1855, 'God is man's fiercest enemy, an enemy to death: according to his wish you must die, destroy yourself, as he hates precisely what is by nature your life, and the joy of your life.' It is the same notion ('man's mortal enemy: but an enemy out of love') which inspires Ibsen's archetypal hero, Brand: 'On the brink of the abyss dance the mindless souls, and not one in a thousand can see what a heap of guilt arises out of this small word: to live.'

If we move to the opposite side of the tragic standpoint, the value judgements obviously change, but the paradigm remains the same. Just as life appeared to be the gross and dull enemy of truth, truth is now perceived as the uselessly cruel destroyer of life. 'Brand dies a saint,' writes Shaw in his *Quintessence of Ibsenism*, 'having caused more intense suffering by his saintliness than the most talented sinner could possibly have done with twice the opportunities.' *The Wild Duck,* the masterpiece in which Ibsen turned his value system upside down, makes the very same point. Here, the antagonist of Gregers Werle, and of his ruthless attempt to force others to stare truth in the face (a behaviour uncannily foreshadowed by Kierkegaard in *The Moment* of 30 August 1855, where he claims that your best friend is the one who would promptly inform you of your spouse's adultery), is Relling, a doctor, a man whose very vocation consists in keeping others *alive* at all costs. It is a point further developed by Thomas Mann, who was a great admirer of *The Wild Duck*: 'Nietzsche and Ibsen, the former in his philosophy, the latter in his plays, have severely questioned *the value of truth for life.'* 'For the radical thinker,' he adds in the same chapter of his *Reflections of an Unpolitical Man,* 'Irony and Radicalism', 'life is a worthless argument. But the ironic attitude would rather ask: "Is *truth* a worthwhile argument, when life is at stake?"'

This opposition of truth and life is a new one: in the long and varied history of tragedy, 'life' had never figured as a power in itself. If it did now, capturing the attention of tragic and anti-tragic thinkers alike, the reason must be sought not so much within tragedy itself, as in its rival literary genre – the novel. This life which can hold truth in check is modern everyday life, saturated with those values of ordinary administration which the novel was quick to perceive, reinterpret and popularize. The sudden paradigmatic elevation of 'life' does therefore bear witness to the centrality of the novel in modern European mentality, while simultaneously throwing light on a kind of relationship between literary forms which has too often been neglected by literary historians. When thinking of 'literary systems', we commonly use the implicit model of the division of labour: each genre accomplishes its own specific task, and they all add up to form the global system of any given period. Yet the *conflict* of genres is in fact just as relevant as their cooperation. The antagonism of truth and life, for instance, is none other than the tragic rendering of the generic struggle between tragedy itself and the novel; while the geographical symmetry described earlier testifies that the 'victory' of one genre may easily imply the total annihilation of its antagonist.

A Darwinian history of literature, where forms fight one another, are selected by their context, evolve and disappear like natural species . . . Here is a fascinating prospect for the moment when literary criticism forsakes its present metaphysical nullity and reverts to some form of materialism.[2] For the time being, let me just add that, of all the difficulties of modern tragedy (and there are many – doesn't the theory of modern tragedy keep reminding us of the near-impossibility of such a genre?) the greatest is precisely its post-novelistic condition. Chekhov, a great playwright belonging to a great novelistic tradition, is the clearest example of such difficulty. In his world, it is not truth but life which leads the dance – a devitalized yet compulsive novelistic life with all its habits, compromises, imprecisions, elusions. In play after play, as the characters approach a 'moment of truth' about themselves, they immediately recoil terrified into the anaesthetized rhythm of the everyday. It is as if the weight of the Russian narrative tradition had made it impossible for Chekhov to conceive of tragedy as a distinct form. With a brilliant ju-jitsu move – the impossibility of modern tragedy is the greatest modern tragedy – he transformed his problem into a viable solution.

Truth versus life, then, and life as the antagonistic 'representative' of the novel within tragic form: let us explore these antinomies in more detail. To begin with a semantic issue: in modern tragedy the opposite of truth is neither a lie nor a secret (think of *Othello*, *King Lear*, or *Phèdre*). No, the opposite of truth is 'half-truth': the form truth takes when it accepts a *compromise with life*. Compromise – the novel's great problematical theme throughout the nineteenth century: yet 'Satan is the soul of compromise', decrees the implacable Brand. The greatest danger for tragic truth is not its violent denial or repression (which in fact, if paradoxically, establishes it), but its dilution in the ordinary course of life. Therefore – Brand again – we need 'a week of seven Sundays', so as to abolish 'the everyday and its mediocrity'. Nor is Brand alone in his attack on compromise. Apart from Nietzsche's repudiation of Apollonian 'measure', which seems to be a variation on the same theme, Kierkegaard exposed the Danish church precisely for its doctrine and practice of compromise. Moreover, the critic who did most to establish Ibsen's international reputation – Georg Brandes – made his debut on the intellectual scene by criticizing Rasmus Nielsen, well known in nineteenth-century Scandinavia for his philosophy of compromise.

A second intractable enemy of modern tragedy is money. Money, of course, is a primary embodiment of compromise and ambiguity: it produces illnesses and the drugs to heal them, it moves from slums to artworks, it is the result of exploitation and can be used for charity. There is definitely no *purity* in money ('Tis yours, 'tis mine, 'tis everybody's slave'), and this is precisely what made it the flexible and irreplaceable medium of the Great Socialization of the nineteenth century. Throughout that age, the formation of the modern individual was more and more entrusted to the new social nexus: to the domain of 'having' as opposed to 'being', to borrow Trilling's terms in *Sincerity and Authenticity*. The novel, for its part, not only acknowledged this development, but in the short span of one generation, from Goethe to Balzac, transformed it into the typical modern myth. But with Ibsen the paradigm is reversed: through money people do not so much shape as deform themselves, and one's truth can be grasped only in the (possibly sudden) *lack* of money.

Whence comes the crowd of creditors and blackmailers so typical of modern tragedy: uninteresting as individuals, but crucial as dramatic functions (or metaphors, as in Strindberg's *Creditors*). These characters take money away from the world, and in so doing force others to their painful but usually regenerative truth.

A further obstacle to tragic truth is to be found in the social convention of *conversation*. Though both are linguistic exchanges, conversation and tragic dialogue incline in opposite directions. As Peter Szondi observed in his *Theory of Modern Drama*, where 'conversation-drama' was strongest (in the novelistic homelands of France and England), the development of tragic language proved impossible – whereas in Germany ('as there was no German society, and no German style of conversation') it could achieve the superb fullness of, say, Friedrich Hebbel. And why this hostility of tragedy and conversation? Because – Szondi again – 'conversation is never binding, never irrevocable': rather than being 'the embodiment of action', as is the case with the tragic language, it suspends action (symptomatically, a conversation can 'go on forever'). Conversation creates an easy and indecisive no-man's-land between subject and object, protecting both from too-deep probings with the conventions of good manners, and giving voice to the slow worldly process by which characters shape themselves in coming to terms with their society. For all these reasons, conversation became the chosen linguistic medium of the novel, and once again Chekhov used the very strength of this novelistic convention to achieve the opposite effect: in his plays, the only way to develop a tragic language lies in not developing it at all, exaggerating the maddening empty drip of aimless talk. In the final scene of *A Doll's House*, though, the two languages – Helmer's socially impeccable commonplaces, and Nora's abrupt, impolite clarity – literally cannot understand each other any longer: appropriately enough, the last 'noise' of the play is the non-linguistic one of a door being shut.

The final opposition between modern tragedy and the novel concerns the kind of *event* most typical of these two genres. As a rule, the novelistic event takes the form of an opportunity: like conversation in the domain of language (and, after all, conversations accompany most novelistic events, or constitute them), an opportunity is a half-subjective, half-objective occurrence, open to a wide variety of different developments. Moreover, a novelistic event is never meaningful in itself, but only within the unbroken diachrony of a longer plot: which is to say that in order to achieve meaning this event requires the fundamentally unchallenged stability of everyday life and ordinary administration. By contrast, the very fissures and chasms which dismantle such stability constitute the most typical instances of the tragic event, whose meaning lies in being a unique turning-point, a sudden illumination after which one's previous existence – one's novelistic existence – appears irredeemably false. It is Kierkegaard's 'moment': the moment of truth, and also truth *as* the moment – something which is lost in the course of ordinary circumstances, and recovered only in discontinuity and crisis.

Tragedy and revolutionary politics

The interdependence of truth and crisis in tragedy anticipates the classical rhetoric of *revolutionary* politics. One of the clearest illustrations of this connection is a text written in the first quarter of our century – nowadays nearly forgotten but then possibly the best-known, and certainly the most legendary, of revolutionary manifestos – Georges Sorel's *Réflexions sur la violence*. Its *leitmotiv* is basically as follows: as a consequence of the 'social *compromises*' dominant everywhere, the West has lived through an age of 'universal cowardice' whose 'peace' and 'stability' have also 'obfuscated the *true* nature of social classes'. But this age is coming to an end, and the *coup de grâce* will come from the General Strike, which, in generating a 'social fissure', a 'crisis', a 'break-up', will force each class to *'be itself'*. The superior 'morality' of the General Strike lies in its forcing social actors to their ultimate forgotten 'truth'. It is never conceived by Sorel as a process (as in Rosa Luxemburg's roughly contemporary writings), but as a single, 'instantaneous' event. As an Apocalypse: the Moment of Truth.

Sorel exemplifies aspects of the continuity between tragic thought and revolutionary politics because he was the most mythical of revolutionary thinkers – the author of the 'book of the age', as Thomas Mann put it in *Doktor Faustus*. But there is a second reason for my choice: Sorel was the *most ambiguous* of revolutionary thinkers – the archetypal ultra-leftist yet the inspirer of reactionary and fascist beliefs. And this was so because that tragic image of revolution as the Moment of Truth – with the inevitable corollary that social truth can only emerge in the crisis of a civil war – was, is and will be shared by large sectors of both Right and Left.

We find this image in the young Lukács – not only in *Soul and Form*, but also in *History and Class Consciousness*, where the economic crisis acts precisely as capitalism's moment of truth: it suddenly unveils the ordinary fetishized 'real structure of society'; it transforms the key concept of totality into something 'which can be grasped within the very domain of praxis'; it operates a de-reification of everyday life, and sets in motion capitalism's 'oedipal progress towards an ineluctable fate.' In the very same years, and in an otherwise wholly different theoretical framework, Carl Schmitt's *Political Theology* ascribes to the notion of crisis just as marked an epistemological prominence. In bringing to light 'the actual possibility of physical killing', Schmitt's 'critical instance' unveils the ultimate horizon – war – of the conceptual pair of Friend and Enemy, which in turn constitutes for him the foundation of all political thought. 'War is thus neither the aim nor the content of politics, but its *premise*, ever present as a real possibility . . . just as in many other cases, exception has here a decisive relevance, such as to unveil the essence of things.'

A few years later Schmitt became the conceptual authority on the connection of politics and tragedy in Walter Benjamin's *The Origin of German Tragic Drama*, the most influential discussion of tragedy ever produced by a left-wing intellectual. And the complicity of the two cultures, under the sign of tragedy, has continued. It has in fact recently become even stronger, considering the extent to which Nietzsche and Heidegger dominate the cultural horizon of the Left intelligentsia. (And yes, Nietzsche and Heidegger cannot be reduced to what European reaction found in them half a century ago: but to 'forget' all that, to pretend that it was a misreading, a misunderstanding! What an exercise in historical blindness!)

Am I trying to imply that Left and Right share the same culture, the same values? Not at all. But I certainly believe that it is virtually impossible to extricate the Left from the Right *whenever the Left adopts a 'tragic' world-view*. In an ironic reversal, the Moment of Truth turns out to be an ambiguous – perhaps the most ambiguous – of political mythologies. Which is, after all, the way it should be, since the vast difference between Left and Right is, first and foremost, a product of temporality: of the weight and memories of the past, the open-ended conflicts of the present, the projects and hopes of the future. Yet when a culture concentrates on the superstitious uniqueness of the moment of crisis (remember Lukács: 'This moment is a beginning and an end, and from it no consequence concerning existence can descend'), temporality will be contracted and abolished: past, present and future will all vanish, and with them all meaningful political determinations.

Does this then mean that the Left must dismiss from its horizon the very notion of a moment of crisis – of open violence, revolution, war? Once again, this is not the point – leaving aside the fact that such events have occurred, occur nowadays, and will occur in the future whether people want them to or not. What I want to stress is that a revolution should be seen neither as a value in itself, nor as a mechanism to generate values: but fundamentally as the possible *consequence* of a given set of values in given circumstances. What I have in mind is a culture of the Left which would consider the moment of crisis neither as the *only* moment of truth, nor as the moment of the *only* truth. For what personal experiences are worth, I can say that this supposed uniqueness, in its superstitious intractability, has left a deep scar on my generation, in my country: it has blinded us to the reality of much of the world around us, because it suggested that it was a 'false' world, an untrue one. In order to escape its misleading appearances, we basically had to make our way, no matter how, towards the moment of crisis, and *then* Social Truth would finally emerge in all its unequivocal clarity: a belief taken to its logical, and practical conclusions, by the most equivocal of contemporary political phenomena – left-wing terrorism. It is of this unhealthy complicity of melodrama and emptiness that the Left must rid itself: the exposure of the relentless yet merely formal desire for Truth being, incidentally, the greatest self-critical achievement – Hamlet, Posa, Herod, Werle – of modern tragedy itself.

No tragic yearning for catastrophe as the well-spring of truth, then: no metaphysical contempt for 'consequences', no Baroque delight in 'exception'. And that this need not lead to unending humiliations and compromises, is shown by an old speech by Max Weber, from which there is probably still a lot to learn: 'From a human point of view [those who feel unconcerned as to the consequences of their actions and are simply inebriated by their romantic sensations] interest me very little, and don't move me at all. What is deeply striking and moving, on the other hand, is the view of a *mature* man – it doesn't matter whether young or old in years – who, feeling truly and wholly his own responsibility for consequences, and acting according to the ethic of responsibility, still, all of a sudden, does say: "I cannot do otherwise: I shall not retreat from here". Here is a truly human and moving behaviour, and such a situation must be possible at any moment for all of us who have not yet lost our inner life.'

Notes

1. A first version of this article was given as a talk at the Literature Program of Duke University in the spring of 1986. My thanks to Jane Tompkins, Fredric Jameson, James Rolleston and all other teachers and students who helped me to improve it by their discussion.

2. [See now Moretti's 'On Literary Evolution', *Signs Taken For Wonders*, 2nd, expanded edn (London: Verso, 1988), pp. 262–78. – *Ed.*]

6 The Bloomsbury Fraction*
(1978)

RAYMOND WILLIAMS

Raymond Williams (1921–88) was, at the time of his retirement, Professor of Drama at the University of Cambridge. His many works of history, theory, criticism and fiction constitute the founding corpus of a distinctive 'cultural materialism'.

The present chapter illustrates one of the main concerns of Williams's later work: the analysis of *intellectual formations*, the socially and ideologically distinct collectivities whose formulating and directing role has been so conspicuous a feature of modern culture. His concrete case – through which he extends the historical characterology of literary liberalism first broached in *Culture and Society* (1958) – is the legendary Bloomsbury Group. Collating different kinds of evidence and resolving their ostensible discrepancies, Williams explains the juncture of social conscience and individual cultivation that defined Bloomsbury as a reforming 'fraction' of the class to which it wholly belonged.

There are serious problems of method in the analysis of cultural groups. When we are analysing large social groups we have some obvious and useful methods at our disposal. The large numbers allow significant statistical analysis. There are usually organized institutions and relatively codified beliefs. There are still many problems in analysis, but we can at least begin with these reasonably hard facts.

In the case of a cultural group, the number of people involved is usually much too small for statistical analysis. There may or may not be organized institutions, through which the group works or develops, but even the most organized institutions are different in scale and kind from those of large groups. The principles which unite the group may or may

* Reprinted from Raymond Williams, *Problems in Materialism and Culture* (London: Verso, 1980), pp. 148–69.

not be codified. Where they are codified, one kind of analysis is immediately relevant. But there are many important cultural groups which have in common a body of practice or a distinguishable ethos, rather than the principles or stated aims of a manifesto. What the group itself has not formulated may indeed be reduced to a set of formulations, but some effects of reduction – simplification, even impoverishment – are then highly probable.

The social and cultural significance of all such groups, from the most to the least organized, can hardly be doubted. No history of modern culture could be written without attention to them. Yet both history and sociology are uneasy with them. We find histories of particular groups, but little comparative or analytic history. In the sociology of culture, we find the effect of general sociology in a tendency to concentrate on groups of a more familiar kind, with relatively organized institutions: churches for the sociology of religion, an educational system for the sociology of education. In other areas of culture – writing, painting, music, theatre, and for that matter philosophy and social thought – there is usually either specialization or neglect. The group, the movement, the circle, the tendency seem too marginal or too small or too ephemeral, to require historical and social analysis. Yet their importance, as a general social and cultural fact, especially in the last two centuries, is great: in what they achieved, and in what their modes of achievement can tell us about the larger societies to which they stand in such uncertain relations.

These are general considerations but they happen to be particularly important in the case of the Bloomsbury Group, if only because, influentially, they went out of their way, by assertion or innuendo, to deflect or deny them. For example, Leonard Woolf:

> What came to be called Bloomsbury by the outside world never existed in the form given to it by the outside world. For 'Bloomsbury' was and is currently used as a term – usually of abuse – applied to a largely imaginary group of persons with largely imaginary objects and characteristics . . . We were and always remained primarily and fundamentally a group of friends.[1]

Of course when Leonard Woolf complained of misrepresentation, he had important things to say. But the theoretical interest of his observation is that, first, in discussing this 'largely imaginary group' he takes for granted the existence and the concept of 'the outside world', and, second, he counterposes 'a group of friends' to a group in some more general sense. But it is a central fact about many though not all such groups that they begin and develop as 'a group of friends'. What we have then to ask is whether any shared ideas or activities were elements of their friendship, contributing directly to their formation and distinction as a group, and, further, whether there was anything about the ways in which they became friends which indicate wider social and cultural factors. It is significant, for example, to continue the quotation:

> We were and always remained primarily and fundamentally a group of friends. Our roots and the roots of our friendship were in the University of Cambridge.[2]

For it is especially significant of Bloomsbury that 'the University of Cambridge' can be taken, in this way, as if it were a simple location, rather than the highly specific social and cultural institution which it was and is. Moreover the social and cultural roots of that particular form of perception – the 'group' and the 'outside world' – have in their turn to be traced to a precise social position and formation.

For this is the real point of social and cultural analysis, of any developed kind: to attend not only to the manifest ideas and activities, but also to the positions and ideas which are implicit or even taken for granted. This is especially necessary in the England of the last hundred years, in which the significance of groups like Bloomsbury or, to take another relevant example, F. R. Leavis and *Scrutiny*, has been widely acknowledged but within an especially weak general perspective. For the concepts to which such groups are referred belong, essentially, to the definitions and perspectives of the groups themselves, so that any analysis which follows tends to be internal and circular.

This is so, for example, in the concept of the 'intellectual aristocracy', which Lord Annan has popularized and documented, and in the concept of 'minority culture', which Clive Bell, of Bloomsbury, and F. R. Leavis, of *Scrutiny*, in their different ways relied on. The point is not to question the intelligence or the cultivation of such self-defining groups. It is rather to relate them, in their specific forms, to those wider conditions which the concepts of an 'aristocracy' or a 'minority' both imply and obscure. This means asking questions about the social formation of such groups, within a deliberate context of a much wider history, involving very general relationships of social class and education. It means asking, further, about the effects of the relative position of any particular formation on their substantive and self-defining activities: effects which may often be presented merely as evidence of the distinction but which, viewed in a different perspective, may be seen as defining in less realized ways.

Thus Annan's presentation of an intellectual aristocracy, defined by a number of intellectually distinguished families, has to be qualified by two different considerations: first, the effect, including the generational effect, of the social position of those families on their members' *opportunities* for intellectual distinction; and, second, the facts of those families as whole numbers of persons, who need not – except on the founding assumption – be described as it were from the most eminent outwards (a method which allows virtually indefinite inclusion by relationship, where inclusion by independent distinction might present more problems) but who, if distinguished families are the *starting point*, can all, by the apparently independent criterion of intellectual achievement, be included and praised. I believe it to be true that indeed, by independent criteria, in the case of many of Annan's subjects, some remarkable clusters of distinction are evident. But these may then be open to quite different kinds of analysis and conclusion from the ideological, and ideologically derived, notion of an 'intellectual aristocracy'.

The same considerations apply to the Bloomsbury Group, especially as we now see it at some historical distance. It can be presented, reasonably, as an extraordinary grouping of talents. Yet in Bloomsbury, quite clearly, there is also now eminence by association. It is interesting to go through Leonard Woolf's list of Old Bloomsbury and its later accessions.[3] It is difficult to be certain in these matters, but it is worth asking how many people on the list would be now independently and separately remembered, in any generally significant cultural sense, apart from their membership of the group. I mean that in one kind of presentation we can lead with Virginia Woolf, E. M. Forster and J. M. Keynes, and then go on through the widening circle to others. But suppose we take the list as it comes: Vanessa Bell, Virginia Woolf, Leonard Woolf, Adrian Stephen, Lytton Strachey, Clive Bell, Maynard Keynes, Duncan Grant, Morgan Forster, Saxon Sydney Turner, Roger Fry, Desmond MacCarthy, Molly MacCarthy, Julian Bell, Quentin Bell, Angelica Bell, David (Bunny) Garnett. It is a list of well-known and some other names. It is indeed exactly what we would expect from Leonard Woolf's accurate description of a group of friends and relations who included some people whose work would be widely respected if the group itself were not remembered, others of whom this is quite clearly not the case, and others again in whom it is difficult to distinguish between independent reputation and the effect of group association and group memoirs.

Yet the point is emphatically not to diminish anybody. That would, indeed, be a gross surrender to some of the very modes of human judgement which Bloomsbury and similar groups effectively popularized. The real point is to see the significance of the cultural group over and above the simple empirical presentation and self-definition as 'a group of friends'. It is to ask what the group was, socially and culturally, as a question distinct from (though still related to) the achievements of individuals and their own immediately perceived relationships. It is indeed just because so many significant modern cultural groups are formed and developed in this way that we have to ask, even against the rising eyebrows of Bloomsbury, certain (heavy) theoretical questions.

For it is clear that no analysis which neglects the elements of friendship and relationship, through which they recognized and came to define themselves, would begin to be adequate. At the same time any restriction to these terms would be a clear evasion of the general significance of the group. We have therefore to think about modes of analysis which avoid collapsing one kind of definition into another, either the generalized group or the empirical assembly. For it is just because of its specific internal formation and its evident general significance – the two qualities taken together – that Bloomsbury is so interesting. It is also an especially important case theoretically, since it is impossible to develop a modern cultural sociology unless we can find ways of discussing such formations which both acknowledge the terms in which they saw themselves and would wish to be presented, and at the same time enable us to analyse these terms and their general social and cultural significance. And because this is so, though I shall mainly discuss Bloomsbury, I shall say something also about Godwin and his circle and the Pre-Raphaelite Brotherhood. This is partly for comparison, including historical comparison, but is also a way of beginning to find terms for the more general discussion.

The formation of Bloomsbury

Let us then notice first that certain of the declared founding principles of Bloomsbury were of a kind which corresponded directly to their precise mode of formation and to the activities for which most of them are remembered. One account after another emphasizes the centrality of the shared values of personal affection and aesthetic enjoyment. For any conscious formulation of these values, we are regularly referred to the great influence of G. E. Moore on the original friends at Cambridge. These shared values were modulated in specific ways. There was a sustained emphasis on candour: people were to say to each other exactly what they thought and felt. There was also great emphasis on clarity: the candid avowal, or any kind of statement, must expect to be met by the question: 'what precisely do you mean by that?' These shared values and habits are then immediately relevant to the internal formation of the group and to some of its external effects. The values and habits which brought them so closely together soon gave them a (self-regarding) sense of being different from others, and these others, in turn, could identify them as a clique. But then, in this as in other important respects, they were also one of the advanced formations of their class:

When I went to Ceylon [*sc.* 1904] – indeed even when I returned [*sc.* 1911] – I still called Lytton Strachey Strachey and Maynard Keynes Keynes, and to them I was still Woolf. When I stayed for a week with the Stracheys in the country in 1904, or dined in Gordon Square with the Stephens, it would have been inconceivable that I should have called Lytton's or Toby's sisters by their Christian names. The social significance of using Christian instead of surnames and of kissing instead of shaking hands is curious. Their effect is greater, I think, than those who have never lived in a more formal society imagine. They produce a sense – often unconscious – of intimacy and freedom and so break down barriers to thought and feeling. It was this feeling of greater intimacy and freedom, of the sweeping away of formalities and barriers, which I found so new and so exhilarating in 1911. To have discussed some subjects or to have called a (sexual) spade a spade in the presence of Miss Strachey or Miss Stephen would seven years before have been unimaginable; here for the first time I found a much more intimate (and wider) circle in which complete freedom of thought and speech was now extended to Vanessa and Virginia, Pippa and Marjorie.[4]

This sense of liberation was a stage in the development of the original Cambridge friends. It was a local realization of their earlier bearings:

> We were convinced that everyone over twenty-five, with perhaps one or two remarkable exceptions, was 'hopeless', having lost the élan of youth, the capacity to feel, and the ability to distinguish truth from falsehood . . . We found ourselves living in the springtime of a conscious revolt against the social, political, religious, moral, intellectual and artistic institutions, beliefs and standards of our fathers and grandfathers . . . We were out to construct something new; we were in the van of the builders of a new society which should be free, rational, civilized, pursuing truth and beauty.[5]

It must of course be clear that this was a very much wider movement than Bloomsbury. In this very account, with a characteristic mixture of honesty and unawareness, Leonard Woolf noted that 'we felt ourselves to be the second generation in this exciting movement', though the attitude to almost everyone over twenty-five seems to have survived this. In fact most of the attitudes and opinions were derived, as here from Ibsen

> saying 'Bosh!' to that vast system of cant and hypocrisy which made lies a vested interest, the vested interest of the 'establishment', of the

monarchy, aristocracy, upper classes, suburban bourgeoisie, the
Church, the Army, the stock exchange.[6]

What Bloomsbury really represented, in the development of this wider
movement, was a new *style*.

It was an effective style for the new critical frankness. But there were
elements in its formation which brought other tones, and not only the
cliquishness of the self-conscious advanced group. The frankness could
modulate into tones of quite extraordinary rudeness about, and to, the
'hopeless'. There is also something very curious about the attachment to
personal affections. This is difficult to estimate, at a distance and from
outside, but 'affection', rather than any stronger word, does, as one
reads, come to seem exact. A cool frankness as a dominant intellectual
tone seems to have had its effect on certain levels of emotional life. This
was, of course, already evident in Shaw, and in the related but wider
Fabian formation. There is an unforgettable moment in a conversation
between Virginia Woolf and Beatrice Webb in 1918:

> Beatrice had asked Virginia what she intended to do now that she was
> married. Virginia said that she wanted to go on writing novels.
> Beatrice seemed to approve and warned Virginia against allowing her
> work to be interfered with by emotional relations. 'Marriage, we
> always say', she said, 'is the waste paper basket of the emotions'. To
> which, just as they came to the level crossing, Virginia replied: 'But
> wouldn't an old servant do as well?'[7]

The fact that in her own record of this conversation Virginia Woolf has
'waste pipe' for 'waste paper basket' only deepens its ironic fascination.
There is a sense in which the rationality and the candour give 'affection'
a limiting though still important definition. On the other hand, what is
quite evident in the group is a significant tolerance in sexual and
emotional matters. This valuable tolerance and the exact weight of
'affection' seem really to be linked.

A final factor which must be added to this initial definition of the
structure of feeling of the group can be precisely represented by the
phrase 'social conscience'. They were not its originators, and in any case
it is a more evident factor after 1918 than before 1914. It relates, certainly,
to the comprehensive irreverence for established ideas and institutions,
in the earliest phase. But it becomes something more. Nothing more
easily contradicts the received image of Bloomsbury as withdrawn and
languid aesthetes than the remarkable record of political and
organizational involvement, between the wars, by Leonard Woolf, by
Keynes, but also by others, including Virginia Woolf, who had a branch
of the Women's Cooperative Guild meeting regularly in her home. The

public record of Keynes is well enough known. That of Leonard Woolf, in his prolonged work for the League of Nations, for the Cooperative movement, and for the Labour Party, especially on anti-imperialist questions, is especially honourable.

It might then come as a surprise, to Bloomsbury and to those formed in its image, to set a mark on 'social conscience'. The phrase itself, from just this period, has become widely naturalized, and it is then very difficult to question it. One way of doing so is to note its widespread association with that other significant phrase, 'concern for the underdog'. For what has most carefully to be defined is the specific association of what are really quite unchanged class feelings – a persistent sense of a quite clear line between an upper and a lower class – with very strong and effective feelings of sympathy with the lower class as victims. Thus political action is directed towards systematic reform at a ruling-class level; contempt for the stupidity of the dominant sectors of the ruling class survives, quite unchanged, from the earliest phase. The contradiction inherent in this – the search for systematic reform at the level of a ruling class which is known to be, in majority, short-sighted and stupid – is of course not ignored. It is a matter of social conscience to go on explaining and proposing, at official levels, and at the same time to help in organizing and educating the victims. The point is not that this social conscience is unreal; it is very real indeed. But it is the precise formulation of a particular social position, in which a fraction of an upper class, breaking from its dominant majority, relate to a lower class *as a matter of conscience*: not in solidarity, nor in affiliation, but as an extension of what are still felt as personal or small-group obligations, at once against the cruelty and stupidity of the system and towards its otherwise relatively helpless victims.

The complex of political attitudes, and eventually of political and social reforms of a certain kind, that flowed from this 'social conscience' has been especially important in England. It has indeed become consensual, from the right wing of the Labour Party through the Liberal Party to a few liberal Conservatives. Bloomsbury, including Keynes, was in this as in other matters well ahead of its times. In its organs, from the *New Statesman* through to the *Political Quarterly*, it was, in its period, second in importance in this consensus only to the closely related Fabian Society. In its hostility to imperialism, where the conscientious identification with victims was more negotiable than in England itself, its contribution was very significant. In its early and sustained hostility to militarism it represented an element of the consensus which was later, and especially in the Cold War, phased out. But what now matters most, in defining the group, is the nature of the connection between these important political bearings and the small, rational, candid group. The true link term is 'conscience'. It is a sense of individual obligation, ratified among civilized friends, which both governs immediate relationships and can be extended, without altering its own local base, to the widest 'social concerns'. It can then be distinguished, as the group itself always insisted, from the unfeeling, complacent and stupid state of mind of the dominant sector of the class. It has also to be distinguished – and this the group and its successors did not see – from the 'social *consciousness*' of a self-organizing subordinate class. These very different political bearings were not so much rejected as never taken seriously. Close contact with them, which the 'social conscience' required, produced a quite un-self-conscious and in its own way quite pure patronage. For if this were not given, these new forces could not be expected to be any more rational and civilized than their present masters.

In these initial definitions of the meanings and values which made this group more than just a group of friends – meanings and values, of course, which at every point, because of what they were, sustained their self-perception as *only* a group of friends, a few civilized individuals – we have come to the edge of the central definition of the social significance of the Bloomsbury Group. They were a true *fraction* of the existing English upper class. They were at once against its dominant ideas and values and still willingly, in all immediate ways, part of it. It is a very complex and delicate position, but the significance of such fractions has been very generally underestimated. It is not only a question of this problematic relationship within any particular section of time. It is also a question of the function of such relationships and such groups in the development and adaptation, through time, of the class as a whole.

Godwin and his circle

It is here that we can look briefly, by way of comparison, at two important earlier English groups. William Godwin and his circle, in the 1780s and 1790s, came out of a quite differently based dissent. Their religious dissent, at the moment of their formation, already carried the specific social implications: of a relatively disadvantaged religious sector, but also the effects of a social and economic position which was very sharply different from that of the ruling and upper class of the day. That is to say, Godwin and his friends were relatively poor working professionals, an emerging small-bourgeois intelligentsia, with no other means of social or political influence. In their basic attempt to establish rationality, tolerance and liberty they were opposing, and knew they were opposing, a whole class and system beyond them. Within their own group they could argue for and try to practise the rational values of civilized equality, including, it should be remembered, for in this with

Mary Wollstonecraft they were especially advanced, sexual equality. In their early phase they were wholly persuaded of the powers of rational explanation and persuasion. Vice was simply error, and error could be repaired by patient inquiry. Virtue could be assured by reasonable institutions. The stupidities and dogmas which now barred the way must be met by steady and careful enlightenment.

What then happened is still very striking. They encountered a ruling class, quite beyond them, which was not only arrogant and cruel but, at just that time, was under a new kind of threat from the effects of the French Revolution. The rational and civilizing proposals were met by the crudest kind of repression: prosecution, imprisonment and transportation. Godwin's novel, *Things as They Are*, is a remarkable evocation of this crisis, in which truth became a literal risk to life, and reasonable explanation was quite ruthlessly hunted down. It is a remarkable moment in English culture, still insufficiently honoured for the bravery of its initial attempt, and this mainly because the repression broke it so thoroughly and drove it underground for a generation. Failed groups are not easily respected, yet this one should be, in the nobility of its aspirations alongside the inherent character of its illusions. What we can so easily call failure was in fact defeat, and it was defeat by a vicious repression.

More generally, and decisively, this group was not a fraction, a break from an upper class. It was an emergent sector of a still relatively subordinate class, the smaller independent commercial bourgeoisie. Questioning everything, but within the assumption of a continuing rational discourse, they were hit by people who hardly even bothered to answer their arguments but who as threat and danger mounted simply bullied or locked them up. And then what we learn theoretically is that we cannot describe any of these cultural groups simply in internal terms: of what values they stood for, what meanings they tried to live. Taken only at this level, Godwin and his circle have some striking resemblances to Bloomsbury, although they were always stronger. But the level that matters, finally, is not that of the abstracted ideas, but of the real relations of the group to the social system as a whole.

The Pre-Raphaelite Brotherhood

The social system as a whole, but of course social systems change: in their general character and in their internal relations. By the time of the Pre-Raphaelite Brotherhood, in the middle of the nineteenth century, an industrial and commercial bourgeoisie was becoming dominant, and some parts of that earlier discourse had found a limited social base. For these and other reasons, the character of this new group was quite different. What they primarily opposed was the conventional philistinism of their day. In their earliest phase they were irreverent, impatient, contemptuous of shams; they were trying to find new and less formal ways of living among themselves. For a moment, which did not last, they were part of the democratic turbulence of 1848. But the central mode of their brief unity as a group was a declaration for truth in art, and a corresponding rejection of the received conventions. Their positive aim was truth to nature, 'rejecting nothing, selecting nothing and scorning nothing'. They defined a return to the old (pre-Raphaelite) as a means to the new. As an immediate group, they practised an easy and irreverent informality, an exceptional and now 'bohemian' tolerance, and some elements of a private group language (in slang such as 'stunner' and 'crib') which deliberately marked them off. They could be described as being, in their chosen area of art, in revolt against the commercial bourgeoisie, yet in majority they came from this same class. Holman Hunt's father was a warehouse manager, William Morris's a bill broker. Moreover, to a surprising extent as they developed, they found their patrons in this same class. Of course in the end they went their separate ways: towards the new and flattering integration represented by Millais, or to the break towards revolutionary socialism – though with the same immediate commercial links – of Morris. But in their effective moment, for all their difficulties, they were not only a break from their class – the irreverent and rebellious young – but a means towards the necessary next stage of development of that class itself. Indeed this happens again and again with bourgeois fractions: that a group detaches itself, as in this case of 'truth to nature', in terms which really belong to a phase of that class itself, but a phase now overlaid by the blockages of later development. It is then a revolt against the class but for the class, and it is no surprise that its emphases of style, suitably mediated, became the popular bourgeois art of the next historical period.

The Bloomsbury fraction

There is always advantage in historical distance, and Godwin and his circle, or the Pre-Raphaelites, are in this sense more easily placed than Bloomsbury, which in certain of its tones and styles has still significant contemporary influence and even presence. Yet the purpose of this brief reference to these earlier groups is to emphasize, past some of the more obvious points in common, not only the ideal differences but the decisive social differences. And these in their turn can be understood only by following the development of the general society. For what happened in the second half of the nineteenth century was a comprehensive development and reform of the professional and cultural life of bourgeois England. The old universities were reformed and made more serious. The administrative services were both developed and reformed, by the new needs of imperial and state administration, and by the competitive examinations which interlocked with the reformed universities. The changing character of the society and the economy built, in fact, a new and very important professional and highly educated sector of the English upper class: very different in its bearings and values from either the old aristocracy or from the directly commercial bourgeoisie. And then – indeed as we look it is no surprise – it was from this sector, and especially from its second and third generations, that novel definitions and new groups emerged; and specifically, in its full sense, Bloomsbury.

The direct connections of the Bloomsbury Group with this new sector are well known. There is a significant frequency of connection with the upper levels of colonial (usually Indian) administration, as in the Stephen family, in Lytton Strachey's father, in Leonard Woolf's early career. There are continuities before and after in this respect: the Mills in the nineteenth century; Orwell in the twentieth. But the period of the emergence of Bloomsbury was the high point of this sector, as it was also the high point of the social order which it served. The sector is distinguishable but is still very closely connected with a wider area of the class. As Leonard Woolf says of the social world of the Stephens:

> That society consisted of the upper levels of the professional middle class and county families, interpenetrated to a certain extent by the aristocracy [Or more generally] The Stephens and the Stracheys, the Ritchies, Thackerays and Duckworths had an intricate tangle of ancient roots and tendrils stretching far and wide through the upper middle classes, the county families, and the aristocracy.[8]

One of the interests of Woolf's account is that he was himself entering this crucial sector from a rather different class background:

> I was an outsider to this class, because, although I and my father before me belonged to the professional middle class, we had only recently struggled up into it from the stratum of Jewish shopkeepers.[9]

He was thus able to observe the specific habits of the class from which Bloomsbury was to emerge:

> Socially they assumed things unconsciously which I could never assume either unconsciously or consciously. They lived in a peculiar atmosphere of influence, manners, respectability, and it was so natural

to them that they were unaware of it as mammals are unaware of the air and fish of the water in which they live.[10]

But that was the class as a whole. What was decisive in the emergence of its professional sector was the social and intellectual atmosphere of the reformed ancient universities. It was here, after liberalization, after a significant recovery of seriousness, and after internal reorganization to assure coached and competitive merit, that the specific qualities of the professional sector emerged within the general assumptions of the class. This allowed some new recruits, like Woolf himself. It promoted many significant and in a sense autonomous continuities, within the old universities. This is why it can still be seen, from a deliberately selective angle, as an 'intellectual aristocracy'.

> The male members of the British aristocracy of intellect went automatically to the best public schools, to Oxford and Cambridge, and then into all the most powerful and respectable professions. They intermarried to a considerable extent, and family influence and the high level of their individual intelligence carried a surprising number of them to the top of their professions. You found them as civil servants sitting in the seat of permanent under-secretaries of government departments; they became generals, admirals, editors, judges, or they retired with a KCSI or KCMG after distinguished careers in the Indian or Colonial Civil Services. Others again got fellowships at Oxford or Cambridge and ended as head of an Oxford or Cambridge college or headmaster of one of the great public schools.[11]

The confusion of this account is as remarkable as the local accuracy of its information. There is the very characteristic admission and yet blurring of the two factors in success: 'family influence', 'high level of . . . individual intelligence'. There is a related blurring of the 'aristocracy of intellect', supported by one range of examples (Fellows and Headmasters; Permanent Under-Secretaries and Editors) and rather different ruling-class figures (Generals, Admirals). Within each range, in fact, the proportionate effect of class provenance, including family influence, and examined or demonstrated individual intelligence would need to be very precisely estimated. For what is really being described is a sectoral composition, and the diversities within this composition need much more precise description than the self-presenting and self-recommending formula – with its deliberate and yet revealing metaphor – of an 'intellectual aristocracy'.

A further relevant point, in this significant sectoral composition, is raised by Woolf's accurate reference to 'male members'. One of the factors that was to affect the specific character of the Bloomsbury Group, as a formation distinguishable from this whole sector, was the delay in higher education for women of this class. Even in its early stages, a few women from these families were directly involved; one of the Strachey sisters, Pernel, became Principal of Newnham. Yet a persistent sexual asymmetry was an important element in the composition of the Bloomsbury Group. As Woolf again puts it:

> Our roots and the roots of our friendship were in the University of Cambridge. Of the 13 persons mentioned above [as members of Old Bloomsbury] three are women and ten men; of the ten men nine had been at Cambridge.[12]

The effects of this asymmetry were ironically and at times indignantly noted by Virginia Woolf, in *A Room of One's Own* and *Three Guineas*.

What we have then to emphasize, in the sociological formation of Bloomsbury, is first, the provenance of the group in the professional and highly educated sector of the English upper class, itself with wide and sustained connections with this class as a whole; second, the element of contradiction between some of these highly educated people and the ideas and institutions of their class as a whole (the 'intellectual aristocracy', in the narrower sense, or at least some or a few of them, were bringing their intelligence and education to bear on the 'vast system of cant and hypocrisy' sustained by many of the institutions – 'monarchy, aristocracy, upper classes, suburban bourgeoisie, the Church, the Army, the stock exchange' – which were elsewhere included as the fields of success of this same aristocracy of intellect); third, the specific contradiction between the presence of highly intelligent and intellectual women, within these families, and their relative exclusion from the dominant and formative male institutions; and, fourth and more generally, the internal needs and tensions of this class as a whole, and especially of its professional and highly educated sector, in a period which, for all its apparent stability, was one of social, political, cultural and intellectual crisis.

The Bloomsbury Group, we can then say, separated out as a distinct fraction on the basis of the second and third factors: the social and intellectual critique, and the ambiguity of the position of women. Taken together, these are the modes at once of its formation and of its achievements. But the first factor, of their general provenance, must be taken as defining the particular qualities of this fraction: their significant and sustained combination of dissenting influence and influential connection. And the fourth factor indicates something of their general historical significance: that in certain fields, notably those of sexual equalization and tolerance, of attitudes to the arts and especially the

visual arts, and of some private and semi-public informalities, the
Bloomsbury Group was a forerunner in a more general mutation within
the professional and highly educated sector, and to some extent in the
English ruling class more generally. A fraction, as was noted, often
performs this service for its class. There was thus a certain liberalization,
at the level of personal relationships, aesthetic enjoyment and intellectual
openness. There was some modernization, at the level of semi-public
manners, of mobility and contact with other cultures, and of more
extended and more adequate intellectual systems. Such liberalization and
modernization were of course quite general tendencies, in changing
social circumstances and especially after the shocks of the 1914–18 war
and, later, the loss of Empire. It is not that the Bloomsbury Group *caused*
either change; it is only (but it is something) that they were prominent
and relatively coherent among its early representatives and agents. At
the same time, the liberalization and modernization were more strictly
adaptations than basic changes in the class, which in its function of
directing the central ruling-class institutions has, for all the changes of
manners and after some evident recruitment of others into its modes, not
only persisted, but more successfully persisted *because* these adaptations
have been made and continue to be made.

The contribution of Bloomsbury

What has then finally to be discussed is the character of Bloomsbury's
cultural, intellectual and artistic contributions within this context of their
specific sociological formation and their historical significance. Yet any
such discussion faces severe theoretical and methodological difficulties.
There can be no question of reducing a number of highly specific
individual contributions to some crude general content. Cultural groups
of this kind – fractions by association rather than fractions or oppositional
groups by manifesto or programme – can in any case never be treated in
this way. Yet neither can the contributions be seen in mere random
association. It is in this careful mood that we have to read Leonard
Woolf's interesting summary:

> There have often been groups of people, writers and artists, who were
> not only friends, but were consciously united by a common doctrine
> and object, or purpose artistic or social. The utilitarians, the Lake
> poets, the French impressionists, the English Pre-Raphaelites were
> groups of this kind. Our group was quite different. Its basis was
> friendship, which in some cases deepened into love and marriage. The
> colour of our minds and thought had been given to us by the climate of

Cambridge and Moore's philosophy, much as the climate of England gives one colour to the face of an Englishman while the climate of India gives a quite different colour to the face of a Tamil. But we had no common theory, system or principles which we wanted to convert the world to; we were not proselytizers, missionaries, crusaders or even propagandists. It is true that Maynard produced the system or theory of Keynesian economics which has had a great effect upon the theory and practice of economics, finance and politics; and that Roger, Vanessa, Duncan and Clive played important parts, as painters or critics, in what came to be known as the Post-Impressionist Movement. But Maynard's crusade for Keynesian economics against the orthodoxy of the Banks and academic economists, and Roger's crusade for post-impressionism and 'significant form' against the orthodoxy of academic 'representational' painters and aestheticians were just as purely individual as Virginia's writing of *The Waves* – they had nothing to do with any group. For there was no more a communal connection between Roger's 'Critical and Speculative Essays on Art', Maynard's *The General Theory of Employment, Interest and Money*, and Virginia's *Orlando* than there was between Bentham's *Theory of Legislation*, Hazlitt's *Principal Picture Galleries in England*, and Byron's *Don Juan*.[13]

At the simplest empirical level this can be taken to be true, though the final comparison is merely rhetorical: Bentham, Hazlitt and Byron were never significantly associated, and their names beg the question. Nor is the characteristic rejection of 'common theory, system or principles' quite as convincing as it looks; Bloomsbury's attitudes to 'system', at least, were among their most evident common, and principled, characteristics.

Indeed there is something in the way in which Bloomsbury denied its existence as a formal group, while continuing to insist on its group qualities, which is the clue to the essential definition. The point was not to have any common – that is to say, general – theory or system, not only because this was not necessary – worse, it would probably be some imposed dogma – but primarily, and as a matter of principle, because such theories and systems obstructed the true organizing value of the group, which was the unobstructed free expression of the civilized individual. The force which that adjective, 'civilized', carries or is meant to carry can hardly be overestimated.

In the decade before the 1914 war there was a political and social movement in the world, and particularly in Europe and Britain, which seemed at the time wonderfully hopeful and exciting. It seemed as though human beings might really be on the brink of becoming civilized.[14]

In this sense, at its widest range, Bloomsbury was carrying the classical values of bourgeois enlightenment. It was against cant, superstition, hypocrisy, pretension and public show. It was also against ignorance, poverty, sexual and racial discrimination, militarism and imperialism. But it was against all these things in a specific moment of the development of liberal thought. What it appealed to, against all these evils, was not any alternative idea of a whole society. Instead it appealed to the supreme value of the civilized *individual*, whose pluralization, as more and more civilized individuals, was itself the only acceptable social direction.

The profoundly representative character of this perspective and commitment can now be more clearly seen. It is today the central definition of bourgeois ideology (bourgeois practice, of course, is something else again). It commands the public ideals of a very wide range of orthodox political opinion, from modern conservatives through liberals to the most representative social democrats. It is a philosophy of the sovereignty of the civilized individual, not only against all the dark forces of the past, but against all those other and actual forces which, in conflicts of interest, in alternative claims, in other definitions of society and relationships, can be quickly seen as enemies and can as quickly be assigned to the far side of that border which is marked by its own definition of 'civilized'. The early confidence of the position, in the period before 1914, has in its long encounter with all these other and actual social forces gone in Leonard Woolf's title – 'downhill all the way'. For all its continuing general orthodoxy, it appears now much more often as a beleaguered than as an expanding position. The repetition of its tenets then in turn becomes more and more ideological.

Bloomsbury's moment in this history is significant. In its practice – as in the sensibility of the novels of Virginia Woolf and of E. M. Forster – it could offer much more convincing evidence of the substance of the civilized individual than the orthodox rallying phrase. In its theory and practice, from Keynesian economics to its work for the League of Nations, it made powerful interventions towards the creation of economic, political and social conditions within which, freed from war and depression and prejudice, individuals could be free to be and to become civilized. Thus in its personal instances and in its public interventions Bloomsbury was as serious, as dedicated and as inventive as this position has ever, in the twentieth century, been. Indeed the paradox of many retrospective judgements of Bloomsbury is that the group lived and worked this position with a now embarrassing wholeheartedness: embarrassing, that is to say, to those many for whom 'civilized individualism' is a summary phrase for a process of conspicuous and privileged consumption. It is not that we can sever the positions of Bloomsbury from these later developments: there are some real continuities, as in the cult of conspicuous-appreciative-consumption;

and certain traps were sprung, as in Keynesian economics and in monetary and military alliances. But we have still to see the difference between the fruit and its rotting, or between the hopefully planted seed and its fashionably distorted tree.

But then, as we see both the connections and the differences, we have to go on to analyse the obscurities and the faults of the original position around which Bloomsbury defined itself. This can be done either seriously or lightheartedly. Let us for a moment choose the latter, in one of Bloomsbury's own modes. It can be said, it was often said, that the group had no *general* position. But why did it need one? If you cared to look, there were Virginia and Morgan for literature, Roger and Clive and Vanessa and Duncan for art, Leonard for politics, Maynard for economics. Didn't these about cover the proper interests of all civilized people? With one exception perhaps, but in the twenties, significantly, this was remedied. A number of associates and relations of the group – Adrian and Karin Stephen, James Strachey – moved into the new practice of psychoanalysis, and Leonard and Virginia Woolf's Hogarth Press – their own direct and remarkable creation – effectively introduced Freudian thinking into English. Thus to the impressive list of Virginia and Morgan for literature, Roger and Clive and Vanessa and Duncan for art, Leonard for politics and Maynard for economics they could, so to say, add Sigmund for sex.

It is tempting to turn any mode back on itself, but the underlying point is serious. The work and thought of the Bloomsbury Group, and that other work and thought which it effectively associated with itself and presented – including, it should be said, the early 'communist' poetry of the thirties – are remarkable, at first sight, for their eclecticism, for their evident *dis*connections. In this sense it is understandable that anyone should turn and ask, rhetorically, what connections there could ever be between Clive Bell on art and Keynes on employment, or Virginia Woolf on fiction and Leonard Woolf on the League of Nations, or Lytton Strachey on history and the Freudians on psychoanalysis. It is true that we cannot put all this work together and make it into a general theory. But of course that is the point. The different positions which the Bloomsbury Group assembled, and which they effectively disseminated as the contents of the mind of a modern, educated, civilized individual, are all in effect *alternatives* to a general theory. We do not need to ask, while this impression holds, whether Freud's generalizations on aggression are compatible with single-minded work for the League of Nations, or whether his generalizations on art are compatible with Bell's 'significant form' and 'aesthetic ecstasy', or whether Keynes's ideas of public intervention in the market are compatible with the deep assumption of society as a group of friends and relations. We do not need to ask because the effective integration has already taken place, at the level of the 'civilized individual', the singular definition of all the best people, secure in their autonomy but turning their free attention this way and that, as occasion requires. And the governing object of all the public interventions is to secure this kind of autonomy, by finding ways of diminishing pressures and conflicts, and of avoiding disasters. The social conscience, in the end, is to protect the private consciousness.

Where this can be assured without that kind of protection – in the privileged forms of certain kinds of art, refusing the 'sacrifice . . . to representation' as 'something stolen from art',[15] or of certain kinds of fiction, as in Virginia Woolf mockingly rejecting social description –

> Begin by saying that her father kept a shop in Harrogate. Ascertain the rent. Ascertain the wages of shop assistants in 1878. Discover what her mother died of. Describe cancer. Describe calico. Describe . . . [16]

– or in the available, significant forms of personal relationships and aesthetic enjoyments – there is still no conflict (in spite of the troublesome 'details') with social *conscience*. Rather this higher sensibility is the kind of life which is its aim and model, after the rational removal of ('unnecessary') conflicts and contradictions and modes of deprivation. For the sake of personal life and of art, as Clive Bell argued,

> Society can do something . . . because it can increase liberty . . . Even politicians can do something. They can repeal censorious laws and abolish restrictions on freedom of thought and speech and conduct. They can protect minorities. They can defend originality from the hatred of the mediocre mob.[17]

It is not always that specific blend of sweet and sour. It is indeed never free from class connotations, as again most explicitly in Bell:

> The liberation will not be complete until those who have already learned to despise the opinion of the lower-middle classes learn also to neglect the standards and the disapproval of people who are forced by their emotional limitations to regard art as an elegant amenity . . . Comfort is the enemy; luxury is merely the bugbear of the bourgeoisie.[18]

At its best it was brave, in its own best terms:

> The least that the State can do is to protect people who have something to say that may cause a riot. What will not cause a riot is probably not worth saying.[19]

Yet after so much saying, there were no riots. Because for all its eccentricities, including its valuable eccentricities, Bloomsbury was articulating a position which, if only in carefully diluted instances, was to become a 'civilized' norm. In the very power of their demonstration of a private sensibility that must be protected and extended by forms of public concern, they fashioned the effective forms of the contemporary ideological dissociation between 'public' and 'private' life. Awareness of their own formation as individuals within society, of that specific social formation which made them explicitly a group and implicitly a fraction of a class, was not only beyond their reach; it was directly ruled out, since the free and civilized individual was already their founding datum. Psychoanalysis could be integrated with this, while it remained an ahistorical study of specific individual formations. Public policies could be integrated with it, while they were directed to reforming and amending a social order which had at once produced these free and civilized individuals but which through stupidity or anachronism now threatened their existence and their indefinite and generalized reproduction. The final nature of Bloomsbury as a group is that it was indeed, and differentially, a group of and for the notion of free individuals. Any general position, as distinct from this special assumption, would then have disrupted it, yet a whole series of specialized positions was at the same time necessary, for the free individuals to be civilized. And the irony is that both the special assumption, and the range of specialized positions, have become naturalized – though now more evidently incoherent – in all late phases of English culture. It is in this exact sense that this group of free individuals must be seen, finally, as a (civilizing) fraction of their class.

Notes

1. LEONARD WOOLF, *Beginning Again* (London: Hogarth Press, 1964), pp. 21, 23.

2. WOOLF, *Beginning Again*, p. 23.

3. WOOLF, *Beginning Again*, p. 22.

4. WOOLF, *Beginning Again*, pp. 34–5.

5. LEONARD WOOLF, *Sowing* (London:Hogarth Press, 1960), pp. 160–1.

6. WOOLF, *Sowing*, p. 164.

7. WOOLF, *Beginning Again*, p. 117.

8. WOOLF, *Beginning Again*, p. 74.

9. WOOLF, *Beginning Again*, p. 74.

10. WOOLF, *Beginning Again*, p. 75.

11. WOOLF, *Sowing*, p. 186.

12. WOOLF, *Beginning Again*, p. 23.

13. WOOLF, *Beginning Again*, p. 26.

14. WOOLF, *Beginning Again*, p.36.

15. CLIVE BELL, *Art* (London: Chatto and Windus, 1914), p. 44.

16. VIRGINIA WOOLF, *Mr Bennett and Mrs Brown*, (London: Hogarth Press, 1924), p. 18.

17. BELL, *Art.*, pp. 274–5.

18. BELL, *Art*, pp. 273–4.

19. BELL, *Art*, pp. 275.

7 Theory of the Avant-garde and Critical Literary Science* (1974)

Peter Bürger

Peter Bürger is Professor of French and Comparative Literature at the University of Bremen. He has written works on Corneille, the French Enlightenment, Surrealism, and – most influentially – *Theory of the Avant-garde* – whose second chapter appears here.

Bürger's historical objective – to specify and explain the artistic departures of the late nineteenth and early twentieth centuries – is pursued with the marked theoretical and methodological self-consciousness of the Frankfurt tradition, which is everywhere present in his text. He begins by revisiting Marx's analysis of the historical relationship between the development of concepts and that of their object and, in so doing, establishes the main lines of his concrete theses. Art in the bourgeois era has been characterized by its *social autonomy*, the particular intentions and contents of particular works notwithstanding. Aestheticism was the moment in which this 'institutional' status became a self-reflecting value and also, therefore, an available object for criticism. The project of the avant-gardes was not merely a variant practice in art, but an effort to overcome its social uselessness through an attack on the art institution itself.

Bürger's reference, it is worth noting, is to 'the historic avant-gardes', a category familiar in much European discussion but not in the Anglo-American tradition, where the notion of 'modernism' has long been canonical. The former is at once more modest than the latter, identifying a plurality of initiatives rather than a period proper, and more demanding, in that the idea of 'avant-garde' implies a cultural radicalism more far-reaching than anything ventured by the iconic English-language modernists.

* Reprinted from Peter Bürger, *Theory of the Avant-garde* (Manchester: Manchester University Press and Minneapolis: University of Minnesota Press, 1984), pp. 15–34.

> *History is inherent in aesthetic theory. Its categories are*
> *radically historical* (Adorno).[1]

The historicity of aesthetic categories

Aesthetic theories may strenuously strive for metahistorical knowledge,
but that they bear the clear stamp of the period of their origin can usually
be seen afterward, and with relative ease. But if aesthetic theories are
historical, a critical theory of art that attempts to elucidate what it does
must grasp that it is itself historical. In other words, it must historicize
aesthetic theory.

It will first have to be made clear what historicizing a theory may
mean. It cannot mean the application to present-day aesthetic theorizing
of the historicist perspective, which understands all the phenomena of a
period wholly as expressions of that period and then creates an ideal
contemporaneity among the individual periods (Ranke's 'equally close to
God'). The false objectivism of the historicist approach has been justly
criticized. To propose bringing it back to life in a discussion of theories
would be absurd.[2] But neither can historicizing mean that one views all
previous theories as nothing more than steps leading up to one's own. In
such an undertaking, fragments of earlier theories are detached from
their original context and fitted into a new one but the change in function
and meaning which that fragment undergoes is not adequately reflected.
In spite of its progressiveness, the construction of history as the
prehistory of the present, a construction that upward-moving classes
characteristically engage in, is one-sided in the Hegelian sense, for it
grasps only one aspect of the historical process, whose other aspect
historicism lays hold of in a false objectivism. In the present context,
historicizing a theory will have a different meaning, that is, the insight
into the nexus between the unfolding of an object and the categories of a
discipline or science. Understood in this fashion, the historicity of a
theory is not grounded in its being the expression of a *Zeitgeist* (the
historicist view) nor in the circumstance that it incorporates earlier
theories (history as prehistory of the present) but in the fact that the
unfolding of object and the elaboration of categories are connected.
Historicizing a theory means grasping this connection.

It might be objected that such an enterprise cannot but lay claim to a
position outside history, so that historicizing simultaneously and
necessarily becomes a dehistoricizing or, in other words, that the
determination of the historicity of the language of a science presupposes
a meta-level from which this determination can be made, and that this
meta-level is necessarily metahistorical (which would then require the

147

historicizing of this meta-level, etc.) We did not introduce the concept of historicization here in the sense of a separation of various levels of the language of science, but in that of reflection, which grasps in the medium of *one* language the historicity of its own speech. What is meant here can best be explained by some fundamental methodological insights that Marx formulated in the introduction to the *Grundrisse der Kritik der politischen Ökonomie* 'The example of labour,' Marx writes, 'shows strikingly how even the most abstract categories, despite their validity – precisely because of their abstractness – for all epochs, are nevertheless, in the specific character of this abstraction, themselves likewise a product of historic relations, and possess their full validity only for and within these relations.'[3] The idea is difficult to grasp because Marx maintained on the one hand that certain categories are always valid, yet also states that their generality is due to specific historical conditions. The decisive distinction here is between 'validity for all epochs' and the *perception* of this general validity (in Marx's terms, 'the specific character of this abstraction'). It is Marx's contention that conditions must have unfolded historically for that perception to become possible. In the monetary system, he says, wealth is still interpreted to be money, which means that the connection between labour and wealth is not seen. Only in the theory of the physiocrats is labour discovered to be the source of wealth, though it is not labour in general but only a particular form of it, namely, agriculture. In classical English economics, in Adam Smith, it is no longer a particular kind of labour but labour in general that is recognized as the source of wealth. For Marx, this development is not merely one in economic theory. Rather, he feels that the possibility of a progress in knowledge is a function of the development of the object towards which insight directs itself. When the physiocrats developed their theory (in France, during the second half of the eighteenth century), agriculture was still the economically dominant sector on which all others depended. Only in economically much more advanced England, where the industrial revolution had already set in and where the dominance of agriculture over all sectors of social production would therefore be eventually eliminated, was Smith's insight possible – that it was not a specific form of labour but labour as such that created wealth. 'The indifference towards a specific form of labour presupposes a highly developed totality of actual forms of labour none of which is any longer the dominant one' (*Grundrisse*, p. 25).

It is my thesis that the connection between *the insight into the general validity of a category* and *the actual historical development of the field to which this category pertains*, which Marx demonstrated through the example of the category of labour, applies also to objectifications in the arts. Here also, the full unfolding of the constituent elements of a field is the condition for the possibility of an adequate cognition of that field. In bourgeois society, it is only with aestheticism that the full unfolding of the phenomenon of art became a fact, and it is to aestheticism that the historical avant-garde movements respond.[4]

The central category of 'artistic means' or 'procedures' can serve to illuminate this thesis. Through it, the artistic process of creation can be reconstructed as a process of rational choice between various techniques, the choice being made with reference to the effect that is to be attained. Such a reconstruction of artistic production not only presupposes a relatively high degree of rationality in artistic production; it also presupposes that means are freely available, i.e. no longer part of a system of stylistic norms where, albeit in mediated form, social norms express themselves. That Molière's comedy uses artistic means just as Beckett does goes without saying. But that they were not recognized as such during Molière's time can be demonstrated by a glance at Boileau's criticism. Aesthetic criticism here is still criticism of the stylistic means of the crudely comic that the ruling social class found unacceptable. In the feudal, absolutist society of seventeenth-century France, art is still largely integrated into the life-style of the ruling class. Although the bourgeois aesthetics that developed in the eighteenth century freed itself of the stylistic norms that had linked the art of feudal absolutism and the ruling class of that society, art nonetheless continued to obey the 'imitatio naturae' principle. The stylistic means therefore do not yet have the generality of means whose single purpose is their effect on the recipient but are subordinated to a (historically changing) stylistic principle. Artistic means is undoubtedly the most general category by which works of art can be described. But that the various techniques and procedures can be *recognized* as artistic means has been possible only since the historical avant-garde movements. For it is in the historical avant-garde movements that the totality of artistic means becomes available as means. Up to this period in the development of art, the use of artistic means had been limited by the period style, an already existing canon of permissible procedures, an infringement of which was acceptable only within certain bounds. But during the dominance of a style, the category 'artistic means' as a general one cannot be seen for what it is because, *realiter*, it occurs only as a particular one. It is, on the other hand, a distinguishing feature of the historical avant-garde movements that they did not develop a style. There is no such thing as a dadaist or a surrealist style. What did happen is that these movements liquidated the possibility of a period style when they raised to a principle the availability of the artistic means of past periods. Not until there is universal availability does the category of artistic means become a general one.

If the Russian formalists view 'defamiliarization' as *the* artistic technique,[5] recognition that this category is a general one is made possible by the circumstance that in the historical avant-garde movements, shocking the recipient becomes the dominant principle of artistic intent. Because defamiliarization thereby does in fact become the dominant artistic technique, it can be discovered as a general category. This is not to say that the Russian formalists demonstrated defamiliarization principally in avant-gardist art (on the contrary, Shklovsky's preferred demonstration objects are *Don Quixote* and *Tristram Shandy*). What is claimed is no more than a connection – though a necessary one – between the principle of shock in avant-gardist art and the recognition that defamiliarization is a category of general validity. This nexus can be posited as necessary because it is only the full unfolding of the thing (here, the radicalization of defamiliarization in shock) that makes recognizable the general validity of the category. This is not to say that the act of cognition is transferred to reality itself, that the subject that produces the insight is negated. What is acknowledged is simply that the possibilities of cognition are limited by the real (historical) unfolding of the object.[6]

It is my thesis that certain general categories of the work of art were first made recognizable in their generality by the avant-garde, that it is consequently from the standpoint of the avant-garde that the preceding phases in the development of art as a phenomenon in bourgeois society can be understood, and that it is an error to proceed inversely, by approaching the avant-garde via the earlier phases of art. This thesis does not mean that it is only in avant-gardist art that *all* categories of the work of art reach their full elaboration. On the contrary, we will note that certain categories essential to the description of pre-avant-gardist art (such as organicity, subordination of the parts to the whole) are in fact negated in the avant-gardist work. One should not assume, therefore, that all categories (and what they comprehend) pass through an even development. Such an evolutionist view would eradicate what is contradictory in historical processes and replace it with the idea that development is linear progress. In contrast to such a view, it is essential to insist that the historical development of society as a whole as well as that within subsytems can only be grasped as the result of the frequently contrariant evolutions that categories undergo.[7]

This thesis needs refining in one further respect. Only the avant-garde, it was said, made artistic means recognizable in their generality because it no longer chooses means according to a stylistic principle, but avails itself of them as *means*. It was not ex nihilo, of course, that avant-garde practice created the possibility of recognizing categories of the work of art in their general validity. Rather, that possibility has its historical presupposition in the development of art in bourgeois society. Since the middle of the nineteenth century, that is, subsequent to the consolidation of political rule by the bourgeoisie, this development has taken a particular turn: the form-content dialectic of artistic structures has increasingly shifted in favour of form. The content of the work of art, its 'statement', recedes ever more as compared with its formal aspect, which defines itself as the aesthetic in the narrower sense. From the point of view of production aesthetics, this dominance of form in art since about the middle of the nineteenth century can be understood as command over means; from the point of view of reception aesthetics, as a tendency towards the sensitizing of the recipient. It is important to see the unity of the process: means become available as the category 'content' withers.[8]

From this perspective, one of the central theses of Adorno's aesthetics – 'the key to any and every content (*Gehalt*) of art lies in its technique' – becomes clear.[9] Only because during the last one hundred years, the relation between the formal (technical) elements of the work and its content (those elements which make statements) changed and form became in fact predominant can this thesis be formulated at all. Once again, the connection between the historical unfolding of a subject and of the categories that grasp that subject area becomes apparent. Yet Adorno's formulation has a problematical aspect and that is its claim to universal validity. If it is true that Adorno's theorem could be formulated only because art since Baudelaire took the course it did, the claim that the theorem applies also to earlier periods of art becomes questionable. In the methodological reflection quoted earlier, Marx addresses this question. He states specifically that even the most abstract categories have 'full validity' only for and within those conditions whose products they are. Unless one wants to see a covert historicism in this formulation, there arises the problem of whether it is possible to have a knowledge of the past that does not fall victim to the historicist illusion of a presuppositionless understanding of the past, that does not simply grasp that past in categories that are the product of a later period.

The avant-garde as the self-criticism of art in bourgeois society

In the introduction to the *Grundrisse*, Marx formulates another idea of considerable methodological scope. It also concerns the possibility of understanding past social formations or past social subsystems. The historicist position that assumes it can understand past social formations without reference to the present of the researcher is not even considered by Marx, who has no doubt about the nexus between the development of the thing and that of the categories (and thus the historicity of cognition). What he criticizes is not the historicist illusion of the possibility of historical knowledge without a historical reference point, but the progressive construction of history as the prehistory of the present. 'The so-called historical presentation of development is founded, as a rule, on the fact that the latest form regards the previous ones as steps leading up to itself, and, since it is only rarely and only under quite specific conditions able to criticize itself – leaving aside, of course, the historical periods which appear to themselves as times of decadence – it always conceives them one-sidedly' (*Grundrisse* p. 106). The concept 'one-sided' is used here in a strictly theoretical sense. It means that a contradictory whole is not being understood dialectically (in its contradictions) but that only one side of the contradiction is being fastened on. The past is certainly to be constructed as the prehistory of the present, but this construction grasps only one side of the contradictory process of historical development. To take hold of the process in its entirety, it is necessary to go beyond the present that first makes knowledge possible. Marx takes this step not by introducing the dimension of the future but by introducing the concept of the self-criticism of the present. 'The Christian religion was able to be of assistance in reaching an objective understanding of earlier mythologies only when its own self-criticism had been accomplished to a certain degree. . . . Likewise, bourgeois economics arrived at an understanding of feudal, ancient, oriental economics only after the self-criticism of bourgeois society had begun' (*Grundrisse* p. 106). Marx speaks of 'objective understanding' here but he certainly does not fall victim to the objectivist self-deception of historicism, for he never doubts that historical knowledge relates to the present. His sole concern is to overcome dialectically the necessary 'one-sidedness' of the construction of the past as prehistory of the present, and to do so by using the concept of the self-criticism of the present.

If one wishes to use self-criticism as a historiographic category as one describes a certain stage of development of a social formation or of a social subsystem, its meaning will first have to be precisely defined. Marx makes a distinction between self-criticism and another type, such as the 'critique Christianity levelled against paganism, or also that of Protestantism against Catholicism' (*Grundrisse* p. 106). We will refer to this type as system-immanent criticism. Its characteristic is that it functions within a social institution. To stick to Marx's example: system-immanent criticism within the institution of religion is criticism of specific religious ideas in the name of other ideas. In contrast to this form, self-criticism presupposes distance from mutually hostile religious ideas. This distance, however, is merely the result of a fundamentally more radical criticism, and that is the criticism of religion as an institution.

The difference between system-immanent criticism and self-criticism can be transferred to the sphere of art. Examples of system-immanent criticism would be the criticism the theoreticians of French classicism directed against Baroque drama, or Lessing's of the German imitations of classical French tragedy. Criticism here functions within an institution, the theatre. Varying concepts of tragedy that are grounded (if by multiple mediations) in social positions confront each other. There is another kind of criticism and that is the self-criticism of art: it addresses itself to art as an institution and must be distinguished from the former type. The methodological significance of the category 'self-criticism' is that for social subsystems also, it indicates the condition of the possibility of 'objective understanding' of past stages of development. Applied to art, this means that only when art enters the stage of self-criticism does the 'objective understanding' of past periods of the development of art become possible. 'Objective understanding' here does not mean an understanding that is independent of the place in the present of the cognizing individual; it merely means insight into the overall process in so far as this process has come to a conclusion in the present of the cognizing individual, however provisional that conclusion may be.

My second thesis is this: with the historical avant-garde movements, the social subsystem that is art enters the stage of self-criticism. Dadaism, the most radical movement within the European avant-garde, no longer criticizes schools that preceded it, but criticizes art as an institution, and its course of development in bourgeois society. The concept 'art as an institution' as used here refers to the productive and distributive apparatus and also to the ideas about art that prevail at a given time and determine the reception of works. The avant-garde turns against both – the distribution apparatus on which the work of art depends, and the status of art in bourgeois society as defined by the concept of autonomy. Only after art, in nineteenth-century Aestheticism, has altogether detached itself from the praxis of life can the aesthetic develop 'purely'. But the other side of autonomy, art's lack of social impact, also becomes recognizable. The avant-gardist protest, whose aim it is to reintegrate art into the praxis of life, reveals the nexus between autonomy and inconsequentiality. The self-criticism of the social subsystem, art, which now sets in, makes possible the 'objective understanding' of past phases of development. Whereas during the period of realism, for example, the development of art was felt to lie in a growing closeness of representation to reality, the one-sidedness of this construction could now be recognized. Realism no longer appears as *the* principle of artistic creation but becomes understandable as the sum of certain period procedures. The totality of the developmental process of art becomes clear only in the stage of self-criticism. Only after art has in fact wholly detached itself from everything that is the praxis of life can two things be seen to make up the principle of development of art in bourgeois society: the progressive detachment of art from real life contexts, and the correlative crystallization of a distinctive sphere of experience, i.e., the aesthetic.

The Marx text gives no direct answer to the question concerning the historical conditions of the possibility of self-criticism. From Marx's text, one can only abstract the general observation that self-criticism presupposes that the social formation or social sub-system to which that criticism directs itself have fully evolved its own, unique characteristics. If this general theorem is transferred to the sphere of history, the result is as follows: for the self-criticism of bourgeois society, the proletariat must first have come into existence. For the coming into being of the proletariat makes it possible to recognize liberalism as an ideology. The precondition for the self-criticism of the social subsystem 'religion' is the loss of the legitimating function of religious world pictures. These lose their social function as feudalism ends, bourgeois society comes into being, and the world pictures that legitimate dominion (and the religious world pictures belong in this category) are replaced by the basic ideology of the fair exchange. 'Because the *social power* of the capitalist is institutionalized as an exchange relation in the form of the private labour contract and the siphoning off of privately available surplus value has replaced *political dependency*, the market assumes, together with its cybernetic function, an ideological function. The class relationship can assume the anonymous, unpolitical form of wage dependency.'[10] Since the central ideology of bourgeois society is one of the base, dominion-legitimating world pictures lose their function. Religion becomes a private affair and, at the same time, the critique of religion as an institution becomes possible.

We now go on to ask what may be the historical conditions for the possibility of the self-criticism of the social subsystem that is art? As one attempts to answer this question, it is most important to guard against a hasty construction of relationships (of the sort, crisis of art, crisis of bourgeois society[11]). If one takes seriously the idea of the relative autonomy of social subsystems *vis-à-vis* the development of society as a whole, one cannot assert that crises affecting society as a whole will necessarily also manifest themselves as crises within subsystems, or vice versa. To grasp the conditions for the possibility of the self-criticism of the subsystem 'art', it is necessary to construct the history of the subsystem. But this cannot be done by making the history of bourgeois society the basis from which the history of art is to be developed. If one proceeded in this fashion, one would do no more than relate the artistic objectifications to the stages of development of bourgeois society, presupposing these latter to be already known. Knowledge cannot be produced in this fashion, since what is being looked for (the history of art and its social effect) is assumed to be known already. The history of society as a whole would then appear to be the meaning of the subsystems, as it were. In contrast to this idea, the non-synchronism in the development of individual subsystems must be insisted on; which means that the history of bourgeois society can be written only as the synthesis of the non-synchronisms in the development of the various subsystems. The difficulties that beset such an undertaking are manifest. They are alluded to simply to make clear why the subsystem 'art' is seen here as having a history of its own.

If the history of the subsystem 'art' is to be constructed, I feel it is necessary to distinguish between art as an institution (which functions according to the principle of autonomy) and the content of individual works. For it is only this distinction that permits one to understand the history of art in bourgeois society as a history in whose course the divergence between institution and content is eliminated. In bourgeois society (and already before the bourgeoisie also seized political power in the French Revolution), art occupies a special status that is most succinctly referred to as autonomy. 'Autonomous art only establishes itself as bourgeois society develops, the economic and political systems become detached from the cultural, and the traditionalist world pictures which have been undermined by the base-ideology of fair exchange release the arts from their ritual use.'[12] Autonomy here defines the functional mode of the social subsystem 'art': its (relative) independence in the face of demands that it be socially useful.[13] But it must be remembered that the detachment of art from the praxis of life and the accompanying crystallization of a special sphere of experience (i.e., the aesthetic) is not a straight-line development (there are significant counter-trends), and that it cannot be interpreted undialectically (as the coming into its own of art, for example). Rather, the autonomous status of art within bourgeois society is by no means undisputed but is the precarious product of overall social development. That status can always be called into question by society (more precisely, society's rulers) when it seems useful to harness art once more. Not only the extreme example of the fascist politics of art that liquidates autonomy but also the large number of legal proceedings against artists for offences against morality testify to that fact.[14] A distinction is to be made here between such attacks and the force that emanates from the substance of individual works as it manifests itself in the form-content totality and aims at eradicating the distance between work and the praxis of life. Art in bourgeois society lives off the tension between the institutional framework (releasing art from the demand that it fulfil a social function) and the possible political content (*Gehalt*) of individual works. This tension, however, is not stable but subject to a historical dynamics that tends towards its abolition, as we will see.

Habermas has attempted to define these contents as they characterize all art in bourgeois society: 'Art is a sanctuary for the – perhaps merely cerebral – satisfaction of those needs which become quasi-illegal in the material life-process of bourgeois society.' Among these needs, he counts the 'mimetic commerce with nature', 'solidary living with others', and the 'happiness of a communicative experience which is not subject to the imperatives of means-ends rationality and allows as much scope to the imagination as to the spontaneity of behaviour' (*Zur Aktualität Walter Benjamins*, pp. 192f.). Such a perspective has its justification within the framework of a general definition of the function of art in bourgeois society that Habermas means to provide, but it would be problematic in our context because it does not permit us to grasp the historical development of the contents expressed in works. I believe it is necessary to distinguish between the institutional status of art in bourgeois society (apartness of the work of art from the praxis of life) and the contents realized in works of art (these may but need not be residual needs in Habermas's sense). This differentiation permits one to discover the period in which the self-criticism of art is possible. Only with the aid of this distinction can our question concerning the historial conditions for the possibility of the self-criticism of art be answered.

Someone may raise the following objection to the attempt to distinguish between the formal determinacy of art[15] (status of autonomy) and the determinacy of its content (*Gehalt*) in individual works: autonomy itself must be understood as content; apartness from the purposive, rational organization of bourgeois society already implies the claim to a happiness society does not permit. There is undoubtedly some justice in such a view. Formal determinacy is not something external to content; independence *vis-à-vis* the direct demand that purposes be served also accrues to the work whose explicit content is conservative. But precisely this fact should prompt the scholar to distinguish between the status of autonomy that governs the functioning of the individual work on the one hand, and the import of individual works (or groups of works) on the other. Both Voltaire's *contes* and Mallarmé's poems are autonomous works of art. But in varying social contexts and for definable historical social reasons, different uses are made of the scope that the status of autonomy confers on the work of art. As the example of Voltaire shows, autonomy certainly does not preclude the artist's adoption of a political position; what it does limit is the chance of effectiveness.

The proposed distinction between art as an institution (whose functional mode is autonomy) and the import of works makes it possible to sketch an answer to the question concerning the conditions for the possibility of the self-criticism of the social subsystem 'art'. As regards the difficult question concerning the historical crystallization of art as an institution, it suffices if we observe in this context that this process came to a conclusion at about the same time as the struggle of the bourgeoisie for its emancipation. The insights formulated in Kant's and Schiller's aesthetic writings presuppose the completed evolution of art as a sphere that is detached from the praxis of life. We can therefore take it as our point of departure that at the end of the eighteenth century at the latest, art as an institution is already fully developed in the sense specified above. Yet this does not mean that the self-criticism of art has also set in. The Hegelian idea of an end of the period of art was not adopted by the young Hegelians. Habermas explains this by the 'special position which art occupies among the forms of the absolute spirit in the sense that unlike subjectified religion and scientific philosophy, it does not take on tasks in the economic and political system but satisfies residual needs which cannot be met in bourgeois society' (*Zur Aktualität Walter Benjamins*, pp. 193f.). I believe that there are historical reasons why the self-criticism of art cannot occur *as yet*. It is true that the institution of autonomous art is fully developed, but within this institution, there still function contents (*Gehalte*) that are of a thoroughly political character and thus militate against the institutional principle of autonomy. The self-criticism of the social subsystem that is art becomes possible only when the contents also lose their political character, and art wants to be nothing other than art. This stage is reached at the end of the nineteenth century, in Aestheticism.[16]

For reasons connected with the development of the bourgeoisie after its seizure of political power, the tension between the institutional frame and the content of individual works tends to disappear in the second half of the nineteenth century. The apartness from the praxis of life that had always constituted the institutional status of art in bourgeois society now becomes the content of works. Institutional frame and content coincide. The realistic novel of the nineteenth century still serves the self-understanding of the bourgeois. Fiction is the medium of a reflection about the relationship between individual and society. In Aestheticism, this thematics is overshadowed by the ever-increasing concentration the makers of art bring to the medium itself. The failure of Mallarmé's principal literary project, Valéry's almost total lack of productivity over two decades, and Hofmannsthal's Lord Chandos letter are symptoms of a crisis of art.[17] At the moment it has shed all that is alien to it, art necessarily becomes problematic for itself. As institution and content coincide, social ineffectuality stands revealed as the essence of art in bourgeois society, and thus provokes the self-criticism of art. It is to the credit of the historical avant-garde movements that they supplied this self-criticism.

Regarding the discussion of Benjamin's theory of art

In his essay 'The work of art in the age of mechanical reproduction',[18] Walter Benjamin uses the concept of *loss of aura* to describe the decisive changes art underwent in the first quarter of the twentieth century, and attempts to account for that loss by changes in techniques of reproduction. Since up to this point we have derived the conditions for the possibility of the self-criticism of art from the historical unfolding of art (institution and content of works), we need to discuss the suitability of Benjamin's thesis, which explains these conditions as the direct result of changes in the sphere of productive forces.

Benjamin's point of departure is a certain type of relation between work and recipient, which he defines as marked by the presence of an aura.[19] What Benjamin means by this can probably most easily be rendered as unapproachability: the 'unique phenomenon of a distance however close it may be' (*Illuminations*, p. 222). The aura has its origin in cultic ritual, but for Benjamin, the mode of reception marked by the presence of aura remains characteristic also of the no longer sacral art that has developed since the Renaissance. It is not the break between the sacral art of the Middle Ages and the secular art of the Renaissance that Benjamin judges decisive in the history of art, but rather that resulting from the loss of aura. Benjamin traces this break to the change in techniques of reproduction. According to him, reception characterized by the presence of aura requires categories such as uniqueness and authenticity. But these become irrelevant to an art (such as the film, for example) whose very design entails reproduction. It is Benjamin's decisive idea that a change in reproduction techniques brings with it a change in the forms of perception and that this will result in a change in the 'character of art as a whole'. The contemplative reception of the bourgeois individual is to be supplanted by the simultaneously distracted and rationally testing reception of the masses. Instead of being based on ritual, art will now be based on politics.

We will first consider Benjamin's construction of the development of art, then the materialist explanatory scheme he proposed. The period of sacral art during which it is an integral part of ecclesiastical ritual, and the period of autonomous art that develops along with bourgeois society and detaches itself from ritual, creating a specific type of perception (the aesthetic), are summarized by Benjamin in the concept of art with an aura. But the periodization of art he proposes is problematic for several reasons. For Benjamin art with an aura and individual reception (absorption in the object) go hand in hand. But this characterization applies only to autonomous art, certainly not to the sacral art of the Middle Ages (the reception of the sculpture on medieval cathedrals and the mystery plays was collective). Benjamin's construction of history omits the emancipation of art from the sacral, which was the work of the bourgeoisie. One of the reasons for this omission may be that with the *l'art pour l'art* movement and Aestheticism, something like a resacralization (or reritualization) of art did in fact occur.

But there is no similarity between this reversion and the original sacral function of art. Art here is not an element in an ecclesiastical ritual within which a use value is conferred on it. Instead, art generates a ritual. Instead of taking its place within the sacral sphere, art supplants religion. The resacralization of art that occurred in Aestheticism thus presupposes art's total emancipation from the sacral and must under no circumstances be equated with the sacral character of medieval art.

To judge Benjamin's materialist explanation of the change in modes of reception as a result of changes in reproduction techniques it is important to realize that he sketches a second explanation which may prove to have greater explanatory efficacy. The artists of the avant-garde, especially the dadaists, he writes, had already, before film was discovered, attempted to create filmlike effects by the means used in painting. 'The Dadaists attached much less importance to the sales [exchange] value of their work than to its uselessness for contemplative immersion. . . . Their poems are a 'word salad' containing obscenities and every imaginable waste product of language. The same is true of their paintings, on which they mounted buttons and tickets. What they intended and achieved was a relentless destruction of the aura of their creation which they branded as reproductions with the very means of production' (*Illuminations*, pp. 237–8). Here, the loss of aura is not traced to a change in reproduction techniques but to an intent on the part of the makers of art. The change in the 'overall character of art' is no longer the result of technological innovation but mediated by the conscious acts of a generation of artists. To the dadaists, Benjamin ascribes only the role of precursors; they create a 'demand' that only the new technical medium can satisfy. But there is a problem here: how is one to explain this pioneering? Differently expressed, the explanation of the change in the mode of reception by the change in reproduction techniques acquires a different status. It can no longer lay claim to explaining a historical process, but at most to being a hypothesis for the possible *diffusion* of a mode of reception that the dadaists were the first to have intended. One cannot wholly resist the impression that Benjamin wanted to provide an ex post facto materialist foundation for a discovery he owed to his commerce with avant-gardist art, the discovery of the loss of aura. But such an undertaking is problematic, for the decisive break in the development of art, which Benjamin fully grasps in its historical significance, would then be the result of technological change. A direct link is established here between emancipation or emancipatory expectation, and industrial technique.[20] But although emancipation is a process that can certainly provide a field of new possibilities for the satisfaction of human needs, it cannot be conceived of as independent of human consciousness. An emancipation that occurs naturally would be the opposite of emancipation.

At bottom, Benjamin is attempting to transfer, from society as a whole to the partial sphere that is art, the Marxist theorem according to which the development of the productive forces 'shatters' the relations of production.[21] The question arises whether this transfer does not ultimately remain mere analogy. In Marx, the concept 'productive forces' refers to the technological level of development of a given society and includes both the means of production as objectified in machines, and the workers' capacities to use these means. It is questionable whether a concept of artistic productive forces can be derived from this idea, because in artistic production, it would be difficult to subsume under one concept the capacities and abilities of the producer and the stage of development of the material productive and reproductive techniques. So far, artistic production has been a type of simple commodity production (even in late capitalist society), where the material means of production have a relatively minor bearing on the quality of the product. They do, however, have a significance as regards its distribution and effectiveness. That, since the invention of film, distribution techniques have affected production in turn cannot be doubted. The quasi-industrial techniques whose dominance in certain areas is a result of this fact have proved anything but 'shattering', however.[22] What has occurred is the total subordination of contents to profit motives, and a fading of the critical potencies of works in favour of a training in consumer attitudes (which extends to the most intimate interhuman relations).[23]

Brecht, in whose *Threepenny Lawsuit* we hear echoes of Benjamin's theorem concerning the destruction of art and its aura by new reproduction techniques is more cautious than Benjamin: 'This apparatus *can be used* better than almost anything else to supersede the old kind of untechnical, anti-technical 'glowing art, with its religious links.'[24] In contrast to Benjamin, who tends to ascribe emancipatory quality to the new technical means (film) as such, Brecht emphasizes that certain possibilities inhere in the technical means; but he suggests that the development of such possibilities depends on the way they are used.

If, for the reasons mentioned, it is a problematical undertaking to transfer the concept of productive forces from the sphere of overall social analysis to that of art, the same holds true of the concept of production relations, if only because in Marx, it unambiguously refers to the totality of social relations that govern work and the distribution of the products of work. But with art as an *institution*, we have already introduced a concept that refers to the conditions under which art is produced, distributed, and received. In bourgeois society, the salient characteristic of this institution is that the products that function within it remain (relatively) free from any pressure that they serve social purposes. It is Benjamin's achievement to have defined, by the concept of aura, the type of relation between work and recipient that evolves in the institution of art in bourgeois society. Two essential insights come together here: first, that it is not in and of themselves that works of art have their effect but rather that this effect is decisively determined by the institution within which the works function; second, that modes of reception must be based in social history: the perception of aura, for example, in the bourgeois individual. What Benjamin discovers is form as a determinant in art (*Formbestimmtheit*, in the sense Marx gives the concept); here, we also have what is materialist in his approach. But the theorem according to which reproduction techniques destroy art that has an aura is a pseudomaterialist explanatory model.

A final comment regarding the matter of periodization in the development of art: above, we criticized Benjamin's periodization because he blurs the break between medieval-sacral and modern, secular art. Given the break between art with and without aura as elaborated by Benjamin, one arrives at the methodologically important insight that periodization in the development of art must be looked for in the sphere of art as institution, not in the sphere of the transformation of the content of individual works. This implies that periodization in the history of art cannot simply follow the periodization in the history of social formations and their phases of development but that it must be the task of a science of culture (*Kulturwissenschaft*) to bring into view the large-scale changes in the development of its subject. Only in this way can cultural science make an authentic contribution to the investigation of the history of bourgeois society. But where that history is taken as an already known reference system and used as such in the historical investigation of partial social spheres, cultural science degenerates into a procedure of establishing correspondences. The cognitive value of such an enterprise must be rated as low.

To summarize: the historical conditions for the possibility of self-criticism of the social subsystem 'art' cannot be elucidated with the aid of Benjamin's theorem; instead, these conditions must be derived from the disappearance of that tension that is constitutive for art in bourgeois society, the tension between art as institution and the contents of individual works. In this effort, it is important not to contrast art and society as two mutually exclusive spheres. For both the (relative) insulation of art from demands that it serve purposes, and the development of contents are social phenomena (determined by the development of society as a whole).

If we criticize Benjamin's thesis according to which the technical reproducibility of the work of art imposes a different mode of reception (one marked by the absence of aura), this does not mean that we deny the general importance of such technical development. But two points must be made: technical development must not be understood as an independent variable, for it is itself dependent on overall social development. Second, the decisive turn in the development of art in bourgeois society must not be traced monocausally to the development of technical reproduction techniques. With these two provisos, one may summarize the importance that technical development has for the evolution of the fine arts in these terms: because the advent of photography makes possible the precise mechanical reproduction of reality, the mimetic function of the fine arts withers.[25] But the limits of this explanatory model become clear when one calls to mind that it cannot be transferred to literature. For in literature, there is no technical innovation that could have produced an effect comparable to that of photography in the fine arts. When Benjamin understands the rise of *l'art pour l'art* as a reaction to the advent of photography,[26] the explanatory model is surely being strained. *L'art pour l'art* theory is not simply the reaction to a new means of reproduction (however substantially it may have promoted the tendency towards the independence of the fine arts) but is the answer to the tendency in fully evolved bourgeois society for works of art to lose their social function (we characterized this development as the loss of the political content of individual works.) There is no intent to deny the significance that changed techniques of reproduction had for the development of art; but the latter cannot be derived from the former. The evolution of art as a distinct subsystem that began with *l'art pour l'art* and was carried to its conclusion in Aestheticism must be seen in connection with the tendency towards the division of labour underway in bourgeois society. The fully evolved, distinct subsystem 'art' is simultaneously one whose individual products tend to no longer take on any social function.

By way of a general formulation, it is probably impossible to go safely further than this: the process by which the social subsystem 'art' evolves into a wholly distinct entity is part and parcel of the developmental logic of bourgeois society. As the division of labour becomes more general, the artist also turns into a specialist. This trend, which reaches its apogee in Aestheticism has been most adequately reflected by Valéry. Within the general tendency towards ever-increasing specialization, it may be assumed that various subsystems impinge on each other. The development of photography, for example, affects painting (withering of the mimetic function). But such reciprocal influences among social subsystems should not be given excessive weight. Although important, especially in explaining non-synchronies in the evolution of the various arts, they cannot be made the 'cause' of that process in which the various arts generate what is specifically theirs. That process is a function of the overall social development to which it belongs and cannot be adequately understood by a cause-effect scheme.[27]

The self-criticism of the social subsystem 'art' to which the avant-garde movements attained has been seen so far primarily in connection with the progressive division of labour that is so characteristic of the development of bourgeois society. The overall social tendency towards the articulation of subsystems and a concurrent specialization of function are being understood as the developmental law to which the sphere of art is also subject. This completes the sketch of the objective aspect of the process. But how the evolution of distinct subsystems is reflected by the subjects must still be inquired into. It seems to me that the concept of a shrinkage of experience can aid us here. If experience is defined as a bundle of perceptions and reflections that have been worked through, it becomes possible to characterize the effect of the crystallization of subsystems resulting from the progressive division of labour as a shrinking of experience. Such shrinkage does not mean that the subject who has now become specialist in a subsystem no longer perceives or reflects. In the sense proposed here, the concept means that specialist 'experiences' can no longer be translated back into the praxis of life. The aesthetic experience as a specific experience, such as Aestheticism developed it, would in its pure form be the mode in which the shrinking of experience as defined above expresses itself in the sphere of art. Differently formulated: aesthetic experience is the positive side of that process by which the social subsystem 'art' defines itself as a distinct sphere. Its negative side is the artist's loss of any social function.

As long as art interprets reality or provides satisfaction of residual needs only in the imagination, it is, though detached from the praxis of life, still related to it. It is only in Aestheticism that the tie to society is finally severed. The break with society (it is the society of imperialism) constitutes the centre of the works of Aestheticism. Here lies the reason for Adorno's repeated attempts to vindicate it.[28] The intention of the avant-gardist may be defined as the attempt to direct towards the practical the aesthetic experience (which rebels against the praxis of life) that Aestheticism developed. What most strongly conflicts with the means-ends rationality of bourgeois society is to become life's organizing principle.

Notes

1. TH.W. ADORNO, *Ästhetische Theorie*, ed. Gretel Adorno and R. Tiedemann (Frankfurt: Suhrkamp, 1970), p. 532.

2. On the critique of historicism, see H.-G. GADAMER, 'The naiveté of so-called historicism consists in the fact that it does not undertake this reflection and in trusting to its own methodological approach forgets its own historicality' *Truth and Method*, p. 266–7. See also the analysis of Ranke by H.R. JAUSS, 'Geschichte der Kunst und Historie' in *Literatureschichte als Provokation*, ed., H.R. Jauss (Frankfurt: Suhrkamp, 1970), p 222–6. (A translation of this essay appears as chapter 2 in H.R. JAUSS, *Toward an Aesthetic of Reception*, trans. T. Bahti, intro. Paul de Man (Minneapolis: Univ. of Minnesota Press, 1982).

3. K. MARX, *Grundrisse*, trans. Martin Nicolaus (New York: Random House, 1973), p. 105.

4. The concept of the historic avant-garde movements used here applies primarily to Dadaism and early Surrealism but also and equally to the Russian avant-garde after the October Revolution. Partly significant differences between them notwithstanding, a common feature of all these movements is that they do not reject individual artistic techniques and procedures of earlier art but reject that art in its entirety, thus bringing about a radical break with tradition. In their most extreme manifestations, their primary target is the art institution as it has developed in bourgeois society. With certain limitations that would have to be determined through concrete analyses, this is also true of Italian Futurism and German Expressionism.

Although cubism does not pursue the same intent, it calls into question the system of representation with its linear perspective, that had prevailed since the Renaissance. For this reason, it is part of the historic avant-garde movements, although it does not share their basic tendency (sublation of art in the praxis of life).

The concept 'historic avant-garde movements' distinguishes these from all those neo-avant-gardist attempts that are characteristic for Western Europe and the United States during the fifties and sixties. Although the neo-avant-gardes proclaim the same goals as the representatives of the historic avant-garde movements to some extent, the demand that art be reintegrated in the praxis of life within the existing society can no longer be seriously made after the failure of avant-gardist intentions. If an artist sends a stove pipe to an exhibit today, he will never attain the intensity of protest of Duchamp's Ready-Mades. On the contrary, whereas Duchamp's *Urinoir* is meant to destroy art as an institution (including its specific organizational forms as museums and exhibits), the finder of the stove pipe asks that his 'work' be accepted by the museum. But this means that the avant-gardist protest has turned into its opposite.

5. See, among others, Victor Shklovsky, 'Art as Technique' (1916), in *Russian Formalist Criticism. Four Essays*, trans. Lee T. Lemon and Marion J. Reis (Lincoln: Univ. of Nebraska Press, 1965).

6. Reference to and comments on the historical connection between Formalism and avant-garde (more precisely, Russian Futurism) in V. Ehrlich, *Russian Formalism* ('s Gravenhage: Mouton, 1955). On Shklovsky, see Renate Lachmann, 'Die "Verfremdung" und das "neue Sehen" bei Viktor Sklovskij', in *Poetica*, 3 (1970), pp. 226–49. But K. Chvatik's interesting remark that there exists 'an inner reason for the close connection between structuralism and avant-garde, a *methodological* and *theoretical* reason' (*Strukturalismus und Avantgarde* (Munich: Hanser, 1970), p. 21) is not developed in the book. Krystyna Pomorska, *Russian Formalist Theory and its Poetic Ambience* (The Hague/Paris: Mouton, Slavistic Printings and Reprintings, 82, 1968) contents herself with a listing of elements Futurism and Formalism have in common.

7. On this, see the important comments by Althusser in Louis Althusser and Etienne Balibar, *Reading Capital*, trans. Ben Brewster (New York: Pantheon Books, 1970), which have hardly been discussed as yet in Germany.

8. See also H. Plessner, 'Über die gesellschaftlichen Bedingungen der modernen Malerei', in *Diesseits der Utopie. Ausgewählte Beiträge zur Kultursoziologie*, ed. H. Plessiers, (Frankfurt: Suhrkamp, 1974), pp. 107, 118.

9. Th. W. Adorno, *Versuch über Wagner* (Munich/Zürich: Knaur, 1964), p. 135.

10. J. Habermas, *Legitimation Crisis* (Boston: Beacon Press, 1975), pp. 25–6.

11. F. Tomberg's 'Negation affirmativ. Zur ideologischen Funktion der modernen Kunst im Unterricht', in Tomberg, *Politische Ästhetik Vorträge und Aufsätze*, ed.

F. Tomberg (Darmstadt/Neuwied: Luchterhand, 1973) may be considered a hasty attempt to create a tie-in between the development of art and that of society, for it is not backed by analyses of the subject. Tomberg constructs a connection between the 'worldwide rebellion against the intellectually limited bourgeois master' whose 'most characteristic symptom' is the resistance of the Vietnamese people against 'North American imperialism', and the end of 'modern art'. This means the end of the period of so-called modern art as an art of creative subjectivity and the total negation of social reality. Where it continues to go on, it must turn into farce. Art can be credible today only if it engages itself in the present revolutionary process – even though this may temporarily be at the price of a loss of form' (TOMBERG, *Politische Ästhetik*, pp. 59f.). The end of modern art here is merely a moral postulate; it is not derived from its development. If, in the same essay, an ideological function is ascribed to commerce with modern art (since it comes out of the experience of 'the unchangeability of the social structure', commerce with it promotes this illusion, TOMBERG *Politische Ästhetik*, p. 58), this contradicts the claim that we have come to the end of the 'period of modern art so-called'. In another essay in the same volume, the thesis of the loss of function of art is affirmed, and we read this conclusion: 'The beautiful world which must now be created is not the reflected world but society as it really is' (Über den gesellschaftlichen Gehalt ästhetischer Kategorien,' TOMBERG, *Politische Ästhetik*, p. 89).

12. J. HABERMAS, 'Bewusstmachende oder rettende Kritik – die Aktualität Walter Benjamins', in *Zur Aktualität Walter Benjamins* ed. S. Unseld (Frankfurt: Suhrkamp, 1972), p. 190.

13. Habermas defines autonomy as 'independence of works of art *vis-à-vis* demands for their use outside art' (*Zur Aktucalität Walter Benjamins*, p. 190), I prefer to speak of social demands for its use because this avoids having the definiendum enter the definition.

14. On this, see K. HEITMANN, *Der Immoralismus-Prozess gegen die französische Literatur im 19. Jahrhundert* (Bad Homburg: Athenäum, 1970).

15. The concept 'formal determinacy' (*Formbestimmtheit*) does not mean here that form is a component of the statement but the determination by the institutional frame within which works of art function. The concept is thus used in the same sense as when Marx speaks of the determination of goods by the commodity form.

16. G. Mattenklott sketches a political critique of the primacy of the formal in Aestheticism: 'form is the fetish which has been transplanted into the political sphere. The total indeterminacy of its contents leaves open the door to any and all ideological accretion' (*Bilderdienst. Ästhetische Opposition bei Beardsley und George* (Munich, 1970), p. 227). This critique contains the correct insight into the political problematic of Aestheticism. What it fails to see is that it is in Aestheticism that art in bourgeois society becomes conscious of itself. Adorno did see this: 'But there is something liberating in the consciousness which bourgeois art finally attains of itself as bourgeois, the moment it takes itself seriously, as does the reality which it is not' 'Der Artist als Stratthalter', in ADORNO, *Noten zur Literatur I* (Bibliothek Suhrkamp 47), p. 188. On the problem of Aestheticism, also see H.C. SEEBA, *Kritik des ästhetischen Menschen. Hermeneutik und Moral in Hofmannsthals Der Tor und der Tod.*' (Bad Homburg/ Berlin/Zürich, 1970). For Seeba, the relevance of Aestheticism is to be found in the circumstance that 'the actual "aesthetic" principle of fictional patterns which are intended to facilitate the understanding of reality but make more difficult its direct, imageless experience leads to that loss of reality from which Claudio already suffers' (SEEBA, *Kritik des ästhetischen Menschen*). The

shortcoming of this ingenious critique of Aestheticism is that in opposing the 'principle of fictional patterns' (which can surely function as an instrument of cognition of reality), it resorts to a 'direct, imageless experience' that is itself rooted in Aestheticism. So that one element of Aestheticism is being criticized here by another! If one listens to authors such as Hofmannsthal, it will be impossible to understand the loss of reality as a result of an addiction to images. Rather, that loss will have to be seen as the socially conditioned cause of that addiction. In other words, Seeba's critique of Aestheticism remains largely rooted in what it proposes to criticize. Further, P. Bürger, 'Zur ästhetisierenden Wirklichkeitsdarstellung bei Proust, Valéry und Sartre', in *Vom Ästhetizismus zum Nouveau Roman. Versuche kritischer Literaturwissenschaft*, ed. P. Bürger (Frankfurt, 1974).

17. On this, see W. JENS, *Statt einer Literaturgeschichte* (Pfullingen, 1962), the chapter 'Der Mensch und die Dinge. Die Revolution der deutschen Prosa', pp. 109–33.

18. In W. BENJAMIN, 'The work of art in the age of mechanical reproduction', in *Illuminations* (New York: Schocken Books, 1969), pp. 217–51. Adorno's letter to Benjamin, dated 18 March 1936 (reprinted in TH. W. ADORNO, *Über Walter Benjamin*, ed R. Tiedemann (Frankfurt: Suhrkamp, 1970), pp. 126–34 is especially important in the critique of Benjamin's theses. R. TIEDEMANN, *Studien zur Philosophie Walter Benjamins* (Frankfurt: Suhrkamp, 1965), pp. 87ff, argues from a position close to Adorno's.

19. See B. LINDER, '"Natur-Geschichte" – Geschichtsphilosophie und Welterfahrung in Benjamins Schriften', *Text + Kritik*, Nos. 31/32 (October 1971), pp. 41–58.

20. Here, we see Benjamin in the context of an enthusiasm for technique that was characteristic during the 1920s of both liberal intellectuals (some references on this in H. LETHEN, *Neue Sachlichkeit 1924–1932* (Stuttgart: Metzler, 1970), pp. 58ff) and the revolutionary Russian avant-garde (an example is B. ARVATOV, *Kunst und Produktion*, ed., trans. H. Günther and Karla Hielscher (Munich: Hanser, 1972).

21. This explains why Benjamin's theses were interpreted by the extreme left as a revolutionary theory of art. See H. LETHEN, 'Walter Benjamins Thesen zu einer' materialistischen Kunsttheorie"', in LETHEN, *Neue Sachlichkeit*, pp. 127–39.

22. Pulp literature is produced by teams of authors, as is well known. There is a division of labour and the work is put out according to criteria that are dictated by the tastes of groups of addressees.

23. This is also the point at which Adorno's critique of Benjamin sets in. See his essay 'Über den Fetischcharakter in der Musik und die Regression des Hörens', in TH W. Adorno, *Dissonanzen. Musik in der verwalteten Welt* (Göttingen: Vandenhoeck 29/29a, 1969), pp. 9–45, which is an answer to Benjamin's essay. See also CHRISTA BÜRGER, *Textanalyse als Ideologiekritik. Zur Rezeption zeitgenössischer Unterhaltungsliteratur* (Frankfurt: Athenäum, 1973), ch. I. 2.

24. B. BRECHT, *The Threepenny Lawsuit* (1931), in John Willett, ed, trans., *Brecht on Theatre. The development of an aesthetic*, (New York: Hill and Wang, 1966), p. 48.

25. This is the reason for the difficulties encountered by attempts to ground an aesthetic theory today in the concept of reflection. Such attempts are historically conditioned by the development of art in bourgeois society, more precisely, by the 'withering' of the mimetic function of art that sets in with the avant-garde. The attempt to provide a sociological explanation of modern

painting is undertaken by A. GEHLEN, *Zeit-Bilder. Zur Soziologie und Ästhetik der modernen Malerei* (Frankfurt/Bonn, 1960). But the social conditions of the development of modern painting as listed by Gehlen remain rather general. In addition to the invention of photography, he mentions the enlargement of living space and the end of the nexus between painting and the natural sciences (GEHLEN, *Zeit-Bilder*).

26. 'With the advent of the first truly revolutionary means of reproduction, photography, simultaneously with the rise of socialism, art sensed the approaching crisis which has become evident a century later. At the time, art reacted with the doctrine of *l'art pour l'art*, that is, with a theology of art' ('The work of art in the age of mechanical reproduction', p. 224).

27. See P. FRANCASTEL, who summarizes his investigations on art and technique as follows: 1. 'There is no contradiction between the development of certain forms of contemporary art and the forms scientific and technical activity takes in contemporary society'; 2. 'the development of the arts in the present obeys a specific aesthetic developmental principle' (*Art et technique aux XIXe et XXe siècles* (Bibl. Meditations 16. 1964), pp. 221f.).

28. See TH W. ADORNO, 'George und Hofmannsthal. Zum Briefwechsel: 1891–1906 in *Prismen, Kulturkritik und Gesellschaft* (Munich: dtv 159, 1963), pp. 190–231; and Adorno, 'Der Artist als Stratthalter,' in *Noten zur Literatur I*, pp. 173–93.

8 Beyond the Cave: Demystifying the Ideology of Modernism*
(1975)

FREDRIC JAMESON

Fredric Jameson (b. 1934) is William A. Lane Jnr Professor of Comparative Literature at Duke University, North Carolina. He is an editor of the journal *Social Text*. His publications include *Marxism and Form* (1971), *The Political Unconscious* (1981) and *Postmodernism* (1991).

The two main coordinates of Jameson's thinking – the early Marxism of Georg Lukács, and the theoretical avant-gardes of latter-day France – are both conspicuous here, as also are his characteristic reach for synoptic understanding and his major preoccupation: the crisis of 'knowability' in the culture of the late-capitalist metropolis. 'Modernism' here is both the familiar period-style and the dominant ideology of organized literary studies. Jameson seeks to displace the latter, to understand the former and its alien predecessors in terms other than its own, and thus to turn our symptomatic 'boredom' to (self-) critical account. Drawing on the analysis of signifying regimes proposed by Deleuze and Guattari, he reconstructs the sequence of pre-modern, realist and modernist cultures as a history of contrasted relationships to the 'coding' of the world, and ends with a commentary on the antinomies of artistic expression and representation in our own time.

There is a novel by Iris Murdoch in which one of the characters – an elderly philosophy professor – reminds us of Plato's conclusions, in the *Phaedrus*, on the use and misuse of language. 'Words,' Socrates is there supposed in essence to have said, 'words can't be moved from place to place and retain their meaning. Truth is communicated from a particular speaker to a particular listener.'[1]

* Reprinted from Fredric Jameson, *The Ideologies of Theory: Essays 1971–1986*, vol. 2: *The Syntax of History* (London: Routledge, 1989), pp. 115–32.

It is an odd remark for a novelist to have one of her characters make. For, of course, if it is true, there could never be such a thing as a novel in the first place. Literature is presumably the preeminent example of words that *can* be moved from place to place without losing their meaning. What else can possibly be meant by the idea of the autonomy of the work of art – one of the great terroristic fetishes of present-day American literary criticism – if it be not this essential *portability* of all literary language? So what we want to ask ourselves first and foremost is not whether the work of art is or is not autonomous, but rather, how it *gets to be* autonomous; how language – in context, in situation – worldly language – gradually manages to separate itself out, to organize itself into relatively self-sufficient bodies of words which can then be grasped by groups and individuals widely divided from one another in space and in time, and by social class or by culture.

Now, although I do not intend here to attempt an answer to the aesthetic and philosophical problem I have just raised – that of the autonomy of the work of art – I think it may be instructive, as a way of leading into my own subject, to tick off a few of the possible solutions to this problem, by way of seeing whether they do not all lead back – however deviously and indirectly – to the social and historical situations that form the absolute horizon of our individual existences.

For it is clear that if you begin by interrogating the origins of a given form, if you take as your object of study, in other words, not the present-day autonomy of a given form or genre, but rather its *autonomization*, you will always end up observing the emergence of such forms from social life in general and everyday language in particular; and this is so whether, with Fischer and Lukács,[2] on the one hand, or with the Cambridge school, on the other, you seek the moment when artistic activity differentiates itself from the unspecialized ritualistic world of primitive social life; or whether, with a writer like André-Jolles, in his *Simple Forms*, you seek the key to some specific genre in a determinate speech act within a determinate social situation – thus, for instance, you might seek to understand how the maxim or epigram separated itself out of the conversational life of a certain type of salon society. In both of these ways of studying autonomization, the worldliness of form is of necessity reaffirmed.

But it may be objected that the forms or genres are only initially a part of the practical world of everyday social life: once differentiated from it, they lose all traces of their origins and become in fact quite independent and autonomous linguistic products in their own right. Yet this is to forget, it seems to me, that genre is itself a social institution, something like a social contract in which we agree to respect certain rules about the appropriate use of the piece of language in question. Far from proving the autonomy of the work of art, therefore, the very existence of the generic convention explains how an illusion of autonomy could come into being, for the generic situation formalizes and thus absorbs into the formal structure worldly elements that would otherwise be passed on in the work of art itself, as content.

Even here, however, I imagine that a final position is possible, one which, while admitting the social nature of the generic situations, declares that the old fashioned genres have ceased in our time to exist and that we no longer consume a tragedy, a comedy, a satire, but rather literature in general in the form of each work, the Book of the world, the text as an impersonal process. The answer here would be, I think, that at that point all the generic situations have been telescoped into one, that of the consumption of Literature itself, which then becomes the hobby of a small group – I won't really call us an élite – centered in the universities and in a few major cultural centers.

What I really want to stress, however, is the way in which our initial question seems to have come full circle. The idea of the autonomy of the work of art – which at first seemed a proud boast and a value to be defended – now begins to look a little shameful, like a symptom into whose pathology one would want to inquire more closely. At this point, then, we are tempted to ask, not whether literary works are autonomous, nor even how art manages to lift itself above its immediate social situation and to free itself from its social context, but rather what kind of society it can be in which works of art have become autonomous to this degree, in which the older social and cultic functions of literature have become so unfamiliar as to have made us forgetful (and this in the strong, Heideggerian sense of the term) of the power and influence that a socially living art can exercise.

A question like this evidently demands that we are able, in some way, to get outside of ourselves and of our own local tastes and literary values, and to see all that with something like a Brechtian estrangement-effect, as though they were the values and the institutions of an utterly alien culture. Were we able to do so, I suggest that we would suddenly become aware of the degree to which a coherent and quite systematic ideology – I will call it the ideology of modernism – imposes its conceptual limitations on our aesthetic thinking and our taste and judgments, and in its own way projects an utterly distorted model of literary history – which is evidently one of the privileged experiences through which we as scholars at least have access to History itself.

When one is the prisoner of such ideology – or *Weltanschauung*, if you prefer – or paradigm or epistémé – how could one ever become aware of it in the first place, let alone patiently undo – or deconstruct – its complicated machinery, through which hitherto we have alone learned to see reality?

I suppose that the first step in doing so is to take an inventory of the things excluded from this ideology, and to make ourselves more acutely aware of the kinds of literary works explicitly rejected from the machine (and which may in many cases not even be classified as Literature at all) such as mass or media culture, lower-class or working-class culture, but also those few surviving remnants of genuine popular or peasant culture from the precapitalist period, and in particular of course the oral storytelling of tribal or primitive societies. Yet to say so is not necessarily to endorse the new-worlds-to-conquer imperialism that has been the spirit of so much of recent Western thought in the cultural realm, for it is not so much a question now of feeling satisfaction at the infinite elasticity and receptivity of our own cultural outlook, but rather of locating the ultimate structural limits of that outlook and coming to terms with its negation, with what it cannot absorb without losing its own identity and wholly transforming itself. For we all know that capitalism is the first genuinely global culture and has never renounced its mission to assimilate everything alien into itself – whether that be the African masks of the time of Picasso, or the little red books of Mao Zedong on sale in your corner drugstore.

No, what I have in mind is a more difficult process than that, one that can be completed successfully only by a painful realization of the ethnocentrism in which we are all, in one way or another, caught. And to put it in its most exaggerated and outrageous form, I will suggest that our first task is not to persuade ourselves of the validity for us of these alien or primitive art forms, but rather to attempt to measure the whole extent of our boredom with them and our almost visceral refusal of what can only be (to our own jaded tastes) the uninventive simplicity and repetition, the liturgical slowness and predictability, or else the senseless and equally monotonous episodic meandering, of an oral tradition that has neither verbal density and opacity, nor psychological subleties and violence to offer us. Not interest or fascination, therefore, but rather that sense of dreariness with which we come to the end of our own world and observe with a certain self-protective lassitude that there is nothing for us on the other side of the boundary – this is the unpleasant condition in which, I suggest, we come to the realization of the Other which is at the same time a dawning knowledge of ourselves as well.

Now I want to borrow a concept from another discipline in order to explain why this should be so, and, perhaps, indeed, to suggest what might be done about it. This is the concept of repression, which, like so much else in Freud's language, is drawn from the political realm, to which, in the medieval languages, its original purely descriptive sense had already been applied. Yet the notion of repression is by no means so dramatic as it might at first appear, for in psychoanalytic theory, whatever its origins, and whatever the final effect of repression on the personality, its symptoms and its mechanisms are quite the opposite of

171

violence, and are nothing quite so much as looking away, forgetting, ignoring, losing interest. Repression is reflexive, that is, it aims not only at removing a particular object from consciousness, but also and above all, at doing away with the traces of that removal as well, at repressing the very memory of the intent to repress. This is the sense in which the boredom I evoked a moment ago may serve as a powerful hermeneutic instrument: it marks the spot where something painful is buried, it invites us to reawaken all the anguished hesitation, the struggle of the subject to avert his or her eyes from the thought with which brutal arms insist in confronting him.

Now, of course, I will make only metaphoric use of this concept, for it cannot be any part of my intention here to assess the possibility of some consequent Freudo-Marxism or to come to terms with the relationship of Freud's own object of study, namely sexuality, to the cultural phenomena that concern us. I would only observe that Georg Lukács's classic analysis of ideology in *History and Class Consciousness* (1923) is very consistent with the description of repression we have just given. Lukács there draws the consequences from his idea that the fundamental category of Marxism is that of Totality, or, in other words, that the fundamental strength of Marxist thinking is its ability – indeed its determination – to make all the connections and to put back together all those separate fields – economics, say, and literature – that middle-class thought had been so intent on keeping apart. It follows, then, that bourgeois ideology, or, in our present terms, the middle-class method of repressing reality, is not so much an affair of distortion and of false consciousness in the sense of outright cynicism or lies (although, obviously there is also enough of that in our discipline to satisfy the most demanding observer), but rather, primarily and constitutively, of leaving out, of strategic omissions, lapses, a kind of careful preliminary preparation of the raw material such that certain questions will never arise in the first place.

This, then, is the sense in which an exploration of repression or of ideological bias in literary criticism demands an attention to the outer and constitutive limits of the discipline just as much as to the positive acts committed on a daily basis in its name and within its confines. I cannot, however, resist an appeal to a very different kind of authority than that of Lukács, and since I have already pronounced the word, I will agree that this problem is on the whole coterminous with what relatively right-wing and theological currents in both France and Germany today have decided once again to call hermeneutics, that is, the whole science of interpretation, the problematics of the encounter with the alien text – whether from the distant past or from other cultures. I will only point out that my own appeal to boredom is not essentially different from that of Hans-Georg Gadamer, Heidegger's principal disciple and the central figure in German hermeneutics, to what he quite deliberately and provocatively calls prejudice, *Vorurteile*,[3] and what we might very quickly describe as the class habits and ideological thought-modes inherent in our own concrete social and historical situation. To say that we understand what is other than ourselves through such *Vorurteile*, or situational prejudice, is therefore to reaffirm the dual character of all understanding and to remind ourselves that it can never take place in the void, 'objectively' or out of situation, that all contact with otherness is also at one and the same time of necessity a return upon ourselves and our own particular culture and class affiliation that cannot but implicitly or explicitly call the latter into question.

Now let us try to see what this would mean in a practical sense, as a way of assessing the organization of literature as a field of study. I have suggested elsewhere that our habit of studying individual writers one by one, in a kind of respectful stylistic isolation, was a very useful strategy in preventing genuinely social and historical problems from intruding into literary study.[4] The position I want to defend here is not unlike this one, but for whole periods rather than individual writers. I suggest that the ghettoization of primitive storytelling is an excellent example of this, but the ambiguity of the word 'myth,' as loosely brandished in our discipline today, makes primitive storytelling a fairly complicated example to use. Our own myth school – or rather, what it might be clearer to call archetypal criticism – obviously has in mind a very different object of study, and a very different kind of textual satisfaction, than that afforded by the primitive storytellers of, say, the Bororo Encyclopaedia. Indeed, whatever the ultimate usefulness of the intellectual brilliance invested in Claude Lévi-Strauss's *Mythologiques*, those four volumes will at least have had the effect of giving us a feeling for those genuinely episodic, molecular strings of events in which the Jungian hero, wearing all his archetypal masks, must inevitably find himself structurally ill at ease.

So we set aside the problem of myth for one much closer to home, which indeed involves that literature most explicitly repudiated by the practice and the values of the ideology of modernism: I refer to realism itself. And perhaps my point about boredom may now make a little more sense to you, when you think, on the one hand, of the inevitable tediousness for us today, programmed by the rapid gearshifts of television, of the old endless three-decker novels; and when, on the other hand, you heave a sigh at the thought of yet another rehearsal of the tiresome polemics waged in the name of realism, to accept the terms of which is perhaps already to find yourself compromised in advance.

Now obviously I share that feeling too to some degree, and am not interested in making some puritanical attack on modernism in the name of the older realistic values; I simply want to underscore the limits of the ideology of modernism in accounting for the great realistic works, and to suggest that to prove Dickens was really a symbolist, Flaubert the first modernist, Balzac a myth-maker, and George Eliot some Victorian version of Henry James if not even of Dostoevsky, is an intellectually dishonest operation that skirts all the real issues.

Modern literary theory has in fact given us what are essentially two irreconcilable accounts of realism. On the one hand, there are the classical apologias for this narrative mode, most dramatically associated with the position of Georg Lukács, but of which Erich Auerbach provides a less controversial and perhaps more patient documentation. For this position, the realistic mode – like the sonata form in music, or the conquest of perspective in painting – is one of the most complex and vital realizations of Western culture, to which it is indeed, like those other two artistic phenomena I mentioned, well-nigh unique. Any reader of Auerbach's *Mimesis* will have retained a vivid picture of the way in which realism slowly takes shape over many centuries by a progressive enlargement and refinement of literary techniques – from the unlimbering of epic sentence structure and the development of narrative perspective to the great plots of the nineteenth-century novels – an expansion of the literary and linguistic recording apparatus in such a way as to make ever larger areas of social and individual reality accessible to us. Here realism is shown to have epistemological truth, as a privileged mode of knowing the world we live in and the lives we lead in it; and for a position of this kind, of course, the modern dissatisfaction or boredom with realism cannot be expected to be taken very seriously.

Yet when we turn to that dissatisfaction itself and to the repudiation of realism in the name of modernism and in the interests of the latter's own developing apologia, we may well find that this other position is by no means dismissed as easily as all that. For the ideologues of modernism[5] do not indeed seek to refute the Lukács–Auerbach defense of the realistic mode in its own terms, which are primarily aesthetic and cognitive; rather they sense its weak link to be preaesthetic, part and parcel of its basic philosophical presuppositions. Thus, the target of their attack becomes the very concept of reality itself which is implied by the realistic aesthetic as Lukács or Auerbach outline it, the new position suggesting that what is intolerable for us today, aesthetically, about the so-called old-fashioned realism is to be accounted for by the inadmissible philosophical and metaphysical view of the world which underlies it and which it in its turn reinforces. The objection is thus, clearly, a critique of something like an *ideology of realism*, and charges that realism, by suggesting that representation is possible, and by encouraging an aesthetic of mimesis or imitation, tends to perpetuate a preconceived notion of some external reality to be imitated, and indeed, to foster a belief in the existence of some such common-sense everyday ordinary shared secular reality in the first place. Yet the great discoveries of modern science – relativity and the uncertainty principle – the movement in modern philosophy toward theories of models and various linguistic dimensions of reality, present-day French investigations of the category of representation itself – above all, however, the sheer accumulated weight and habit of the great modern works of art from the cubists and Joyce all the way to Beckett and Andy Warhol – all these things tend to confirm the idea that there is something quite naive, in a sense quite profoundly *un*realistic, and in the full sense of the word ideological, about the notion that reality is out there simply, quite objective and independent of us, and that knowing it involves the relatively unproblematical process of getting an adequate picture of it into our own heads.

Now I have to confess that I find both these positions – the defence of realism just as much as the denunciation of it – equally convincing, equally persuasive, equally true; so that, even though they would appear to be logically incompatible, I cannot persuade myself that they are as final as they look. But before I suggest a resolution that has seemed satisfactory to me, I want to remind you again of the reason we brought the subject up in the first place. The quarrel we have evoked is more fundamental, it seems to me, than a mere difference in aesthetic theories and positions (or else, if you prefer, such mere differences are perhaps themselves more fundamental than we have been accustomed to think): to be sure, in one sense, they simply correspond to differences in taste – it is clear that Lukács and Auerbach, for whatever reasons of background and upbringing and the like, deep down really don't like modern art. But again: perhaps what we call taste is not so simple either. I want to suggest that these two conflicting aesthetic positions correspond in the long run to two quite different cultures: there was a culture of realism, that of the nineteenth century – and a few of its inhabitants still survive here and there, native informants who provide us with very useful reports and testimony about its nature and values – and there is today a different culture altogether, that of modernism. Alongside these two, as we suggested earlier, there is yet a third kind, namely what we called in the most general way primitive or at least precapitalist, and whose products – incomprehensible to both modernist and realist aesthetics alike – we call myths or oral tales. So the limits of our own personal tastes have brought us to the point where we can see our need, not to pick and choose and assimilate selected objects from the older aesthetics or cultures into our own, but rather to step outside our own culture – outside the culture of modernism – entirely and to grasp its relationship to the others and its difference from them by means of some vaster historical and supracultural model.

Before I suggest one, however, I have an obligation, even in the most sketchy way, to complete my account of the quarrel between the realists and the modernists: what both leave out, you will already have guessed, is simply history itself. Both positions are completely ahistorical, and this in spite of the fact that *Mimesis* is a history, one of the few great contemporary literary histories we possess, and in spite of the fact, also, that Lukács is a Marxist (that the modernists are ahistorical will probably be less surprising, since after all by and large that is exactly what they set out to be). Briefly, I would suggest that realism – but also that desacralized, postmagical, common-sense, everyday, secular reality which is its object – is inseparable from the development of capitalism, the quantification by the market system of the older hierarchical or feudal or magical environment, and thus that both are intimately linked to the bourgeoisie as its product and its commodity (and this is, it seems to me, where Lukács himself is ahistorical, in not positing an exclusive link between realism and the life of commerce, in suggesting that a wholly different social order like that of socialism or communism will still want to maintain this particular – historically dated – mode of reality-construction). And when in our own time the bourgeoisie begins to decay as a class, in a world of social anomie and fragmentation, then that active and conquering mode of the representation of reality which is realism is no longer appropriate; indeed, in this new social world which is ours today, we can go so far as to say that the very object of realism itself – secular reality, objective reality – no longer exists either. Far from being the world's final and definitive face, it proves to have been simply one historical and cultural form among many others, such that one might argue a kind of ultimate paradox of reality itself: there once was such a thing as objective truth, objective reality, but now that 'real world' is itself a thing of the past. Objective reality – or the various possible objective realities – are in other words, the function of genuine group existence or collective vitality; and when the dominant group disintegrates, so also does the certainty of some common truth or being. Thus the problem about realism articulates in the cultural realm that profound ambivalence that Marx and Engels have about the bourgeoisie in history in general: the secularization and systematization that capitalism brought about is both more brutal and alienating, *and* more humane and liberating, than the effects of any previous social system. Capitalism destroys genuine human relationships, but also for the first time liberates humankind from village idiocy and the tyranny and intolerance of tribal life. This simultaneous positive and negative coding of capitalism appears everywhere in the works of Marx, but most strikingly and programmatically perhaps in the *Communist Manifesto*; and it is this very complex and ambivalent, profoundly dialectical assessment of capitalism that is reflected in the notion of the historical necessity of capitalism as a stage; whereas in the literary realm it takes the form of the hesitations just expressed about the realistic mode that corresponds to classic nineteenth-century capitalism, hesitations which can be measured in all their ambiguity by the simultaneous assertion that realism is the most complex epistemological instrument yet devised for recording the truth of social reality, and also, at one and the same time, that it is a lie in the very form itself, the prototype of aesthetic false consciousness, the appearance that bourgeois ideology takes on in the realm of narrative literature.

The model I now want to submit to you derives no doubt ultimately from Engels also, who had it himself from Morgan's *Ancient Society*, who in turn drew it from a still older anthropological tradition. But the form in which I am going to use this model – which in essence is nothing more than the old classification of cultures and social forms into the triad of savage, barbarian, and civilized types – comes more directly from a recent French work that gives us the means of transforming his otherwise purely historical typology into a rather sensitive instrument of practical literary analysis.

Now I should preface all this by saying that I don't intend here to give anything like a complete account, let alone a critique, of this more recent work – the *Anti-Oedipus* of Gilles Deleuze and Félix Guattari[6] – around which there has been a great deal of controversy, and whose usefulness for us lies in its reintroduction of genuinely historical preoccupations into the hitherto resolutely a- or antihistorical problematics of structuralism. Deleuze and Guattari, indeed, give us a vision of history based once more firmly on the transformation of fundamental social forms, and on the correlation between shifts in meaning and conceptual categories, and the various types of socioeconomic infrastructures.

But I must at least explain that, as the book's title, *Anti-Oedipus*, suggests, its official theme is the now familiar one of the reactionary character of Freud's doctrine of the Oedipus complex – a position for which Karl Kraus's famous aphorism might serve as a motto: 'Psychoanalysis is that illness of which it believes itself to be the cure.' I will content myself with observing that the violence with which this rather hysterical assertion is argued goes a long way toward making me suspect that Freud must have been right about the Oedipus complex in the first place. The real interest of the book, I would think, lies elsewhere, in its energetic attempt to synthesize a great number of contemporary intellectual trends and currents which have not all been confronted with one another before in quite so systematic a way. Here the alternative title, *Capitalism and Schizophrenia*, may suggest the approach, and indeed, within these pages, we find, alongside Freud and Marx, in both original and dubbed versions, phenomenological reflections on the body, Mumford on the city, linguistics and anthropological materials, studies of the commodity society, but also of kinship systems, theories of genetic codes, references to modern painting, and all this bathed in the familiarity of the great contemporary literary works like those of Beckett and Artaud, of which, of course, the term 'schizophrenic' is meant to furnish both a description and a relatively new literary classification which is of no little practical interest.

Schizophrenia, however, has a more fundamental strategic value for Deleuze and Guattari, one which is very directly related to the historical typology with which we are ourselves concerned. For schizophrenia provides something like a zero degree against which we can assess the various – shall I call them more complex? – forms of human life, and by comparison serves as a kind of base line against which we can then measure and deconstruct the various determinate structures of individual and social reality which in their unending succession make up what we call history. Schizophrenia is, then, for Deleuze and Guattari something like the primordial flux that underlies existence itself; and clinically, to be sure, what characterizes the schizophrenic is this almost druglike dissolution of the bonds of time and of logic, the succession of one experiential moment after another without the organization and perspective imposed by the various kinds of abstract orders of meaning – whether individual or social – which we associate with ordinary daily life. So – to begin to construct our model – we can say that schizophrenia is something like a flux which is then, in the various social forms, ordered into some more elaborate, but also clearly, in one way or another, more repressive structure; to put it in the terminology of Deleuze, we will say that organized social life in one way or another then *codes* this initial flux, organizes it into ordered hierarchical meanings of one kind or another, makes the hallucinatory landscape suddenly fall into meaningful perspectives and become the place of work but also of the kinds of determinate values that characterize a given social order.

Now at this point we come upon our now-familiar triad of savage, barbarian, and civilized societies, and here also the approach of Deleuze and Guattari – this terminology of flux and codes – adds a handle that suddenly makes this rather antiquated piece of historical typology into a relatively sophisticated item of technical equipment. Let us remember what we needed to have our model do: we needed something like a unified field theory of the various hitherto wholly unrelated bodies of literature, something that would give us a terminology sufficiently responsive to deal in the same breath with primitive storytelling, precapitalist literatures, bourgeois realism, and the various modernisms of the present postindustrial world of late monopoly capital and of the superstate; such a common terminology or unified field theory ought then to allow us to see all these social and literary forms somehow as permutations of a common structure, or at least rearrangements of terms they hold in common.

Now it is clear that Deleuze and Guattari understood Engels's and Morgan's old historical triad in a fairly free and loose way: for Morgan, savagery was the first stage of human social life, which ran from the invention of language to that of the bow-and-arrow; barbarism is the next, more complex stage, in which agriculture and pottery are developed, and which is characterized above all by the use of metals; civilization, finally, begins with the invention of writing. Yet it seems to me that within the purely archaeological confines of the paradigm, there lies a deeper imaginative truth, and this poetic or Viconian vision of human societies is what is used and exploited by Deleuze and Guattari, and what presently interests us. On this view, peoples living in the state of savagery are those we generally call primitive cultures, neolithic tribes, village societies of all kinds, of which, in the golden age of American anthropology in the nineteenth century, the supreme example was the American Indian, and for which, particularly since Lévi-Strauss and *Tristes tropiques*, we have developed a nostalgia that does not shrink from an explicit invocation of Rousseau himself. Now barbarian society is somehow thought to be more complex than that of savagery, but also more dynamic, and, if I may put it that way, more fearsome and dangerous; it is not an accident that with barbarism we instinctively associate cruelty, whether it be on the level of the raids of nomadic predators or of the great inhuman Asiatic city-states and oriental despotisms; and here cruelty – whether it be that of Attila or of Babylon – is a code-word for a war machine, that is to say, essentially for the poetic truth of metals and metallurgy. When we arrive at length at what is called civilization, it is clear that for Deleuze and Guattari, that it is to be measured, not so much by inscriptions, as rather simply by the primacy of commerce, by the progress of a money economy and a market system, of organized production and exchange, in short, of what must sooner or later answer to the name of capitalism.

Let me quickly resume their hypothesis: the savage state is the moment of the coding of the original or primordial schizophrenic flux; in barbarism we have, then, to do with a more complex construction on this basis, which will be called an overcoding of it; under capitalism, reality undergoes a new type of operation or manipulation, and the desacralisation and laicization, the quantification and rationalization of capitalism will be characterized by Deleuze and Guattari precisely as a decoding of these earlier types of realities or code-constructions; and finally, our own time – whatever it may be thought to be as a separate social form in its own right, and it is obviously to this question that we will want to return shortly – our own time is marked by nothing quite so much as a recoding of this henceforth decoded flux – by *attempts* to recode, to reinvent the sacred, to go back to myth (now understood in Fry's archetypal sense – in brief, that whole host of recoding strategies which characterize the various modernisms, and of which the most revealing and authentic, as far as Deleuze and Guattari are concerned, is surely the emergence of schizophrenic literature, or the attempt to come to terms with the pure primordial flux itself.

Now I will try, not so much to explain these various moments, as to show why this way of thinking and talking about them may be of use to us (and if it is not, of course we have been mistaken in our choice of a model, and there remains nothing but to jettison this one and to find some paradigm better able to do the work we require from it).

The application of the terminology of flux and codes to primitive life and storytelling may be overhastily described in terms of symbolism or of Lévi-Strauss's conception of the 'primitive mind,' of that *pensée sauvage* or primitive thought which has not yet invented abstraction, for which the things of the outside world are, in themselves, meaning, or are indistinguishable from meanings. The medieval conception of the world as God's book, in which, for example, the beasts are so many sentences in a bestiary, is still close enough to this naive coding to convey its atmosphere to us. Yet in the primitive world, the world of the endless oral stories and of the simple and naively or, if you prefer, 'naturally' coded flux, none of those things are really organized systematically; it is only when this omnipresent and decentered primitive coding is somehow ordered and the body of the world *territorialized*, as Deleuze and Guattari put it, that we find ourselves in the next stage of the social (but also the literary) order, namely that of barbarism, or of the despotic machine. Here the world-book is reorganized into what Lewis Mumford calls a megamachine, and the coded flux, now overcoded, acquires a center; certain signifiers become privileged over others in the same way that the despot himself gradually emerges from tribal indistinction to become the very center of the world and the meeting place of the four points of the compass; so a kind of awesome Forbidden City of language comes into being, which is not yet abstraction in our sense either, but far more aptly characterized, in my opinion, by that peculiar phenomenon we call allegory, and in which a single coded object or item of the outside world is suddenly overloaded with meaning, lifted up into a crucial element of a new and complicated object-language or overcoding erected on the basis of the older, simpler, 'natural' sign-system. So in the passage from savagery to barbarism, it may be said that we pass from the *production* of coded elements to the *representation* of them, a representation that indicates itself and affirms its own splendor as privilege and as sacred meaning.

Civilization, capitalization, then come as an attempt to annul this barbaric overcoding, this despotic and luxurious sign-system erected parasitically upon the basis of the older 'natural' codes; and the new social form, the capitalist one, thus aims at working its way back to some even more fundamental and uncoded reality – scientific or objective – behind the older signs. This changeover is, of course, a familiar historical story, of which we possess a number of different versions, and I have the obligation clearly enough to explain what advantages there are to us – in our practical work as teachers and students of literature – in the one I am proposing here. For we know that the ideologues of the rising bourgeoisie – in that movement called the Enlightenment – set themselves the explicit task of destroying religion and superstition, of extirpating the sacred in all of its forms; they were then quite intensely aware of the struggle to *decode*, even if they did not call it that and even if subsequent generations of a bourgeoisie complacently installed in power preferred to forget the now rather frightening corrosive power of that ambitious effort of negativity and destructive criticism.

So gradually the bourgeois invents a more reassuring, more positive account of the transformation: in this view, the older superstitious remnants simply give way to the new positivities of modern *science*; or, if you prefer – now that a model-building science in our own time has seemed a less reliable ally – to the positive achievements of modern technology and invention. But both these accounts – that of the Enlightenment itself and that of positivism – are concerned more with abstract knowledge and control than with the facts of individual existence. From the point of view of our particular discipline, in other words, this positive science- or technology-oriented account of the secularization of the world seems more appropriate to the history of ideas than to narrative analysis. The dialectical version of the story – that of Hegel as well as of Marx and Engels – still seems to provide the most adequate synthesis of these older purely negative or purely positive accounts. Here the changeover is seen in terms of a passage from quality to quantity: in other words, the gradual substitution of a market economy for the older forms of barter or payment in kind amounts to the increasing primacy of the principle of generalized equivalence, as it is embodied in the money system. This means that where before there was a qualitative difference between the objects of production, between, say, shoes and beef, or oil paintings and leather belts or sacks of grain – all of them, in the older systems, coded in unique and qualitative ways, as objects of quite different and incommensurable desires, invested each with a unique libidinal content of its own – now suddenly they all find themselves absolutely interchangeable, and through equivalence and the common measure of a money system reduced to the grey tastelessness of abstraction.

The advantage now of the addition to this view of Deleuze and Guattari's concept of the decoded flux is that we will come to understand quantification, the pure equivalence of the exchange world, henceforth no longer as a reality in its own right, but rather as a process, an outer limit, a secular ideal, a kind of absence of quality that can never really be reached once and for all in any definite form, but only approached in that infinite and teasing approximation of the asymptote to a curve with which it will never completely coincide. This is why the periodization of the ideologues of modernism, when they talk about the break with the classical novel, or the realistic novel or the traditional nineteenth-century novel, always proves so embarrassing, because, of course, as a positive phenomenon the classical novel is not there at all when you look for it, realism proving to be, as Darko Suvin put it, simply the zero degree of allegory itself.

Now I can give only two brief illustrations of the usefulness of the view for practical criticism of these so-called realistic novels. In the first place, it seems to me that the idea of a decoded flux for the first time gives content to the very formalistic suggestions – in the Jakobson – Tynjanov theses on realism, for instance – that each realism constitutes a demystification of some preceding ideal or illusion. Obviously, the prototype for such a paradigm is the *Quixote* of Cervantes, but it would seem to me that the idea of realism as a decoding tends to direct our attention far more insistently to the very nature of the codes thus canceled, the older barbaric or savage signifiers thus dismantled; this view, in other words, forces us to attend far more closely to the page-by-page and incident-by-incident operations, whereby the novel effectuates this desacralization, thus effectively preserving us, at the same time, from any illusion that secular reality could be anything but provisional terminus of the narrative process.

The other point I want to make is the close identity between realism and historical thinking, an identity revealed by the model of decoded flux. It has been claimed – by the tenets of the rise-of-science explanation I mentioned a moment ago – that the new scientific values, particularly those of causality and causal explanation, are responsible for the new perspectivism shown by critics like Auerbach to constitute the very web of the new realistic narrative texture. Let me suggest, on the contrary, that causality is not a positive but rather a negative or privative concept: causality is simply the form taken by chronology itself when it falls into the world of quantification, of the indifferently equivalent and the decoded flux. Angus Fletcher's book *Allegory*, (1964) gives us an excellent picture of the literary phenomena that played the role in the older high allegory or barbaric overcoding of what will later become causality in realism: action by contiguity, emanation, magical contamination, the hypnotic and in-gathering spell of a kosmos or spatial form – all of these must then disappear from the decoded narrative, and the continuity of time must be dealt with in some more secular way, if it is not to decay and disintegrate back into the random sequence of unrelated instants which is the very nature of the primordial schizophrenic flux itself.

Historical thinking, causality, is now a way of making things yield up their own meanings immanently, without any appeal to transcendental or magical outside forces; the process by which a single item deteriorates in time is now seen to be meaningful in itself, and when you have shown it, you have no further need of any external or transcendental hypotheses. Thus realism is par excellence the moment of the discovery of changing time, of the generation-by-generation and year-by-year dynamics of a new kind of social history. Realism is at one, I am tempted to say, with a world of *worn things*, things among which, of course, one must number people as well, and those discarded objects that are used-up human lives.

At length, as the nineteenth century itself wears on, we begin to detect signs of a kind of fatigue with the whole process of decoding; indeed, as the very memory of feudalism and the ancien régime grows dim, there appear perhaps to be fewer and fewer codes in the older sacred sense to serve as the object of such semiotic purification. This is, of course, the moment of the emergence of modernism, or rather, of the various modernisms, for the subsequent attempts to *recode* the henceforth decoded flux of the realistic, middle-class, secular era are many and varied, and we cannot hope even to give a sense of their variety here. So I will simply attempt to make one point, which seems to me absolutely fundamental for the analysis of modern literatue, and which, to my mind, constitutes the most useful contribution to our future work of the model here under consideration. It is simply this: that it follows, from what we have said, and from the very notion of a recoding of secular reality or of the decoded flux, that all modernistic works are essentially simply canceled realistic ones, that they are, in other words, not apprehended directly, in terms of their own symbolic meanings, in terms of their own mythic or sacred immediacy, the way an older primitive or overcoded work would be, but rather indirectly only, by way of the relay of an imaginary realistic narrative of which the symbolic and modernistic one is then seen as a kind of stylization; and this is a type of reading, and a literary structure, utterly unlike anything hitherto known in the history of literature, and one to which we have been insufficiently attentive until now. Let me suggest, in other words, to put it very crudely, that when you make sense of something like Kafka's *Castle*, your process of doing so involves the substitution for that recoded flux of a realistic narrative of your own devising – one which may be framed in terms of Kafka's supposed personal experience – psychoanalytic, religious, or social – or in terms of your own, or in terms of some hypothetical destiny of 'modern man' in general. Whatever the term of the realistic narrative appealed to, however, I think it's axiomatic that the reading of such work is always a two-stage affair, first, substituting a realistic hypothesis – in narrative form – then interpreting that secondary and invented or projected core narrative according to the procedures we reserved for the older realistic novel in general. And I suggest that this elaborate process is at work everywhere in our reception of contemporary works of art, all the way from those of Kafka down to, say, *The Exorcist*.

And since I mentioned chronology a moment ago, let me briefly use the fate of chronology in the new artistic milieu of the recoded flux to give you a clearer sense of what is meant by the process. It has been said, for instance, that in Robbe-Grillet's novel *La Jalousie*, chronology is abolished: there are two separate sets of events that ought to permit us to reestablish the basic facts of the story in their proper order, only they do not: 'the crushing of the centipede which, in a novel telling a story, would provide a good point of reference around which to situate the other events in time, is [in fact] made to occur *before* the trip taken by Frank and A., *during* their trip, and *after* it.'[7] Yet it would be wrong to conclude that Robbe-Grillet had really succeeded thereby in shaking our belief in chronology, and along with it, in that myth of a secular, objective, 'realistic' reality of which it is a sign and a feature. On the contrary, as every reader of Robbe-Grillet knows, this kind of narrative exasperates our obsession with chronology to a veritable fever pitch, and the absence of any realistic 'solution,' far from being a return to the older non-causal narrative consciousness of primitive peoples, as in allegory for instance, in fact drives us only deeper into the contradictions of our own scientific and causal thought-modes. So it is quite wrong to say that Robbe-Grillet has abolished the story; on the contrary, we read *La Jalousie* by substituting for it a realistic version of one of the oldest stories in the world, and its force and value come from the paradoxical fact that by canceling it, the new novel tells this realistic story more forcefully than any genuinely realistic, old-fashioned, decoded narrative could.

Now from a sociological point of view it is clear why this had to happen with the breakdown of a homogeneous public, with the social fragmentation and anomie of the bourgeoisie itself, and also its refraction among the various national situations of Western or Nato capitalism, each of which then speaks its own private language and demands its own particular frame of reference. So the modern work comes gradually to be constructed as a kind of multipurpose object, Umberto Eco's so-called *opera aperta* or open form[8] designed to be used by each subgroup after its own fashion and needs, so that its realistic core, that 'concrete' emotion, but also situation, which we call, simply, *jealousy*, seems the most abstract and empty starting point of all, inasmuch as every private audience is obliged to recode it afresh in terms of its own sign-system.

The first conclusion one would draw from this peculiar historical and aesthetic situation is that Lukács (whose limits I hope I have already admitted) turns out in the long run to have been right after all about the nature of modernism: very far from a break with that older overstuffed Victorian bourgeois reality, it simply reinforces all the latter's basic presuppositions, only in a world so thoroughly subjectivized that they have been driven underground, beneath the surface of the work, forcing us to reconfirm the concept of a secular reality at the very moment when we imagine ourselves to be demolishing it.

This is a social and historical contradiction, but for the writer it is an agonizing dilemma, and perhaps that would be the most dramatic way of expressing what we have been trying to say. No one here, after all, seriously wants to return to the narrative mode of nineteenth-century realism; the latter's rightful inheritors are the writers of bestsellers, who – unlike Kafka or Robbe-Grillet – really do concern themselves with the basic secular problems of our existence, namely, money, power, position, sex, and all those humdrum daily preoccupations that continue to form the substance of our daily lives all the while that art literature considers them unworthy of its notice. I am not suggesting that we go back and read or write in the older way, only that in their heart of hearts – as the Goldwater people used to say – everyone knows that John O'Hara's novels still give a truer picture of the facts of life in the United States than anything of Hemingway or Faulkner, with all their tourist or magnolia exoticism. Yet – yet – the latter are palpably the greater writers. So we slowly begin to grasp the enormity of a historical situation in which the truth of our social life as a whole – Lukács would have said, as a totality – is increasingly irreconcilable with the aesthetic quality of language or of individual expression; of a situation about which it can be asserted that if we can make a work of art from our experience, if we can tell it in the form of a story, it is no longer true; and if we can grasp the truth about our world as totality, as something transcending mere individual experience, we can no longer make it accessible in narrative or literary form. So a strange malediction hangs over art in our time, and for the writer this dilemma is felt as an increasing (structural) incapacity to generalize or universalize private or lived experience. The dictates, not only of realism, but of narrative in general, tend gradually to restrict writing to sheer autobiography, at the same time that they transform even autobiographical discourse itself into one more private language among others: reduced to the telling of the truth of a private situation alone, that no longer engages the fate of a nation, but merely a single locality; and no longer even for that, but a particular neighbourhood – and even that only as long as it still remains a neighbourhood in the traditional, ethnic or ghetto, sense; even therein, speaking henceforth only for a specific family, and then not even for its older generations; at length reduced to a single household, and finally, within it, to a single gender. So little by little the writer is reduced to so private a speech that it is henceforth bereft of any public consequences or resonances, so that only symbolic recoding holds out the hope of saying something meaningful to a wider and more heterogeneous public. Yet, as we have seen, that new kind of meaning is quite different from the old one. But in this wholly subjectivized untruth, the modern writer nonetheless in another sense remains profoundly true and profoundly representative: for everyone else is equally locked into his or her private language, imprisoned in those serried ranks of monads that are the ultimate result of the social fragmentation inherent in our system.

Many are the images of this profound subjectivization and fragmentation of our social life, and of our very existences, in the world of late monopoly capitalism. Some strike terror and inspire us with a kind of metaphysical pathos at our condition, like that persona of Lautréamont sealed since birth in an airtight, soundproof membrane, dreaming of the shriek destined to rupture his isolation and to admit for the first time the cries of pain of the world outside.

All are, of course, figures, and it is a measure of our dilemma that we cannot convey the situation in other than a figurative way; yet some figures seem more liberating than others, and since we began with a reference to Plato, let us conclude with a Platonic vision, which was once itself the foundation of a metaphysic,but which now, today, and owing to historical developments quite unforeseeable in Plato's time, seems – like the gravest of all figures and metaphors – henceforth to have been intended in the most *literal* sense.

> Imagine [says Socrates], an underground chamber, like a cave with an entrance open to the daylight and running a long way underground. In this chamber are men who have been prisoners there since they were children, their legs and necks being so fastened that they can only look straight ahead of them and cannot turn their heads. Behind them and above them a fire is burning, and between the fire and the prisoners runs a road, in front of which a curtain-wall has been built, like the screen at puppet-shows. . . .Imagine further that there are men carrying all sorts of artefacts along behind the curtain-wall, including figures of men and animals made of wood and stone and other materials . . .
>
> An odd picture [responds Socrates' listener] and an odd sort of prisoner.
>
> They are drawn from life, I replied. For tell me, do you think our prisoners could see anything of themselves or their fellows save the shadows thrown by the fire upon the wall of the cave opposite?[9]

There are, of course, ways of breaking out of this isolation, but they are not literary ways and require complete and thoroughgoing transformation of our economic and social system, and the invention of new forms of collective living. Our task – specialists that we are in the reflections of things – is a more patient and modest, more diagnostic one. Yet even such a task as the analysis of literature and culture will come to nothing unless we keep the knowledge of our own historical situation vividly present to us: for we are least of all, in our position, entitled to the claim that we did not understand, that we thought all those things were real, that we had no way of knowing we were living in a cave.

Notes

1. IRIS MURDOCH, *The Unicorn* (London: Chatto and Windus 1963), p. 118.

2. See, for example, ERNEST FISCHER, *The Necessity of Art* (London: Penguin, 1963), or GEORG LUKÁCS *Aesthetik* (Berlin, 1963).

3. HANS-GEORG GADAMER, *Wahrheit und Methode* (Tubingen: Mohr 1965), pp. 255–61

4. FREDRIC JAMESON, *Marxism and Form* (Princeton: Princeton UP, 1972), pp. 309–26

5. The modernist position is resumed in RENATO POGGIOLI, *Theory of the Avant-Garde* (Cambridge, Mass:Belknap Press, 1968) and eloquently defended in Nathalie Sarraute, *The Age of Suspicion* (New York, 1963). I should add that any really consequent treatment of it would also have necessarily to come to terms with what might be called the left-wing modernism of Brecht or of the *Tel Quel* group.

6. GILES DELEUZE and FELIX GUATTARI, *Anti-Oedipe* (Paris: Minuit, 1972); translated as *Anti-Oedipus* by R. Hurley, M. Seem, and H. R. Lane (Minneapolis: U Minnesota Press, 1983).

7. GERALD PRINCE, *A Grammar of Stories* (The Hague, 1973), p. 23.

8. See UMBERTO ECO, *Opera Aperta* (Milan, 1962).

9. *The Republic*, Book VII, trans. H. D. P. Lee (Baltimore, 1955), pp. 278–79.

9 Marxism and Popular Fiction*
(1981)

TONY BENNETT

Tony Bennett (b. 1947) teaches social and cultural theory at Griffith
University, Australia. He has written *Formalism and Marxism* (1979)
and, with Janet Woollacott, *Bond and Beyond* (1987).

Bennett's work has concerned 'popular fiction' – though not the
degraded, heteronomous object so named in the bourgeois critical
tradition and, by replication, in much Marxist writing. 'Popular
fiction', Bennett argues here, is the conceptual residue of the dominant notions of 'Literature' and 'literary value', which must be
displaced in the interests of a materialist rethinking of written culture
and a genuinely political practice of criticism. The theoretical positions
developed here adumbrate Bennett's later analyses of the making and
remaking of textual 'effects' in historical 'reading formations'.

Literature, popular fiction and the bourgeois literary formation

It is usual to assume, when confronted by the formula 'Marxism and
. . .', that a relationship is to be argued for in which Marxism will figure
as the analytical donor and the other bit, the bit which comes after the
'and', as the beneficiary. In this case, it suggests that what might be on
offer is a Marxist theory of popular fiction. I should stress, therefore, that
this is not the approach adopted here. Indeed, rather than proposing a
Marxist theory of popular fiction, I want to argue against the need for
such a theory or for a theory formulated in those terms.

To be more specific, my overriding purpose is to outline the part that
the study of popular fiction (so called) might play within a critical

---

* Reprinted from Tony Bennett, 'Marxism and Popular Fiction', *Literature and
History*, 7 (1981), pp. 138–56; see continuation, pp. 156–65.

Marxism and Popular Fiction

strategy aimed at deconstructing the category of Literature and at dismantling those critical procedures which currently produce for literary texts their political and ideological effects. By 'Literature' here, I have in mind not the literary as, in Tony Davies's words, 'a neutral totality of imaginative or fictional writing', but Literature as 'an ideologically constructed canon or corpus of texts operating in specific and determinate ways in and around the apparatus of education';[1] in short, the canonized tradition. And I would regard such a project as a Marxist one; indeed, it is perhaps the most important task currently facing Marxist criticism. As Stuart Hall has argued, the conventional ordering of the system of intertextual relationships implied by the concept of Literature needs to be made 'the first object of interrogation' within any radical critical practice:

> Why is it that the text, the many texts, the many signifying practices which are present in any social formation have yielded, as the administered curriculum of literary studies, these ten books up to the top; then these twenty books with a question mark above them; then those fifty books which we know about but which we only need to read very quickly; and then those hundreds and thousands of texts nobody ever reads? That hierarchy itself, which constitutes the selective tradition in literary studies, becomes the first object to be interrogated.[2]

Whilst there are signs that such a critical project is well underway, it should be stressed that it is the full range of 'that hierarchy' and not just the top of it – not just 'Literature' – that needs to be problematized. Indeed, this is unavoidable: to take on the concept of Literature by way of analysing its critical effects *necessarily* involves a critical reconsideration of those other categories – such as 'popular fiction' – which have conventionally been ranged alongside or opposed to it. For 'Literature' does not merely denote a particular body of texts. It is, rather, the central, co-ordinating concept of the discourse of literary criticism, supplying the point of reference in relation to which relationships of difference and similarity within the field of writing are articulated. So much so that most other forms of writing have been defined negatively: only in the respects in which they differ from Literature. Thus the concept of popular fiction conveys – beyond the notion of numerical appeal – nothing so much as that it is *not* Literature. It is, in fact, a residual concept – the residue which remains once the sphere of Literature has been described and accounted for: in most instances, attempts to articulate the specific qualities of popular fiction consist of a listing of those attributes (such as lack of character or standardization of plot) which supposedly distinguish it from the already established characteristics of Literature.

It follows that any attempt to unsettle the concept of Literature necessarily and simultaneously involves unsettling the concept of popular fiction in that it calls into question the ways in which relationships of difference and similarity within the field of writing have conventionally been constructed. What is at issue, then, is not just a dismantling of the category of Literature, or the ways in which the texts thus labelled have usually been studied, but a study and critique of the bourgeois literary formation – of the ways in which the relations of intertextuality have been constructed within that formation; of the ways in which different practices of writing have been caught, held and defined in relation to one another; and of the ways in which critical and institutional practices have borne upon the reproduction of those differences. It also involves an attempt to think outside that formation, to construe the internal economy of the field of writing in terms which by-pass the distinctions posited by the concept of Literature.

My purpose, then, is not to develop a Marxist theory of 'popular fiction', but to suggest some ways in which what is commonly referred to as popular fiction may be analytically occupied by Marxists in order to call into question the system of critical concepts of which popular fiction itself forms a part. As a prelude to doing so, however, it will be necessary to indicate that Marxist criticism has, for the greater part of its history, been an essentially bourgeois enterprise at the level of its founding theoretical assumptions, if the kind of critical strategy suggested above is to be developed and inserted within Marxism as part of a substantially reformulated critical problematic. It will also be necessary to consider the relationship between Marxism and popular fiction from another angle: historical and critical rather than strategic. My contention, here, will be that the neglect of popular fiction within Marxist criticism (or, where it has been dealt with, the terms in which it has been addressed) is regrettable not merely in itself and not merely for political reasons, but because it is symptomatic of a faulty conception of the Marxist critical project, which has proved debilitating even for the way the study of canonized texts (ever the Marxist critic's preferred stalking ground) has been conceived and executed.

Against Literature

I have stated that popular fiction has been a neglected area of study within Marxist criticism; that the bulk of Marxist critical attention has focused on the canonized tradition is incontestable. However, and especially of late, there *are* Marxists who have concerned themselves with the study of popular texts – Eco and Barthes, for example. Even so, it is noticeable that popular texts have figured more prominently within the project of developing a general semiology than within the distinctively literary-critical region of Marxist theory. So far as the *historical formation* of Marxist criticism is concerned, however, the degree of critical attention devoted to the study of recognizably popular forms within those major schools of Marxist criticism which – at least until recently – have defined the central terms of reference of Marxist critical debate has been, to say the least, cursory.

Take Lukács. He has nothing at all to say on the subject, not a word. His critical attention moves unremittingly within the confines of 'world historical literature', pausing only momentarily to take the odd, largely uninformed, swipe at the degenerate 'mass culture' of the West; or, in the gestures of a familiar organicism, to invoke 'the people' – creative, it would seem, not in their own right but only by proxy – as a necessary support for all truly great world literature. Goldmann, makes one or two oblique references to popular fiction in attempting to explain why the methods of world-view analysis should be 'valid only for the great works of the past'.[3] But in resolving this problem definitionally – Goldmann squares his circle with remarkable candour: world-view analysis can only be used in relation to great works because, so it happily turns out, only great works contain or express world-views – he puts popular fiction safely back in the box labelled 'ideology' from whence he took it. And Althusser, having posited an unargued-for distinction between 'authentic art' and 'works of an average or mediocre level' ignores the latter entirely.[4]

The only major school of Marxist criticism that can claim to have seriously and sustainedly studied the domain of non-canonized texts – although more in the field of music than of fiction – is the Frankfurt School. However, the Hegelianized version of the mass-culture critique which informed the Frankfurt theorists' approach to popular texts resulted chiefly in a leftward inflected version of the terms in which such texts had already been condemned. All the elements which inform the mass-culture critique – the lack of a controlling centre of culture, aesthetic barbarism, and so on – are present in the Frankfurt critique, but shuffled to the left in being recast within the Frankfurt perspective of containment. And sometimes not so very far to the left either: the terms of reference of Lowenthal's *Literature, Popular Culture and Society*[5] are not so very dissimilar from those of that more recognizably culturally conservative work, *Fiction and the Reading Public*.[6]

There are other exceptions – Gramsci and, perhaps most notably, Raymond Williams, who, at a theoretical level if not at the level of his 'practical criticism', has done more than any other single figure to contest the concept of Literature by tracing the stages and processes of its historical formation. Nonetheless, the point that Marxist critics have, for the greater part, merely mirrored bourgeois criticism, accepting its valuations and duplicating its exclusions, remains valid. If the gravitational pull of the concept of Literature has proved well-nigh irresistible with regard to the way the 'canon' has been approached and conceptualized, the pull of the mass-culture critique has proved equally strong in relation to the way Marxists have studied popular forms. The result has been, for a science which claims to be revolutionary, a highly paradoxical history in which Marxist criticism has functioned largely corroboratively in relation to the distinctions forged by bourgeois criticism: approving of the same body of canonized works but for different reasons, and disapproving of the rest – lumped together as a residue – but, again, for different reasons. Bourgeois criticism has thus been simultaneously patted on the back for having recognized which works are truly great and taken to task for having misrecognized the reasons for their greatness. The *real* reason for Tolstoy's greatness, it turns out, has nothing to do with the eternal verities of the human condition, but to his having given coherent expression to the world-view of the peasantry (Lukács) or to his supplying us with a vision of the contradictions inscribed in the ideology to which his works allude (Macherey). Mulhern has warned that 'it would be astonishing if the judgements of Marxist criticism turned out to be so many materialist *doppelgänger* of those made current by the foregoing idealist tradition'.[7] Yes, astonishing indeed; nonetheless, so far as the question of literary evaluation is concerned, that has been the main heritage of the tradition so far.

This mimicry of the evaluations of bourgeois criticism is symptomatic of the complicity with the defining assumptions of bourgeois criticism which marked the foundation of Marxist criticism. For a variety of reasons, see for example, Anderson, *Considerations of Western Marxism*,[8] Marxist criticism's basic orientation in relation to bourgeois criticism has been to compete with it on its own ground rather than to dispute or displace that terrain. At the level of ideological polemic, the main claim of Marxist criticism has been that the central problem of bourgeois criticism – the specificity of Literature – can be satisfactorily accounted for only by the application of Marxist (that is, historical and materialist) principles of analysis. It would be mistaken to argue that this strategy (as distinct from a theoretical position) has been wholly in error or wholly negligible in its consequences. If bourgeois criticism is currently in crisis (and I do say 'if'), this is due in no small part to the fact that it has been forced, by the challenge of Marxism, to evacuate, or at least to share, the critical terrain over which it once reigned supreme. Yet the price paid for this has been that Marxist criticism has distinguished itself from bourgeois criticism solely at the level of method (addressing the same set of problems by means of different analytical principles), and not at all at the crucial level of the theoretical constitution of its object. It has, in this respect, constituted the least Marxist region of Marxist theory, still experiencing the strong gravitational pull of a bourgeois problematic in a way that has not been true of Marxist economic or political theory.

I have argued in *Formalism and Marxism*[9] why I think the problem of Literature is a mistaken one for Marxism. There are, in the main, two reasons. First, to constitute as a problem the specificity of the mode of writing embodied in the selected canon is to neglect both the critical and institutional processes bearing on the selection and reproduction of that canon and the historical relativity of the way in which the concept of Literature suggests the internal organization of the sphere of writing should be viewed. It is to subscribe to an ideological problem that is produced and is only visible within a specific ideological orchestration of the system of intertextual relationships and which answers in advance questions pertaining to the internal economy of the sphere of writing. Hence the important relations of difference within the field of writing are *necessarily* held to be those between the canonized and non-canonized traditions, whilst the important relations of similarity are *necessarily* held to be found within each of these categories. No other orchestration of relationships of similarity and difference (except those concerning minor stylistic devices or questions of genre classification) is possible.

Second, whilst a historical and materialist approach to the study of literary texts requires that the focus should be on explaining the differences between forms of writing, by way of the historically specific material and ideological constraints which have regulated their production, the problem of Literature pulls in the opposite direction. For it suggests that those texts which constitute Literature can be abstracted from the historically specific circumstances of their production and be grouped together under the heading 'Literature' precisely because they share some uniquely distinguishing set of formal properties which marks them off from other, 'non-literary', forms of writing. This has resulted, for Marxism, in either a truncated materialism, which stops short of those crucially differentiating attributes which constitute the 'literariness' of Literature and which, by definition, transcend any rigorous historical determination, or a one-sided materialism, which focuses on conditions of production at the expense of those conditions of consumption which reproduce specific texts as valued texts.

Quite apart from being a mistaken problem in itself, this concern with 'Literature' has seriously distorted the ways in which other areas of critical interest have been conceived and addressed within Marxism. It has resulted, first, in an obsessive degree of concern with the problem of value. This, at least in the way it has usually been formulated, is, I shall contend, not a proper problem for Marxism and, more important, has impeded the development of what should occupy its place – the analysis of the *social contestation of value* as a means of making *strategically calculated* interventions within that process of contestation. Equally debilitating, the degree of centrality accorded the problem of value has 'overdetermined' – and with harmful consequences – the way in which three related areas of Marxist critical concern have been conceptualized: the analysis of the historical determination of literary forms; the calculation of the political and ideological effects that might be attributed to different practices of writing; and the problem of the relative autonomy of literature (as a general category) and of the diverse relations which exist between the literary and the ideological.

Marxist criticism: a deformed materialism

The problem of value

The statement that Marxists have been obsessively concerned with the problem of value is, of course, contestable. Terry Eagleton, for one, has argued that Marxism 'has maintained a certain silence about aesthetic value'.[10] Whilst it is true that attempts to pose the problem of value at an explicitly theoretical level have been few and far between, the problem of value has nonetheless saturated Marxist critical practice in the sense that it has been routinely there, present in the background, even when other problems have been addressed. It has been massively present in the way the problem of reductionism has been posed within Marxist criticism. For this has been conceived as a problem only in relation to valued texts; outside this restricted sphere of writing, reductionist formulations have been actively embraced. Reductionism, that is to say, has been shunned less for theoretical reasons than for tactical ones, particularly – in the context of an ideological contest with bourgeois criticism – the need to ward off the ever-ready equation between materialism and philistinism.

I will return to this point later. Meanwhile, it should be noted that to maintain that the problem of value is an improper one for Marxism is not thereby to assert the equivalence or parity of all forms of writing – a self-evident absurdity. Statements to the effect that Joyce opened up the possibilities of language in a way that Conan Doyle, say, did not seem to me to be quite unproblematic. However, such purely technical assessments of the formal effects of different practices of writing do not, of themselves, offer grounds for valuing the one above the other. That is a further step which requires the intervention of a discourse of value which argues reasons for preferring forms of writing which stretch the possibilities of language over those which do not (for not all discourses of value have produced such criteria for valuation). Still less is it to advocate a neo-Kantian stance which abdicates the realm of value in the name of a pseudo-neutrality. This is not merely a question of arguing that judgements of value can and should be made; it is more one of recognizing that they inevitably *will* be made and that Marxists cannot afford to stand aloof from the ever ongoing process of the social valorization – and counter-valorization – of texts.

Rather, my chief objection is to the form which the debate about value has predominantly taken within Marxist criticism where it has been conceived as *identical with* and *addressed through* the problem of Literature. This has resulted in the conflation of a whole series of analytically separate problems: the problem of explaining the source of a work's value has been run in with that of explaining its 'literariness' – those formal characteristics which uniquely distinguish it from other forms of fiction – and, worse, problems of aesthetic evaluation and political calculation have been implicitly merged, as in Lukác's attempt to construct a realist aesthetic that would recruit all great realists to the banner of progressivism in art. Most disquieting of all, however, has been the tendency – consistent with an acceptance of the valuations of bourgeois criticism – to view value as essentially *static*, at least over large periods of time; to regard it as a property that is inherently inscribed within conventionally revered texts; and, as a part of an ideological polemic with bourgeois criticism, to contend that such properties can only be explicated by returning the text, analytically, to the conditions of its production.

This way of posing the problem is mistaken for a number of reasons, all of which cluster around the fact that value is not – nor, logically, can it be – a property of the text *alone*. One cannot pose the question of value without introducing into the analysis the problem of the valuing subject. Texts do not *have* value; they can only *be valued* by valuing subjects of particular types and for particular reasons, and these are entirely the product of critical discourses of valuation, varying from criticism to criticism. What has been offered within Marxist criticism, under the guise of *theories of value*, are in fact merely *specific reasons for valuing*, specific discourses of value begetting valuing subjects of particular types, which cannot logically (although they may, of course, politically) be preferred above those produced by competing critical discourses of valuation.

In the case of Lukácsian aesthetics, for example, texts are valued – that is, they are alleged to contain a value which Marxist critical judgement merely accurately reflects – in proportion to the degree to which they approximate the norm of historical self-knowledge which constitutes the Lukácsian model of literariness. In the case of the Althusserians, value is explained in terms of the extent to which texts distance or rupture the ideological discourses to which they allude; if they do this significantly, they're 'in', they count as Literature and are valued; if they do not, they are consigned elsewhere. As specific political reasons for valuing, such arguments are unexceptionable; they can be debated with politically at the level of a strategic calculation of their effects – of the practices of writing they support, of the types of valuing subject they produce, of the categories of readers they imply and so on. However, in so far as they are presented as theories of value (and they *are* so presented) they are singularly impertinent. For such are not all the grounds upon which the revered texts of the great tradition have, predominantly, been valorized. It is only possible to present such *reasons for valuing as theories of value* by simply discounting the positions of valuing subjects produced by and within competing critical discourses. We can see here the way in which the logic of false consciousness has exerted its presence in Marxist aesthetic debate. For attempts to construct a theory of value have necessitated that the valuing subjects produced by the discourses of bourgeois criticism should be dismissed as illusory subjects, mistaken in their reasons for valuing.

A theory of value (as opposed to an analysis of the social and ideological processes of valorization) is only possible on condition that one escapes from the plurality of different reasons for valuing, the plurality of discourses producing different valuing subjects, by means of the discursive construction of the category of a universal valuing subject. This, of course, has been the central tactic of bourgeois criticism: value resides in the relationship between the universal values embodied in great works and the universal subject buried deep within us all. The more usual tactic within Marxism has been that of historicism as manifested in the formation of teleological theories of value pivoted on the construction of a universal valuing subject which, situated at the end of history, beyond the conflict which currently separates us as valuing subjects (and, of course, as much more than that), will, come the day, vindicate the provisional judgements currently made on its behalf. This is very clearly the case with Lukács whose entire critical practice – where texts are conceived as being historically related to one another as the baton of aesthetic totalization is passed on from class to class – required, for its very constitution, the concept of the proletariat as the identical subject-object of history waiting, with its judgements in hand – but always just around the next historical corner.

Interestingly enough, Terry Eagleton is finally obliged to gesture in the direction of just such a historicism (despite his repudiation of it) in his discussion of aesthetic value in the final chapter of his *Criticism and Ideology*. Despite its lucidity and cogency, it is also a deeply troubled account of the problem, one which pulls – or is pulled – in contradictory directions, seemingly ever on the brink of jettisoning the connection between value and Literature yet, finally, always brought back to affirming that connection. This tension is most clearly visible, as Francis

Mulhern points out, in Eagleton's uneasy oscillation between two contradictory positions. On the one hand, Eagleton asserts, value neither is nor can be 'immanent'; it can only be 'transitive' or 'relational'. This would seem to, imply, as Mulhern puts it, that 'the question of value must always be posed historically, in the form, valuable *to whom* and *in what conditions?*'[11] This perspective is, however, immediately undercut as Eagleton goes on, to cite Mulhern again, to imply 'that value is imparted to the work by its historical conditions of production and that this value is constant – in a word, that value is after all, in this sense at least, "immanent"'.[12] It will be instructive to trace, in a fairly detailed way, how the tension between these two positions is handled and how the slippage from the one to the other takes place.

It is worthy of note that, from the outset, Eagleton poses the problem of value only in relation to already-valued works. There is, he argues, nothing 'to be gained by that form of literary ultra-leftism which dismisses received evaluations merely because they are the product of bourgeois criticism'; nor should it 'be a matter of embarrassment that the literary texts selected for examination by Marxist criticism will *inevitably* overlap with those works which literary idealism has consecrated as "great".'[13] The task of Marxist criticism is rather 'to provide a materialist *explanation* of the bases of literary value', to challenge the inability of idealist criticism 'to render more than subjectivist accounts of the criteria of value'.[14] These formulations contain a crucial ambiguity which runs throughout the remainder of the chapter, for the phrase 'provide a materialist *explanation* of the bases of literary value' proves to be liable to two different interpretations which support, I would argue, two contradictory projects. According to the first interpretation, the bases of literary value are to be accounted for by focusing on the reasons for valuing proffered within different 'ideologies of value'. The focus here is on the production of value within the process of the ideological consumption of the text. According to the second interpretation, it is the value that is actually 'in' the work that is to be explained in terms of the conditions of its production. Depending on which interpretation is to the fore, what is on offer turns out to be either a 'science of the ideologies of value' or a 'science of value' – formulations which necessarily undercut one another inasmuch as the former necessarily dissolves the object, 'value', which the latter requires in order to constitute itself.

Yet Eagleton makes it clear that he is no friend of Literature. The function of the centrality accorded to the 'value-question' within literary studies, he argues, has been to dissolve the materialist analysis of literary texts into the moment of individual consumption:

Criticism becomes a mutually supportive dialogue between two highly valorized subjects: the valuable text and the valuable reader. . . .

Valuable text and valuable reader are reversible: in a mutual complicity, such a text writes its reader and such a reader writes the text. The valuable reader is constituted as valuable by the texts which he constitutes as such; ideological value is projected into the Tradition to re-enter the present as metaphysical confirmation or critique. The name of this tautology is Literature – that historical invention whose ideological tyranny is more supple and deep-seated for us than that of any other art-form.[15]

Historical invention though 'Literature' may be, however, Eagleton is, in the end, obliged to align himself with it. The crux of the dilemma which impels this consists in the status that is to be accorded the text in relation to its readings. At this crucial point in the argument, two problems are implicitly merged: the problem of value and the problem of meaning or interpretation. Eagleton is, at least initially, forthright in declaring himself against any fetishization of 'value as an immanent quality of the product'[16] and refers both the problem of discrepant interpretations and that of discrepant valuations to the ideological conditions of reading:

> For the literary text is always the text-for-ideology, selected, deemed readable and deciphered by certain ideologically governed conventions of critical receptivity to which the text itself contributes . . . If the text itself is the overdetermined product of a structural conjuncture, so indeed is the practice of reading; the problems of textual meaning and value pose themselves precisely in the series of historical conjunctures between these two moments. Reading is the operation whereby a particular historical ideology so puts to work the materials of the text as to fashion it into a readable product, an ideological object, a text-for-ideology.[17]

Yet, and rightly, anxious to avoid dissipating the text amongst its diverse and plural readings, Eagleton immediately stresses that the text necessarily constrains the possible ways in which it may be read, that it is a determinate factor in the equation – 'not that it dictates a single sense to the reader, but that it generates a field of possible readings which, within the conjuncture of the reader's ideological matrix and its own, is necessarily finite'.[18] The conclusion drawn from this is that the question of value must be posed in relation to the articulation of two distinct moments: 'the ideological matrix of our reading and the ideological matrix of their [the texts'] production'.[19] What is called for is 'a science of the ideological conditions of the production of value' which, rather than inserting 'value "within" the product' would 'reinsert the conditions of textual production within the "exchange relation" of value'.[20]

This formulation of the problem is substantially correct, and a major advance on previous statements of the issue. And it is easy to see how, by proceeding in this way, a materialist account of 'the ideological conditions of the production of value' might be produced which would steer between the Scylla and Charybdis of historicism and immanentism. Provided, that is, that two further conditions are met: one, that such an analysis, instead of restricting itself to the canonized tradition, would examine the ideological conditions of the production of value in operation within the evaluation of different groups of texts by different groups of readers in different texts-ideology conjunctures; two, the supposition that the plurality of different reasons for valuing produced within different ideologies of value might in some way be integrated to yield a unified set of reasons for valuing, in turn subscribed to by a unified valuing subject, be abandoned.

In fact, Eagleton complies with neither of these conditions.This is not merely to say that his analysis remains resolutely within the confines of the great tradition (although it does). Far more pertinent is the fact that having, in an important innovation, redefined the 'problem of value' as a problem of 'the ideological conditions of the production of value', he then, *as if by way of addressing that problem*, conflates it with another, quite separate issue: the problem of relative autonomy – of the irreducible specificity of the aesthetic (as a general category) – and, leading on from this, the problem as to why *some* texts are not limited by the conditions of their production but continue to register long-term effects within a culture. It is in this way that the category of Literature, having been shown the front door, is smuggled in through the back. When the chips are down, the problem of value *is* the problem of Literature. For there is after all, it would seem, a 'basis for value' within the text (or, more accurately, within specific texts); a basis for value which is no more and no less than the text's literariness construed, in this case, as those properties (the internal fracturing of ideologies) which distinguish such texts from other forms of writing (those which, moving within the withered ideological matrices of dominant social myths, preclude 'that transformative textual production of such myths which might alone "redeem" them').[21]

Those works which have conventionally been valued, it turns out, have been rightly valued (albeit for the wrong reasons), because, come the reckoning, they do have value inscribed within them. They are valuable not despite their historical limitations but 'by *virtue of them*'[22]; by virtue, that is, of those determinations which produce that internal troubling of ideology which constitutes 'the literary'. Beneath the diverse ideologies of value which produce the text as a text-for-ideology, there is a core residuum of 'real value' soliciting merely partial recognition from the ideologically-deluded subjects which constitute its readers pending the day when its true nature will be recognized. For, Eagleton finally confesses, 'if Marxism has maintained a certain silence about aesthetic value, it may well be because the material conditions which would make such a discourse fully possible do not as yet exist'.[23] Far from the twin perils of historicism and immanentism being avoided they are, in effect, combined. The value that is immanent within the text awaits a final historicist consummation in order, at last, to be truly recognized by a valuing subject worthy of the name.

In his review of *History and Class Consciousness*, Josef Révai argued that the conception of the proletariat as the identical subject-object of the historical process meant, in regard to the totality of past history, 'an unsupersedable transcendence of its historicity with respect to its being for itself',[24] as the real history that has taken place is overridden by and referred to the history that is yet to be. In the same way, the categories required to sustain a Marxist theory of value – chiefly, the category of a universal valuing subject in its historicist variant – necessarily undercut any materialist *credo*. The real history of valuation – of competing and contesting evaluations – is retrospectively nullified by the impending integrative judgements of a post-historical valuing subject. Clearly, the effect of any such theory is to exorcize conflict from the sphere of the aesthetic – even if only in the form of a visionary goal looming at the end of history.

In place of a theory of value, then, Marxism's concern should be with the analysis of 'the ideological conditions of the social *contestation* of value'. So far as the *making* of evaluations is concerned, this is a matter for strategic calculation – a question of politics and not of aesthetics.

The literary and the ideological

I would not pretend to have disposed of the problem of value in the above remarks; rather, I have aimed merely to open up a debate which seems long overdue. To avoid misunderstanding, I should therefore stress, once again, that to take issue with the problem of value does not entail arguing that the sphere of writing is lacking in internal differentiation. Faced with this problem by his *New Left Review* inquisitors, Raymond Williams replied:

> The mistaken assumptions which lie hidden in the old concepts have to be cleared away for us to be able to begin searching again for a more tenable set of emphases within the range of writing practices – I agree that you could not go on with an undifferentiated range. On the other hand it seems to me that from now on we have to accept it as a true range, without any categorial division between what is done on one side of a line and what is done on the other.[25]

Clearly, then, relationships of similarity and difference within the sphere of writing need to be established. The crucial questions concern the criteria which should govern the construction of such relationships. In subscribing to the problem of value, as mediated through the category of Literature, Marxist critism has taken on board an already established principle for their construction. And it is one which sits ill at ease with – and has, indeed, seriously distorted or obfuscated – the contending principles, dictated by Marxism's own theoretical and political requirements, which ought to govern the way in which these relationships are articulated. The price that the centrality accorded the problem of value has exacted can be seen in relation to the way adjacent areas of Marxist critical concern have been conceived and addressed.

I have already alluded to its influence on the way in which problems of determination have been posed. Its most discernible effect is that Marxists have been less concerned with explaining specific works (those of, say, Tolstoy or Racine in the case of Lukács and Goldmann respectively) as the product of specifically constrained signifying practices, than with the problem of explicating their 'greatness'; or, more accurately, the foregrounding of the latter concern has 'overdetermined' the way in which the former has been posed. The result has been a highly paradoxical enterprise in which the role allotted to the conditions of textual production has been to explain why and how some conditions of production enable the texts produced within them to break free from their restraining hold in order to achieve a universal appeal. Either that, or, as with Plekhanov, the towel is thrown in from the outset: materialist principles of analysis can take one only so far – up to the text but not into it or into the source of the aesthetic pleasure it affords.

It is easy to see how, in both options, the problem of value has distorted the way in which the issue of relative autonomy has been posed in the literary-critical region of Marxist theory. For it has resulted in this issue being regarded not as one pertaining to the *specificity of the determinations bearing on literary practice* but, rather, as one concerning the *limitations of any account which focuses on the analysis of determinations per se.* It has been viewed not as a problem of how to articulate the relationships between those determinations specific to literature and the more general economic, political and ideological determinations which Marxism sees as relevant to the analysis of any practice, but of how to resolve the tension between any determinist account which focuses on the analysis of conditions of production and the apparently contradictory evidence afforded by those texts which continue to register their effects when the originating conditions of their production have passed away.

In sum, it has been posed less as a problem *within* Marxism than as one *between* Marxism and bourgeois criticism; less as a problem concerning the articulation of different levels of determination within a social formation, than as one of reconciling Marxism's materialism with the idealist theories of value propounded within pre-Marxist criticisms. The result has been that the role allotted to conditions of textual production has been shamefacedly curtailed, as it has been acknowledged that texts do break free from the conditions of their production in registering continuous and long-term effects within a culture, whilst, at the same time, it has been ludicrously extended as it has been argued that whether or not texts do thus break free from their conditions of production is 'finally' determined by those conditions of production themselves. Such a materialism is a materialism purchased at a price: first, because it results in a one-sided historical approach to the study of literary texts, as if the history that flowed into the text through the conditions of its production were the only one that counted, overriding or cancelling out in advance the history which might bear on it through the history of its consumption; second, because the reductionism that is avoided in one area of fiction is actively endorsed in relation to other since, by the *very force of the argument*, non-canonized texts are *necessarily* collapsed back into the conditions of production from which they derive. Here, it would seem, culture works by reflex – not so much because detailed textual study has supported this conclusion but because it is *necessitated* by the attempt to render a materialist account of the specificity of Literature in terms of the uniqueness of its relations to the conditions of its production.

This 'necessitarianism' is most clearly seen in the way Marxist critics have addressed the problem of the relative autonomy of 'the literary' and the diverse modes of its relations to the ideological. No matter which school of criticism – Lukácsian, Frankfurt, Althusserian – the position advanced is substantially the same: Literature is not ideology and is relatively autonomous in relation to it, whereas popular fiction is ideology and is reduced to it. Literature, it is usually argued, either rises above ideology because of its social typicality or the depth of its historical penetration (Lukács), or consists of a specific set of formal operations upon it (Althusser): but 'popular' or 'mass' fiction is viewed as simply a reflection or formulaic reproduction of the ideology on which it is dependent and which it simply passes on. 'Popular literature', as Roger Bromley has put it, 'is one among many of the material forms which ideology takes (or through which it is mediated) under capitalism, and is an instance of its social production through the medium of writing.'[25]

The difficulties with such formulations are numerous. It is just not possible to contend, to take Althusser's proposition, that it is only in the case of 'truly authentic' art, and not at all in the case of 'average or mediocre' works, that a distance is opened up between the 'literary' and the 'ideological'. For instance, quite an elaborate play with the dominant forms of narrative ideology is to be found in the detective novel[27], whereas the detective film, as Stephen Neale has put it, 'dramatizes the signification process itself as its fundamental problem'.[28] More generally, the entire field of popular fiction – especially film and television – is replete with parodic forms in which considerable 'distancing', 'alluding', 'foregrounding' and so on takes place. Whilst an exact categorization of programmes such as *Monty Python's Flying Circus*, *Not the 9 o'clock News* and *Ripping Yarns* may be difficult, it is clear, first, that they are *popular* and they are *fiction*; and second, that they are not *just* ideology: they disrupt not merely conventional narrative forms but are often profoundly, if anarchically, subversive of the dominant ideological discourses of class, nation, sexism and so on.

Such empirical difficulties apart, the very attempt to found a distinction between Literature and popular fiction – so that one is differentiated from, and the other flattened against, ideology – results in a crucial theoretical inconsistency according to which the effectivity that is granted to formal and aesthetic strategies in relation to ideological categories in one area of fiction is withheld from often not dissimilar strategies in other areas of fiction. Such a formulation is, at best, illogical: any area of writing in which fictional devices and strategies are in evidence must, in some way or other, effect a specific *production* of the ideological discourses contained within it. It cannot, if the concept of 'fiction' is to retain any usefulness as a differentiating term, simply be equated with such ideological discourses. Nor, if the logic of reflection theory is faulty elsewhere, can it be construed as a mere reflection or formulaic reproduction of them. At worst, however, it is self-fulfilling, the product of a rift within the critical strategy of Marxism which guarantees that popular texts be viewed reductively. If 'literary' texts have been distinguished from ideology whereas popular texts have been collapsed back into it, this is partly attributable to the fact that these different regions of textual production have received different types of critical attention which serve to buttress the supposition that the distinctions between them are, indeed, organized and explicable in these terms. In their treatment of canonized texts, Marxists have focused on the specifically formal means and mechanisms by which such texts either distance themselves from, or lift themselves above, the merely ideological. When dealing with popular texts, however, they have tended to read through such specifically formal operations, to plunder the texts for the evidence of the 'falsifications' or reality which they contain, and, in doing so, have joined hands with bourgeois criticism in reproducing, in the very form of their critical practice itself, the Literature/popular fiction distinction in its ideological form.

Such contradictions are attributable, ultimately, to the pressure which 'Literature' has exerted on the way the problem of relative autonomy has been conceived and addressed. Rather than being posed as a problem

concerning the complex and diverse articulation of two different regions
of the ideological, the literary (or fictional) and the discursive, it has been
construed as a problem concerning the relationship between Literature
(as a specific and privileged area of fictional practice) and Ideology
viewed, variously, as the domain of false consciousness, as the opposite
of Marxism, or as a specific practice producing specific 'imaginary'
subject positions which give rise to the effect of 'misrecognition'. Such a
project is misconceived because the categories with which it deals –
Literature and Ideology – are, inasmuch as they have their provenance in
different bodies of theory (bourgeois criticism and Marxism respectively),
mismatched from the outset. Put simply, there is no *necessary* reason why
a space should exist within Marxist theory for the concept of Literature,
and the attempt to clear such a space has resulted in the problem of the
relationship between the literary or the fictional (in their diverse modes)
and the ideological being resolved by definitional *fiat*. Ultimately, the
proffered equation of popular fiction with ideology within Marxism is a
tautology, a *necessary* definition entailed by the way in which the relations
between Literature, Science (Marxism) and Ideology have already been
constituted. Once Literature has been distinguished from Ideology and
from Science (Marxism) in the formulations of classical Marxism's
favoured 'holy trinity of the superstructure', then there is, quite simply,
nowhere that popular fiction can be placed, other than within the ideological,
which does not call into question the category of Literature and the terms
in which its specificity has been theoretically constructed. The effect of
the category of Literature has been, to so constrain Marxists theoretically
that they have had *no option* but to argue, time and again, that since
popular fiction is not Marxism (it does not contain any analysis of social
relationships), and since it is not Literature either (it does not have the
critical 'edge' of Literature), then it *must* be ideology.

These difficulties are evident in Roger Bromley's 'Natural Boundaries:
the Social Function of Popular Fiction' (see note 26), an attempt to
develop and insert a theory of popular fiction within an *already mapped-
out* system of relations between Literature, Science (Marxism) and
Ideology. 'Popular literature', Bromley suggests, 'should be regarded as a
specific ideological practice within an ideological apparatus (publishing,
communications, media, etc.), and as such participates in the permanent
insertion of individuals and their actions in practices governed by
ideological apparatuses'.[29] This would seem to constitute popular fiction
as a specific region of ideology, housed within specific apparatuses and
with specific means of production giving rise to specific effects. It
appears, however, that its specificity consists in its secondariness:
popular fiction 'is not a primary site of ideology (cf. the educational
system) but is one of the secondary areas where ideological components
are represented, and reinforced . . .'.[30] Popular fiction, then, is that

region of ideology within which the permanent insertion of individuals and their actions in practices governed by ideological apparatuses' is buttressed and reinforced by the ways those discourses which occupy 'the primary sites of ideology' are reproduced and passed on. The specific effectivity of popular texts, Bromley suggests, consists in their naturalization of the ideological discourses they contain and relay – they function in the same way as Barthes's category of 'myth'. In naturalizing the order of ideological signifiers contained within it, the popular text does 'operate' on ideology, but only by way of passing it on unnoticed, 'uniform, unambiguous and non-contradictory'.[31]

This being so, the task of a Marxist reading of such forms is to penetrate beneath the occluding workings of the text, to pull out and identify the primary ideological discourses they conceal, and, having done so, to reveal them as distortions of – well, reality, what else? It is in this way, Bromley suggests, that popular fiction 'achieves its plausibility by working basically with a paradigm of two parallel absences and presences':

ABSENT	PRESENT
The current relations of production.	Personal relations.
The bourgeoisie (the real ruling class) as personified in economic categories.	Aristocracy (fraction offered at the level of style and code as *real* ruling class).
The working classes, defined in relation to capitalism as economic personifications of *labour*. That is to say: Capital and Labour in its fundamental relations of antagonism under capitalism.	The petit-bourgeoisie personified in the *woman* particularly (and in authorial ideology.)
Exchange Relations in the economy.	Marriage: non-antagonism. House as property, self-owning and self-growing.
Division of labour.	No divisions other than the natural.
Society.	Nature. Self consciousness.[32]

A number of problems coalesce in this argument. It is clear, first, that the formal and aesthetic strategies Bromley describes are not at all specific to popular texts. They are rather those general strategies of classical realism as theorized by Colin MacCabe. The essay thus offers not an analysis of the ideological effects of popular fiction, but an analysis of the ideological effects which might be attributed to all texts – whether canonized or popular – within which such realist strategies predominate. Second, although clearly concerned to develop a general theory of popular fiction, Bromley does so entirely by means of extrapolation from features exhibited by a single genre: the late-nineteenth-century feminine romance. This is, in fact, a reflex of that inherited cast of mind which, in presupposing the essential distinction traversing the sphere of writing to be that which runs between Literature and 'the rest', assumes that analysis of a part of this residue will suffice for generalization about the whole. Yet it is clear that, had a different genre been studied – science fiction, say – Bromley's right-hand column would be entirely differently filled, and, as a consequence, the present/absent relations supposedly constitutive of popular fiction would collapse from within. Perhaps most important of all, however: the 'limit text' which furnishes the point of comparison for popular fiction, and in relation to which it is found wanting, is none other than *Capital*. The system of oppositions in the chart makes one point and one point only: popular fiction is not Marxism; it does not represent social relations in the same way as Marxism does and, accordingly, is a falsification of the version of reality which Marxism offers. All of which is no doubt true, but it is hardly surprising, or even necessarily regrettable; at least, not unless one subscribes to the requirements of a realist aesthetic.

But it is, of course, politically that the effects of this approach are most damaging. For its *en bloc* categorization of popular fiction as a sphere of writing which contributes to the reproduction of dominant ideological formations entails that it be abandoned as a field of struggle. The only relation of political calculation it permits is that of struggling *against* popular fiction (by unmasking it, by opposing to it the knowledge of Marxism or the critical insights of Literature), rather than *within* it. It is necessary to insist, in the face of the essentialism that has blighted much Marxist discussion of the internal economy of the superstructure, that conflict and struggle take place *within* and not just *between* the different regions and spheres of the superstructure. Beating popular fiction over the head with the three volumes of *Capital* is, politically, beside the point; what is needed are terms of theorization which will enable writers and critics to intervene, in a strategically calculated way, *within* the processes of popular reading and writing. Hegemony is to be won, not by sailing against the prevailing wind but by plotting a course across it.

Questions of political calculation

This brings me to the influence that the problem of value (and, through that, the category of Literature) has had on the way in which questions of political calculation have been posed within Marxist criticism. If the problem of value has been implicitly equated with, and addressed through, the problem of the specificity of Literature, questions of political calculation have been merged with both in the assumption that the determination of an aesthetic carries with it the determination of a politics. This has yielded a series of competing equations (different in substance but similar in kind) proffered by contending theoretical tendencies; equations of the type 'politically progressive texts' = 'valued texts' = 'those texts which most closely approximate to the model of literariness' (as posited by the critical tendency concerned). Political debates have, thus, been inextricably bound up with debates as to what, precisely, constitute the distinguishing characteristics of the aesthetic, with the result that political calculations have been advanced from within, and as emanations of, opposing theories of the specificity of the aesthetic. In fact, in Marxist criticism it is with aesthetic issues that the real base-lines of disagreement have been drawn, political disputes often being epiphenomenal in relation to these.

The assumption of a correlation between the determination of an aesthetic and of a politics has supported the view that a text's political effects can be read-off from, or calculated solely on the basis of, an analysis of its formal properties. This assumption lies behind those debates whereby one is expected to decide, in an abstracted way, either for or against realism or modernism, for or against texts of *plaisir* or texts of *jouissance*, or to weigh in the balance the effects of the semiotic chora; in short, behind that entire tradition in which essentialism vies with essentialism. It is easy, as Terry Eagleton has admonished, to struggle free of such essentialism only to fall foul of 'an "extreme conjuncturalism" which merely collapses the work into its various moments of reception'.[33] Nonetheless, the decisive objection to such purely formal approaches to literary politics is that the conjuncture constitutes *the only possible political 'place'* into which a text can play and register its effects. Still, Eagleton is right to warn against an unpardonable reduction of the conditions of reception to the political circumstances of the conjuncture. The way in which the text is inserted and has effects in relation to any given conjuncture needs to be viewed as being mediated through the systems of intertextuality – the changing articulations of text-ideology relations – which bear upon the moment of reception. It is as it is accessible through these that the text enters back into history – is historically 'redetermined' – during the process of its reception, figuring not as the *source of an* effect, but as the *site* on which *plural and even contradictory* effects may be produced during the course of its history as a received text.

The calculation of political effects, however, requires not only that the conjuncture or the prevailing system of intertextual relations be taken into account; there is also the question of the reader – of his/her position in the conjuncture, and of how s/he is placed in relation to the systems of intertextuality which regulate the act of reading. Whilst the 'effects' tradition within media sociology is seldom laudable, it has given serious consideration to questions of the audience; and in recent years, the input of semiological perspectives to the process of 'decoding' has yielded a climate of opinion in film and television studies which is more cautious than that discernible in literary-critical circles concerning the extent to which effects can be inferred from form. Put simply, there are, as yet, no serious readership studies, a project which the literary left has culpably neglected.

This is not to suggest that readership studies should replace textual analysis; the text clearly constrains the possible ways in which it may be read, although these limits can never be specified in advance. Nor is it to suggest that existing models of audience research should simply be borrowed; these clearly place too much reliance on simple-minded questionnaire techniques. It is rather to recognize that the ground on which the text produces its effects consists not of naked subjectivities but of individuals interpellated into particular subject positions within a variety of different – and sometimes contradictory – ideological formations. This further entails recognizing that such positions vary in accordance with considerations of race, class and gender and, concerning their insertion within the system of intertextual relations, on the degree to which, within the educational apparatus, the institution of Literature has borne upon their ideological formation, upon their positioning as readers. As John Hill has argued:

> The early claim of semiotics to be in some way able to account for a text's functioning through an immanent analysis was essentially misfounded in its failure to perceive that any textual system could only have meaning in relation to codes not purely textual, and that the recognition, distribution and activation of these would vary socially and historically. . . . We would want to argue that readership must be understood in terms of broader patterns of socio-cultural consumption whereby texts are read both 'aesthetically' in terms of codes specifically 'artistic', and 'socially', in relation to the broader contours of life-experience engendered via class, race, sex and nation, where again these are not conceived as homogeneous but variegated. . . .[34]

If such considerations are not allowed a determining role in relation to the process of reading, the result is liable to be an approach to the calculation of the text's effects which, implicitly, is orientated to an assumed reader: white, male and bourgeois. Indeed, only too often (think of Adorno) the implied reader has been none other than the critic himself. More than a theoretical point is at issue here; consideration of the reader also requires that the very practice of Marxist criticism itself be re-thought. If texts do not have effects but serve as the site on which effects may be produced, then the question of effects is pre-eminently a practical problem; the problem as how best to intervene within the social process of the production of textual effects. 'In analysing literature', Colin MacCabe has argued, 'one is engaged in a battle of readings, not chosen voluntaristically but determined institutionally. The validity of interpretation is determined in the present in the political struggle over literature'.[35] The object of Marxist criticism is not that of producing an aesthetic, of revealing the truth about an already pre-constituted Literature, but that of intervening within the social process of reading and writing. It is no longer enough, if ever it was, to stand in front of the text and deliver it of its truth. Marxist critics must begin to think strategically about which forms of critical practice can best politicize the process of reading. This may mean different forms of criticism, and different forms of writing, for different groups of readers. As Brecht said: 'You cannot just "write the truth"; you have to write it *for*, and *to* somebody, somebody who can do something with it'[36]. Not a sufficient antidote, perhaps, to a theoreticism which has made, in Willemen's words, 'discursive activities immune from the necessity of planning and strategy in favour of a radical a-historicist opportunism that abdicated, in theory, any responsibility for the effects discursive practices may have'[37] – but a start. [. . .]

Notes

1. T. Davies, 'Education, Ideology and Literature', *Red Letters*, No. 7 (1978), p. 13.

2. S. Hall, 'Some Paradigms in Cultural Studies', *Annali*, xxi (3) (1978), p. 26.

3. L. Goldmann, *The Hidden God: A Study of Tragic Vision in the Pensées of Pascal and the Tragedies of Racine* (London: Routledge and Kegan Paul, 1964), p. 314.

4. L. Althusser, 'A Letter on Art', in *Lenin and Philosophy, and Other Essays* (London: New Left Books, 1971), p. 204.

5. L. Lowenthal, *Literature, Popular Culture and Society* (California: Pacific Books, 1961).

6. Q.D. Leavis, *Fiction and the Reading Public* (London: Chatto and Windus, 1965).

7. F. Mulhern, 'Marxism in Literary Criticism', *New Left Review*, No. 108 (1978), p. 68.

8. P. Anderson, *Considerations on Western Marxism* (London: New Left Books, 1976).

9. T. Bennett, *Formalism and Marxism* (London: Methuen, 1979).

10. T. Eagleton, *Criticism and Ideology* (London: New Left Books, 1976), p. 187.

11. Mulhern, 'Marxism in Literary Criticism', p. 86.

12. Mulhern, 'Marxism in Literary Criticism', p. 86.

13. Eagleton, *Criticism and Ideology*, p. 162, my emphasis.

14. Eagleton, *Criticism and Ideology*, p. 162 my emphasis.

15. Eagleton, *Criticism and Ideology*, p. 164.

16. Eagleton, *Criticism and Ideology*, p. 166.

17. Eagleton, *Criticism and Ideology*, p. 167.

18. Eagleton, *Criticism and Ideology*, p. 167.

19. Eagleton, *Criticism and Ideology*, p. 169.

20. Eagleton, *Criticism and Ideology*, pp. 168–9.

21. Eagleton, *Criticism and Ideology*, pp.185–6.

22. Eagleton, *Criticism and Ideology*, p. 179.

23. Eagleton, *Criticism and Ideology*, p. 187.

24. J. Revai, 'A Review of George Lukács's 'History and Class Consciousness', *Theoretical Practice*, 1 (Jan. 1971), p. 28.

25. R. Williams, *Politics and Letters* (London: New Left Books, 1979), p. 326.

26. R. Bromley, 'Natural Boundaries: the Social Function of Popular Fiction', *Red Letters*, No. 7 (1978), p. 40.

27. See comments on the Sherlock Holmes stories in C. Belsey, *Critical Practice* (London: Methuen, 1980).

28. S. Neale, *Genre* (London: BFI, 1980), p. 26.

29. Bromley, 'Natural Boundaries', p. 42.

30. Bromley, 'Natural Boundaries', p. 40.

31. Bromley, 'Natural Boundaries', p. 39.

32. Bromley, 'Natural Boundaries', pp. 52–3.

33. T. Eagleton, 'What is Literature', *New Statesman*, (6 July 1979), p. 20.

34. J. Hill, 'Ideology, Economy and the British Cinema', in *Ideology and Cultural Reproduction*, ed. M. Barrett, P. Corrigan, A. Kuhn and J. Wolff (London: Croom Helm, 1979), p. 122.

35. C. MacCabe, *James Joyce and the Revolution of the Word* (London: Macmillan, 1978), p. 26.

36. Cit. P. Slater, *Origin and Significance of the Frankfurt School. A Marxist Perspective* (London: Routledge and Kegan Paul, 1977), p. 141.

37. Cit. Neale, *Genre*, p. 4.

10 Licensed to Look: James Bond and the Heroism of Consumption* (1987)

Michael Denning

Michael Denning (b.1954) teaches American studies at Yale University. As well as *Cover Stories*, he has written *Mechanic Accents: Dime Novels and Working-class Culture in America* (also 1987).

Denning acknowledges the ancestry of Ian Fleming's Bond novels in the Imperial spy thriller, and affirms their part in a typically racist and sexist cultural politics; but his particular purpose is to read them as an historically specific variant of the genre, belonging to the era of the Cold War and the consumer–capitalist 'society of the spectacle'. Mass tourism and mass pornography are the distinctively post-war cultural codes that these texts reiterate and, through the image and activity of their protagonist, render meaningful and even heroic.

Thrillers of the spectacle

With James Bond, the spy thriller enters its moment of greatest popularity. Just as earlier espionage themes came to dominate the thriller generally, now the espionage thriller comes to dominate the entire field of popular fiction. Tales of spies are no longer one part of popular culture; they are its center. James Bond transcended the novels and films which brought him to life, and joined that small group of fictional characters who are known by many who never read or saw the 'original' texts – figures like Robinson Crusoe and Sherlock Holmes. But this presence of Bond in the popular imagination is itself only one part of the presence of espionage in the culture of the late 1950s and early 1960s: spy stories proliferated in novels, on film and on TV; in the daily

---

* Reprinted from Michael Denning, *Cover Stories: Narrative and Ideology in the British Spy Thriller* (London: Routledge and Kegan Paul, 1987), pp. 91–113.

newspapers, the sensational cases of George Blake and Kim Philby marked the spy fever of the 1960s. Christopher Booker, in a history of the period's culture, writes:

> The curious way in which the Bond phenomenon had become a shadow to the history of the age, had been given a further twist in March 1961 when an American magazine had revealed that one of the most fervent Bond readers was President Kennedy. Partly aided by this revelation, in 1961 and 1962, the sales of Bond books on both sides of the Atlantic had soared. Now, by the end of 1962, with the arrival of new authors such as Len Deighton (north London) and John le Carré (Oxford early 50s), a Foreign Office official, 'spy literature', like satire, seemed to be turning into an industry. It was also in November 1962, that with the arrival of James Bond on the screen, played by the former Carnaby Street model and Royal Court actor Sean Connery (Glasgow), the record-breaking *Dr. No* marked the beginning of a turn in British cinema away from 'Northern Realism' and indeed 'naturalism' of any kind towards an altogether more colourful and sensational kind of fantasy. The real explanation for this new popularity of spy stories, in fact, was not so much that they were a reflection of the increase in real life spying, as a more subtle reflection of the *Zeitgeist*.[1]

Though the *Zeitgeist* is easier to invoke than to define, the spy novel is in a sense the war novel of the Cold War, the cover story of an era of decolonization and, particularly after the débâcle at Suez in 1956, the definitive loss of Britain's role as a world power.

Ian Fleming's first novel about James Bond, *Casino Royale*, was published in 1953; twelve more novels and the two collections of short stories were published by 1965. But the moment of Bond does not really begin until the publication of *Casino Royale* in Pan paperback in 1956, and the serialization of *From Russia, With Love* in the *Daily Express* in 1957; after which the sales of the Bond books took off, reaching a peak in 1964 and 1965 in the wake of the release of the first Bond films. For it was the Bond books that brought the American paperback revolution to Britain. 'They were', John Sutherland writes, 'a breakthrough comparable in some ways to Lane's, thirty years earlier', that is, to Allen Lane's Penguins. Pan claimed that ten of the first eighteen million-sellers in Britain were Bond novels.[2]

And just as this qualitative leap in the mode of production of popular fiction must be marked off from the fiction that preceded it, so there is also a discontinuity between the spy thrillers of the first half of the century and this new expansion of the thriller – a discontinuity that ought not be effaced by the conventions of literary histories of the genre. For no formal account of the genre's progress explains the Bond books and their enormous popularity. Surely the logic of increasing verisimilitude, the sense that each new breakthrough in the spy novel marks a more convincing code of realism, does not account for Fleming's fantastic tales, despite his skill at using the reality-effect in details, a skill that led Kingsley Amis to define that device as the 'Fleming effect'.[3] Rather what is remarkable is the way that the earlier spy thriller had spent much of its force; both Greene and Ambler had largely given up the spy thriller by the late 1940s, and they were to return to the genre in the 1960s because of the new centrality accorded it by the work of Fleming, le Carré, and Deighton.

So how are we to account for this new thriller, and how describe its constituents? The obvious place to begin would be with the figure of James Bond himself, particularly in light of the way that he managed to transcend his textual embodiment and join Sherlock Holmes as a major character in the popular imagination. The difficulty lies in the variety of James Bonds there are. Some critics find him essentially a continuation of the tradition of snobbery with violence, an all too familiar aristocratic clubman with an even greater degree of sadism thrown in. Others see him as a modern and modernizing hero, the 'perfect pipe-dream figure for organization man', as Julian Symons put it.[4] Some see him as a 'cold warrior', a racist and a sexist; others stress the moments when he seems to parody these. Is he really an amateur out defending the realm, an updated Richard Hannay (after all, Hannay's amateur status did not preclude his working for the government), or is he the consummate professional, totally subordinate to the service? Is his amateurism maintained by his game-like attitude toward his missions and his sense of improvisation, or do his training and competence together with his lack of developed self-consciousness put him firmly in the camp of the professional, doing a job? Or, to put it another way, is he really an upper-class clubman, trained in the public school ethic, or is he an Americanized 'classless' modernizer, bringing 'the white heat of technology' to the spy thriller? Is he a superhero, or is he, as Ian Fleming thought, absolutely ordinary?

No doubt readers will answer these questions in part through their sense of the character, their after-image of the tales, and in part by citing pieces of evidence, kernels of character, the attributes mentioned in one place or another that build the narrative illusion which is 'a character'. So an Amis will point out that Bond is not really an aristocrat because he never drinks port or sherry. The point is that each set of attributes can be countered with another; Bond is a contested figure who has been accented in a number of ways. Indeed, the story of the casting for the film Bond illustrates this well: Fleming himself preferred David Niven, a figure who had played upper-class characters. However, after the choice of Sean Connery, Fleming remarked, 'Not quite the idea I had of Bond, but he would be if I wrote the books over again'.[5] Connery was meant to give more of a 'man of the people' image to Bond, and Christopher Booker argues that Connery's Bond was part of a 'new class' of image producers that dominated the culture of the late 1950s and early 1960s, mixing lower-class origins with media affluence and consumerism. The later casting of Roger Moore as Bond returned the character to an older, more class-ridden paradigm since Moore was strongly identified with his television portrayal of the gentleman outlaw of the 1930s, the Saint.

But the contest over Bond's public image was already a part of the novels. In *From Russia, With Love*, the 1957 tale which I will examine in some detail, the point of the Russian plot is to kill Bond 'WITH IGNOMINY'. They wish to humiliate and destroy not only the man but the image, the myth which is important to the British secret service. The strength of the British, we are told, 'lies in the myth – the myth of Scotland Yard, of Sherlock Holmes, of the Secret Service . . . this myth is a hindrance which it would be good to set aside . . . Have they no one who is a hero to the organization? Someone who is admired and whose ignominious destruction would cause dismay? Myths are built on heroic deeds and heroic people. Have they no such men?. . .' The answer, of course, is: 'There is a man called Bond'.[6]

The plot to destroy Bond's image itself employs that image: the Russians convince the British secret service that one of their women agents has fallen in love with a photograph of Bond. The manifest absurdity of this plot is explained away by Bond's superior, M., who invokes a 'common' behaviour in a society of images: 'Suppose you happened to be a film star instead of being in this particular trade. You'd get daft letters from girls all over the world stuffed with Heaven knows what sort of rot about not being able to live without you and so on. Here's a silly girl doing a secretary's job in Moscow . . . And she gets what I believe they call a "crush" on this picture [of Bond], just as secretaries all over the world get crushes on these dreadful faces in the magazines.' Therefore Bond's job is to behave like the image: 'It is with an image she has fallen in love. Behave like that image'.[7]

In a way, our relation to Bond as readers is not far removed from that of Tatiana Romanova, investing our own energies in a mere image. This has two different effects. First, and less significantly, it means that Bond is something of a cipher which can be invested with a variety of content. But, more importantly, these different investments do not seem to distort an original Bond, for the effect of the Bond image is to efface its origins. Bond is a character of the present, not one with a particular class history, or regional rootedness. He is not a type, and we feel the self-mocking humor when, at one point in *The Man With the Golden Gun*, Bond claims that 'EYE AM A SCOTTISH PEASANT AND EYE WILL ALWAYS FEEL AT HOME BEING A SCOTTISH PEASANT'.[8]

Here we do find his link with that new class that Booker speaks of: though they are not so much a class as themselves avatars of a particular image of affluence, fashion, modernity, and classlessness. These 'New Aristocrats' were creators of images: Booker cites pop singers (the Beatles, Mick Jagger), photographers (David Bailey), interior decorators, spy novelists (Deighton), actors (Michael Caine, Connery), and fashion designers. Though they may have come from working-class, lower-middle-class and northern back-grounds, the effect of the aristocracy of images was to efface their origins: the jacket notes on Len Deighton's novels which variously claim that he is the son of a chauffeur or the son of the Governor General of the Windward Islands, which have him educated at either the Royal College of Art or at Eton and Oxford, and which attribute to him a variety of jobs, are a playful example of this effacement and confusion of origins.

Nevertheless, the analogy between Bond as image and the brief reign of the 'New Aristocrats' is merely the beginning of an explanation of the cultural meaning and power of Bond: what it does is point us to the crucial term, the production and proliferation of images. In what follows I will look at the way two central aspects of the thriller, the game and the empire, are reconstructed in the tales of Fleming in the terms of a society of the spectacle, and will then look at the meaning of the new prominence of the codes of sexuality in the Fleming thriller.

Killing time

In *The Spy Who Loved Me*, James Bond tries to explain the enterprise of spying to Vivienne Michel:

> It's nothing but a complicated game, really. But then so's international politics, diplomacy – all the trappings of nationalism and the power complex that goes on between countries. Nobody will stop playing the game. It's like the hunting instinct.[9]

In many ways this is, as we have seen, the oldest trope in the book. The figure of the Great Game for spying and international intrigue comes in a heroic version in the early thrillers of Buchan and Sapper, but it is no less present when it is unveiled as a mystification in the cynical tales of Ambler and Maugham. In Fleming, we find a new inflection: it is still a heroic and necessary game and one that Bond enjoys playing; nevertheless, it is clearly a deadly serious game, one for professionals not amateurs.

But much as the Bond thrillers draw on these older paradigms of the game and the ethic of sportsmanship and fair play, reworking them and at times parodying them, the game also takes on a new significance through the foregrounding of two sorts of game: first, the way the plot structure itself resembles a game, and second, the attention to the representation of a variety of games in the books.

The game-like nature of the Bond tales was the subject of Umberto Eco's important and influential essay on narrative structure in Fleming's novels. He argued that the novels were structures like a game with a set of rules, pieces, and conventional moves: the reader knows the rules, the pieces, and the moves – even the outcome is not a surprise – and watches the game unfold. The sequence of moves is strictly determined with only the slightest variation. And not only is the story constructed like a game but the story itself is a game, a contest, a series of what Eco calls 'play situations'.[10]

This game-like nature of the tales, which Bond himself recognizes in his oft-repeated comment about his 'playing Red Indians', also makes for the formalism of the books (and indeed licenses the formalism of Eco's analysis). All existential or psychological elements are carefully excluded, as we can see if we think of neighboring genres. The tradition of the thriller as a hunt, for example, which the Bond books resemble, usually takes the extremity of men hunting men as an example of an existential confrontation with the primitive, the instinctual, and so forth. In Geoffrey Household's *Rogue Male* (1939), for example, we see the reduction of all life to a 'kill or be killed' situation, as the hunter-hunted narrator progressively sheds all trappings of civilization. One can see a similar process in more recent hunt tales such as Desmond Bagley's *Running Blind* (1970) or Gavin Lyall's *The Most Dangerous Game* (1964) (where the most dangerous game – in the sense of prey – is men). Bond's adventures, though similar, do not evoke this. They are, first of all, of a serial nature; far from being the exceptional reduction of civilized man to his 'true' primitive nature, his adventures are all part of the job. They are closer to that other popular formula, 'capers', which are elaborately and professionally planned operations, the accomplishment of a particularly difficult coup, as in the assassination of de Gaulle in Frederick Forsyth's *The Day of the Jackal* (1971) or the *coup d'état* in his *The Dogs of War* (1974). There is little mystery involved in these adventures: suspense reigns. Rather than the continually deferred question of whodunnit, we have the continually repeated question of what happened next or even the technical question of how was it accomplished.

If this begins to explain the absence of an existential explanatory system, we can see the lack of real psychological motivation by comparing Bond to the formula of the avenger, exploited in a paradigmatic way in the stories of Mickey Spillane, stories which are often linked to those of Fleming and which had a significant influence on

Fleming. By exploiting the desire for revenge, Spillane produces books which are fully as formulaic as the Bond tales but which are by no means game-like.

This game-like structure comes to a sort of narrative self-consciousness in *From Russia, With Love*. In *From Russia, With Love*, Bond's Turkish ally, Kerim, tells Bond: 'But I was not brought up to "be a sport" . . . This is not a game to me. It is a business. For you it is different. You are a gambler.' Like the Hairless Mexican in Maugham's *Ashenden*, Kerim 'hasn't had the advantages of a public-school education'. But it is his metaphor that marks the limit of the text:

> This is a billiard table. An easy, flat, green billiard table. And you have hit your white ball and it is travelling easily and quietly towards the red. The pocket is alongside. Fatally, inevitably, you are going to hit the red and the red is going into that pocket. It is the law of the billiard table, the law of the billiard room. But, outside the orbit of these things, a jet pilot has fainted and his plane is diving straight at that billiard room, or a gas main is about to explode, or lightning is about to strike. And the building collapses on top of you and on top of the billiard table. Then what has happened to that white ball that could not miss the red ball, and to the red ball that could not miss the pocket? The white ball could not miss according to the laws of the billiard table. But the laws of the billiard table are not the only laws, and the laws governing the progress of this train, and of you to your destiny, are also not the only laws in this particular game.[11]

Indeed, this sense of different levels of rules is more pronounced in *From Russia, With Love* than in most Fleming tales. Here we find a less pronounced version of the formula found in the other books: there is no game between Bond and the villain, no fantastic plot for world domination by the villain. Both the original plot – to destroy not so much Bond as the image of Bond – and the final struggle with Red Grant in the curious 'battle of the books' show a self-consciousness about the laws of Fleming's own 'billiard table'. And the ending, the quite unexpected and unrelieved death of Bond, seems to be a stepping outside of those laws. Ironically, perhaps, though *From Russia, With Love* killed off Bond, it surely didn't kill off his image: the peak of Bond's celebrity began with the serialization of *From Russia, With Love* in the *Daily Express*. So Fleming dutifully resurrected Bond at the beginning of the next novel, *Dr. No*, setting him up for new games.

However, the appearance of the game in the narrative structure is not the only aspect of the game figure that is new in the Fleming tales. So too is the extraordinary amount of space devoted to representing games and sports. One of Fleming's talents is as a sportswriter, whether he is writing about Bond's golf match with Goldfinger, the baccarat game against Le Chiffre, the bridge game against Drax, or the ski chase in *On Her Majesty's Secret Service*. In part, these are used to play out the conventions of the ethic of sportsmanship. In *Moonraker*, for example, Sir Hugo Drax is introduced as a quite extraordinary man – with one reservation: he cheats at cards. As M. says, 'don't forget that cheating at cards can still smash a man. In so-called Society, it's about the only crime that can still finish you, whoever you are'. Nevertheless, Bond's victory over Drax, and over Goldfinger, who cheats at golf, comes not through revealing the cheater to Society, the arbiter, but through cheating in return. After all, as Bond thinks in the course of his deception of Goldfinger, 'there was more to this than a game of golf. It was Bond's duty to win'.[12]

A second use of the games is to establish a system of national characters. National characters are in part delineated by the sorts of games that are played. So the Russians are chess players: Kronsteen in *From Russia, With Love*, the 'Wizard of Ice', is a chess master and spymaster who sees people as pawns and recalls cases as he does gambits. Bond and the British, on the other hand, are gamblers, both in the casino and in the field.

But the representation of games and sports has less to do with either the older public school ethic or the stereotypes of national character than with the new ethic of consumption and leisure. For the games Bond plays, like the liquor he drinks and the automobiles he drives, serve as a kind of guide to leisure. The sports represented are not the public school cricket pitch, nor the aristocratic blood sports and yachting, nor the working-class spectator sport of football: they are the consumer sports of golf, skiing, and casino gambling. They have the glamor of being the sports of the wealthy, the sports of the holiday on the Continent, yet are relatively free from traditional class connotations. Like Bond's vodka martinis, they are neither port nor a pint at the pub.

But though these books are themselves for killing time, they are not simply guides to consumption, 'how-to' books, rehearsals for leisure. Rather they are also redemptions of consumption, an investing of the trivial contests of the fairway with global intrigue. If, in *Goldfinger*, Fleming devotes three times as much space to the golf match as to the robbery of Fort Knox, this is surely because the detail and attention to the contest the reader can imagine not only prepares him or her for the absurdity of the Fort Knox plot, but is also a more interesting story than the Fort Knox plot. For just as the spy stories of le Carré tell tales of white-collar work, so Fleming's adventures are really tales of leisure, tales where leisure is not a packaged, commodified 'holiday', filling up a space of 'time off' from work, an acceptable moment to 'kill time', but is

an adventure, a meaningful time, a time of life and death – in the words
of *From Russia, With Love*, a killing time.

Thrilling cities

All my life I have been interested in adventure and, abroad, I have
enjoyed the *frisson* of leaving the wide, well-lit streets and venturing
up back alleys in search of the hidden, authentic pulse of towns. It was
perhaps this habit that turned me into a writer of thrillers, and by the
time I made the two journeys that produced these essays, I had
certainly got into the way of looking at people and places and things
through a thriller-writer's eye.

– Ian Fleming, *Thrilling Cities* (1964)

In his essay on James Bond, Tony Bennett examines the narrative codes
that structure the stories and argues

that the ideologies of sexism and imperialism are inscribed within the
very form of the Bond novels . . . As the relations between Bond and
the villain and between Bond and the girl develop and move toward
their resolution, a series of collateral ideological tensions is thus
simultaneously worked through and resolved. It is in this way that the
Bond novels achieve their 'ideological effect' – the effect, figuratively
speaking, of placing women back in position beneath men and putting
England back on top.[13]

His account of the relation between ideologies and narrative codes is, I
think, a persuasive and productive one; and his focus on the 'imperialist
code' and the 'sexist code' is well taken: these are surely codes that unite
larger ideological themes with the detail of the narratives of Fleming.
However, the very names he gives these codes seems to elide the
specificity of Fleming's reconstruction of ideologies of Empire and the
novelty of his construction of an ideology of sexuality. So rather than
seeing the tales as a modernized version of the imperialist adventure tale,
it seems to me that their clearly imperialist and racist ideologies are
constructed through a narrative code of tourism; and rather than seeing
the sexual codes as a 'sexist code', the repositioning of the 'girl', who is
'out-of-place sexually', in the traditional ordering of sexual difference,
one can see that the 'girl' is put into place in a new ordering of the sex/
gender system, through the narrative code of pornography. In both
cases, I will argue in the following two sections, Bond's 'licence to kill' is
less significant than his 'licence to look'.

Travel and tourism make up much of the interest and action of a Bond thriller. The final and climactic quarter of *From Russia, With Love* takes place on the fabled Orient Express; the final struggle with Goldfinger occurs aboard a BOAC airliner; and in almost all the novels some space is given to narrating Bond's travels by plane and train. Umberto Eco argues that the 'Journey' is one of the principal 'play situations' in the novel. And indeed, the representation of travelling also works in capturing the reader, a reader who is often travelling himself or herself. From the W. H. Smiths at the nineteenth-century railway station to those at the twentieth-century airport, the sale and consumption of cheap fiction has been tied to the means of transport. Bond himself exemplifies this as he reads a copy of Eric Ambler's *The Mask of Dimitrios* on the flight into Istanbul in *From Russia, With Love* and when he picks up the 'latest Raymond Chandler' for his flight in *Goldfinger*.

Furthermore, the stories have a relation to tourism in that almost all of them take place in exotic locales. Only one Bond novel, *Moonraker*, takes place primarily in Britain, in striking contrast to the clubland thrillers of Buchan, Sapper, Dornford Yates, and Leslie Charteris. In part, this is a consequence of the post-war fiction market, which, as John Sutherland has remarked, was oriented to international Anglophone sales and encouraged international settings in writers as unalike as Fleming and Graham Greene. The loss of British world economic and political hegemony was accompanied by the loss of a cultural centrality; the obverse of imaginary centrality to the world of the British agent Bond is the marginality of Britain as a place of adventure.

But tourism takes its place as a central narrative code in the Fleming novels in a deeper way by infiltrating Fleming's prose and organizing the Fleming 'world system'. For the prose of the travel book and the tour guide is present in Fleming's work far beyond his own travel book, *Thrilling Cities*. In some cases, as in *Live and Let Die*, tourist guides supplant Fleming's prose entirely as the reader is treated to several pages about Haitian voodoo lifted directly from Patrick Leigh Fermor's *The Travellers Tree*; a footnote tells us that this is 'one of the great travel books'. In other cases, as in *You Only Live Twice*, there are tedious sections of straightforward travelogue by Fleming, filling up a sketchy plot with what one chapter title aptly terms 'Instant Japan'. But even in less extreme cases, the prose of the tourist guide inflects much of these novels, often lending them their interest and a certain degree of verisimilitude. So in *From Russia, With Love* we often find passages like this one of Bond awakening in Istanbul:

Bond got out of bed, drew back the heavy plush red curtains and leant on the iron balustrade and looked out over one of the most famous views in the world – on his right the still waters of the Golden Horn, on his left the dancing waves of the unsheltered Bosphorus, and, in between, the tumbling roofs, soaring minarets and crouching mosques of Pera. After all, his choice had been good. The view made up for many bedbugs and much discomfort.[14]

Here we find an epitome of the tourist's experience: the moment of relaxed visual contemplation from above, leaning on the balustrade; the aesthetic reduction of a social entity, the city, to a natural object, coterminous with the waves of the sea; the calculations of the tourist's economy, exchanging physical discomfort for a more 'authentic' view; and the satisfaction at having made the right exchange, having 'got' the experience, possessed the 'view'. Indeed, if we see Fleming's travel writing, like his sports writing, as the presence of the discourse of the spectacle, the discourse of consumer society, we can see how its effect is to redeem these activities of consumption, to heroize them. For the tourist is caught in a constant and inescapable dilemma: he or she is there to see, to capture the authenticity of the object in a moment of individual self-development. But he or she is caught in the fact that tourism is a mass spectacle, that he or she is only one of many tourists who have passed this way for the 'view', that, indeed, those other tourists may well be blocking the view and rendering impossible the solitary experience. This dilemma – to be superior to the 'tourists' while at once recognizing one's kinship with them – is what is solved by Bond, the ideal tourist, always alone and always superior. His tourism has an ostensible purpose, though the line between tourism and spying is a fine one.

Tourism and touristic ways of seeing are not only inscribed in Fleming's prose but also organize what might be called the Fleming 'world system', a world system dependent upon Cold War and imperialist ideologies but not entirely congruent with them. For the setting of the Bond books is not entirely established either by the Cold War axis of East and West – to which England is not central – or by the imperialist axis of British metropolis and colonial periphery. Rather it is established in large part by what Louis Turner and John Ash have termed the 'pleasure periphery', the tourist belt surrounding the industrialized world including the Mediterranean, the Caribbean, the Philippines, Hong Kong, Indonesia.[15] Much of this world is dependent upon the neo-colonialism of the tourist industry; it stands, for Bond, as an idyllic paradise, as a more authentic culture, and as a source of threat and upheaval.

As an idyllic paradise, these locations are the settings for sports, elaborate meals, and sexual adventure. The women who are 'out-of-place sexually', 'deviant' politically or sexually in that they are in league with the villain or are lesbians, are encountered in these 'pleasure

221

peripheries', and it is here, away from Miss Moneypenny and May, Bond's 'treasured Scottish housekeeper,' that Bond is free to battle, seduce, and then retreat to London. These women, as their names indicate (Pussy Galore, Tiffany Case, Honeychilde Rider, Kissy Suzuki), are apparently outside of the British sex/gender system entirely (though we will examine this more closely in the next section); they are part of the 'view'. Here Fleming's setting is not far from the tourist advertisements of a holiday in the sun.

The second meaning of these settings invokes a more complex version of tourism, the viewing of a more vital, more authentic culture. For tourism has often meant the encounter with another, non-capitalist (or non-monopoly capitalist) mode of production with its kinship structures, its handicrafts, its street life and marketplaces. And here Bond is given a more privileged access than the average tourist. He is taken, by his secret work, into secret worlds – the Harlem of Mr Big in *Live and Let Die*, the Jamaica of Dr No, and the Istanbul of Kerim in *From Russia, With Love*. These are the environs of the grotesque Fleming villains, who are, as Eco has shown, usually of mixed blood, obscure origins, abnormal sexuality, and physical monstrosity, and work in obscure alliances with the KGB. But they are also the home of those figures that we might call, after Propp, the donors: the characters – quintessentially Kerim in *From Russia, With Love* and Quarrel in *Dr No* – with whom Bond makes indispensable alliances, alliances that allow him access to the non-Western cultures and therefore give him the strength to defeat the villain on his home territory. Darko Kerim, for example, who heads the secret service's Istanbul office, mediates England and Turkey, having a Turkish father and an English mother. His knowledge of the territory is indispensable to Bond; he serves as a kind of tour guide not only to the presence of the Russians but also to the clubs and taverns of Istanbul. The visit to a gipsy restaurant leads to a supper with the gipsies and to Bond's witnessing a fight between two gipsy women, the settling of a family affair. As Kerim says to Bond, 'It will not be for the squeamish, but it will be a remarkable affair. It is a great privilege that we may be present. You understand? We are *gajos* [foreigners]. You will forget your sense of proprieties? You will not interfere? They will kill you, and possibly me, if you did.'[16] This is a tourist's view beyond that of the Bosphorus, a view of an 'older,' more thorough patriarchy, a fight between two women of the 'tribe' over the rights to the son, supervised by the father. It is a patriarchy that is seen in a less crude form in Kerim himself, all of whose operatives are sons. This world is seen as being surpassed – Kerim will be killed – but its secrets are needed by Bond, who has only the metaphoric institutional father, M.

But this world is also a threatening world to Bond. *Dr No* opens in Jamaica, where Fleming himself lived, and the narrator writes of the mansion that houses Kingston 'Society': 'Such stubborn retreats will not survive long in modern Jamaica. One day Queen's Club will have its windows smashed and perhaps be burned to the ground, but for the time being it is a useful place to find in a sub-tropical island – well run, well staffed and with the finest cuisine and cellar in the Caribbean.'[17] This sense of doom comes from the shadow of a real history hanging over the stories. The grotesque villains, each defeated in turn, are avatars of a more profound threat to the wellbeing, not only of England or the West, but of the tourist. We can mark this objectively as decolonization, the emergence of the character of the 'Third World' as the result of protracted liberation struggles throughout Asia, Africa, and Latin America. Frantz Fanon has written that the psychic equivalent of decolonization is the reversal of the look, the refusal to be the object of the colonizer's gaze. And this indeed is the anxiety of the tourist: as Felix Leiter, Bond's American helper, says to Bond: 'Harlem's a bit of a jungle these days. People don't go up there anymore like they used to . . . One used to go to the Savoy Ballroom and watch the dancing . . . Now that's all changed. Harlem doesn't like being stared at anymore.' A little later, 'Bond suddenly felt the force of what Leiter had told him. They were trespassing. They just weren't wanted'.[18] The narrative of tourism here finds its limits; Bond's licence to look is revoked.

For Your Eyes Only

But the new prominence of sex in the late Fifties was not just a concern with the realities of sex; even more, it was a preoccupation with the idea of sex, the image of sex; the written image, the visual image, the image that was promulgated in advertisements, in increasingly 'daring' films, in 'controversial' newspaper articles and 'frank' novels; the image purveyed by the strip-tease clubs and pornographic book shops that were springing up in the back streets of Soho and provincial cities; and the image that, mixed with that of violence, was responsible in the years after 1956 for the enormous boom in the sales of Ian Fleming's James Bond stories.

– Christopher Booker, *The Neophiliacs* (1969)

Probably the most striking innovation of the thrillers of Ian Fleming for contemporary readers lay in their codes of sexuality. Both critics and enthusiasts of James Bond focused on his sexual adventures; they all noted that the Bond tales were the first British thrillers to make sexual encounters central to the plot and to the hero. The thrillers of Buchan, Sapper, and Ambler all avoided anything but the most fleeting accounts of sexual relations, and whatever erotic energy they had was covert or displaced into other codes, particularly into representations of violence and torture. Nevertheless, striking as this shift seemed to contemporary readers and reviewers, one wonders about its meaning. For the sexual politics of the Bond thrillers are in many ways very traditional, and the representations of sexuality are, by the conventions of the 1980s, tame. The apparent novelty of Bond was, one might conclude, another version of a persistent and recurrent masculine fantasy dressed up in the latest fashions of a consumer society. This is the view taken by Tony Bennett in his illuminating discussion of the 'sexist code' in the Bond narratives, which details how the plots work to reposition a woman who is 'out-of-place' sexually and politically into a traditional ordering of sexual difference. As an example he cites Bond's view of the recent history of gender:

> Bond came to the conclusion that Tilly Masterton was one of those girls whose hormones had got mixed up. He knew the type well and thought they and their male counterparts were a direct consequence of giving votes to women and 'sex equality'. As a result of fifty years of emancipation, feminine qualities were dying out or being transferred to the males. Pansies of both sexes were everywhere, not yet completely homosexual, but confused, not knowing what they were. The result was a herd of unhappy sexual misfits – barren and full of frustrations, the women wanting to dominate and the men to be nannied. He was sorry for them, but he had no time for them.

Faced with this world, Bond's mission is to 'rescue' these women, to re-establish order in the world of gender. And he has few doubts as to the nature of that order, as one sees in this passage from *Casino Royale*:

> He sighed. Women were for recreation. On a job they got in the way and fogged things up with sex and hurt feelings and all the emotional baggage they carried around. One had to look out for them and take care of them. 'Bitch', said Bond . . .[19]

Yet the very crudeness of Fleming's fantasies of male power should not obscure their historical specificity; nor should the manifest absurdity of Bond's history of gender in the twentieth century lead us to forget Bond's place in the history of gender. For *Casino Royale* (1953) takes its place alongside *Playboy* (1953) as the mark of the first mass pornography. To say this is to define pornography not simply as a depiction of male power (in which case it surely predated Bond or *Playboy*) nor as any particular representation of sexuality (for the conventions of these representations change over time and the conventions of both Bond and the 1950s *Playboy* now scarcely qualify as pornographic); rather what characterizes these representations and the era of mass pornography are, first, a narrative structured around the look, the voyeuristic eye, coding *woman* as its object, and second, a culture whose every discourse is dominated by, indeed translated into, a code of sexual signifiers.

The argument that pornography is better defined as a version of voyeurism than as a representation of sexuality is drawn in part from the fact that much of what passes as pornography is not the representation of sexual activities but the representation of women's bodies in various states of undress. Thus, as Annette Kuhn puts it, 'in an address to male spectators, the body of woman is constructed as a spectacle and the *mise en scène* of representations of women's bodies coded in various ways as both to be looked at by the spectator and, in the same process, to evoke sexual arousal in him'. This line of thought owes much to Laura Mulvey's important essay which attempted to show how the classic Hollywood cinema constructs woman as an object of looking and constructs the spectator as male. The conclusion that Kuhn draws, a conclusion that is central to an understanding of James Bond, is that pornography is not exceptional, not qualitatively different from other representations in the culture. Rather pornography occupies 'one point on a continuum of representations of women, a continuum along which are also situated such commonly available and highly socially visible representations as advertisements'.[20] Thus, the James Bond tales can rightly be seen as an important early form of the mass pornography that characterizes the consumer society, the society of the spectacle, that emerges in Western Europe and North America in the wake of post-war reconstruction.

For Bond's pornographic imagination is structured not so much around explicit depictions of sexual acts as around Bond as voyeur, Bond as spy. We see this in the scene where Bond first encounters Honeychilde Rider:

> It was a naked girl, with her back to him. She was not quite naked. She wore a broad leather belt around her waist with a hunting knife in a leather sheath at her right hip. The belt made her nakedness extraordinarily erotic. She stood not more than five yards away on the tideline looking down at something in her hand. She stood in the classical relaxed pose of the nude, all the weight on the right leg and the left knee bent and turning slightly inwards, the head to one side as she examined the things in her hand.[21]

This picture of Bond the voyeur is related, of course, to the tourist Bond; but it also structures the actions of Bond the secret agent.

If we take *From Russia, With Love* as an example, we can see how the permutations of the voyeur, of Bond's licence to look, organize a series of loosely connected, virtuoso anecdotes that make up the heart of Bond's adventures in Istanbul. Bond's first action after arriving and taking in the 'view' is to accompany Kerim through an underground tunnel in order to spy on the Russian Embassy through a periscope; it is through this periscope that he first glimpses Tatiana Romanova, the Russian filing clerk who has supposedly fallen in love with his photograph. This episode is followed by the celebrated scene, entitled 'Strong Sensations', in which Bond, together with Kerim, watches the fight between the gipsy women: 'Bond held his breath at the sight of the two glistening, naked bodies, and he could feel Kerim's body tense beside him. The ring of gipsies seemed to have come closer to the two fighters. The moon shone on the glittering eyes and there was the whisper of hot, panting breath.' Since Bond is pledged, as a tourist, not to interfere with the women, this scene ends in an orgy of gunfire only tangentially related to the plot. The assassination of Krilencu follows this episode; but what is memorable here is not the assassination but its location, the 'mouth of Marilyn Monroe':

'Sniperscope. German model,' whispered Kerim. 'Infra-red lens. Sees in the dark. Have a look at that big film advertisement over there. That face. Just below the nose. You'll see the outline of a trap door.'. . . Bond rested his forearm against the door jamb and raised the tube to his right eye . . . The outline of a huge woman's face and some lettering appeared . . . Bond inched the glass down the vast pile of Marilyn Monroe's hair, and the cliff of forehead, and down the two feet of nose to the cavernous nostrils. A faint square showed in the poster. It ran from below the nose into the great alluring curve of the lips . . . Out of the mouth of the huge, shadowed poster, between the great violet lips, half open in ecstasy, the dark shape of a man emerged and hung down like a worm from the mouth of a corpse.

The sight of Krilencu is dwarfed by the look of the spectacle, doubly magnified: the voyeur Bond with the Sniperscope, the pin-up as a grotesque but alluring poster. Bond only watches the assassin, Kerim; indeed, the narrator informs us that Bond has never killed in cold blood. Bond's licence to kill is here clearly less important than his licence to look.[22]

Bond then returns to his hotel to find the compliant Tatiana Romanova, naked in his bed; but this final episode of his Istanbul adventures has an ironic twist. Rather than an explicit representation of Bond and Tatiana in bed, the spy Bond is spied upon, and the reader finds himself sharing a view with SMERSH itself:

Above them, and unknown to both of them, behind the gold-framed false mirror on the wall over the bed, the two photographers from SMERSH sat close together in the cramped cabinet de voyeur, as, before them, so many friends of the proprietor had sat on a honeymoon night in the stateroom of the Kristal Palas. And the viewfinders gazed coldly down on the passionate arabesques the two bodies formed and broke and formed again, and the clockwork mechanism of the cine-cameras whirred softly on and on as the breath rasped out of the open mouths of the two men and the sweat of excitement trickled down their bulging faces into their cheap collars.

These films are part of the Soviet plot to destroy the image of Bond.[23]

This brief account of Bond's adventures in Istanbul shows the ways in which the presence of sexuality manifests itself in figures of looking, in spying and being spied upon. But this does not account for the historical specificity of these figures; surely, the dynamics of voyeurism predate the appearance of James Bond, as much as they contribute to his success. The novelty is signaled by the poster of Marilyn Monroe; the object of the gaze is not a woman but a commodified image, an image from the world of film. Thus the novelty of the Bond tales, and that of mass-produced pornography generally, is its place in the new organization of sexuality in consumer capitalism. This takes two forms. On the one hand, one of the characteristics of consumer capitalism is, as the social theorist Herbert Marcuse pointed out, the libidinalization of the workplace and daily life, what he termed 'repressive desublimation'.[24] In this situation, sexuality becomes the master code into which all discourses – commercial, political, philosophical, even religious – are translated. And just as a society which translated all economic, political, and philosophical discourse into a religious code found its ideological boundaries defined and contested in terms of heresy, so this consumer capitalism which relentlessly transcodes politics, religion, and philosophy into sexual terms fights its ideological battles under the sign of pornography. These battles are not, despite appearances, merely battles between the forces of 'liberation' and the forces of 'repression.' The apparent liberation of sexuality from patriarchal norms – the so-called 'sexual revolution' – is both a genuine change in sexual practices and a reconstitution of sexuality in a fetishized mode that continues to subordinate and oppress women. Nevertheless there is a kinship between the appearance of Bond and *Playboy* and the celebrated trials of *Lady Chatterley's Lover* and the works of Henry Miller. Indeed, John Sutherland tells us that the 'paperback revolution' arrived in Britain with the mass sales of the Bond books *and* the mass sales of these literary works the libraries wouldn't carry.

But the other part of the reorganization of sexuality in consumer capitalism is tied to a shift in the sex/gender system itself, that contradictory combination of a particular sexual division of labor and certain dominant sexual ideologies. The new sex/gender system which has emerged in consumer society has yet to be named fully, but it is characterized by the expansion and industrialization of the service sector with its largely female workforce, the creation of a sexual market less marked by the formal institutions of marriage and prostitution, and the demise of the family wage system; this has generated an ideological revolt by men against the 'breadwinner ethic', the self-organization of women in the feminist movement, and indeed the construction of a new culture, a culture that might be figured in the names *Playboy* and *Cosmopolitan*.[25] It is in this context that the sexuality and masculinity of Bond appears: a masculinity defined by freedom from marriage, an easy familiarity with the brand names that are the accompaniments to a consumer lifestyle – cars, cigarettes, liquor – and a licence to look.

Notes

1. CHRISTOPHER BOOKER, *The Neophiliacs: A Study in the Revolution in English Life in the 1950s and 1960s* (London: Collins, 1969), p. 179.

2. TONY BENNETT, 'James Bond as Popular Hero,' U203 *Popular Culture: Unit 21* (Milton Keynes: Open University Press, 1982), p. 6; John Sutherland, *Fiction and the Fiction Industry* (London: Athlone Press, 1978), p. 176.

3. KINGSLEY AMIS, *The James Bond Dossier* (New York: New American Library, 1965), p. 111.

4. JULIAN SYMONS, *Bloody Murder* (Harmondsworth: Penguin, 1974), p. 246.

5. Quoted in BENNETT, 'James Bond as Popular Hero', p. 18.

6. IAN FLEMING, *From Russia, With Love* (St Albans: Triad Panther, 1977), pp. 47, 40.

7. FLEMING, *From Russia, With Love*, pp. 87–8, 123.

8. IAN FLEMING, *The Man With the Golden Gun* (New York: New American Library, 1966), p. 157.

9. IAN FLEMING, *The Spy Who Loved me* (London: Pan Books, 1967), p. 118.

10. UMBERTO ECO, 'Narrative Structures in Fleming', in *The Role of the Reader* (Bloomington: Indiana University Press, 1979).

11. FLEMING, *From Russia, With Love*, pp. 169, 170.

12. IAN FLEMING, *Moonraker* (London: Pan Books, 1956), p. 29; IAN FLEMING, *Goldfinger* (London: Pan Books, 1961), p. 90.

13. BENNETT, 'James Bond as Popular Hero', pp. 18–20.

14. FLEMING, *From Russia, With Love*, pp. 98–9.

15. LOUIS TURNER and JOHN ASH, *The Golden Hordes: International Tourism and the Pleasure Periphery* (London: Constable, 1975).

16. FLEMING, *From Russia, With Love*, p. 126.

17. IAN FLEMING, *Dr No* (London: Pan Books, 1960), pp. 5–6.

18. IAN FLEMING, *Live and Let Die* (London: Pan Books, 1957), pp. 41, 50.

19. BENNETT, 'James Bond as Popular Hero', pp. 13–14; FLEMING, *Goldfinger*, p. 189; IAN FLEMING, *Casino Royale* (London: Pan Books, 1955), p. 33.

20. ANNETTE KUHN, *Women's Pictures: Feminism and Cinema* (London: Routledge & Kegan Paul, 1982), p. 113; LAURA MULVEY, 'Visual Pleasure and Narrative Cinema,' *Screen*, 16 (1975): pp. 6–18; KUHN, *Women's Pictures*, p. 115.

21. FLEMING, Dr No, p. 67.

22. FLEMING, *From Russia, With Love*, pp. 131, 139–40.

23. FLEMING, *From Russia, With Love*, pp. 149–50.

24. HERBERT MARCUSE, *One-Dimensional Man* (Boston: Beacon Press, 1964).

25. A good deal of contemporary cultural history and analysis is condensed in this account: see in particular the work of JANICE WINSHIP: 'Advertising in Women's Magazines, 1956–1974', Centre for Contemporary Cultural Studies Occasional Paper no. 59 (1980); 'Woman Becomes an Individual: Femininity and Consumption in Women's Magazines, 1954–1969', Centre for Contemporary Cultural Studies Occasional Paper No. 65 (1981); 'Sexuality for Sale', in S. Hall and others, *Culture, Language, Media* (London: Hutchinson, 1980); 'A Woman's World', in Women's Studies Group, *Women Take Issue* (London: Hutchinson, 1978); BARBARA EHRENREICH, *The Hearts of Men* (London: Pluto Press, 1983); and ROSALIND COWARD, ' "Sexual liberation" and the family', *m/f*, 1 (1978) pp. 7–24.

11 Lessons from Brecht*
(1974)

STEPHEN HEATH

Stephen Heath teaches in the English Faculty of the University of
Cambridge. He was for some years an editor of *Screen*. His publications include *The Nouveau Roman: a Study in the Practice of Writing*
(1972), *Vertige du déplacement* (1974), *Questions of Cinema* (1981) and
The Sexual Fix (1982).

The reading of Brecht given here is rather more than an act of
philological retrieval. It attempts to specify the meaning and actuality
of his theoretical writings by 'mobilizing' them in relation to subsequent political cinema (Godard, Oshima, Straub) and semiotic
theory (Barthes – see note 32 below); to the Marxist theory of ideology
as rendered by Althusser, and to Freud. In this setting, Brecht's
theory-practice emerges as an intervention in and against the fundamental terms of the dominant artistic culture: *representation* and
narrative, which jointly work to deny contradiction and to confirm the
ideological position of the subject. The artistic counter-strategy of
'distanciation' implies a ceaseless practice of displacement, a production of contradictions, that is, of necessity, 'theoretical' in its process
and effects.

Heath's essay comes from a period of rarely concentrated politico-
cultural debate. The prospective manner of its closing paragraphs
bears witness to the 'once and future' possibility of coordinated
intellectual work that, 'inaccessible' as it must sometimes be, goes on
outside the contemplative frame and disciplinary terms of the academic institution.

---

* Reprinted from *Screen*, 15 (1974), pp. 103–28.

> '*A defect? I've never been able to endure anything*
> *but contradiction.*' (XIX, 414)

Lessons from Brecht. The following notes are no more than that: a series
of readings (the very etymology of the word *lesson*) across the range of
Brecht's writings on literature and art, politics and society, in the
interests of the discussion of one or two questions which are of
importance to us in our work today and which those writings pose
clearly and crucially. It is this purpose that gives these notes their sole
coherence; to read Brecht (making of Brecht the 'subject') is to appeal
neither to a person nor, *a fortiori*, to what Brecht called, in a note on
'reactionary writing', the 'trimmings' (*Beilage*) of personality (XVIII, 82) –
did Brecht himself, indeed, ever show the slightest regard for the author,
for artistic authority? throughout his work there runs a kind of practical
disrespect, a 'fundamental laxity in matters of intellectual property'
(XVIII, 100), the constant plagiaristic appropriation of previous works as
material to be recast, rethought in new articulations: simply, it is to recall
certain ideas, certain formulations, the example of a truly dialectical
practice, a ceaseless process of theoretical production in the conjuncture
of specific problems, specific situations.

The determining questions here are thus Brecht's own, raised at every
moment of that practice: what is the use of this and for whom? will it aid
in restructuration? *Was nützt der Umgruppierung?* (XVIII, 112); which
means for us the opening out of Brecht's formulations into fresh
problems, into a new situation – those of film, that of our reflection on
cinema and on the whole nature of the relations of artistic practices and
ideology, of the particular interventions of such practices in – and on –
ideology. The method adopted in these notes is, however timidly, that
'mobilisation of quotations' regarded by Brecht as basic to dialectical
argument, being listed as one of the objectives of his proposed 'Society of
Dialecticians' (XX, 147).

Distance and separation

In *Loin du Viêt-nam*, an entire section of the film is occupied by – as
though held in the hollow of the spoken discourse which accompanies it
– the split eye of Godard, face half-hidden by the enormous mass of the
Mitchell camera which fills the screen. The split eye: one eye towards us,
its gaze refracted by a pair of glasses and already partially concealed; one
eye glued to the sight, on the other side of us who are glued to the
screen through the sight of the invisible camera eye of the film, our point
of view. Centre frame, the lens of the Mitchell, dominating, blind spot of

the image, gulf of the representation, sightless and with nothing to see – 'taking' us, and losing 'us': the distance of negation.

Godard, it is often said, here addresses himself directly to the spectator, 'fiction is jettisoned in favour of direct speech'. This ideology of the direct dies hard – though Godard has tried to demonstrate precisely that no speech, no image, is 'direct'; witness, for instance, *Lettre à Jane*. There is no question in this section of *Loin du Viêt-nam* of a nod and a wink between subjects in speech (as one talks of 'comrades in arms'), nothing of that 'directness' that made the name of a Richardson (*Tom Jones*). Indeed, what have we, *subjects*, to say about Vietnam? what positions of consequence does ideology give us as subjects to take? But this camera – American Mitchell – , this film – American Eastman Colour – have a great deal to say, something to tell us about Vietnam, about the reality of the struggle and about the reality of our struggle in ideology against the representations it produces and the positions of the subject they hold (representation is exactly a fixing of positions). Godard's section is not in Vietnam but far from Vietnam, which is to pose the problem differently, specifically. What Godard pulls out of true – *distances*, in Brecht's sense of the term, this giving the extent of the 'far from' – is the 'directness' of representation; not direct speech but distance in speech (distance should be introduced everywhere, says Brecht, even into words themselves). Vietnam is not a crisis of consciousness – a problem of direct speech (a reduction into which, in a different area of concern, a film like *State of Siege* can fall) – but a crisis of the subject, of the ideology through which we live – a problem of representation; the section interpellates-disinterpellates us and Godard, refuses the position of the camera/I, negates: imposition of ideology, deposition through interrogation; in short, *distanciation*.

Distance, negation, deposition. Looking at Chinese painting (xvɪɪɪ, 278–9), Brecht notes the lack of monocular perspective, the absence of a fixed point of focus, its dependence on juxtaposition: 'several things are juxtaposed together, dispersed over the paper as the inhabitants of a town are dotted around in that town, not independently of one another but neither in a dependence of a kind that would threaten their very existence'. Such painting thus provides an image of an order without constraint: 'Chinese composition lacks the element of constraint which is so familiar to us; its order costs no violence'. Placing things side by side, with no attempt at totality, at uniformity ('the artist does not deny the basic surface by covering it over completely'; think in this respect of the poverty of objects and expressions in *Tout va bien* which allows image and sequence of images to produce a certain space of reading, a certain movement of argument and contradiction – the recurrent scenes in Godard's films of covering over and effacing are perhaps a symptomatic counterpoint in this connection – and then think – the particular example matters little – of *Mourir d'aimer*, with its décors of abundance, the image constantly covered by the expression of Annie Girardot, the stifling definitions of all-informing essence; or equally of *Last Tango in Paris*, where the bare apartment is entirely congealed in the expression of the absence it suggests, the discovery of the world 'outside' inside: for Brando hotel, wife, the past; for Schneider childhood, paternal house, the General father). Chinese painting leaves room, the eye can wander, dispersed: 'the things represented play the role of elements which could exist separately and independently, yet they form a whole through the relations they sustain among themselves on the paper without, however, this whole being indivisible'. Not an organic unity – a meaning – but a series of meanings and remeanings (a tabularity), a multi-perspective without the fixity of depth. Instead of representations, displacement – of eye, of subject (in both senses of the term), a materiality of texture which baffles the 'innocence' of reflection:

> in the gaps between objects, the grain of paper or linen is brought out with its own particular value. . . . The mirror in which something is here reflected stays in the forefront as mirror and this implies amongst other things a laudable renunciation of the complete subordination of the spectator, whose illusion is never complete.

Negation, distance, is precisely that: the demonstration of relations, of structures; the overturning movement, as in the Godard section, between representation and production, image and material, subject and language, a *critical* dialectics.

Everyone knows about Brecht and distanciation but it is not always apparent that this knowledge is very Brechtian (that is, held within a political theory concerning the necessity of a specific intervention in representation and ideology). The two habitual weaknesses in this respect – ways of smoothing over the terms of this specific intervention – are the reduction of distanciation to a technique (leaving the illusion of representation intact: witness the symptomatic appearance and conservation of the image of the illusionist in the following declaration by Resnais concerning *Stavisky*: 'Just as with Brecht you knew you were at the theatre, so I want you never to forget in my work that you are at the cinema. What I show on the screen is filmed images which announce themselves as such. This is my anti-illusionist side; a conjurer does not hide his skill, and neither do I';[1] the confusion here is indicative: the illusion is identified as such, but distanciation is taken as the simple demonstration of the illusion and Resnais can claim to be both anti-illusionist *and* conjurer, *and* illusionist) and the equation of distance and separation.

Separation is the mode of the classic – 'Aristotelian' – theatre which Brecht seeks to oppose, as it is also of classic cinema; the very mode of representation. The structure of representation is a structure of fetishism: the subject is produced in a position of separation from which he is confirmed in an imaginary coherence (the representation is the guarantee of his self-coherence) the condition of which is the ignorance of the structure of his production, of his setting in position. To understand the mechanism of this, we need to refer back to the account given by Freud, notably in the 1927 paper entitled 'Fetishism'.[2]

The paper opens with what Freud describes as a 'most extraordinary case': a young man who spent his early years in England before being taken to Germany where he forgot his mother-tongue almost entirely, erects as the condition of his sexual fulfilment the appearance of 'a shine on the nose'. This 'shine' is revealed in analysis as a displacement from the English *'glance* at the nose' to the German *'Glanz* – gleam, brilliance, shine – auf der Nase', a displacement that holds – and checks – the moment of the discovery by the patient as child of the lack of a penis in women; glancing upwards, a saving substitute is found on the face, and the glance produces the shine, the renewal of which is then the basis of future sexual activity. The fetish, that is, disavows the fearful knowledge of the lack; Freud writes: 'the subject's interest comes to a halt as it were halfway; it is as though the last impression before the uncanny and traumatic one is retained as a fetish'.

It is this procedure of disavowal (*Verleugnung*) that is of particular importance. Comments Freud:

> In the conflict between the weight of the unwelcome perception and the force of his counter-wish a compromise has been reached, as is only possible under the dominance of the unconscious laws of thought – the primary processes. Yes, in his mind the woman *has* got a penis, in spite of everything; but this penis is no longer the same as it was before. Something else has taken its place, has been appointed its substitute and now inherits the interest which was previously directed to its predecessor. But this interest suffers an extraordinary increase as well, because the horror of castration has set up a memorial to itself in the creation of this substitute.

Knowledge is disavowed in horror of what it entails (the woman lacks a penis, she is castrated, therefore I too may be castrated); the fetish assures the subject's position, his identity. All this is to say that fetishism is a structure – popular accounts of fetishism with reference simply to objects are thus extremely misleading – and that this structure focuses a centre, the subject it represents, which derives its unity, its untroubled centrality, from the split it operates between knowledge and belief, between knowledge which disperses the stability of the subject, opens a production of desire in which the subject has everything to lose, and belief in which the subject positions himself in his structural plenitude. Freud notes the *happiness* of fetishism: people are usually 'quite satisfied with it'; they even 'praise the way in which it eases their erotic life'. The fetish is a token of triumph over the threat of castration and a protection against it; moreover, it avoids homosexuality in that it does endow women with the characteristic that makes them possible sexual objects.

If we look closely at Freud's exemplary case, we can see that it is truly most extraordinary, providing as it does in the play on *glance/Glanz* a little résumé of the fetishistic effect. The fetish is indeed a brilliance, something lit up, heightened, depicted, as under an arc light, a point of (theatrical) representation; hence the glance: the subject is installed (as at the theatre or at the movies) *for* the representation (which is why, perhaps, the representation in turn of fetishism – in Strick's *Ulysses* or in sexploit films such as *La Punition* – has a flatness that creates unease); identity in separation, the very geometry of representation.

Think in this respect of the *photograph*, which seems to sustain exactly this fetishistic structure. The photograph places the subject in a relation of specularity – the glance – , holding him pleasurably in the safety of disavowal; at once a knowledge – this exists – and a perspective of reassurance – but I am outside this existence (the curious tense of the photo: the anterior present), the duality rising to the fetishistic category par excellence, that of the beautiful. This is the success of the photo in the *Sunday Times Magazine* or *Paris-Match*, the constant glance at the world which can sublime anything into the security of beauty. We need to consider carefully the complex of determinations evident in the contemporaneity of the development of the photograph, the definitive establishment of the ideology of subject, representation and exchange, and the eventual emergence of fetishism as a theoretical concept in Marx (analysis of the fetishism of commodities) and then in Freud (theory of the construction of the subject); what is in question in Marx and Freud being the function of representation: not the alienation of essence, but the essential denial of work, production, the refusal to grasp the positions of subject and object within that process. As far as film is concerned, one of the crucial factors in the form of its development was exactly this ideology and its exploitation of the photographic image in this way. The resistance to the coming of sound, for example, was then readily expressed in the name of sublimity, an expression of which the following declaration by Chaplin is indicative: 'it's beauty that counts most in the cinema. The screen is pictorial. Images. Lovely young girls, beautiful young men in self-sufficient scenes'.[3] It seems, moreover, that such a feeling retains its dominance today, both in realisation and reception: consider the style of the films of Claude Chabrol and the kind of acclaim they receive. Thus one of the key battles in the cinema has been – and is – precisely that against fetishism (Godard's *Le Gai Savoir* poses the problem concisely) and this is a battle brought very much to the forefront in Brecht's own work, as is made clear by Walter Benjamin in his essays on Brecht where he does, indeed, refer to the specific example of the photograph. Describing the technical development of the photograph, Benjamin comments on the absorption of that development into the establishment of a flawless perfection, of 'aura' (*die Aura*):

> let us follow the subsequent development of photography. What do we see? It has become more and more subtle, more and more modern, and the result is that it is now incapable of photographing a tenement or a rubbish-heap without transfiguring it. Not to mention a river dam or an electric cable factory: in front of these, photography can now only say: 'How beautiful'. *The World is beautiful. . . .*[4]

The problem is, therefore, according to a constant Brechtian emphasis, not to continue to supply the production apparatus of photography as it is, but to change it; without a radical restructuration, the attempt to join photograph – or film – and revolutionary commitment is a contradiction in terms, and this tranformation is what Brecht refers to as 'literarisation' (*Literarisierung*): here, the breaking down of the barrier between image and writing, depiction and meaning: 'Literarising entails punctuating "representation" with "formulation"';[5] it being this that could give to photography its 'revolutionary use value'[6] and, following Brecht, Benjamin talks of montage in this connection as a form of such punctuation, as 'the agitational use of photography'.[7] There is no need to stress the importance of montage for this purpose in early Russian cinema, where it goes along with the use of slogans, notions of intellectual film and so on, nor its new importance today, providing as it does, for instance, the specific texture of the explorations of political cinema in Godard whose own reference to Brecht is, moreover, quite explicit.

Let us come then to this reference, to Brecht's own practice in its theoretical formulations. Fetishism describes, as we have seen, a structure of representation and exchange and the ceaseless confirmation of the subject in that perspective, a perspective which is that of the spectator in a theatre – or a movie-theatre – in an art of representation. It is this fixed position of separation-representation-speculation (the specularity of reflection and its system of exchange) that Brecht's distanciation seeks to undermine. Thus there is no call for surprise if, contrary to received ideas, Benjamin opens a discussion of epic theatre (the Brechtian theatre of distanciation) by describing a certain *refusal of separation* which it entails:

The point at issue in the theatre today . . . concerns the filling-in of the orchestra pit. The abyss which separates the actors from the audience like the dead from the living, the abyss whose silence heightens the sublime in drama, whose resonance heightens the intoxication of opera, this abyss which, of all the elements of the stage, most indelibly bears the traces of its sacral origins, has lost its function. The stage is still elevated, but it no longer rises from an immeasurable depth; it has become a public platform. Upon this platform the theatre now has to install itself.[8]

In Brecht's own words, it is a question of 'creating a new contact between the stage and the auditorium and thus giving a new basis to artistic pleasure' (xv, 301), of abandoning the 'fourth wall, that fictitious wall that separates stage and audience' (xv, 341).

It is this breaking down of separation on which the establishment of distance depends, the repositioning – depositioning – of the spectator in a critical – multi – perspective, and it is identification (*Einfühlung*; 'the identification of the spectator with the characters imitated by the actors' xv, 240) which therefore bears the brunt of Brecht's attack. The reasons for this lie in turn in the *effect* of such identification, that of *catharsis*, the spiritual absolution of the spectator as this can be seen most notably in tragedy which gleans from a consideration of human suffering a harvest of essence – this is 'how it is', the Reality of Man's Condition.[9] One of Brecht's favourite examples of this curve of tragedy is *King Lear*, which moves from a specific socio-political situation – the division of the kingdom – to the stripping away of the social and political until Lear is left naked on the heath, a universal representative of mankind, the poor, naked 'forked animal', dying *'abgestreift und aufgeopfert'* as Hegel would put it. In tragedy, that is, suffering is essentialised and so, as it were, *redeemed*, the spectator absolved in the laying bare of an absolute pattern of meaning: separation, identification, the pity-and-fear of catharsis. It must be emphasised, however, that though tragedy is, in this way, a major point of attack ('humanity must not be smeared with tragedy' xviii, 10), identification, depending on separation in the face of the scenic representation, and the catharsis it sustains are of general definition for Brecht: it is the whole context of cathartic drama that he is concerned to reject.

Such a rejection, it may be worth noting, is one of the crucial factors of difference between Brecht and Lukács, marking the 'debate' between the two men in the thirties and continuing into Lukács's subsequent estimates and misappreciations of Brecht's work, as well as into his later attempts to found a general aesthetic theory.[10] For both men, catharsis is a wide-embracing aesthetic category, but from totally different patterns of understanding; in Lukács, that is, catharsis is a validly transforming crisis of subjectivity: the receiver of the art-work (spectator, reader) feels a sorrow, and even a sort of shame, at never having perceived in reality, in his own life, something which is given so 'naturally' in the work. It is not necessary to go into the detail of how an initial fetishising consideration, its destruction by an unfetishised image in the work of art, and the autocriticism of subjectivity are contained in this setting up of contrast and this perturbation. Rilke gives a poetic description of an ancient Apollo. The poem culminates – exactly in line with our discussion – with an appeal by the statue to the person contemplating it: 'You must change your life'.[11]

Subject and representation are assumed and the objective image (given as non-fetishising on this assumption) re-presents the subject to himself in a totality absent – alienated – in the initial point of departure, thus suggesting that transformation of subjectivity (and not of the subject, which would be to pose the problem of representation, to pose it as problem) defined by the Rilke poem – 'You must change *your* life.' In the context of this urge to totality, the idea of essence quickly reappears – 'Catharsis addresses itself to the essence of man'[12] – and it is to be noted that Lukács's revaluations of Brecht's work depend precisely on its recasting into such terms of catharsis, the discovery of 'a complex dialectic of good and evil. Problems of society have become problems of humanity, subsuming the inner conflicts and contradictions of the warring parties'.[13] In no sense, however, do Brecht's theory and theatre hinge on subjectivity and humanity; it is a question rather of introducing distance into subject and representation and so of producing not a totality, but a series of social, political and ideological interruptions; the motto of such a theatre is not 'You must change your life' but, to adapt as does Brecht the eleventh of the *Theses on Feuerbach*, the point is to change the world'.

The gap between Brecht and Lukács can be seen again – in direct consequence of their respective handling of catharsis – in their attitudes to the idea of the hero. For Lukács, the biographical form of the novel, the process of the conflict between hero and world, is a guarantee of totality; the reader is given consciousness through that movement. For Brecht, on the contrary, it is this mediation through the hero, the pattern of individuation-essentialisation-consciousness, that must be displaced; as the character Jesse puts it in *Mann ist Mann*: 'Man is indeed at the centre of things, but relatively.' Significantly, that work of Brecht that probably comes nearest to the Lukácsian conception of the experience of the novel, the very early *Trommeln in der Nacht*, is later criticised heavily from the standpoint of distanciation: 'I did not manage to make the spectator see the revolution with different eyes from my *hero* Kragler, and he saw it as something romantic. The strategy of distanciation was not yet at my disposal.' Such a strategy of distanciation, moreover, demands the examination of the effect of the hero in all its material extensions. In the French film *Septembre chilien* the voice of the woman militant in the final interview is spoken over by Simone Signoret; where the woman's voice is flat, anonymous almost, *political* (that of a specific struggle), Signoret's brings with it emphatic emotion and individual pain, a heroisation, a certain non-political 'human message', the feeling of those Signoret roles of today, the resolutely determined yet deeply – and fraily – affected Woman (eg *Les Granges brûlées*). It is these effects that Brecht's theory seeks to locate and to *refuse*.

Distanciation, then, is the work of this location and refusal, a work against separation-and-identification. As such, it stands dialectically away from the notion of a simple opposition: it is not a question of positing separation against identification (we have seen the real inter-dependence of these two poles in the fetishistic structure) and it is thus erroneous to suppose that identification is somehow excluded in a mechanical gesture: 'a way of acting which does not aim at the identification of the spectator with the actor (this way of acting is what we call 'epic') has no interest in *totally* excluding identification' (xv, 387). Brecht's particular reference here is to the mode of acting as quotation which he proposed and by which he had been impressed in Chinese theatre (once again, and like Eisenstein continually, Brecht turns to Oriental art for examples of an alternative economy of the sign, of meaning and representation); the Chinese actor represents but represents also the process of representation:

> The Chinese show not only the behaviour of men, but also the behaviour of actors. In this way, they show how actors present the actions of men; for the actors translate the language of everyday life into their own language. So when one watches a Chinese actor, one sees no less than three characters at once, one who shows and two who are shown (xv, 428).

Or, as Marina Vlady puts it at the beginning of *Deux ou trois choses que je sais d'elle*: 'Yes, speak like truth quotations. That's what old Brecht said. Actors must quote.'

What is important, the exact context of this presentation-as-quotation, is the ceaseless *displacement* of identification ('man is indeed at the centre of things, but relatively'), the introduction precisely of a constant distance, a critical movement that produces not a totality but a play of contradictions, an idea of transformation ('the custom that one must think afresh in every new situation', *Der Neinsager*). The aim is no longer to fix the spectator apart as receiver of a representation but to pull the audience into an activity of reading; far from separating the spectator, this is a step towards his inclusion in a process: the spectator must be included, his attitude modified';

> It is also as spectator that the individual loses his epicentral role and disappears: he is no longer a private person 'present' at a spectacle organised by theatre people, appreciating a work which he has shown to him; he is no longer a simple consumer, he must also produce. Without active participation on his part, the work would be incomplete (and if it were complete, then it would *today* be imperfect). Included in the theatrical event, the spectator is 'theatralised': thus less goes on 'within him' and more 'with him' (xv, 222).

It is significant in this respect that it is to the principle of montage that Brecht continually refers to suggest the realisation of this *active* inclusion (a reference which, again, distinguishes him sharply from Lukács for whom montage is a potential destruction of essential forms), for the practice of montage in cinema (the practice of a Godard, or, differently, of the early Resnais – *Muriel*) offers exactly a way of cutting the spectator into and beyond the film in a (multi-) position of reading; moreover, it is as this that the combat against montage is waged in the history of cinema, the refusal of montage going hand in hand with the fetishisation of Reality and its observer, the cult of the sequence-shot, of, in short, that ideology of the 'direct'.

We should remember, then, as Barthes reminds us, Brecht's admiration for Eisenstein (he talks of 'the enormous impression that the first films of Eisenstein made on me' xx, 46) but in doing so we should also grasp, as Barthes again reminds us, the difference between the two bodies of work on the common ground of montage: in Brecht, the question is not that of the production of adherence (the synthesis of two montage elements into a realised and directed concept); rather, it is that of the production of contradictions already mentioned, a dialectical procedure by which the spectator is placed in that *critical* position on which Brecht lays so much importance and which means not simply that the spectator criticises but also that his own position is given as critical, contradictory, that he is pulled out of his fixity. Which is to say that distanciation for Brecht is not a 'form' but a mode of analysis, the very mode of understanding of dialectical materialism. Little wonder that 'Marx was the only spectator I could imagine for my plays' (xv, 129).

In this perspective, it is possible to correct two more misunderstandings (or reductions): that distanciation is a form and that to define distanciation is to define a series of techniques, the presence or absence of which marks a play or a film as 'Brechtian' or 'non-Brechtian', as 'distanciating' or 'non-distanciating'. The first, although clearly in the long run the two are directly linked, leads to the characteristic saving irony of contemporary bourgeois cinema, from *La Nuit américaine* to *O Lucky Man*, from *Stavisky* to Jodorovsky's *La Montagne sacrée* (an irony which is generally a transposition of the novelistic devices dear to a Gide – *Les Faux-monnayeurs* – or a Huxley – *Point Counter Point*; there is a work to be done one day on the history of the cinema in its appropriations and reappropriations of the novelistic, such a history being not, as it were, a literary history of cinema but, precisely, a history of the forms of the ideological institution of representation). Each of these films clearly demands individual analysis, yet in every case such an analysis would show how a representation (a set of coherent and totally assumed positions) is confirmed (and *not* infirmed) by a reference to the illusion of its presentation, an effect that need cause no surprise if we think back to the previous description of fetishism and to the knowledge/belief split on which that was shown to depend. Indeed, as has been so often pointed out from at least Dr Johnson on, no one (except the mythical spectator of Rymer's *Othello*) has ever taken the illusion as reality; the point is always the illusion *of* reality, and we saw the foundation of identification and catharsis in separation: 'the spectator never loses consciousness of the fact that he is at the theatre. He remains conscious of the fact that the illusion from which he derives his pleasure is an illusion. The ideology of tragedy lives on this deliberate contradiction' (xv, 386–7). What is important in Aristotelian theatre is the reality of the illusion and it is this reality that is the real target for distanciation; which is then to say that the notion of distanciation as simply a set of techniques is an ideological refusal of the actual force of the analysis – of the *intervention* – it effects on ideology, reducing it to a mere decorativism according to a common process of inoculation bitterly described by Brecht himself: 'Capitalism has the power to turn into a drug, immediately and continually, the poison that is thrown in its face and then to enjoy it' (xx, 37). Distanciation is the recognition of the need for a ceaseless work of displacement and this even – constantly – within the forms of its own production.

The reality of the illusion: it is this that is the very area of that work in its critical ambition; its object, that is, can be seen as *ideology*, or, more accurately, the relations of men to reality and to themselves in ideology, in so far as 'in ideology is represented not the system of real relations that govern the existence of individuals, but the imaginary relation of these individuals to the real relations under which they live'.[14] There is room here for only the most sketchy account of ideology and the following points are given simply in the context of the immediate argument with regard to Brecht's theory of distanciation. Briefly, then, to expand that definition in this direction, ideology plays an effectively *active* role in a given mode of production (which is to recognise ideology as being indispensable to any society); it functions as 'a set of practical

norms which govern the attitude and the practical stance adopted by
men with regard to the real objects and the real problems of their social
and individual existence, and of their history'. To grasp this is to
acknowledge the material existence of ideology; it is not a question of a
kind of cloud of ideas hanging over the economic basis but of a specific
social reality – a set of *representations* – defined in a series of specific
institutions (ideological state apparatuses). To analyse a particular
ideology is to analyse this existence within the dynamic – the process – of
a mode of production. It was said, however, that what is represented is
the *imaginary* relation between men and the real conditions of their
existence. 'Imaginary' here refers to an effect of recognition-miscognition
(*reconnaissance-méconnaissance*): recognition because ideology is anchored
in reality, embraces the conditions of existence, furnishes a practical
guide for intervention on reality (is not a pure realm of the imagination);
miscognition because it seizes reality in order to represent it according to
its own purposes: 'In ideology the real relation is inevitably invested in
the imaginary relation, a relation that *expresses a will* (conservative,
conformist, reformist or revolutionary), a hope or a nostalgia rather than
describing a reality'; 'Ideology, then, is the expression of the relation
between men and their "world", that is, the (overdetermined) unity of
the real relation and the imaginary relation between them and their real
conditions of existence'.

It is the process of the establishment of *subjects* within – *by* – this
representation that is crucial; ideology takes up individuals and *places*
them as subjects, puts them in positions of subjectivity, *subjects them*. We
need a very fine understanding here: the distinction between individual
and subject is (methodologically) real, but individuals always are
subjects; there is no simple state of anteriority of some pure individuality;
even before birth, the individual has already been placed as subject,
enveloped in a discourse that names him in his subjection. What is
required is a way of thinking that is subtle enough – dialectical enough –
to grasp that the individual is always the subject of ideology but that he
is always more than simply that figure of representation (just as the
social cannot be reduced to the ideological which nevertheless is the very
form of its representation as society). Similarly, we must also realise that
this process of ideology is not to be described as the interiorisation of
norms (of 'roles') by the subject (this is the description given in popular
existential analyses – from which it is not completely certain that
Althusser himself manages to escape – which very quickly refinds such
notions as alienation and constantly supposes a preceding and
underlying, authentically reassertable subjective project); the subject only
has his existence because he is positioned in a set of structures which
determine experience for the subject *whom they include*.

It is this structural positioning of the individual as subject, his defining inclusion in ideological formations, that Althusser describes as the mechanism of *interpellation*; through a range of ideological state apparatuses – family, school, church, press, art, etc – the individual is ceaselessly called upon as subject, solicited, interpellated by these institutions in the interests of the reproduction of the social formation, of the agents of production. The subject is thus the fundamental category of ideology:

> the category of the subject is constitutive of all ideology, but immediately, at the same time, we must add that the category of the subject is constitutive only in so far as all ideology has as its function (this function defining it as ideology) the 'constitution' of concrete individuals as subjects. It is in this play of a dual constitution that the functioning of all ideology is to be found.

In fact, the problem is more difficult: such an account would have to be supplemented by a consideration of the whole question of the construction of the individual as subject-support for ideological formations in the symbolic, the question, that is, of the subject in language (where language is at once constitutive and not reducible to the ideological) and which gives the necessity for the articulation within historical materialism of psychoanalytic theory (as science of the construction of the subject).

Something of this difficulty will make itself felt, indeed, as we look in the context of this discussion of ideology at the Brechtian theory and practice of critical intervention. To work on the reality of the illusion is effectively to work on the ideology of representation and the subject-positions it determines. This is the very point of the attacks on identification, separation, catharsis, passivity, and distanciation is the dialectical realisation of such attacks; thinking within and without, in and beyond the play – or the film – is the mode of critical displacement: the play represents – is held within ideology – but that representation, that series of received formations, – is itself represented (so that we have, as it were and to adapt a Brechtian expression, *complexes* of representation – *Vorstellungscomplexe*) and this grounds the work not in 'Truth' but in an objective concrete political knowledge (defined in the precise context of a theory – distanciation – and its object – ideology). Barthes put it well in an early essay:

> Distanciation is this: going all the way in the representation, to the point where the meaning is no longer the truth of the actor but the political relation of the situation. In other words distanciation is not a form, it is the link between a form and a content. In order to distance, a support is required – meaning'.[15]

243

Brecht's is a theatre of representation but of representation *for meaning* (and so a theatre of pleasure, 'pleasure comes from giving meaning to things' XIX, 551; the admiration for Diderot, mentioned by Barthes, stems from this commitment to an art of instruction and pleasure, of transformation); representations are shown and distanced, seized in the complex of reality and attitude they produce. This is that decentring to which reference was made in discussing the loss of the organising status of the hero in epic theatre: it is not that the spectator is held separate to the action of the play and, from there, effectively placed in a relation of identification to the hero as totalising consciousness, but rather that the spectator is himself included in the movement from ideology to real, from illusion to objective truth (the political analysis of forms of representation in their determinations, the activity of the play); there are no heroes in such a theatre, not even the spectator (as judge, as unifying consciousness): as subject, the spectator is taken up in the representation – the play creates an effect of recognition – but that representation, that position taken up are pulled out of true (of 'Reality') and distanciation is exactly this (critical) operation.

> The play itself *is* the spectator's consciousness – for the essential reason that the spectator has no other consciousness than the content that unites him to the play in advance, and the development of this content is the play itself: the new result which the play *produces* from the self-recognition whose image and presence it is. Brecht was right: if the theatre's sole object were to be even a 'dialectical' commentary on this eternal self-recognition and non-recognition – then the spectator would already know the tune, it is his own. If, on the contrary, the theatre's object is to destroy this intangible image, to set in motion the immobile, the eternal sphere of the illusory consciousness's mythical world, then the play is really the development, the production of a new consciousness in the spectator – incomplete, like any other consciousness, but moved by this incompletion itself, this distance achieved, this inexhaustible work of criticism in action; the play is really the production of a new spectator, an actor who starts where the performance ends, who only starts so as to complete it, but in life.[16]

Film theatre

Let us consider an apparent paradox. One of the decisive definitions of film in its classic ideology, the ideology dependent on the production and exploitation of the effect of the 'impression of reality', was made *against* theatre, in terms of the power of film for the illimitation of the visible constraints of the stage (of the *scene*, giving that word the two senses – stage and tableau – that it so often takes in the Barthes piece; where the stage has 'wings', fixed limits, the screen, as it were, knows only the implied continuation of the reality of the image:

> The screen is not a frame like that of a picture (*tableau*), but a mask (*cache*) which allows us to see only a part of the event. When a person leaves the field of the camera, we recognise that he is out of the field of vision, but he continues to exist identical to himself in another part of the scene which is hidden from us. The screen has no wings . . .'
> (Bazin);[17]

such an illimitation moving out of the shot (the exit and re-entry of characters, objects continuing off the frame)[18] into the shot (deep focus), over the shot (sequence-shot). Thus one way of restating the limitations of cinema (of posing its specificity as signifying practice) has been precisely the *theatralisation* of film (in Straub, for example; the 'theme' itself comes to the surface in *Othon* or *The Bridegroom, the Comedienne and the Pimp*, but the activity is a factor of all the films). In other words, one mode of distanciation in film has often, and centrally, been the exact reference to theatre.

The paradox that might be seen here is to be understood along what could be called the bond of representation. Aristotelian theatre and classic cinema are held together in this bond according to a series of shared aims (the effect of 'Reality') and devices (note the importance of the *scene* in classic American cinema, for which sequence-shot and deep focus provide the very possibility) but, as in Bazin, the development of film and the specification of its artistic independence are made by asserting the differences of the one from the other. Hence Barthes is right to hold film and theatre (as well as literature) together in a general discussion of representation, at the same time that the theatralisation of film can be seen as a certain way of demonstrating the particularity of film, its forms, of opening a distance within its flow of representation.

Such notions as framing and *découpage* on which Barthes insists are indeed significant in this respect. Effectively, the screen does reproduce the conditions of Italian fourth-wall theatre, which is to say that it disposes – that it lays out – the coherence of subject-spectator whom it holds in position. It is in the very terms of this reproduction that cinema 'technology' is developed: from the perfecting of the camera itself as instrument to the elaboration and codification of the rules of film making and construction (the 30° rule is an easy example), it is this coherence of the subject-eye in its relation to the image that is crucial. Concerning the camera, for instance, recent work has stressed the ideological determinations operative in its history.[19] Thus we can note that the photograph knows a development contemporaneous with the growing awareness in painting of the dependence of the scientific perspective defining its form on a specific cultural structure established in the Renaissance (Hegel's *Lectures on Aesthetics* provide an account of this awareness), that the photograph itself poses questions about the reliability of the eye, produces a certain scientific doubt, and that this doubt is accompanied – compensated – by a massive bolstering of the eye and its perspective in the realm of ideology – the ideological exploitation of the camera to reproduce, to confirm, the vision of the eye. As has already been suggested, it is this exploitation that guides the subsequent modifications of the camera which is 'perfected' towards such a reproduction, the placing of the subject in a fixed relation to a stable 'Reality'. The camera is invisible, a window objectively framing reality, the means of the representation to the subject of his position, and this is the very *moral* of the frame; the German for the French *cadrage*, the centring and adjustment of the image, is precisely *Einstellung* which also means attitude, moral standpoint. Everything in the mainstream (commercial) development of camera, movie camera, editing and continuity techniques and so on is then fashioned to this position – lenses, camera height, strategies for linking shots (the manuals are entirely based on the reference to the confirmation of the subject, to the maintenance of continuity; failure to observe the rule of 30° will lead to 'too brutal a modification of the spectator's vision . . . a disagreeable effect').[20] It is indicative, moreover, that the character perspective (ie the subjective shot) is classically possible but only within certain very restricted limits, those exactly of an identification with a figure who himself occupies at that point a position analogous to that of a (and hence of the) spectator; films like *The Lady of the Lake*, shot in the first-person, are rare, regarded as 'aberrations', and aberration is indeed the intended signification of the use of the marked first-person elsewhere – blindness, in the scene in the apartment between girl and killer in *Wait until Dark*; short-sightedness, in the comically clumsy bathing scene in *Ssssnake*. What is fundamental is separation, the fetishistic position of representation: the power of the camera is that it traces the dividing line in such a way as to hold the spectator as it were with the wings behind him and not to his side, whence that effect of illimitation to which Bazin refers.

The apparent paradox again is that the destruction of the effect in its ideological complicity can pass through the theatralisation of the camera: representational fixity, the continuity of separation, the third-person on which classic cinema turns, is broken down by the dislocation of illimitation, a demonstration of the limits imposed on the camera that can be made in the name of an extreme subjectivism. This is the characteristic of a certain form of American underground cinema (of which a film like

Flaming Creatures would be typically representative) where exploration against the pattern of camera continuity goes along with – as though the one were the term of the other – a non-aligned sexuality, the irruptive reference to an energy not accessible in the geometry of the self-representation of the subject in the fetishistic structure. The problem is that produced in this way such an energy actually re-enters – re-confirms finally – the positions of the old alignments; hyperidentification blocks analysis in the myths of spontaneity, authenticity, free-wheeling subjectivity. In a note on the force and the weakness of 'destructive and anarchist lyricism' Brecht provides us with an effective summary of this:

> All the productivity of men is not contained in the actual production, which is always limited. Those elements that are not directly absorbed into it, however, do not simply fall outside, they contradict; they are not simply lacking in meaning, they disturb. Thus only a very attentive scheme (*ein sehr weit gespannter Plan*) will be able to grasp their activity, and you need an ear which is extremely sensitive to what is productive. It is a real achievement to keep these elements from destruction, that is, from destroying *and* from being destroyed' (xix, 408).

What constitutes that achievement is the posing of the problem of representation politically, of the political problem of representation, and it is exactly this that the idea of distanciation invokes. It is not sufficient to wield the lyric force of an immediate freedom (which is not to deny its possible local efficacy but to recognise the weakness of the only reference it can produce, that of an anarchic subjectivity, the very destruction of its own potential destructive force); the need is for a work in and on representation, for, that is, the introduction of distance, a work within representation that produces an understanding of its formations and of the construction of the subject in the positions assigned by those formations. It is this understanding that would characterise a Brechtian film theatre: theatralisation is not just *An Actor's Revenge* with its visible – theatrical – organisation of the frame as *limited and limiting space*, but also, more crucially, *Dear Summer Sister* with its *critical heterogeneity* (Oshima's films are attacked as hybrid, bastard forms, as lacking in the artistic purity of the true Japanese cinema), its exploration of the contradictions and ideological positions of contemporary Japanese society, including those of cinematic practice in that situation; is not just *Othon* but also *Nicht Versöhnt (Not Reconciled)*;[21] is a film like *British Sounds* with its discordance of language *from within language* ('the struggle of an image against a sound and of a sound against an image'), its refusal of *figuration* (note the uncentred, non-vocal framing in the Ford workers' discussion sequence, the absence of deep focus, the use of repetition and discontinuity).

Representation, language, theory: the problems crystallise in these terms. As Barthes shows, film and theatre are 'in' representation; the task is to displace that representation politically, not to reproduce its coherence but to demonstrate the contradictions that coherence avoids, the liaisons it assumes and guarantees. Such a demonstration – distanciation – is a work that is *theoretical*, the constant production of a reflexive knowledge that transforms particular representations, displaces them *in their forms* (for Brecht the production of theory is one of the main demands made by the proletariat on intellectuals and to assent to advice of the 'no theory, just get on with writing plays' variety is to fall into the trap of what, following Lenin, he calls 'rampant empiricism', xv, 276), and the objective focus of that transformation, of that displacement, the area of work, is then language: 'the theory of knowledge must above all be criticism of language' (xx, 140); 'the critical examination of language is of major importance when it considers the latter as an instrument of harm' (xix, 432). What is in question in these last quotations, the first a note on reading Kant, the second a comment on the force of the satire of Karl Kraus, is, finally, a general emphasis on the need for a ceaseless attention to language, to languages in their specific productions, to their reality as *specific signifying practices*.[22] The harm is precisely their instrumentalisation, their homogenisation as direct reflection/expression, immediate – and so unquestionable – 'Truth'. Against this, distanciation as heterogeneity: film theatre, the film text as hybrid, impure, process of contradictions; the 'end of cinema' in Godard's phrase, the end, that is, of that established language which is given as *the* language of cinema, as the realisation of the essential genius of film form, fixing the position of director and spectator, the conditions of reading (or not reading), ideologically determined (in the interests of the 'impression of Reality') and itself determining, by a movement in return, the history of cinema, the forms of its development, its 'progress', its *exploitation*. The destruction that marks the practice of a Godard, an Oshima, a Straub (as, in theatre, that of a Brecht) is to be understood here, against the language of this exploitation: 'Unfortunately, cinema is a language, but I try to destroy that language, to make films that do not take any account of that language.'[23] Not to take account of that language, however, is a *critical* enterprise, exactly a destruction, a *depropriation* ('Language is a form of colonisation. No?'[24]): what falls, what is destroyed, is the unity of film founded in the acquired orders of representation and the subject of their expression. This is the sense of Straub's idea of the practice of film as *negativity at work*, 'la mort au travail': 'At every moment a film must destroy what it was saying the moment before; we are stifling in stereotypes and it is important to help people to destroy them. In this respect, I hope the last shot will signify nothing. This for a start.'[25] No longer the illusion of the continuum of plenitude ('Reality speaks') but the discontinuity of the series of articulations that cross the cinetext in which the 'fullness' (the *property*, the imaginary projections of the subject as punctual source of meanings) equally of director and spectator is implicated. The films of such a textual practice are themselves a constant process of reading, this process then itself demanding new modes of reading, displacing the spectator from the positions in which he is interpellated in the classic film. This again is often the very 'argument' of Godard's films – at a high level of theory in *Le Gai Savoir* or in *Lettre à Jane*: how is the audience to be deployed in a reading other than that of the unfolding of image sequences in the direction of its own knowledge? Classic film is finally less a question of mise-en-scène than of mise-en-*place*, and anything that disturbs that place, that position, the fictions of myself and my 'Reality' can only be theoretical, the theatralisation of representation in its forms; film theatre, critical cinema, a cinema of crisis and contradiction.

Narrative/montage

What better way to avoid contradiction than narrative? It is not by chance that the 'impression of Reality' depends so closely on the development of cinema as 'unique narrative art form',[26] that it is, indeed, in the terms of narrative that the very language of classic cinema is defined and worked out ('it is in one and the same movement that cinema made itself narrative and that it gained some of the attributes of a language').[27] Narrative joins and aligns, smooths reading into the forward flow of its progress, and there need be no surprise if narrative can be seen as more 'realistic' than, say, documentary (which is anyway very often a narrative genre), for narrative is, as it were, the transformation of representation into 'Reality', the demonstration of its truth, the discovery of its meaning. Against the passionate interest in the *dénouement* (the revelation), Brecht opposes an interest in the choices and determinations of the action; against the rush of each scene into the next, a concentration on each scene for itself; against the straight evolution of a linear progression, an uneven movement of jump cuts, a complex montage of moments that proceeds 'by fits and starts, in a manner comparable to the images on a film strip.'[28] 'The relationship of epic theatre to its story, he says, is like that of a ballet teacher to his pupil; his first task is to loosen her joints as far as they will go.'[29]

The effect of narrative is exactly that of a tightening, action is moulded in a *destiny*, an inevitable coherence of the real. Whence its dual impulse of suspense and motivation, the very crux of its logic (and it is just such a logic that differentiates narrative from pure chronicle). When in *Ssssnake* we are informed early on that only the mongoose can stand up to the king cobra, this guarantees at once the eventuality of a battle in the film between the two, and its sense; when, at the fair, a scene is devoted to the prowess of one of the policemen at rifle-shooting, this creates an expectation of the use of this prowess later in the film (narrative is a mode which strives to leave no waste) and gives a retrospective credibility to the final scene in which he saves the girl by killing the cobra with one shot; when the sick boa is installed in the cellar with the warning that it will curl up in the rafters, we know that it will later appear from above, and when it does appear, crushing the over-inquisitive faculty member, it is, therefore, with a natural inevitability that replaces our sudden shock in a sphere of rational explanation; when we are told 'in passing' that death from a mamba's bite resembles death from heart attack, then the use later on of the mamba as the weapon for the perfect crime is assured and the crime itself when it comes is justified in return. What is important in all this is the two-way – 'unbeatable' – oscillation: if we realise the initial motivation, suspense is created (we wait for the boa to appear); if we do not, then the final event has a full shock effect and at the same time sends us back to the motivation, makes us see the link (we remember the boa's installation in the cellar); either way, the narrative produces a totality, offers an impregnable coherence. This may be unimportant in *Ssssnake*, but it is less so in a film like *State of Siege* where the force of narrative actually changes an apparent political message: suspense – whether or not to kill the American agent (and what we need to look at is how and why the fact of having announced the agent's death from the beginning of the film does not deter the subsequent creation of narrative suspense) – gives a *dramatisation* of the action (the drama played out between Bideau and Montand, the expression of the predicament of consciousness) – which is in fact the corollary of the real feeling of the film, manifested in the mediating figure of the old journalist, the view of reason.

For Brecht, it is the interrogation of reason and its forms that is crucial. Narrative must be interrupted; the focus is to be not on action and character in their irresistible momentum but on the 'intellectual decisions' of every action:

> the pattern of the action is complicated by actions *that might have been*: destiny is no longer a monolithic power; rather one is given to observe fields of force across which run contradictory currents; the power-groups themselves are not only taken up in movements which oppose them but are subject to internal contradictions, etc. (xv, 197).

One seeks 'the contradiction within what forms a unity' (xv, 361) and for this Brecht has a name borrowed precisely from cinema, *montage*, to be understood as a principle of distanciation, the production of contradiction at every moment of the work, from the individual gesture of the actor to the overall organisation of the scenes. Montage is the *dialectical* form of the work.

Tradition and domination

'A work that does not dominate reality and that does not allow the public to dominate it is not a work of art' (xix, 411). It is this emphasis that provides Brecht's criterion of value: the work is a work in so far as it produces a specific knowledge, a certain domination of reality. This moreover is a question of form as well as of content: 'the domination of reality. Everything could be measured against that demand, including the formal aspect, for no artist can dominate reality if his work errs in its form' (xix, 413). Distanciation is the form in Brecht of the domination of reality; opposed as such to any crude notion of realism, to the idea of 'reflection'.

Practically, the problem then posed is that of artistic heritage, of tradition. There is no domination of reality without an interrogation of reality in its forms, including those of its representation in art, and this interrogation is itself a formal process, a production, not a reflection. Thus Brecht stands against the Lukácsian vision of modernism as *decadence* – the breaking up of traditional forms seen as barbarism – in the interests of an avant-garde activity of the exploration of reality in the production of new forms of its definition. For Brecht, the role of the artist, as of the intellectual, is the overthrow of the weight of the heritage; to the question 'What does the proletariat expect of its intellectuals?', the first point of the answer is that they 'disintegrate bourgeois ideology' (xx, 54). The relation to tradition has to be one of destruction and, eventually, reconstruction, of depropriation and reappropriation where possible; 'In every age we have to try to tear tradition away from the conformism which seeks to appropriate it', writes Benjamin.[30] Brecht gives the complexity of his position in a fine passage entitled 'The proletariat was not born in a white waistcoat':

Culture naturally reflects the conflict that has arisen between the productive forces and the mode of production . . . There is no doubt that today a good number of those who are the bearers of culture are linking themselves ever more closely with the proletariat, the most powerful of the productive forces. The manifestations of the proletariat

251

in the domain of culture, its apprenticeship, its intellectual productivity do not go on on some ground exterior to bourgeois culture and totally distinct from it. Certain elements of culture are common to both classes. Certainly, we must maintain that some habitual elements of culture have played out their role and are become elements of unculture (*Unkultur*). But there are other elements that remain which are in difficulty and which we need to defend. Our position with regard to culture has for basis the same process of expropriation which is to be carried on in the material domain. To take over culture means to transform it decisively. It is not only the owner who changes but the property too. And this is a very complicated process. So, which part of culture are we defending? The answer must be: those of its elements which the actual relations of production must suppress in order to carry on as they are (xx, 89–90).

We come back here to our discussion of ideology; ideology is not to be replaced by some area of pure knowledge; rather, from within ideology, art, as realism in Brecht's sense, attempts to displace the formations of ideology by posing the specific relations of those formations in the mode of production (this is again the basis of Brecht's notion of the social *gestus*). But such a production encounters immediately the ideological definition of representation; it is not simply that what is represented is ideological but that the terms of representation itself are equally so. This is where we need to recall Althusser's account of the dominant ideology in a given conjuncture as providing *the ideological threshold common to all classes*; the massive representation of 'the world', of the social formation in which individuals find themselves, the very realm of the 'natural'. This is Brecht's point concerning culture: there is no immediate productivity 'on some ground exterior to bourgeois culture and totally distinct from it', 'certain elements of culture are common to both classes'. From then on, the struggle is, as it were, on the very ground of representation – on the very ground of the interpellations of the subject in reality by ideology; art as *displacement* in so far as it holds representation at a distance – the distance, precisely, of politics.

Cinema

There are discussions elsewhere [in the same issue of *Screen*] of Brecht's own interventions in the field of cinema – the 'sociological experience' of the *Threepenny Opera* lawsuit, the making with Dudow of *Kuhle Wampe*. It may be worth adding to these a brief indication of one or two emphases scattered through the writings and concerning Brecht's conception of cinema.

Brecht values cinema as providing a close focus on exterior action, as being a non-introspective and potentially non-identificational art:

> The fact is that the cinema demands exterior action and not introspective psychology. Thus it is that capitalism, by provoking, organising and automatising certain needs on the scale of the masses, acts in a manner that is quite simply revolutionary. By concentrating solely on 'exterior' action, by reducing everything to processes, by no longer recognizing in the hero a mediator nor in man the universal measure, it demolishes the introspective psychology of the bourgeois novel; it devastates wide expanses of ideology. This exterior point of view is adequate for the cinema and makes of it something of importance. Cinema can well admit of the principles of a non-Aristotelian dramaturgy (one, that is, not based on a phenomenon of identification, of *mimesis*) (XVIII, 170–1).

Coupled with this is the definition of cinema as an art of relative immobility; it is 'by nature static and must be treated as a succession of tableaux' (XV, 283).

The difficulty of this is apparent: it is easy to say that Brecht (as Benjamin too in 'The work of art in the age of mechanical reproduction', an essay heavily influenced by Brechtian theses) was totally mistaken as to the actual development of cinema under the hegemony of Hollywood (and Brecht's own misadventures in Hollywood, the difficulties encountered by his various projects bear witness to the fact of this mistaken estimation), that cinema became precisely the mode of the reconfirmation of the structures of the novel, of the novelistic, this bringing with it the whole paraphernalia of mimesis, identification, introspective psychology, hero as consciousness and so on. Again, it is easy to view with surprise the idea of cinema as fundamentally static when more or less the whole weight of thinking about film has identified its specificity as lying precisely in its movement ('What has the film maker to correspond to the colour and visual design of the painter, the solid masses of the sculptor, the musical sounds of the composer, and the word sounds and stresses of the writer and poet? Undoubtedly the answer to this question is, *movement*')[31] but we can begin to see here that Brecht is really grasping at a new conception of film or, better, at a *possibility* suggested by film against the straight terms of representation (those of the 'novelistic' of bourgeois novel and theatre) into which it was being firmly cast. The focus of this possibility seems to be the capacity of film to hold back the narrative, not to exhaust the images in the momentum of revelation, and this is the meaning of Brecht's emphases on the static nature of film and its potential for non-introspection, the presence of the image against the consciousness of developing presence. Such a possibility, moreover, might be seen as Brecht's own immediate experience of cinema at the time of *Kuhle Wampe*: the silent and early post-silent comedies in which the gag functions exactly as a constant narrative interruption; the films of Eisenstein which, as Barthes has shown, produce a certain effect of obtuseness, a friction of image and diegesis in the production of a 'third sense'.[32] The problem is not then a simple one of misunderstanding (of Brecht being 'right' or 'wrong'); rather it is one of the context of political intervention. Brecht's own oft-repeated principle of conduct needs to be remembered: the question can never be one of merely producing *for* a medium (theatre, radio, cinema or whatever); it is always fully one of *changing* that medium. It is the process of this transformation (which takes up dialectically medium and work), and this process alone, that is truly revolutionary.

Critical theory

There is a short text written by Brecht in connection with a projected magazine to be called *Kritische Blätter* (XVIII, 85–6) which deserves to be copied out in full at this point, providing as it does a sharp indication of the emphases and options that should be those of a review such as *Screen* today. It will perhaps suffice, however, and this will form the only 'conclusion' to this piece, simply to bring forward some passages from this text in conjunction with one or two brief annotations.

The magazine, says Brecht, must be critical in the widest sense of the term: there is not an established criticism that can be immediately and validly applied; criticism is to be created: 'the first task is to render criticism *possible*'. It is exactly the production of this possibility that is important for *Screen*: film criticism abounds, *critical* theory of film is rare; it is the development of the latter as the displacement of the former that is needed; indeed there is a case to be made for the constant *explication* of this displacement through analyses of the ideological structures of existing 'criticism', from the pages of the weekly papers to the new aesthetic radical-conservatism of this or that review. Evidently, the elaboration of critical theory – the rendering possible of criticism – means the posing of film as specific object, specific signifying practice, and the grasping from within that perspective of the problems of intervention in ideology, of a political cinema.

It is such an intervention on the part of critical theory itself on which Brecht lays the key stress (*Kritische Blätter* is to teach an *eingreifendes*

Denken): 'criticism is here understood in its double sense, the *dialectical* transformation of the totality of subjects into a *permanent crisis,* and hence the conception of the age as a 'critical period' in both meanings of the term'. It is here that *theory* is crucial: 'This makes necessary the rehabilitation of *theory* in its productive rights'. We come back to a previous point: there can be no question for Brecht – for us – of recommending and selecting ('Critics' Choice'), of moving, that is, in the circuit of a criticism of a cinema whose products it exists to sell; nor even of establishing a critical pantheon of alternative films. The struggle, the real work, is the attempt at a ceaseless transformation; 'today there is a new way of learning, a critical way, in which one transforms what one learns, a revolutionary way of learning. The new exists but it is only born out of the struggle with the old, not without it, in a void':

> The theory, or rather, in the beginning, the theories are not extracted from 'finished' works; they are developed at the points where works 'bring together' cinema and life, taking life in the economico-sociological sense of the term. Such a criticism transforms finished works into unfinished works, it proceeds analytically.

It is the production of this analysis that has occupied variously the films of a Straub or a Godard; it is this analysis that should occupy *Screen* now over the whole area of cinema. Such are the critical lessons of Brecht.

Notes

1. ALAIN RESNAIS, Interview: *Le Nouvel Observateur*, No. 496 (13–19 May 1974), p. 74.

2. S. FREUD, 'Fetishism', *Standard Edition of the Complete Psychological Works*, vol. XXI, (London: Hogarth Press) pp. 152–7.

3. CHARLES CHAPLIN, Interview: cit. MARCEL LAPIERRE, *Anthologie du cinéma*, Paris 1946, p. 228.

4. WALTER BENJAMIN, *Understanding Brecht*, (London 1973), pp. 94–95; cf. BENJAMIN's 'Short History of Photography', *Screen*, 13 (1), (Spring 1972).

5. BENJAMIN, *Understanding Brecht*, p. 7.

6. BENJAMIN, *Understanding Brecht*, p. 95.

7. WALTER BENJAMIN, *Schriften* I (Frankfurt 1955), p. 411 ('Montage als agitatorische Verwertung der Photographie').

8. BENJAMIN, *Understanding Brecht*, p. 1.

9. Cf. the very Brechtian definition of tragedy given by Barthes: 'Tragedy is simply a way of gathering up human suffering, of subsuming it and thus of justifying it under the form of a necessity: the refusal of this recuperation and the search for the technical means for not succumbing to it treacherously is

today an important undertaking'; R Barthes, *Essais Critiques* (Paris: Seuil, 1964), p. 102.

10. A very helpful acccount of something of this debate, together with translations of some key texts by Brecht, is given in *New Left Review* (March–April), pp. 39–53.

11. G. Lukács, *The Meaning of Contemporary Realism* (London: Merlin Press, 1962), p.88

12. G. Lukács, *Die Eigenart des Ästhetischen*, p. 868.

13. G. Lukács, *The Meaning of Contemporary Realism* (London: Merlin Press, 1962), p. 88.

14. This and the following quotations are taken from two essays by Louis Althusser, *For Marx*, pp. 150–1.

15. Roland Barthes, 'Sept photo-modèles de *Mère Courage*', *Théâtre populaire*, No. 35 (1959), p. 18.

16. Althusser, *For Marx*, pp. 150–1.

17. André Bazin, 'Théâtre et cinéma', *Qu'est-ce que le cinéma?* Vol. II, (Paris: Cerf, 1959), p. 100.

18. Sirk seems to have tried to use this as a means of producing distanciation: 'A fragment running out of shot puts the observer into the picture in a way. The moment you have the whole table and drawer there you just become a voyeur.' *Sirk on Sirk* (Interviews with Jon Halliday) (London: BFI/Secker and Warburg, 1971), p. 79. Cf. Paul Willemen, 'Distanciation and Douglas Sirk', *Douglas Sirk*, eds L. Mulvey and J. Halliday, (Edinburgh: Edinburgh Film Festival/NFT, 1972), pp. 23–29.

19. The discussion can be found in: Marcelin Pleynet, 'Le point aveugle', *Cinéthique*, No 6 (1970); Jean-Louis Baudry, 'Cinéma: effets idéologiques produits par l'appareil de base', *Cinéthique*, No 7–8 (1970); J.-L. Comolli. 'Technique et idéologie: caméra, perspective, profondeur de champ', *Cahiers du Cinéma*, Nos 229, 230, 231, 233, 234–5, (1970–72) Cf Christopher Williams, 'Ideas about film technology and the history of the cinema', BFI/SEFT seminar paper (April 1973).

20. *Apprendre le cinéma*, special number of *Image et son*, (Paris, May 1966), p. 152. In fact, there is a great need for a detailed analysis of the way in which this kind of rule was established in cinema and permissibly transgressed. In an essay on Walsh's *Pursued* published in the Edinburgh Film Festival book, 1974 Paul Willemen examines an extremely interesting example of the use or misuse of the 30° rule leading to *discontinuity*.

21. As for Godard, so too for Straub the reference to Brecht is extremely important: *Not Reconciled* has a quotation from Brecht attached to the script similar to that with which Marina Vlady begins *Deux ou trois choses*, *History Lesson* is based on Brecht's 'novel', *The Business Deals of Mr Julius Caesar*, his interviews make continual use of Brechtian formulations and insights.

22. Each word in this term is important: 'signifying' is the recognition of a language as a systematic articulation of meanings; 'practice' refers to the process of this articulation, to the *work* of the production of meanings, and in so doing it brings into the argument the problem of the relations of the subject within that work; 'specific' gives the necessity for the analysis of a particular signifying practice in its specific formations (which is not a commitment to some 'purity'; in film, for instance, what is important is to analyse the particular

heterogeneity of languages it subsumes – its combination of codes – and the particular forms by which it achieves this subsumption – its coherence).

23. JEAN-MARIE STRAUB, 'Entretien', *Cahiers du Cinéma*, No. 223 (Aug – Sept 1970), p. 51

24. STRAUB, 'Entretien', p. 50.

25. STRAUB, 'Entretien', pp. 53–4, 49.

26. J. H. LAWSON, *Film: The Creative Process*, 2nd edn (New York, 1967), p. xx.

27. CHRISTIAN METZ, *Essais sur la signification au cinéma* I (Paris 1968), p. 99. (For discussion, see 'The Work of Christian Metz', *Screen*, 14, (3) (Autumn 1973), pp. 22–4).

28. BENJAMIN, *Understanding Brecht*, p. 21.

29. BENJAMIN, *Understanding Brecht*, p. 16.

30. BENJAMIN, *Schriften*, I, p. 497. [Cf. WALTER BENJAMIN, 'Theses on the Philosophy of History', *Illuminations*, ed. Hannah Arendt and trans. Harry Zohn (London: Collins/Fontana, 1973), p. 257. – *Ed.*]

31. E. LINDGREN, *The Art of the Film*, 2nd edn (London, 1963), p. 92.

32. ROLAND BARTHES, 'Le troisième sens', *Cahiers du Cinéma*, July 1970), pp. 12–19. ['The Third Meaning', in ROLAND BARTHES, *Image-Music-Text*, trans. Stephen Heath (London: Fontana/Collins, 1977). In the same volume see also 'Diderot, Brecht, Eisenstein', first translated in the same issue of *Screen* (the first of two devoted to Brecht) and cited – no longer with visible provenance – on pp. 240, 244–5, 248 above. – *Ed.*]

33. [All quotations from Brecht are referred to the *Gesammelte Werke in 10 Banden* (Frankfurt: Suhrkamp Verlag, 1967) and identified in the text by volume and page, thus: (xv, 51). Translations are by the author. – *Ed.*]

Further Reading

This short bibliography consists of:

(1) A list of authors and titles from the broad Marxist tradition of thinking about literature and culture, including the contributors and other writers referenced in this volume, and subsectioned *(a)*, *(b)* and *(c)* according to the three-phase analysis of the Introduction.

(2) A heterogeneous list of historical and critical discussions of the tradition, together with some 'contextual' Marxist writings, not literary in focus, chosen for their particular intellectual impact upon it (with the large but obvious exception of the Marxist classics).

(3) A list of contemporary journals for reference and continuing reading. None of these listings aims at completeness; those for more prolific authors are particularly selective; many of the works included contain more detailed bibliographies.

(1) The tradition

(a)

BUKHARIN, NIKOLAI *Historical Materialism: a System of Sociology*. Ann Arbor: University of Michigan Press, 1969.

CAUDWELL, CHRISTOPHER *Illusion and Reality: a Study in the Sources of Poetry*. London: Lawrence & Wishart, 1946.

——— *Studies and Further Studies in a Dying Culture*. New York: Monthly Review Press, 1971.

CRAIG, DAVID *Marxists on Literature: an Anthology*. Harmondsworth: Penguin, 1975.

ENGELS, FREDERICK (see MARX, KARL).

FISCHER, ERNST *The Necessity of Art*. Harmondsworth: Penguin, 1963.

GRAMSCI, ANTONIO *Selections From Cultural Writings*, David Forgács and Geoffrey Nowell-Smith (eds). London: Lawrence & Wishart, 1985.

KAUTSKY, KARL *The Materialist Conception of History*, John H. Kautsky (ed.). New Haven: Yale University Press, 1988.

LENIN, VLADIMIR *On Literature and Art*. Moscow: Progress Publishers, 1967.

LIFSCHITZ, MIKHAIL *The Philosophy of Art of Karl Marx*. London: Pluto, 1973.

MARX, KARL *Grundrisse: Foundations of the Critique of Political Economy (Rough Draft)*. Harmondsworth: Penguin, 1973.

———— (and ENGELS, FREDERICK) *On Literature and Art*. Moscow: Progress Publishers, 1976.

NIZAN, PAUL *Pour une nouvelle culture*. Paris: Grasset, 1971.

PLEKHANOV, GEORGII *Unaddressed Letters and Art and Social Life*. Moscow: Progress Publishers, 1957.

TROTSKY, LEON *Literature and Revolution*. Ann Arbor: University of Michigan Press, 1960.

(b)

ADORNO, THEODOR *Prisms*, trans. Samuel and Shierry Weber. London: Neville Spearman, 1967.

———— *In Search of Wagner*, trans. Rodney Livingstone. London: NLB, 1981.

———— (with BENJAMIN, W., BLOCH, E., BRECHT, B., and LUKÁCS, G.) *Aesthetics and Politics*. London: NLB, 1977.

BENJAMIN, WALTER *The Origin of German Tragic Drama*, trans. John Osborne. London: NLB, 1977.

———— *Illuminations*, trans. Harry Zohn. London: Fontana/Collins, 1973.

———— *Understanding Brecht*, trans. Anna Bostock. London: NLB, 1973.

———— *Charles Baudelaire: A Lyric Poet in the Era of High Capitalism*, trans. Harry Zohn. London: NLB, 1973.

BLOCH, ERNST 'Discussing Expressionism', in ADORNO et al., *Aesthetics and Politics*.

BRECHT, BERTOLT 'Against Georg Lukács', in ADORNO et al., *Aesthetics and Politics*.

GOLDMANN, LUCIEN *The Hidden God: a Study of Tragic Vision in the Pensées of Pascal and the Tragedies of Racine*. London: Routledge and Kegan Paul, 1964.

———— *Towards a Sociology of the Novel*. London: Tavistock, 1975.

———— *Method in the Sociology of Literature*. Oxford: Blackwell, 1981.

LUKÁCS, GEORG *Theory of the Novel*, trans. Anna Bostock. London: Merlin Press, 1978.

———— *History and Class Consciousness*, trans. Rodney Livingstone. London: Merlin Press, 1971.

———— *The Historical Novel*, trans. Hannah and Stanley Mitchell. London: 1962.

———— 'Realism in the Balance', in ADORNO et al., *Aesthetics and Politics*.

———— *The Meaning of Contemporary Realism*. London: Merlin Press, 1963.

MARCUSE, HERBERT *Negations*, trans. Jeremy J. Shapiro. London: Allen Lane, 1968.

———— *The Aesthetic Dimension*. London: Macmillan, 1979.

SARTRE, JEAN-PAUL *What Is Literature?* London: Methuen, 1950.

———— *The Problem of Method*. London: Methuen, 1963.

———— *Essays in Aesthetics*. London: Peter Owen, 1964.

WILLIAMS, RAYMOND See (c)

(c)

BALDICK, CHRIS *The Social Mission of English Criticism 1848–1932*. Oxford: Clarendon, 1983.

BALIBAR, RENÉE *Les français fictifs: le rapport des styles littéraires au français national*. Paris: Hachette, 1974.

BARRETT, MICHÈLE *Women's Oppression Today: Problems in Marxist–Feminist Analysis*. London: Verso, 1980).

———— 'The Place of Aesthetics in Marxist Criticism'. NELSON AND GROSSBERG (see below).

BATSLEER, J., DAVIES, T., O'ROURKE, R. and WEEDON, C. (eds) *Rewriting English: Cultural Politics of Gender and Class*. London, Methuen, 1985.

BELSEY, CATHERINE *Critical Practice*. London: Methuen, 1980.

BENNETT, TONY *Formalism and Marxism*. London: Methuen, 1979.

———— (with WOOLLACOTT, JANET) *Bond and Beyond*. London: Macmillan, 1987.

BÜRGER, PETER *Theory of the Avant-garde*, trans. Michael Shaw. Manchester: Manchester University Press/Minneapolis: University of Minnesota Press, 1984.

―――― 'Aporias of Modern Aesthetics'. *New Left Review*, 184 (1990), pp. 47–56.

COWARD, ROSALIND and ELLIS, JOHN *Language and Materialism*. London: Routledge and Kegan Paul, 1977.

DENNING, MICHAEL *Cover Stories: Narrative and Ideology in the British Spy Thriller*. London: Routledge and Kegan Paul, 1987.

―――― *Mechanic Accents: Dime Novels and Working-class Culture in America*. London: Verso, 1987.

DOLLIMORE, JONATHAN *Radical Tragedy*. Brighton: Harvester, 1984.

DOLLIMORE, JONATHAN and SINFIELD, ALAN (eds.) *Political Shakespeare: New Essays in Cultural Materialism*. Manchester: MUP, 1985.

DRAKAKIS, JOHN (ed.) *Alternative Shakespeares*. London: Methuen, 1985.

EAGLETON, TERRY *Criticism and Ideology*. London: NLB, 1976.

―――― *Walter Benjamin, or Towards a Revolutionary Criticism*. London: Verso, 1981.

―――― *Literary Theory: an Introduction*. Oxford: Blackwell, 1983.

―――― *The Function of Criticism*. London: Verso, 1984.

―――― *Against the Grain: Essays 1975–1985*. London: Verso, 1986.

―――― *The Ideology of the Aesthetic*. Oxford: Blackwell, 1990.

ENZENSBERGER, HANS MAGNUS *The Consciousness Industry*, trans. Michael Roloff. New York: Seabury Press, 1974.

―――― *Dreamers of the Absolute*. London: Hutchinson Radius, 1988.

FEKETE, JOHN *The Critical Twilight: Explorations in the Ideology of Anglo-American Literary Theory From Eliot to McLuhan*. London: Routledge & Kegan Paul, 1978.

FORTINI, FRANCO *Verifica dei Poteri*. Milan:Il Saggiatore/Garzanti, 1974.

FROW, JOHN *Marxism and Literary History*. Oxford: Blackwell, 1986.

GOODE, JOHN *George Gissing: Ideology and Fiction*. London: Vision Press, 1978.

HALL, STUART (ed.) *Culture, Media, Language: Working Papers in Cultural Studies*. London: Hutchinson, 1980.

HEATH, STEPHEN *The Nouveau Roman: a Study in the Practice of Writing*. London: Elek, 1972.

―――― ed. and trans. Roland Barthes *Image-Music-Text*. London: Fontana/ Collins, 1977.

―――― *Questions of Cinema*. London: Macmillan, 1981.

―――― *The Sexual Fix*. London: Macmillan, 1982.

JAMESON, FREDRIC *Marxism and Form*. Princeton: Princeton University Press, 1972.

―――― *The Political Unconsciousness*. London: Methuen, 1981.

―――― *The Ideologies of Theory. Vol. 1 Situations of Theory*. Vol. 2 *The Syntax of History*. London: Routledge & Kegan Paul, 1988.

―――― *Postmodernism, or the Cultural Logic of Late Capitalism*. London: Verso, 1991.

KAPLAN, CORA *Sea Changes: Culture and Feminism*. London: Verso, 1986.

―――― (with BURGIN, VICTOR and DONALD, JAMES, eds) *Formations of Fantasy*. London: Methuen, 1986.

LENTRICCHIA, FRANK *After the New Criticism*. Chicago: University of Chicago Press, 1980.

LOVELL, TERRY *Pictures of Reality: Aesthetics, Politics, Pleasure*. London: BFI, 1980.

―――― *Consuming Fictions*. London: Verso, 1987.

MACCABE, COLIN *Theoretical Essays: Film, Linguistics, Literature*. Manchester: Manchester University Press, 1985.

MACHEREY, PIERRE *A Theory of Literary Production*, trans. Geoffrey Wall. London: Routledge & Kegan Paul, 1978.

MORETTI, FRANCO *Signs Taken For Wonders: Essays in the Sociology of Literary Forms* (2nd edn). London: Verso, 1988.

―――― *The Way of the World: the Bildungsroman in European Culture*. London: Verso, 1987.

MULHERN, FRANCIS 'The Marxist Aesthetics of Christopher Caudwell'. *New Left Review*, 85 (1974), pp., 37–58.
____ 'Marxism in Literary Criticism'. *New Left Review*, 108 (1978), pp. 77–87.
____ *The Moment of 'Scrutiny'*. London: Verso, 1981.
NELSON, CARY and GROSSBERG, LAWRENCE (eds) *Marxism and the Interpretation of Culture*. London: Macmillan, 1988.
RUDICH, NORMAN (ed.) *Weapons of Criticism*. Palo Alto, 1976,
SAID, EDWARD W. *Orientalism*. New York: Pantheon, 1978.
____ *Covering Islam*. London: Routledge & Kegan Paul, 1981.
____ *The World, the Text, and the Critic*. Cambridge, Mass: Harvard University Press, 1983.
SINFIELD, ALAN *Literature, Politics and Culture in Post-war Britain*. Oxford: Blackwell, 1989.
SPRINKER, MICHAEL *Imaginary Relations: Aesthetics and Ideology in the Theory of Historical Materialism*. London: Verso, 1987.
SZONDI, PETER *Theory of the Modern Drama*. Minneapolis: University of Minnesota Press, 1988.
TAYLOR, JENNY BOURNE *In the Secret Theatre of Home*. London: Routledge, 1988.
TEL QUEL *Théorie d'ensemble*. Paris: Seuil, 1968.
WIDDOWSON, PETER (ed.) *Re-reading English*. London: Methuen, 1982.
____ *Hardy in History: a Study in Literary Sociology*. London: Routledge, 1989.
WILLIAMS, RAYMOND *Culture and Society 1780–1950*. London: Chatto and Windus, 1958.
____ *The Long Revolution*. London: Chatto and Windus, 1961.
____ *Drama From Ibsen to Brecht*. London: Chatto and Windus, 1968.
____ *The English Novel From Dickens to Lawrence*. London: Chatto and Windus, 1970.
____ *The Country and the City*. London: Chatto and Windus, 1973.
____ *Television: Technology and Cultural Form*. London: Fontana/Collins, 1974.
____ *Communications* (3rd edn). Harmondsworth: Penguin, 1976.
____ *Marxism and Literature*. Oxford: Oxford University Press, 1977.
____ *Modern Tragedy* (second edition). London: Verso, 1979.
____ *Problems in Materialism and Culture*. London: Verso, 1980.
____ *Keywords: a Vocabulary of Culture and Society* (second edition). London: Fontana/Collins, 1983.
____ *Writing in Society*. London: Verso, 1984.
____ *What I Came to Say*. London: Hutchinson Radius, 1989.
WOLFF, JANET *The Social Production of Art*. London: Macmillan, 1981.
WOLLEN, PETER *Signs and Meaning in the Cinema*. London: Secker and Warburg/BFI, 1968.
____ *Readings and Writings: Semiotic Counter-strategies*. London: Verso, 1982.
WOTTON, GEORGE *Thomas Hardy: Towards a Materialist Criticism*. Goldenbridge: Gill and Macmillan, 1985.

(2) Historical, critical and other

ALTHUSSER, LOUIS *For Marx*. London: NLB, 1977.
____ *Lenin and Philosophy*. London: NLB, 1971.
ANDERSON, PERRY *Considerations on Western Marxism*. London: NLB, 1976.
____ *Arguments Within English Marxism*. London: Verso, 1980.
ATTRIDGE, DEREK, BENNINGTON, GEOFF and YOUNG, ROBERT (eds) *Post-structuralism and the Question of History*. Cambridge: Cambridge University Press, 1987.
COLLETTI, LUCIO *From Rousseau to Lenin*. London: NLB, 1972.

EASTHOPE, ANTONY *British Post-structuralism since 1968*. London: Routledge, 1988.

FORGÁCS, DAVID 'Marxist Literary Theories', in Ann Jefferson and David Robey (eds), *Modern Literary Theory*. London: Batsford, 1982.

GILROY, PAUL *There Ain't No Black in the Union Jack: the Cultural Politics of Race and Nation*. London: Hutchinson, 1987.

JAY, MARTIN *The Dialectical Imagination: a History of the Frankfurt School and Institute of Social Research*. London: Heinemann, 1973.

LUNN, EUGENE *Marxism and Modernism*. London: Verso, 1985.

SLATER, PHIL *Origins and Significance of the Frankfurt School: a Marxist Perspective*. London: Routledge & Kegan Paul, 1977.

THOMPSON, E. P. *The Poverty of Theory and Other Essays*. London: Merlin Press, 1978.

TIMPANARO, SEBASTIANO *On Materialism*. London: NLB, 1975.

(3) Journals

Literature and History
New Formations
New Left Review
New German Critique
News From Nowhere
Radical Philosophy
Red Letters
Screen
Screen Education
Social Text
Telos
Textual Practice
Working Papers in Cultural Studies

Index